WE HAVE NO LEADERS

SUNY SERIES IN
AFRO-AMERICAN STUDIES

JOHN HOWARD AND ROBERT C. SMITH,
EDITORS

WE HAVE NO LEADERS

AFRICAN AMERICANS
IN THE
POST–CIVIL RIGHTS ERA

ROBERT C. SMITH

FOREWORD BY RONALD W. WALTERS

STATE UNIVERSITY OF NEW YORK PRESS

Parts of Chapters 1 and 8 are based on "Politics Is Not Enough: The Institutionalization of the African-American Freedom Movement" which appeared in *From Exclusion to Inclusion: The Long Struggle for African American Political Power* edited by Ralph Gomes and Linda Faye Williams, Greenwood Press, © 1992.

Published by
State University of New York Press, Albany

For information, address State University of New York Press,
State University Plaza, Albany, N.Y. 12246

Production by M. R. Mulholland
Marketing by Theresa A. Swierzowski

Library of Congress Cataloging-in-Publication Data

Smith, Robert Charles, 1947-
     We have no leaders : African-Americans in the post-civil rights
era / Robert C. Smith ; foreword by Ronald W. Walters.
        p.   cm. — (SUNY series in Afro-American studies)
     Includes bibliographical references and index.
     ISBN 0-7914-3135-5 (HC : acid-free). — ISBN 0-7914-3136-3 (PB :
acid-free)
     1. Afro-Americans—Politics and government. 2. United States-
-Politics and government—1945-1989. 3. United States—Politics and
government—1989-   4. Civil rights movements—United States-
-History—20th century. 5. Afro-Americans—Civil rights-
-History—20th century. I. Series.
E185.615.S5828 1996
324'.,089'96073—dc20   95-52681
                                                                          CIP

10 9 8 7 6 5 4 3 2 1

To the women who
have made and make
my life:

Blanch
Scottie
Tahirih
Cleo Juanita
Thelma
Bernice
Blanch Elizabeth
Jessica Juanita
Scottus-Charles

Contents

Part V

Tables

Foreword

Professor Robert C. Smith has produced a work, the breadth and depth of which accomplish an important milestone in the scholarship of black politics. While the summarizing of a significant part of the political history of the black community for the past thirty years is, in itself, an important feat, he subjects the discrete events which comprised this history to a most aggressive, exacting and on the whole superb analytical microscope. In doing so, he teases out some of the most important questions in the field, and consequently, in the use of politics by the black community. Along the way, he produces some gems of insight and theoretical importance. For example, on his way to defining the essence of the ideology of "black power," he also develops a thought that may be useful in defining the project of black politics in general. Smith's thesis is that struggle over racial meaning is a constant and dynamic tension between the black perspective and the attempt by whites to impose the dominant perspective on a racial event.

Dr. Smith uses this paradigm to examine the civil rights movement in order to determine its impact on the political agenda of the 1970s and concludes that it fell short in many respects. The most significant impact, he suggests, is that it furthered the process of political incorporation to the point that a new generation of leaders have emerged within major American political institutions at every level of government. He concludes, correctly, that this alone did not have much of an effect on the quality of life in the black community. The historical irony must be noted, however, that the civil rights movement ushered in an electoral politics movement at a time when resources began to be withdrawn from major urban areas.

He also looks at major events of the 1970s such as the Black Political Convention of 1972 and the agenda it produced, the other Black Political Conventions which took place in the 1970s and the Humphrey-Hawkins Bill—the centerpiece of the policy agenda of the 1970s. In all of these, he concludes, the process of political incorporation which was supposed to be the instrument of their realization has had nearly the opposite effect. In fact, it has been so ineffectual as to be incapable of shielding the black community from the conservative politics of the "Reagan revolution" of the early 1980s and from its attempt to foist upon the black community a new black conservatism as its authentic voice. Nevertheless, Smith's rather harsh judgment on the politics of the 1970s which suggests that black agendas, conventions, and so forth may be unnecessary or even useless, captures the frustration most have felt for the "yield" of black politics. However, these tools have been useful in helping to define what black politics was all about, even if it could not be achieved.

Here, there are two central issues: The first is an evaluation of the instrument, or the strategies which comprise black politics that have sought to implement the black agenda, and the second is one of the objectives, or the agenda itself. With respect to the first issue, it may well be asked, acknowledging that the civil rights movement may have created a great wish list of unrealistic desires, just what constitutes realistic expectations for the various methods by which blacks have sought to develop influence in the political system. One assumes that black electoral politics has been an instrument for improvement in the quality of black life. However, this assumption, Smith suggests, is at various points open to question, and he makes the harsh judgement that it has often failed and that at all ends, it may even be *irrelevant*.

If he is correct about the marginal influence of black politics, this is an acknowledgement that, while it has been important in generating agenda-setting activity within the black community, may not be sufficient in achieving the objectives themselves. In the political arenas of the Congress, a state legislature or city council, the process for gaining access by campaigning to win election in majority black districts has yielded significant black representation. But is the politics of representation sufficient, when effectiveness—that is, the acquisition of tangible, perhaps inordinately tangible results, given the problems the black community—is demanded? For some, symbolic politics, which widens the base of representation as a public good of the construction of a democratic society, is often accepted over politics with hard tangible results.

The pursuit of effectiveness in a legislative body requires the tools of agenda setting such as coalition building and negotiation, and then, one must often "catch a favorable wind" of public opinion as well. These requirements, however, generally have the effect of diluting agendas, sometimes considerably beyond recognition, as was the case with the Humphrey-Hawkins Bill. And this is especially true where the sponsoring group is so relatively powerless that it necessitates the support of a more powerful group. This is why the Humphrey-Hawkins Act came to be "Humphrey-Hawkins" in the first place, and also why it was eventually passed in the negotiations that followed, but never heard from again.

Then, public opinion is important and Smith clearly illustrates that in a period of unfavorable, antiblack public opinion, the resulting agenda of black politics, containing such objectionable measures as urban financing and civil rights enforcement, for example, has been weakened or killed altogether. Smith's analysis, therefore, appears to capture the rationale for the re-emergence of black nationalism, especially among black youth, as a politics not requiring negotiation or dilution and which can be used as a weapon of defense against public racism.

At all ends, Professor Smith raises a series of critical concerns about the means and ends of black politics. And while one response to its failure to deliver a bouquet of substantive tangible results is despair and cynicism, what may also be inferred from this volume is that we should take another look, as a community, at the whole range of political ideologies and strategies, such as boycotts, real demonstrations, more effective lobbying, civil disobedience, and the like, in an effort to break out of the moderate returns from an over-reliance on moderate instruments such as electoral politics and the tactic of political incorporation alone. If there is merit in such a suggestion, it is clearly informed by this volume.

Ronald W. Walters, Professor
Political Science
Howard University
Washington, D.C.

Preface

The civil rights movement, what I refer to more generically as the Afro-American freedom struggle, is one of the most thoroughly researched and carefully documented events in the twentieth-century history of the United States. Much of this work focuses on the origins and evolution of the movement, dealing with important individuals, organizations, strategies and events from the Montgomery bus boycott in 1955 to the Selma voting rights demonstrations in 1965. There are also studies of the executive and legislative decision-making processes that resulted in the passage of the major civil rights acts of the period. And there are studies of the implementation of these laws, especially the Voting Rights Act and Titles VI and VII of the 1964 Civil Rights Act. This book takes a broader approach, examining the processes and consequences of the institutionalization of the civil rights movement; of the shifting of the central dynamic of black politics from protests in the streets to the corridors of power in Washington and elsewhere. It has been twenty-five years since this process got under way; thus it is appropriate to stand back and take stock of what happened, why, and with what consequences for the historic struggle of the African people for freedom and equality in the United States. This is the principal purpose of this volume, to present for the first time a systematic and comprehensive study of the institutionalization of the civil rights movement.

The book has three major objectives. First, to specify and apply to the civil rights movement a theoretical framework for understanding the outcomes of protest movements in terms of processes of institutionalization, incorporation and cooptation. Second, to present a detailed history or chronicle of black politics in the United States during the last twenty-five years. Third, to integrate analysis of the black movement into an understanding of the political and policy contexts in which the problem of race is dealt with in the American democracy. The book is divided into five parts. Part One includes one chapter, which lays out a general theory or framework for analysis of social movement outcomes and then applies it to the civil rights movement. This chapter also includes a model of political incorporation that is used to analyze post civil rights era black politics in terms of issue agendas, political mobilization, coalition formation and policy outcomes.

One of the major requirements of effective social movement incorporation is the development of new institutions and the mobilization of the constituent group. Part Two, in two chapters, examines the efforts of blacks to do this in the post–civil rights era. The failure of this institution building and mobilization effort is traced through a detailed history of the National Black Political Convention, 1972–84. Given this history, a chapter is devoted to the current state of black organization and institutional development, focusing on the traditional civil rights organizations, the church, black nationalist groups, the Congressional Black Caucus and the Joint Center for Political Studies.

Part Three contains five chapters. The first examines black incorporation into systemic political institutions and processes and its consequences for the black leadership group and the internal dynamics of black politics. Then in several chapters I examine the policy consequences of incorporation in terms of the role of black officials in executive policy making and in congressional decision making with respect to civil rights, social and economic reform and a case study of the Humphrey-Hawkins Act.

In Part Four, black incorporation in the party system and Jesse Jackson's campaigns for president and his National Rainbow Coalition are examined in terms of issues, strategies, coalition formation and the responsiveness of the Democratic party. Finally, in this part a chapter is devoted to analysis of the role of race and racism in shaping post–civil rights era partisanship, the party system and the election of Bill Clinton in 1992 and a Republican congressional majority in 1994.

The final part and chapter of the book discusses the consequences of the institutionalization of the Afro-American freedom movement for the internal life and organization of the black community and for the future of race relations in the United States. The book ends on a rather pessimistic note. It finds that the black movement has been almost wholly encapsulated into mainstream institutions; coopted and marginalized. As a result it has become largely irrelevant in terms of a politics and policies that would address the multifaceted problems of race in the post–civil rights era. Meanwhile, the core black community has become increasingly segregated, and its society, economy, culture and institutions of internal governance and communal uplift have decayed.

As perhaps is already clear, this book is normatively informed. It is also didactic. Gunnar Myrdal writes, "The social scientist faces the further problem: how can he be in this sense objective and, at the same time practical? What is the relation between wanting to understand

and wanting to change society? How can the search for true knowledge be combined with moral valuations?" His answer is that the "logical means available for protecting ourselves from biases are broadly these: to raise the valuations actually determining our theoretical as well as our practical research to full awareness [and] to scrutinize them from the point of view of relevance, significance and feasibility in the society under study. . . ."[1] Three biases are relevant to understanding my approach to this study. First, I should like to change American society so as to bridge the enormous gap in social and economic well-being between blacks and whites. To create what Matthew Holden, Jr., calls an integrated polity; one where "race would not predict the distribution of either material benefits or psychic esteem in any significant degree."[2] Second, it is my view or bias that more government intervention in the operations of the market economy and more redistributive tax and social welfare policies are requisite to achieving the objective of integration. Finally, to achieve this objective or at least to make progress toward its attainment I believe that blacks in America must engage in militant political action and rely on the nationalist principles of self help, self reliance and group solidarity. These biases inform the theoretical, empirical and practical approaches I have taken in this research.

In its present form this book came about in the last several years. However, in a sense I have been working on this study and a related book since I completed graduate work in 1976.[3] Inevitably then I have acquired a number of debts in the course of thinking, researching and writing. Professor Donn Davis at the University of California at Berkeley and Professor Harry Scoble at UCLA first introduced me, each in different ways, to the limits and possibilities of the scientific study of Afro-American politics. At Howard University my mentor, friend and colleague Ronald Walters has been a constant source of support and inspiration and a model of commitment to scholarship and activism in the Afro-American freedom struggle. Although Professor Walters and I disagree in our interpretations of certain aspects of post–civil rights era black politics, (especially the National Black Political Convention), his detailed chapter-by-chapter critique based on his broad knowledge and experience was extremely valuable. I am therefore especially pleased that he consented to write the book's forward. Other colleagues at Howard that over the years provided information and conversation useful in thinking and researching the book include Linda Williams, William Ellis, Charles Harris, Walter Hill, James Sulton, Richard Seltzer, Lorenzo Morris, Ralph Gomes and Alvin Thornton. I owe special debts to Joseph McCormick, II, Mack Jones and Kwasi Harris for the extended time each has devoted to discussions with me on the nature of post–civil rights era black leadership and politics. The indefatigable Hanes Walton, Jr., was always available to help me track down obscure literature and data and has been a reliable source of constructive criticism and advice. At San Francisco State University, my colleagues Rufus Browning and David Tabb engaged in numerous discussions and rendered a detailed critique of the theoretical chapter, which builds to some extent on their earlier prize-winning study *Protest Is Not Enough*. Professor Browning also took the time to read and comment on the entire manuscript.

Richard Shingles, Debbie LeVeen, Aaron Wildavsky and Georgia Persons also rendered detailed critiques of the theoretical chapter that led to improvements in its substance and organization. Professors Persons and Wildavsky also read and made useful comments on Chapter 2, as did Professor Harold Cruse at the University of Michigan, David Covin at Sacramento State and Lorenzo Morris at Howard. Professor Dianne Pinderhughes of the University of Illinois, Clarence Lusanne of Howard and Professor John R. Howard of the State University of New York read the entire manuscript and offered suggestions that led to its improvement. I am especially grateful to Professor Pinderhughes for her detailed chapter-by-chapter comments. Finally, my dear and abiding friend Larry Mason, a sophisticated student of Afro-American politics in his own right although by training an attorney, provided a critical reading of several chapters and was a constant source of critical discussion and debate as the work slowly progressed.

The ideas in this book were tried out initially on the students in my black politics classes at Howard and San Francisco State Universities. I am grateful to those many students for listening and questioning, and to Howard for providing me the unparalled opportunity to spend all of my time teaching in the black politics field. This teaching experience at both the undergraduate and graduate levels was enormously helpful in thought and research for this book. At Howard I also benefitted from the work of three able research assistants, Bernice Taylor, Sadu Sowa and Abraham Poole. At San Francisco State, Paul Anderson was an able and diligent research assistant, and the students in my Congress and Presidency classes assisted me in locating and analyzing memoirs, books and studies on race-related issues in the Carter and Reagan administrations. This study was supported by several modest grants from the faculty research committees at Howard and San Francisco State. I should also like to thank the many black leaders who over the years consented to interviews or completed questionnaires related to this study. Finally, I would be remiss if I did not thank Victoria St. Ambrogio for an especially good job of copyediting.

As with virtually everything I have written beginning with my dissertation, my wife, Scottie, typed the manuscript through its several drafts and provided critical substantive and editorial advice. This book is dedicated to her, my mother, sisters and daughters. Their love and support is the sustaining grace of my life.

Part I

My paramount object in this struggle is to save the Union, and is not either to save or destroy slavery—If I could save the Union without freeing any slave I would do it, and if I could save it by freeing all the slaves I would do it; and if I could save it by freeing some and leaving others alone I would also do that—what I do about slavery and the colored race, I do because I believe it helps to save the union—I shall do less whenever I shall believe what I am doing hurts the cause, and I shall do more whenever I shall believe doing more will help the cause—I shall try to correct errors when shown to be errors; and I shall adopt new views so fast as they shall appear to be true views—I have here stated my purpose according to my view of official duty; and I intend no modification of my oft-expressed personal wish that all men everywhere could be free.

—Abraham Lincoln (1862)

1

From Protest to Incorporation: A Framework for Analysis of Civil Rights Movement Outcomes

In 1905 W.E.B. DuBois and his colleagues issued the Niagara Manifesto, initiating the modern civil rights movement. Four year later the NAACP was created as the movement's principal organizational vehicle. Fifty-nine years later the civil rights movement was over, its basic goals and objectives having been achieved with the passage of the Fair Housing Act of 1968. Two years before, in 1966, factionalism began to overtake the movement as the civil rights establishment was challenged, first by the advocates of black power and then by larger, more diverse factions of radicals, revolutionaries and black nationalists. For a brief period the center of gravity of the movement shifted sharply toward radicalism and nationalism. But by 1980 the radical wing of the movement was in disarray and retreat, and the historic black freedom struggle was largely coopted into routine institutions and processes of American political life. In this chapter I develop a framework and model to analyze these transformations in the nature and character of the modern black freedom struggle.

Although there is a substantial social science literature on social movements,[1] sadly, as one recent review concludes, "our models for understanding the emergence of new social movements and their spread and outcomes are woefully inadequate."[2] This is in part a function of the division of labor in the social sciences between sociologists who focus on movements and political scientists who focus on institutional politics (interest groups, parties, elections and legislatures), leaving relatively unexplored the nexus between these two processes of politics. As the sociologist McAdams puts it in his book on the origins of the civil rights movement, there is an "absence of any real dialogue between political scientists and sociologists. . . . political scientists have traditionally conceptualized power almost exclusively in institutional terms. Accordingly they have failed to adequately explain or take account of the impact of social movements on the institutionalized political establishment."[3] This absence of dialogue, McAdams suggests, may result from the generally negative view of social movements in the early social science research, where they were often viewed as irrational, fanatical expressions of individuals in groups alienated or disconnected from the society.[4] Whatever the reason, McAdams is correct in saying, "It is time the links between institutionalized and insurgent politics were established and insights from both sociology and political science be brought to bear on a complete analysis of the topic of power in America."[5] This is a principal objective of this study, to explain the outcome of the civil rights movement in terms of institutional politics in the United States.[6]

A Framework for Analysis of Social Movement Outcomes

My concern is with the outcomes of the civil rights movement, rather than its origins.[7] First, an abstract model of system responses to social movements is developed and specified. This model is then applied to the civil rights movement from 1905 to 1968 and to its progeny, the black power movement from 1966 to 1972.

In the 1960s in three books David Easton developed a highly abstract model designed to unveil "the basic processes through which a political system, regardless of its generic or specific type, is able to persist as a system of behavior in a world of stability or change."[8] In incomplete and unpublished work, the late Professor Harry Scoble of UCLA developed what he called a "process model" to analyze system responses to insurgent movements.[9] Scoble's model is essentially a further specification and refinement of the output side of the Easton model. It is a modified version of this model that I employ as the framework to analyze the responses of the American political system to the civil rights movement, using it as a bridge or link between insurgent and institutional politics.

Easton's model or framework is simple and straightforward. It is principally concerned with system "persistence" and "maintenance." System persistence involves the "perpetuation of *any* means through which values may be allocated" or binding decisions made for a society.[10] That is, all governments wish to be able to continue to govern in some fashion, that is, persist. Historically, however, Easton notes that system persistence is rarely at issue. Political systems may undergo revolutions or radical changes in values and structures but "seldom is there at stake the survival of any system at all."[11] Political systems may be thoroughly transformed or for a time anarchy may prevail, but government—some authoritative structure to make binding decisions for a society—does not for long completely disappear.[12] Thus the relevant concept is system maintenance. Political systems wish not only to persist but to preserve or maintain a particular kind of system, usually the existing pattern of values, relationships and structures.[13] That is, governments seek to maintain the basic values and relationships that characterize the society, economy and polity. This requires, for any given society at any given time, the identification of these basic or "system" values and relationships. I will do this for the United States shortly; but first Easton's model calls attention to the notion that systems from time to time confront "stress" or "disturbances." Stress is defined as "those conditions that challenge the capacity of a system to persist" while disturbances are those "activities in the environment or within a system that can be expected to or do displace a system from its current pattern of operation."[14] Like our understanding of the emergence of social movements, Easton writes that "At the outset it is necessary to recognize that the precise identification of a stressful condition in a system raises major problems some of which are not amendable to solution."[15] Which is to say that it is difficult beforehand to identify what conditions will give rise to system stress or disturbance. Rather, the model is most useful historically as one can look back and conclude that "Any time a disturbance leads to change of the essential characteristics of a type of system—those that best define the characteristic way in which a system operates—we can say that the system has been put under stress and succumbed."[16] This is essentially how I use the framework to explain the outcomes of the civil rights movement, except I modify it to say that any time a disturbance *threatens* or appears to the authorities to threaten the characteristic operation of a system, then it is under stress and may or may not succumb depending on how it responds.

Stresses or disturbances in the environments (social, economic, cultural, etc.) give rise to demands by individuals and groups on the political system: in the terminology of the system model, "inputs." Theoretically, demands may be categorized as either systemic or nonsystemic. Systemic demands are those that do not challenge or threaten or appear to challenge or threaten the basic values or essential characteristics of the system, while nonsystemic demands are those that do challenge basic system values or characteristics. Typically, then, in the United States systemic demands are the routine inputs of organized interest groups, while nonsystemic demands are frequently the result of social movements. In addition to the substantive character of the demands, the method or methods employed to pursue them may be categorized as systemic and nonsystemic, depending on the nature of

the political system. In the United States systemic methods include elections, lobbying, litigation and nonviolent or peaceful protests, while
nonsystemic methods include any form of violence, organized or spon-
taneous, and forms of nonviolent protest that threaten to disrupt the
routine operations of the system.[17] Systems, or more precisely the elites
or authorities that manage systems, respond to demands on the basis of
their substantive content and the methods employed in pursuit of them.
Clearly, systemic demands pursued through systemic methods are eas-
ier to process than those that challenge basic system values and that
are pursued through violence or other forms of disruption. But in addition, elites respond to demands on the basis of a calculus of the relative
resources (size, money, status, solidarity, weapons, etc.) of the group
(and its allies) making the demands in relationship to the group or
groups that may be opposed to the group and/or its demands. Depending on the relationship of these input variables in terms of demand
type, methods and the relative balance of power or resources between
the proponents and the opposition, Scoble identified five logically possible systemic responses or outputs: neglect, symbolism, substantive
policy, cooptation and political repression.

Scoble's five outputs in many ways simply specify or make
explicit what is implicit in Easton's model. Easton notes that a system in
response to demands has "the capacity to call up a variety of responses"
or "repertories of options."[18] For example, Easton refers to the substantive policy output, or response, as when the system responds by "mod-
ifying the conditions so that the original circumstances that gave rise to
the demands no longer exist," and to the symbolic option as when the
system takes steps "to create this impression [of substantive policy] in
the minds of the members, even though in fact nothing other than
image has changed."[19] In addition, neglect is possible. In response to
demands the system may do nothing, act as if there is no input. This
option is possible if the group's demands and its methods are such that
they do not constitute any form of threat or pressure, or when a
response to the demands of one group might result in opposition from
other groups with greater resources or the capacities to impose counter-
demands or pressures on the system. The authorities then may calculate
that system maintenance requires ignoring one group's demands
because of the opposition or potential opposition of others.

Cooptation is defined as the "process of absorbing new elements
into the leadership-determining structure of an organization as a means
of avoiding threats to its stability."[20] Two types are identified: formal
and informal. Formal cooptation occurs when there is a need to publicly
absorb new elements in response to mass discontent and a threat or

perceived threat to system maintenance or legitimacy. Thus, highly visible appointments are made, new organizations established, all with great fanfare in order to signify participation or inclusion within the system. Informal cooptation, on the other hand, occurs not as a result of mass movements or perceived threats to system legitimacy or maintenance but when powerful groups have sufficient resources to more or less impose their demands on the system. Here the problem is not a response to mass discontent but to organized power. Cooptation is, therefore, informal, nonpublic, because the group is interested in the substance of power, not its trappings. In addition, an open capitulation to organized power may itself undermine legitimacy since it may be perceived as an undemocratic bowing to powerful special interests.[21] In dealing with system response to the civil rights movement my concern is with formal cooptation. First, because blacks, relatively speaking, were not a powerful group during the period under consideration and the movement in its final phase did pose or at least was perceived by the authorities to pose a threat to system stability, legitimacy or maintenance.

Formal cooptation often occurs simultaneously with political repression. Groups that pose a threat to system stability may be repressed, but since every system wishes to govern by consent rather than repression cooptation is usually the preferred alternative. That is, if drawing leadership elements of the dissident group into the system has the effect of restoring stability and legitimacy, then it is preferred. But, it may be that in some circumstances cooptation is not enough—necessary, but not sufficient—and therefore repression becomes necessary as well. Repression may also be employed prophylactically so as to prevent the emergence of ideas, groups or demands that might eventually pose a threat to the system. What is repression? Wolfe proposes that it be understood as "A process by which those in power try to keep themselves in power by attempting to destroy or render harmless organizations and ideologies that threaten their power," while Goldstein writes that repression is "government action which grossly discriminates against persons or organizations viewed as presenting a fundamental challenge to existing power relationships or key government policies because of their perceived beliefs."[22] In a narrower vein Scoble defines it as simply the "negative sanctioning of political opinion and action."[23] All these definitions call attention to the fact that elites seek to preserve the system (and their power within it) by imposing sanctions on ideas and organizations that may threaten it and this is done through sanctions, more or less severe, as the circumstances call for. In every system, certain ideas or ideologies are stigmatized and persons holding them are considered "outside of the mainstream" and are ignored or are denied opportunities otherwise available to citizens. This has the effect of artificially foreshortening the range of permissible political thought and behavior within the system. The sanctions employed to achieve these objectives may range from denial of employment opportunities and access to the media, to attempts to infiltrate, subvert and disrupt political organizations; harass and discredit political leaders; legal or judicial repression; forced exile and, in extreme cases, death.

The ideas, ideologies or values that are nonsystemic, outside of the mainstream, vary by systems and by historical circumstances in a given system. It is important therefore to identify, for any given system at any given time, its systemic values, relationships or structures. Thus, at the outset, before using this framework in analysis of system responses to the civil rights movement, it is necessary to identify such values in the context of the American system. But first, of the five system responses, Scoble emphasizes that they seldom occur singularly or sequentially (except perhaps neglect); rather, they tend to occur in some combination, what Scoble calls a "judicious mix." That is, depending on the nature of the demands, their methods of expression and the relative balance of forces between the group and its opposition, the system will respond with the full repertoire of options; some cooptation and symbolism with a bit of repression and a dash of substantive policy in order to arrive at the appropriate recipe for system stability and maintenance.

Systemic Responses to the Civil Rights Movement, 1905–1968

System response to the demands of a group are a function to a significant degree of the nature of the demand, particularly whether it is systemic or nonsystemic. A substantive policy response, other things being equal, is a much more likely response to systemic demands while repression, other things being equal, is the more likely response to nonsystemic demands. The demand for civil rights was a challenge to racism. The question therefore is whether racism—the subordination of blacks on the basis of their color—was systemic. That is, was racism, like for examples democracy, constitutionalism and capitalism, a basic value or relationship essential to the characteristic operations of the system, its society, economy and polity? The answer is difficult. Hardly anyone would disagree that during the civil rights era and today that democracy, constitutionalism and capitalism are basic values or essential characteristics of the American system. Racism is more problematic. Some would argue that during the civil rights era (and today as well) racism was (is) a basic value or set of characteristics of the system.

Others would disagree. No serious student would argue that racism historically was not systemic but some would contend that with ratification of the Civil War amendments racism became contrary to system values, unconstitutional, un-American. Although it was widely practiced and officially sanctioned in the southern region especially but to some extent throughout the country, it might be argued that this practice was contrary to principle, a violation of the nation's creed as Myrdal put it in *An American Dilemma*. Indeed, the principal thesis of Myrdal's famous study was this alleged conflict between the systemic values of democracy, equality and constitutionalism and the "group prejudices against particular persons or types of people and all sorts of miscellaneous wants, impulses and habits that dominate his outlook."[24] This was the view, at least the stated view, of Martin King as he invoked the Bible and the Constitution in support of his claim that the demands of the civil rights movement were systemic. President Kennedy invoked these same principles in his 1963 television address proposing the Civil Rights Act, declaring that the movement's demands were "as old as the scriptures and as clear as the American Constitution." But both King and Kennedy might have made these assertions because of their strategic efficacy rather than because they corresponded to systemic realities. For example, it might be argued, to put it colloquially, that actions speak louder than words, that behavior is a more relevant indicator of essential system characteristics than abstractly invoked principles. It is possible for systems, like individuals, to deny themselves, to live with contradiction and paradox. As Silberman put it in 1964 referring to Myrdal's alleged dilemma, "The tragedy of race relations in the United States is that there is no American dilemma. White Americans are not torn and tortured by the conflict between their devotion to the American creed and their actual behavior. They are upset by the current state of race relations, to be sure, but what troubles them is not justice being denied but that peace is being shattered and their business interrupted."[25] This problem does not lend itself to a neat conceptual or empirical resolution. To some extent, whether racism was systemic in the civil rights era or even today in the post-civil rights era is a matter of intellectual or ideological tastes. Perhaps all that can be said with certainty is that in the southern region of the country the elites of this subsystem viewed racism as systemic, as part of the "southern way of life." Thus, to the extent that the civil rights movement was targeted on and in the south, its demands were nonsystemic.

As I indicated at the outset of this chapter, contrary to much popular, journalistic and academic opinion the civil rights movement did not begin in the 1950s and 1960s; rather, it entered its final phase and came to an end during this period. It is difficult to locate the origins of a social movement in any exact manner. My starting point is the early part of this century with the 1905 Niagara Conference, the formation of the NAACP in 1909 and the death of Booker Washington in 1915. It is during this period that the basic goals, strategies and organizational bases of the modern movement for civil rights were developed. At the conference at Niagara, DuBois, William Monroe Trotter and other Afro-American intellectuals and political activists challenged the dominant conservative, accommodationist, anti–civil rights philosophy of Booker Washington and laid out an alternative agenda of civil rights activism. The goals of the movement were summed up in the Niagara Manifesto: "We will not be satisfied to take one jot or title less than our manhood rights. We claim for ourselves every single right that belongs to free born Americans, political, civil and social; and until we get these rights we will never cease to protest and assail the ears of America."[26] The document raised specific demands for the right to vote, an end to discrimination in public accommodations, equal enforcement of the law and quality education. As for strategy or methods, the Manifesto declared, "These are some of the things we want. How shall we get them? By voting where we may vote; by persistent, unceasing agitation, by hammering at the truth; by sacrifice and hard work."[27]

Although the influence of Booker Washington's accommodationist philosophy was to continue (in the rural south into the 1950s and early 1960s), in large part as a result of the "hammering" propaganda of DuBois in the NAACP's magazine *The Crisis* a consensus developed among the northern Afro-American intelligentsia and civic, church and fraternal leadership around the basic goals and strategies of the Afro-American freedom struggle as sketched out in the Niagara Manifesto. The formation of the interracial NAACP provided a centralized organizational vehicle for the struggle and by the time of Washington's death several years later, the civil rights leadership of DuBois and his NAACP colleagues were well on their way to displacing the accommodationist leadership of Washington's "Tuskegee Machine" in the eyes of the Afro-American leadership and the national structure of white power.[28] And despite sometimes vigorous challenges from the nationalist tendency (most effectively, the Garvey movement) and the socialist left in the Afro-American community, the liberal integrationist civil rights protest consensus endured, providing the intellectual and organizational groundwork for the coalition of white liberals, labor and religious groups that yielded the enactment of the basic items of the Niagara agenda in the mid-1960s civil rights laws.

For purposes of analyzing system responses to the civil rights movement (1905–68), the movement may usefully be divided into three relatively distinct phases—lobbying, litigation and protest—although there is of course overlap.[29] To be effective, a group that engages in lobbying must have certain resources: a degree of status, money, skills, organization, access to the media and government decision makers and the vote. Compared to its opposition—principally although not exclusively the white power structure of the south—the civil rights movement had relatively few resources. At a time when white supremacist thought was dominant in the culture, blacks had relatively low status; the group was disproportionately poor and uneducated; the NAACP was just getting off the ground organizationally in terms of staff and affiliates (a fully staffed Washington office was not established until the 1950s) and access to the mainstream media and key government decision makers in the Congress and the executive was seldom routine and frequently nonexistent. And finally, until the 1940s near 90 percent of the black electorate, concentrated in the southern region, was disenfranchised. The absence of the ballot is critical because effective lobbying in the United States depends on the ability of the group to threaten decision makers with the ultimate sanction—deprivation of office. Given this calculus of resources between the movement and its opponents, neglect or symbolism are the predictable systemic responses.

Simultaneous with and in a sense a precondition to the initiation of its lobbying strategy, the NAACP under DuBois's leadership launched a campaign of education and propaganda in order to alter the inferior status of blacks and to shape a favorable climate of public opinion on the Afro-American and his civil rights. White supremacist doctrine and propaganda was at its zenith; the historian Rayford Logan called this period at the turn of the century the "nadir" of the Negro in American life and thought.[30] Thus, DuBois and others used the pages of *The Crisis* (and the mainstream media where accessible) to "hammer at the truth" about the notions of black inferiority, about the democratic impulses of Reconstruction and generally about the moral and political imperative of civil rights and racial justice.[31] It is difficult to gauge the effects of these efforts on elite and mass public opinion but they certainly provided reasoned and occasionally eloquent rebuttals to racist and white supremacist propaganda.

In 1909 the NAACP launched its fifty year campaign to secure passage of federal anti-lynching legislation.[32] Lynching—the ritualistic murder of blacks who challenged or allegedly challenged their subordinate place in the southern social system—was an abomination. Thousands of blacks were lynched from the 1870s through the 1950s as part of the southern strategy to use fear and intimidation to maintain the racist social system. It worked. Again, the purpose of lynching was political: to maintain the subordination of blacks by demonstrating the terrible things that might happen to anyone, man, woman or child, who challenged the system. Katznelson writes:

> Most lynch victims were hanged or shot, but often other means, grotesque in their horror, were employed. The humiliations and tortures were often incredible. In Waco, Texas, in 1916, Jesse Washington, a retarded adolescent, was burned at the stake in the public square while thousands watched and cheered. In South Carolina in May 1918, after three innocent men had been hanged for murder, the lynch mob "strung up" the pregnant widow of one by the ankles, doused her clothing with gasoline, and after it burned away, cut out the unborn child and trampled it under-foot, then riddled her with bullets. Of the 416 blacks lynched between 1918 and 1927, forty-two were burned alive, sixteen burned after death and eight beaten to death and cut to pieces.[33]

Although under the federal Constitution the punishment for mur-der is the responsibility of the states, the NAACP sought federal inter-vention since it was clear that state authorities were either unable or, more likely, unwilling to enforce the law. The response of the system from 1909 until the demand for this legislation was dropped in the 1960s was neglect. The legislation was twice passed in the House but died in the Senate as a result of southern filibusters. The role of Presi-dent Franklin Roosevelt shows the limits of the lobbying strategy.[34] Roosevelt was not overtly hostile to the black demand for civil rights but in his long tenure as President he never supported a legislative civil rights demand. Rather, he argued, as did President Kennedy a genera-tion later, that to support the anti-lynching bill or other civil rights leg-islation would antagonize the powerful white southerners who con-trolled important congressional committees and thereby jeopardize his social welfare legislation, which, he pointed out, disproportionately benefitted blacks. In addition, Roosevelt was aware that the white south played pivotal roles in the Democratic Party nominating process and constituted an important bloc of votes in the electoral college. By con-trast, blacks had no comparable resources. They throughout this period had only one or two members of the House, no representation in the Senate, little representation or leverage in the Democratic nomination process and only marginal leverage on the electoral votes of the states outside the southern region. Thus, the system's response was neglect.

Although blacks continued to press for anti-lynching legislation during the Truman and Eisenhower administrations, in the 1930s the NAACP began to shift from a strategy of lobbying to litigation. This was in part a result of the Association's recognition of the severe resource constraints it faced in trying to effectively lobby the Congress and the president.[35] President Truman proposed a major civil rights package in 1948 but it was rejected by the Congress, and it precipitated a third-party revolt by the party's southern wing and the loss of several deep-south states in the fall election. Thus, gradually, civil rights strategy shifted from the lobbies of Congress to the courts. The shift was gradual but by the late 1940s litigation had become the dominant method or strategy of the movement. Lobbying efforts continued but more resources were allocated to the legal effort than lobbying; for example more resources to the NAACP Legal Defense Fund under Thurgood Marshall than to the Association's Washington bureau under Clarence Mitchell.[36] The lobbying strategy continued and, in part as a result of the patient and skillful work of Mitchell, the Congress in 1957 and again in 1960 passed civil rights bills, the first since Reconstruction. These bills, however, represented a symbolic rather than substantive response to the civil rights demand, providing an image of action or change rather than any real modifications in the conditions of blacks in the United States.

In 1939, in recognition of the importance of the shift to litigation and to take advantage of new laws granting tax-exempt status to organizations that did not engage in lobbying, the NAACP created a separate organization—the NAACP Legal Defense Fund—to pursue exclusively the demand for civil rights through the courts. From this point until the protests of the 1960s, litigation was the dominant strategy of the movement and Thurgood Marshall the movement's preeminent leader. In terms of resource mobilization, this strategy shift was a rational response to the resource constraints of lobbying. Unlike lobbying, litigation requires comparatively few resources in terms of money (relatively speaking, since the series of cases consolidated as *Brown* probably cost in excess of $100,000, not counting the free legal and other expertise provided) and votes. Rather, litigation requires only a skilled pool of legal talent, organized systematically. In the 1930s Charles Hamilton Houston transformed the Howard University Law School into a civil rights laboratory and clearinghouse.[37] The result was the training of a cadre of lawyers committed to using the courts to press the demand for civil rights. With the formation in 1939 of the Legal Defense Fund, this resource was mobilized in a systematic strategy to use the due process and equal protection clauses of the Fourteenth Amendment, and the Fifteenth Amendment to restructure race relations in the south.

The use of litigation was not an entirely new strategy. The NAACP in fact won a major Court victory in 1917 when in *Buchanan v. Warley* the Supreme Court invalidated a Louisville, Kentucky ordinance requiring residential segregation.[38] What was new in the 1940s was the priority and systematic pursuit of the strategy in a series of test cases in the areas of voting and school segregation.[39] Simultaneously with the NAACP's strategy shift, the Supreme Court was in the process of shifting its jurisprudence away from the protection of property rights toward a concern with individual rights and the protection of the rights of insular and isolated minorities. This came about partly because of the Court's losing its bitter battle with Roosevelt over the constitutionality of several major New Deal programs. In addition, Roosevelt's several appointments gradually transformed the conservative court toward liberal activism. By the 1940s then, the NAACP and the Court were converging in their approaches to litigation.

In 1944 in *Smith v. Allwright* the NAACP won a major victory, when the Court invalidated the Texas Democratic Party's whites-only primary, a reversal of its decision in *Grovey v. Townsend* (1935) which had sanctioned such primaries. Ten years later in the *Brown* school desegregation cases the Court reversed the doctrine of separate but equal established in the 1896 *Plessy v. Ferguson* case. These were important victories but they were largely symbolic, providing an image of action and change but with little effect on the conditions of southern blacks in terms of voting or schools.[40] Southern schools were not effectively desegregated until the late 1960s, largely as a result of enforcement of Title VII of the 1964 Civil Rights Act; and blacks did not get the effective right to participate in Democratic primaries in the south until implementation of the 1965 Voting Rights Act. Symbolic responses, however, are not necessarily inconsequential in political life. The *Brown* case does not stand as a landmark in the Afro-American freedom struggle because of its impact on the education of blacks but precisely because of its symbolic value. What the unanimous decision of the Court in this case said was that racism and segregation were not systemic; they were unconstitutional and un-American. This symbolism of *Brown* probably gave impetus and inspiration to those who would launch the final, protest phase of the movement. In a sense it provided an additional resource to the movement, intangible but a resource nevertheless since for the first time since Reconstruction the Constitution could be said to be on the side of blacks rather than southern segregationists. Perhaps then it is no accident that the final and most effective phase of the movement was launched one year after *Brown*.

Protest in the form of boycotts, sit-ins and mass demonstrations had been employed before in the civil rights struggle. The significance of the year-long Montgomery bus boycott in 1955 was that it resulted in the emergence of a charismatic leader, an organization and a systematic strategy of protest. After the success at Montgomery, Martin Luther King, Jr. and his colleagues in the Southern Christian Leadership Conference, CORE and the Student Nonviolent Coordinating Committee began thinking through and testing out the strategic use of protest as a means to press the movement's demands. The demonstrations at Birmingham in 1963 and at Selma in 1965 were the fruits of this decade of systematic planning.

The strategy of nonviolent protest as a means to "demonstrate" to the nation and its leadership the nature of southern racism was rooted in the philosophy and strategy of Mohandas Gandhi but also in the thesis of Myrdal that most Americans, if forced to choose, would repudiate racism rather than democratic principles. The purpose of the demonstrations was to force Americans and their leaders to choose. Although nonviolence was the guiding principle and practice of King and his colleagues, the strategy depended on a violent response by southern authorities in order to be effective. In effect, the strategy employed systemic methods of peaceful protests as a means to invoke a nonsystemic or violent reaction on the part of the opposition.[41] Racist violence—transmitted to the nation and the world through television—would elicit sympathy, support and allies who would then use their resources to pressure national authorities to enact and implement policies that would alter the racist values and operating practices of the southern subsystem.[42] This is essentially what happened in the decade between Montgomery in 1955 and Selma in 1965.

In 1962 Dr. King led a series of demonstrations in Albany, Georgia. They failed, having no effect on segregation practices locally and, more importantly, on national decision makers in Washington. They failed because Albany's police chief apparently understood that King's strategy of protest required a violent response on the part of the authorities. Therefore, throughout the several weeks of the Albany campaign, the police not only did not themselves respond violently but also protected the demonstrators from the threat of violence from white citizens. Albany was important, however, in the lessons learned. As the next target of the movement, King in 1963 choose Birmingham, in large part because of its police commissioner's reputation for violent repression of the local civil rights movement. Commissoner Eugene "Bull" Connor acted like a bull, unleashing a wave of violent assaults on peaceful demonstrators including school children. The Birmingham campaign received worldwide television coverage and the desired strategic consequence.

Despite the demands of the civil rights lobby and the pivotal role blacks had played in his narrow election, President Kennedy in 1963 had tentatively decided to postpone sending comprehensive civil rights legislation to Congress until after 1964. First, because he had other domestic legislative priorities—tax cuts, medicare, trade—that would (so he thought) be held hostage by the southerners who controlled key committees of the Congress if he proposed a civil rights bill. Second, the President, while generally sympathetic to the aspirations of blacks, was not passionately committed to the cause and judged that even if he proposed legislation it would not pass. From this perspective, his proposing such legislation would be a useless symbolic exercise that might damage his entire legislative agenda and perhaps his prospects for reelection. Calculating that he would be reelected by a substantial margin in 1964, Kennedy had tentatively decided to delay any civil rights legislation until his second term, when he thought the chances of passage would be greater and he would not have to worry about the impact on his political future. The demonstrations at Birmingham dramatically changed these calculations and forced the reluctant president to reorder his priorities and make civil rights the principal item on his domestic agenda. First, because Birmingham resulted in the activation of powerful elements of the Democratic coalition—labor, liberals and religious groups—in support of the black demands. These forces served to counterbalance the influence of the white south on Kennedy's political calculations. Second, and most critically, Kennedy judged that the demonstrations at Birmingham and elsewhere represented what, in his June 1963 nationwide television address, he called a "rising tide of discontent" that threatened system stability. Thus, he said it was time for the system to respond and take the issue from the streets into the Congress. Shortly thereafter he proposed what was to become the Civil Rights Act of 1964, the first substantive response to the demands of the civil rights movement since its inception in 1905.

This pattern of national policy elites responding to protests and disorders in the streets rather than routine lobbying or litigation also characterized the enactment of the other major civil rights bills of the 1960s. Although President Johnson had in 1965 instructed the Justice Department to begin drafting voting rights legislation, the violence and brutality of the authorities at Selma during the demonstrations led by King resulted in earlier-than-planned submission of the legislation, a stronger bill and its speedier passage by the Congress. Similarly, the 1968 Fair Housing Act appeared stalled in Congress until the violent rebellions in the aftermath of Dr. King's murder resulted in its unexpected quick passage.

The principal theoretical points to be made about the system's response to the demands of the civil rights movement are that it was slow and when there was a response it was most often symbolic. Further, it responded substantively *only* when protests, violence and disorders threatened or at least were perceived by national elites to threaten system maintenance or stability. Finally, it should be noted that even as the system was responding in the 1960s with substantive policies, there was also what Scoble describes as the "judicious mix" of other responses including cooptation and repression. Both cooptation and repression became more pronounced as the decade progressed and the civil rights movement turned toward radical, nonsystemic demands and strategies, but they were present throughout the decade. Indeed, repression as a systemic response was more or less a response to the movement from its inception at the beginning of the century.[43]

In any event, the civil rights movement came to an end in the middle 1960s. After more than a half century of lobbying, litigation and protest, the basic goals of the Afro-American freedom struggle as articulated in the 1905 Niagara Manifesto had been achieved. The focus of this book is on what happened next. Tarrow writes:

> Protest cycles can either end suddenly, through repression, or more slowly, through a combination of features: the institutionalization of the most successful movements, factionalization within them and between them and new groups which rise on the crest of the wave and the exhaustion of mass political involvement. The combination of institutionalization and factionalization often produce determined minorities, who respond to the decline of popular involvement by turning upon themselves and—in some cases—using organized violence.[44]

These combination of features characterized the end of the civil rights movement. With the passage of the basic civil rights laws the movement was at a crossroads; A. Phillip Randolph, its elder statesman, said it suffered from a "crisis of victory." Simply put, although the movement had achieved its fundamental goal of equal rights under law, blacks still were not equal in fact, as the long-standing problems of racism and poverty in the big city ghettos (dramatically manifested two weeks after signing of the Voting Rights Act by the Watts riot) now became the principal concern of the civil rights leadership. As Dr. King put it in the title of his last book, "Where do we go from here?" was the question of the moment. Answers to this question sparked more than a decade of intense internal debate and factionalism in the movement (see Chapter 2).

Dr. King sought to continue the movement style of politics, with a focus on economic rights (and the Vietnam war) and the problems of poverty and ghettoization, conducting demonstrations in Chicago while planning a national poor peoples campaign to end with a march on Washington for economic justice (specifically a full employment and guaranteed income program). This approach, a continuation of movement style protests—although not the substantive demand for full employment—was opposed by the other major leaders in the civil rights establishment (Roy Wilkins of the NAACP and Whitney Young of the Urban League), the young Jesse Jackson and most vigorously by Bayard Rustin, the movement's principal strategic planner. Rustin in his writings and in internal debates sharply criticized the idea of the poor peoples campaign and when he did not prevail refused, despite continued pleading from King, to assist in any way with the campaign's planning (see Chapter 7). Instead of protest Rustin argued for a strategy shift from protest to institutional or systemic politics in the form of a progressive electoral coalition as the most effective way to achieve King's economic justice agenda. Rustin's position as to the movement's new direction was to eventually prevail, but not without much debate, turmoil and violence sparked by the black power revolt, the ghetto rebellions and a turn toward radical and revolutionary activism by elements of the movement's more radical wing.

The Student Nonviolent Coordinating Committee (SNCC), the most self-consciously radical of movement organizations, started the black power debate on the 1966 Meredith March in Mississippi.[45] For several years the more nationalist SNCC staffers had been attempting to bring more separatist principles into the movement, principles drawn from Frantz Fanon, Malcolm X and the Nation of Islam. Under the leadership of Bill Ware, a small group of SNCC Atlanta staffers, organized to mobilize support for ousted Georgia State Representative and former SNCC worker Julian Bond, began to develop ideas around these more nationalist themes.[46] In 1966 the group prepared a position paper that set forth the fundamental themes and a rudimentary proposal that constituted the basic manifesto of black power. Although Stokely Carmichael initially joined with a majority of the staff in rejecting the separatist themes of the position paper, after his defeat of the incumbent Chairman John Lewis in a bitter and divisive election he embraced the principles and rhetoric of black power. Carmichael's victory was widely interpreted in the press as a triumph of black radicalism and national-ism. Carmichael then persuaded SNCC to join the Meredith March in order to use it as a forum to articulate and build support for black power.[47] As a result of the Mississippi march, black power immediately became the focus of widespread debate (elite and mass, black and white) and controversy regarding the future of the freedom struggle.[48]

Although black power ultimately came to represent the employ-ment of systemic interest or pressure group strategies to pursue post–civil rights era objectives,[49] in its first several years it was inter-preted as a radical, violence-prone revolutionary break with the civil rights status quo and the established political order. That is, in its demands and its methods black power came to represent a system-challenging movement. Simultaneous with the growing radicalism of the movement, the urban black lower class revolted in a series of riots from 1965 to 1968. And in 1967 the Black Panther Party "picked up the gun" and became an explicitly nationalist, Marxist-Leninist political formation, posing a direct violent challenge to basic system values and procedures.[50] This threatening symbolism of black power, its clear break with systemic rhetoric and routines, was made emphatic for the author-ities by Carmichael's attendance as guest of honor at the Organization of Latin-American Solidarity (OLAS) in Havana in August 1967. At this meeting of communists, socialists and revolutionaries from through-out the hemisphere, Carmichael declared, "America is going to fall and I only hope I live long enough to see it."[51] In this situation an intensifi-cation of repression as a systemic response was predictable; there was a perceived threat to system stability, and in the minds of army intelli-gence and the head of the nation's police/domestic intelligence appa-ratus—J. Edgar Hoover—there was a real danger that the Afro-Ameri-can freedom struggle might be transformed into a genuine revolution.

Political repression may take any number of forms, from denial of employment opportunities and access to the media, to attempts to infil-trate, subvert and disrupt political organizations, harass and discredit movement leaders, legal repression and murder. All of these forms of repression were used against the black movement in the late 1960s and early 1970s.[52] The major goal of this campaign of repression was, as Hoover wrote, to "prevent the coalition of militant black nationalist groups . . . which might be the first step toward a real mau mau in America, the beginning of true black revolution."[53] It is unlikely that Hoover's musings about revolution were well founded, but in any event the government was by and large successful in its campaign to "expose, disrupt and otherwise neutralize" the movement's radical wing, ren-dering it near impotent by the early 1970s.

Simultaneous with this pattern of repression the system responded with cooptation, a systematic and highly visible effort to absorb blacks into the system as a means of system maintenance and stability. Again, cooptation in the formal sense occurs when there is a need to publicly absorb new elements in response to mass discontent and the loss or perceived loss of legitimacy. Thus, while the radical wing of the movement was being repressed, more moderate elements were being drawn into highly visible systemic offices. This has the purpose over time of restoring confidence in the system in the eyes of the movement's mass base.[54] Since the early 1970s, while repression has abated the process of cooptation is ongoing, so that today we have only marginalized remnants of movement-style politics as the phenomenon is now nearly wholly encapsulated in the routines of systemic institutions and processes.

In ordinary discourse cooptation is a pejorative term. However, as Selznick writes, cooptation is often the "realistic core of avowedly democratic procedures."[55] In other words, it is part of the structural adjustment of democratic systems to the claims of new groups for inclusion, integration or incorporation. Integration in this sense was certainly high on the list of the priorities of the traditional civil rights establishment with its emphasis on the right to vote and participate in the political process. As Dr. King said, "Give us the ballot" and we will transform the social structure of oppression. Thus, from the perspective of the movement's radical wing cooptation is pejorative, a negative response or output; but from the perspective of the movement's center or establishment it is viewed, as Rustin argued, as the fulfillment of a long-held movement goal, akin to ending segregation in public facilities. This is also the view of virtually all students of protest and social movements in the United States: that protest is not enough; that social movements inevitably exhaust themselves; that if the causes represented by mass movements are to be sustained and advanced it must be through institutional structures and processes or not at all. Whatever the reasons for this outcome of the movement, it is clear that since the death of Dr. King, the Afro-American freedom struggle has become incorporated into systemic institutions and processes.

Incorporation and Coalition Formation: Afro-American Political Strategy in the Post–Civil Rights Era

A variety of concepts—cooptation, integration, incorporation and institutionalization—have been employed to describe the system-oriented character of the Afro-American freedom struggle since the end of the civil rights era. There is in the social science literature no clear-cut distinctions between these concepts. They are all used by scholars to describe the same phenomenon. A group previously excluded from systemic institutions and processes is brought into those institutions and processes, either because it poses a threat to system stability or maintenance or because it is part of the normal, evolutionary adjustments of a democratic society to the claims of new groups for inclusion, incorporation or integration. If the group is incorporated in response to its perceived threats to system stability, legitimacy or maintenance, then Selznick describes it as cooptation; however, it has also been labeled by some scholars as institutionalization.[56] In addition to distinguishing the phenomenon on the basis of why it occurred—as a natural adjustment of democratic societies to the claims of new groups for inclusion or in response to disruptions and instability—the concepts may be distinguished on the basis of their substantive outcomes, whether inclusion represents a gain or loss for the group. Inclusion may be viewed as cooptation, a "sellout," when it results in relatively few substantive gains for the group and when it has the tendency to decrease or undermine the capacity of the group to press its demands for gains in the future.[57] Incorporation or integration, on the other hand, is viewed positively because it is believed to result in substantive gains for the group and, more importantly, by "working within the system" it increases the capacity of the group to press effectively for further gains. Thus, whether the inclusion of blacks since the 1960s into systemic institutions and processes is cooptation or integration/incorporation is an empirical question and a matter of interpretation. The empirical questions involve the extent to which blacks have made substantive gains since the 1960s and the extent to which their inclusion in the system has helped or hurt their capacities to press their demands on the system. The bulk of this book is devoted to answering these two questions. But the empirical data are not unambiguous; whether blacks in the post–civil rights era have enhanced their capacities to press their demands on the system and whether the system has responded substantively to those demands is also a matter of interpretation of the empirical data. Is the proverbial glass since the 1960s half full or half empty? The data and analysis presented in this book on the last twenty-five years of the black freedom struggle leads me to conclude that the results of incorporation are that blacks have lost the capacity to effectively press their demands on the system and that the system has consequentially responded to their demands with symbolism, neglect and an ongoing pattern of cooptation. Consequently, black politics has become largely irrelevant in terms of a politics and policies that would address effectively the problems of the race in the post–civil rights era.

Whatever the concept used, no one disputes that since the 1960s the black movement has shifted from protest to politics. Bayard Rustin was a key figure in this strategy shift. Rustin had vigorously opposed Dr. King's planned poor peoples campaign, arguing that while its goal of full employment was appropriate, protest as a strategy to achieve it was counterproductive. Instead, he argued that full employment and other major social reforms could only be achieved through what he called "political power." In his seminal article "From Protest to Politics: The Future of the Civil Rights Movement" published in *Commentary* in 1965, Rustin laid out the strategic rationale for the movement's transformation as well as a rudimentary post–civil rights era agenda. First, Rustin argued that the movement could not be "victorious in the absence of radical programs for full employment, the abolition of slums, the reconstruction of our educational system, new definitions of work and leisure. . . . How are these radical objectives to be achieved? The answer is simple, deceptively so: through political power."[58] More specifically, Rustin maintained that the 1964 Civil Rights Act had destroyed the legal foundations of racism; that the Economic Opportunity Act of 1964 and the war on poverty furnished the means for attacking the cumulative effects of racism; and that the Voting Rights Act of 1965 provided the tools for the enfranchisement of millions of potential progressive voters. Thus, he argued, the movement should turn to electoral activism in an effort to build a "coalition of progressive forces which becomes the effective political majority in the United States . . . Negroes, trade unions, liberals and religious groups."[59] By the early 1970s Rustin's position as to the movement's new direction had become dominant, displacing strategies of protest and violent rebellion.

What Rustin called for was a strategy of incorporation. Political incorporation, Stinchcombe writes, is "The capability [of a group] of influencing elections so that one's party has a chance to enter a majority coalition on at least some issues of most importance to it, and that majority is able to control the government."[60] According to Stinchcombe, an empirical index of a group's incorporation includes (1) the proportion of the group with the vote, (2) the chances that the parties the group votes for have of getting into a majority coalition and (3) the powers of the parliament, legislature or the government generally.[61] Browning, Marshall and Tabb, in a study dealing specifically with the incorporation of blacks in local politics, identify three necessary steps if excluded groups are to move toward political incorporation. Following Stinchcombe, these steps include (1) the mobilization of the black electorate, (2) the development and maintenance of a multiethnic coalition of other minorities and progressive whites and (3) winning elections and becoming the governing majority.[62] These, stated simply, are the essential components of post–civil rights era black politics. It is a politics that has largely failed, resulting in either neglect of the black agenda or symbolic responses as in the case of the Humphrey-Hawkins Act. The remainder of this book details this failure; but to summarize briefly here in terms of the Stinchcombe index or the steps in the Browning, Marshall and Tabb theory: the strategy of incorporation has failed because (1) the black community has not been effectively mobilized; (2) the progressive coalition of whites and other ethnic minorities envisioned by Rustin has not materialized, (3) the party supported by blacks has not had a good chance of controlling the national government and when it has controlled the government—as in the case of the Carter Administration—it has tended to ignore black demands or respond with symbols.

Finally, putting this discussion in the context of the system framework developed at the outset of this chapter: The strategy or methods employed by blacks to press their demands in the post–civil rights era have been wholly systemic—voting, elections, and efforts at multiethnic coalition formation. Protests and mass demonstrations are occasionally employed but without the strategic purposes of the 1960s demonstrations, that is, as a means to bring pressure on the system to respond with substantive policy outputs. Rather, protests in the post–civil rights era have become institutionalized and those that have occurred in the last twenty-five years have been largely symbolic or ceremonial.[63] Violence, of course, is eschewed by the post–civil rights era black establishment, as it was, in principle at least, by the civil rights establishment.[64] In terms of the substantive dimension of the post–civil rights era black agenda, although many of its elements are systemic there is underlying its principal item—full employment—a nonsystemic quality. In his 1965 essay Rustin wrote, ". . . while most Negroes in their hearts—unquestionably seek only to enjoy the fruits of American society as it now exists, their quest cannot be *objectively* satisfied within the framework of existing political and economic relations."[65] Rather, Rustin said that adding up the costs of a full employment program and a program of ghetto reconstruction, "we can only conclude that we are talking about a refashioning of our political economy."[66] Rustin, a democratic socialist, was probably correct; an effective full employment program would likely require some restructuring of the political economy. This was the evolving view of Dr. King and as will be shown in Chapter 7, it was also the view of both liberal and conservative critics of the 1976 Humphrey-Hawkins Act. This is the crux of the problem of post–civil rights era black politics: trying to achieve a nonsystemic demand by routine, systemic methods. The predictable response is neglect, or at best, symbolism.

Blacks in the post–civil rights era have had a dual agenda that includes not only fundamental social and economic reforms around programs of full employment and ghetto reconstruction but also a narrower race-specific agenda that seeks to maintain and extend the civil rights gains of the 1960s. By and large they have been successful in this narrow area of civil rights, even in the face of hostile presidents, courts and public opinion (see Chapter 6). In this sense the glass is half full. That is, on civil rights, blacks have been effectively incorporated into the system. However, unlike the fairly narrow, race-specific agenda of the civil rights era, the new agenda of black politics is broad and multi-faceted.

Since the late 1960s a bewildering series of conventions, meetings, leadership summits, assemblies, congresses, institutes and so forth have replaced rallies, marches and demonstrations and lawsuits as the principal routine activity of the black leadership establishment. These meetings and gatherings of the 1960s and 1970s have yielded an equally bewildering set of documents variously described as the black agenda (see Chapter 2). Out of this process, by the mid 1970s a consensus black agenda had emerged. It is best articulated in a document issued by the Joint Center for Political Studies in 1976. In that year the center brought together a bipartisan assembly of more than one thousand black elected and appointed officials. At its conclusion the group issued a "Seven Point Mandate" that it said represented a leadership consensus on the post–civil rights era black agenda. It included:

1. A full employment program that "guarantees the right to useful and meaningful jobs for those willing and able to work."
2. Welfare reform to include a "guaranteed annual income . . . not laden down with punitive counterproductive (forced) work requirements."
3. Comprehensive national health insurance.
4. Tax reform to remove loopholes that permit wealthy individuals and corporations to pay no taxes or less than fair rates.
5. Increased funding for higher education, elementary and secondary education, and vocational education, and support for busing as a "means to insure high quality education for children in integrated settings."
6. Minority business initiatives, including support for government set asides and a "one year moratorium on federal loan repayments."
7. Support for international sanctions on South Africa; repeal of the Byrd amendment allowing the importation of Rhodesian chrome in

violation of United Nations sanctions and support for the new International Economic Order, specifically assuring "just and stable prices for primary commodities."[67]

With minor changes in emphasis and specifics (less concern with busing, more with affirmative action, successful repeal of the Byrd amendment, imposition of South African sanctions) these items remain the principal demands blacks have advanced in the post–civil rights era. And it is a consensus agenda, although like the agenda of the civil rights era it is sometimes challenged (vigorously throughout the 1970s) by the nationalist and radical tendencies in black America (see Chapter 2) and in the 1980s by a vocal but small group of new black conservatives. However, at both the mass level and among the leadership of blacks, the essentials of this agenda constitute the "mainstream" of post–civil rights era black politics. This means that in the post–civil rights era the black community, without respect to class, is strikingly more liberal on economic and social welfare issues than are whites.[68] Yet the mainstream in white politics during this twenty-five year period has moved toward the right, making it extraordinarily difficult for blacks to become a part of the dominant or governing coalition in Washington that exercises long-term control over policy issues of central concern to them. Blacks in the post–civil rights era are not just a racial minority then, but, perhaps more critically, an ideological one as well.

Finally, what is striking about the black agenda is that it is not really black. That is, relatively few items on it are race specific; rather, it is best described as a broadly liberal or social democratic agenda including progressive tax reform, national health insurance, increased education funding and full employment. This is no accident. At the outset of the post-civil rights era black leaders recognized that a racialized "black" agenda could not attract the necessary support to become a majority. Charles Hamilton articulated the analytic and strategic basis for the full employment priority in a paper prepared for the Urban League's first national conference to consider the post–civil rights black agenda. He argued that full employment should become the "new major focus" of the movement because of the obvious long-standing "crisis" of joblessness in black America and its correlation with other socioeconomic problems, but also because it would facilitate moving beyond the limits of 1960s-style protest toward more efficacious electoral activism. Hamilton also argued that this issue would create a consensus and thus "rise above the devastatingly divisive ideological debates now wracking traditional civil rights circles because it applies to the total society, not only to blacks and other traditionally stigmatized minorities, who are seen as wanting only hand-outs. It would, in other words, recognize the critical factor of race and racism, but it offers a deracialized solution."[69]

The problem with Hamilton's deracialized solution to the problems of race is that there is not in the United States a majority coalition that favors progressive social and economic policies and programs that would substantially meliorate the conditions of the so-called underclass. The long struggle for the civil rights agenda teaches two clear lessons. First, social change in the United States, especially where race is concerned, takes a long time. Second, such change occurs only in times of systemic crisis or when sufficient pressure is brought to bear on policy makers so they cannot engage in neglect. Blacks and their allies in the post–civil rights era have not found a way to bring such pressure to bear. If they cannot do so—and this study shows that it is not likely that they can—then the conditions of blacks and the nation's cities will continue their ominous decline. This decline in the long run, however, is likely itself to pose a threat to system stability. Perhaps then and only then will political authorities act, as Lincoln did during the Civil War, on its race problem. Act because it is necessary to try to maintain a system in crisis.

PART II

We should form an institution that will bring the most distant and detached portions of our people together, embrace their varied interests, and unite their whole moral power. Our collected wisdom should be assembled, to consult on measures pertaining to the general welfare; and so direct our energies, as to do the greatest good for the greatest number. Thus united, and thus directed, every weapon that prejudice has formed against us, would be rendered powerless; and our moral elevation would be as rapid, as it would be certain. Without a national institution of some description, our affairs can never attain any degree of consistence or permanence. . . . The noble and praiseworthy efforts of the *few*, must continue to be partial, imperfect and unsuccessful, for want of the support and cooperation of the *many*. I have already expressed myself in favor of a convention, but if a society can be so modified as to meet our wants, I shall be perfectly willing to acquiesce. I will not object to any institution which may meet the views of a majority, provided it will unite and harmonize the distant and discordant parts of our population.

—Reverend Lewis Woodson (1838)

2

The National Black Political Convention, 1972–84

The proximate historical roots of the 1970s convention process may be traced to the black power rebellion sparked by Stokely Carmichael and the SNCC on the 1966 Meredith March in Mississippi.[1] The black power symbol stimulated a critical debate on the future of black politics in the post–civil rights era, in some ways as important as the nineteenth-century debate between Washington and DuBois on the future of the race in the post-Reconstruction era. Black power essentially represented a variety of reformist black nationalism, appealing to race group consciousness and solidarity, cultural revitalization and independent organization as means to establish blacks as an independent force in American politics.[2] This essential meaning of black power was obscured in the initial historically and contextually uninformed debate surrounding the symbol. First, the press coverage was generally slanted, painting black power as a dangerous form of radical black separatism. Second, both the black and white political establishments, reacting to some extent to the slanted press coverage, distorted the import of black power; Roy Wilkins and Whitney Young for example charged extremism and "racism in reverse." And finally, at the time of the Meredith March Carmichael and his colleagues did not themselves have a clear understanding of black power's significance. Caught off guard by the immediacy of the slogan's rise to national prominence, it was, as Carson writes, "only after Carmichael attracted national attention as an advocate of black power did he begin to construct an intellectual rationale for what initially was an inchoate statement of conclusions drawn from SNCC's work."[3] Then, in a series of articles and the book with Charles Hamilton, Carmichael elaborated a pragmatic black power formulation that was essentially a race version of the familiar interest group, pluralist model of American politics, which called for the mobilization of the groups' resources so that blacks could become an independent force, capable of extracting concessions within the pressure-group-based American polity.[4]

Within a year, however, Carmichael had abandoned this reformist variety of black nationalism and his name (becoming Kwame Toure), and had adopted the revolutionary ideology of Pan Africanism linked to the notion of socialist revolution.[5] Carmichael's ideological shift was to have a seminal effect on nationalist and radical thinking in the 1970s, contributing to much babble and confusion; however, its most important effect was to facilitate the cooptation of black power in its reformist version by the black and white political establishments. Carmichael's colleague Hamilton in his lectures and writings became a highly visible and articulate advocate of this reformist notion of black power,[6] and by the end of the decade this version had been adopted by virtually the entire black establishment and by important elements of the liberal power structure that plays such an important patron role in black establishment leadership.[7]

Actually this process of establishment cooptation of black power began immediately after the Meredith March in the person of Harlem Congressman Adam Clayton Powell, then Chairman of the House Committee on Education and Labor but something of an iconoclast within the establishment, who immediately seized on the national momentum occasioned by black power and sought to give it his pragmatic content.[8] In the fall of 1966 Powell, acting own his own initiative, called a black power planning conference at his Washington office. SNCC's executive committee declined to take part in this meeting, wary of what it saw as an effort by establishment black leaders to coopt black power's momentum for their own purposes.[9] At Powell's meeting more than a hundred "delegates" representing more than fifty black organizations agreed to call a National Black Power Conference the following year under the leadership of Nathan Wright, a conservative clergyman associated with the Newark Episcopal Diocese's Social Work program.

The conference was held a year later in Newark just days after the suppression of that city's massive 1967 black rebellion. More than a thousand delegates (from twenty-six states, more than a hundred cities and nearly three hundred organizations) registered for the four-day meeting. Anticipating the 1972 Gary convention, relatively few black establishment figures were present; most notably the major civil rights leaders—Martin King, Whitney Young, Roy Wilkins and Bayard Rustin—declined invitations.[10] Otherwise, as Chuck Stone, the journalist and Powell aide, reported, the full "ideological eclecticism" of black people was represented, from revolutionaries to conservatives.[11] Fourteen workshops dealing with black power in terms of economics, culture, politics, and so forth were held and there was as usual much speech making but only one formal resolution was adopted. It in part read:

Black people who live under the racist governments of America, Asia, Africa and Latin America stand at the crossroads of either an expanding revolution or ruthless extermination. It is incumbent on us to get our own house in order, if we are to fully utilize the potentialities of revolution, or to resist our own execution. . . . It is, therefore, resolved that the National Conference on Black Power sponsor the creation of an International Congress, to be organized out of the soulful roots of our peoples and to reflect the new sense of power and revolution now blossoming in black communities in America and black nations throughout the world.[12]

Aside from this formal resolution, the conference adopted an eclectic series of "spirit of the conference" resolutions calling for such things as the election of more black congressmen, the reseating of Adam Powell, a buy black campaign, the restoration of Muhammad Ali's title, a national guaranteed income, community control of black education and the police, the establishment of a national think tank or clearinghouse on black affairs and a "national dialogue on the desirability of partitioning the U.S. into separate and independent nations, one to be a homeland for white Americans and the other for black Americans."[13] Finally, the conference called for the holding in 1972 of a "national black grassroots political convention" following the conventions of the two major parties.[14]

In its origins, ideologies, organization and leadership styles, this black power conference anticipated the dilemmas and contradictions of the convention process initiated at Gary in 1972. Yet many of these problems were overlooked by the leaders of this process as in the next four years they set about to implement the conference's call for a "national grassroots convention." In the meantime SNCC, wary of the unpredictable charismatic leadership of Carmichael and his successor H. Rap Brown, was now under "collective leadership" and on the verge of collapse as a result of internal conflict, financial insolvency and police repression. In its final days the group debated the idea of forming a black political party that would forthrightly address the problems of race and class exploitation, but by the time this idea was given serious consideration at the Gary convention, SNCC as an organization was history.

Another important event in this pre-Gary period was the 1967 National Conference for New Politics held in Chicago. This was an effort to build a coalition between the largely white new left of students and antiwar activists and activists of the black movement. Indeed, there was some hope that Martin King might become the new politics presidential candidate in 1968. But this first effort at a post–civil rights era "Rainbow Coalition" foundered on the crest of the emergent force of a reactionary black nationalism and the infantile disorders then emerging among elements of the new left (as represented by the yippies and the Weathermen). For example, at the convention King was shouted down by black delegates who yelled "Kill Whitey." H. Rap Brown, then SNCC Chair, declined an invitation to address the conference on the grounds that he did not speak to white audiences and the black caucus, although representing less than a fifth of the delegates, demanded and received 50 percent representation on all convention decision-making bodies. Thus, this effort at multiracial progressive coalition formation was stillborn, with consequences that still linger today in terms of cooperation between blacks and the white left. Indeed, there is hardly today any sustained work between blacks and the white left.[15]

The 1972 Convention at Gary:
Origins, Actors, Processes and Outcomes

The period 1967 to about 1975 was one of great ideological and organizational ferment in black America—perhaps, for so short a period of time, the greatest such intense period of political discussion and movement in the history of the Afro-American freedom struggle. The ferment was occasioned by several discrete factors that came together in this period to create the conditions that made the effort to create an all-inclusive national negro congress-type organization seem almost inevitable, in spite of the failure of thirty years earlier.

The first of these factors was the achievement of the fundamental agenda of the civil rights movement. As discussed in Chapter 1, there had been since early in the century a basic consensus within the national black and white liberal establishments about the basic goals of the civil rights struggle, with differences largely over strategy and tactics plus the conflicts of personality, organizational primacy and resource mobilization and allocation that are typical of any social movement. The passage of the basic civil rights laws of the 1960s shattered that consensus among the black leadership and ruptured the relationship with important elements of the white liberal establishment. Instead of debates about strategy and tactics in pursuit of the common goal of fundamental citizenship rights, the debate centered now on new goals and directions for the movement. Although the civil rights movement had always paid attention to the non–civil rights issues of joblessness, poverty and urban ghettoization, the securing of elementary civil and citizenship rights was always more prominent. Thus, with their achievement in the 1960s, leaders could now turn to these other issues. The 1965 Watts rebellion and subsequent riots in other large northern cities reinforced concern with these issues, making it clear that the civil rights revolution was in many ways irrelevant to the problems of urban blacks outside of the south.

The second factor in this mix was the emergence and fairly rapid acceptance of the black power philosophy at both the elite and mass level of the black community and among important patrons within the liberal establishment. With its emphasis on race consciousness, cultural revitalization, race exclusive organization, self-reliance and unity, black power pointed to a new, more nationalistic direction in black society and politics. One result of this was a massive increase in organizations founded on the principles of black power. Between 1967 and 1970 more than seventy national black organizations were formed, most of which were racially exclusive and at least quasi-political. But more than this simple expression of nationalism, black power was at the cutting edge of revitalization of all varieties of the nationalist ideology—political (reform and revolutionary), cultural, territorial separatism and Pan Africanism. National organizations and leaders like Elijah Muhammad and the Nation of Islam (religious, economic, cultural nationalism and territorial separatism), Ron Karenga and US (cultural nationalism), Huey Newton and the Black Panthers (revolutionary nationalism), Imari Obadele and the Republic of New Africa (territorial separatism) and Pan Africanist leaders and groups like Kwame Toure and the African Liberation Support Committee all became increasingly prominent during this period. All of these groups, while divided over ultimate goals and strategies, emphasized core nationalist ideological principles such as the saliency of racism, the importance of positive group-specific cultural traits and the need for self-reliance and unity.

The third factor was the nationalization of the black electorate as a result of the implementation of the 1965 Voting Rights Act. The first year since Reconstruction that there was widespread black voter participation in the states of the southern region was 1972. This had two effects on the development of the momentum for a national political convention. First, it suggested the prospects of enhanced leverage of the black vote—if it could be unified around a common agenda and strategy—in presidential elections both within and between the two major parties. Second, the Voting Rights Act and scores of black power inspired voter mobilization campaigns, north and south, resulted in the election of a sizeable number of blacks to political office; including several big city mayors and a tripling of the size of the black congressional delegation, from four to thirteen. These black elected officials, following the principle of black power, quickly organized themselves into a variety of caucuses. They began immediately jockeying to displace the civil rights leaders as the principal black political leaders. They argued that in the post–civil rights era, "politics not protest" was the new direction of the struggle; and as elected officials they were specialists in politics and their election gave them a greater degree of legitimacy than nonelected civil rights or protest leaders. This view was vigorously articulated by some members of the Congressional Black Caucus who contended that as "the highest body of black elected officials" they were the legitimate representatives of the entire national black community.

The final ingredient that completes the recipe for the convention was the death of Martin King. Dr. King, although his prestige had declined from its peak at Selma in 1965, was still recognized by elite and mass, black and white, as the preeminent leader of the race. Operating on the aegis of charismatic authority, King's heroic presence tended to eclipse the strategy and thinking of other black leaders as he continued to embrace protest not only as a method of struggle on issues of race and poverty but increasingly the Vietnam War as well. The removal of his presence thus opened up considerable political space for new ideas about strategy and new claimants for leadership. The most immediate consequence, however, was to give currency to the notion that there was not now after King nor little prospect in the future for a single dominant charismatic leader; rather, in the post–civil rights era black leadership would be collective, drawing on elected officials, traditional civil rights leaders and grassroots, nationalist-oriented persons.

These are the factors, taken together, that produced the environment leading to a series of meetings of black leaders in late 1970 and throughout 1971, resulting in the decision to hold a national convention. A key figure in this process was Amiri Baraka, the poet, playwright and cultural nationalist. Baraka, the former Leroi Jones, is a pivotal figure in both the rise and fall of the convention. Starting his political activism in the left-progressive integrationist milieu of Greenwich Village "beat" politics, by the 1970s he had changed his ideology—with his usual vituperative assaults on his former associates—to a variety of cultural nationalism inspired and later popularized by Ron Karenga and his west coast organization US. This ideology sought to have blacks adopt what Baraka and Karenga saw as an African value system based on what was called the seven principles of Kawida.[16] This utopian and reactionary version of cultural nationalism was for a brief time given organizational expression in a group Baraka founded called the

Congress of African People (CAP). But by the early 1970s he was trying to subsume his cultural nationalist approach within the broader framework of Pan Africanism, which was increasingly in vogue, in part as a result of Kwame Toure's adoption of it after his brief exile in West Africa. In addition, Baraka had been a guiding force in the organization of an umbrella black political convention in 1970 in Newark, his hometown, that resulted in the election of Kenneth Gibson as the city's first black mayor. This Newark experience in electoral politics suggested a possible model for a national organization that would unite the disparate ideological and institutional factions of the black community into a cohesive force that could exercise independent leverage in national politics.[17]

Fresh from his victory in the Newark mayoral election, Baraka's Congress of African People in September 1970 organized what was described as the first modern Pan African Congress. This meeting in Atlanta, in many ways a precursor of the Gary convention two years later, brought together the range of institutional and ideological forces in black America, from newly elected black mayors Kenneth Gibson and Gary's Richard Hatcher to the separatist nationalists such as Imari Obadele of the Republic of New Africa and Louis Farrakhan of the Nation of Islam, and establishment leaders like the Urban League's Whitney Young, Ralph Abernathy and Jesse Jackson. The basis for such disparate groups coming together was the notion of "operational unity" or "unity without uniformity" then being advanced by Baraka's cultural nationalist colleague Ron Karenga. As Baraka put it:

> It is the way of thinking that allows the Urban League's National Executive Director to exchange views frankly with a Minister Farrakhan or a Kenneth Gibson to reflect on the concepts of more orthodox Pan Africanists. There is health in such an approach. It is much like the united liberation front of the Vietnamese people, called "Viet Cong," in which all walks of Vietnamese unite themselves, whether they are Catholics, or Buddhists, socialists or speak of free enterprise, unite themselves around ideas which are mutually beneficial to all, ideas that finally will liberate all.[18]

Another important basis for the gathering at Atlanta was the nationalist principle of black unity, especially as expressed in the then growing influence of Pan Africanism—the unity of all African peoples everywhere. The Pan Africanist expression of the nationalist ideology had become increasingly influential in black activists and intellectual circles since Stokely Carmichael (Kwame Toure) proposed it in his

essay published a year before in *The Black Scholar*. In his exile in West
Africa, Toure had come under the influence of Ghana's Kwame
Nkrumah and Sekou Toure of Guinea, two of the leading figures in
the African independence struggle. On his return to the United States
he in effect argued that the black liberation struggle in this country
could not be won until all Africa was liberated and completely united
as one nation under scientific socialism. He suggests, then and now,
that the appropriate strategy for blacks in this country was to organize first around this goal of African liberation and unity on the
assumption that the inevitable result would be to speed up the liberation process in the United States. Thus, internal black struggle in the
United States was largely irrelevant.[19] Even Toure's thoroughly establishment colleague Charles Hamilton, who had done so much to moderate the radical potential of black power, jumped on the Pan Africanism bandwagon, arguing that "Pan Africanism is clearly the next viable
stage of the historical struggle of black people to assert themselves on
the world scene" and that electoral politics' ultimate long-term function
was to "politicize the masses rather than obtain mass benefits."[20] Thus,
Hamilton appears to adopt Toure's view on the essential irrelevance of
electoral politics in the larger black struggle. Essentially, the rhetorical
spell cast by Pan Africanism dulled critical faculties in terms of the
limited role black Americans could play in Africa and as a consequence
distracted critical discussion away from the concrete realities of internal
U.S. black politics.[21]

Thus, many of the speeches by nationalist as well as integrationist
invoked Pan Africanism and the then-popular slogan, "It's Nation
Time." For example, in his address Jesse Jackson said, "I want to deal
with going back home and Pan Africanism because I believe it is the
penultimate protection and security for our people. I believe strongly in
Pan Africanism."[22] And Gary's Mayor Hatcher stated, "The underlying concept, I think, which guides all of us today and these last two
days is the concept that we are all African people; the concept that we
are working together to build a strong united African nation wherever
we may be; the concept that we must work toward the unification of
Africa; in other words the concept of Pan Africanism."[23]

The conference, as usual for such meetings, included in addition to
the plenary speech making a series of workshops dealing with such
topics as education, the family, technology, law and justice, etc. The
workshop on politics or "Political Liberation" as it was called was led
by Baraka. Each workshop was charged with proposing resolutions
that would create institutions to implement the principles of Pan
Africanism. Baraka's politics group proposed the creation of a black

political party. The party as proposed was a curious blend of Pan Africanist and Baraka's cultural nationalism themes. Its rationale was stated as follows:

> Since Africans can only defeat white supremacy by creating alter-
> native institutions which in actuality will be the replenishment
> and reorganization of inert traditional African institutions (of
> course redefined by our confrontation with western traditions and
> technology, but African never the less, and able to answer the
> needs of the contemporary African where ever in the world). We
> sought to answer the questions: what is a contemporary African
> Political Institution (the answer, in this case, was an International
> African Political Party) able to run candidates for elections, build
> schools and housing and hospitals, or fight a war.[24]

The Atlanta CAP meeting was important in several respects in the development of the convention two years later. First, it reinforced Baraka's status as an important figure in the process. This was to be critical in the origins but especially the collapse of the convention, since Baraka brought to it a proclivity for ideological oscillation and vituper-ative rhetoric but also a well-organized, disciplined and dedicated cadre of activists willing to work to organize and sustain a convention. Sec-ond, the meeting suggested that it might be possible to bring together the range of black institutional and ideological groups in a common structure, using the ideology of Pan Africanism and "unity without uniformity" as the basis for overcoming the sharp divisions in the black community. As a prototype for what was to come, the Atlanta Pan African Congress clearly manifested the internal contradictions in black politics that the slogan *unity without uniformity* and the rhetoric of Pan Africanism sought to conceal, contradictions that suggested the inevitable failure of the process. To take one example, Whitney Young of the Urban League made a moderate speech in the tradition of liberal integrationism, rejecting what he called "chauvinistic appeals" to African virtues and European vices and the ideas of separatism. On the latter point Young told the plenary:

> On segregation or separatism, I believe my views are well known.
> I believe that any time an educationally and economically disad-
> vantaged group can be isolated it can always be, and without
> exception has been, subject to gross discrimination, exploitation
> and oppression. As for America, Black people have been here for
> more than four hundred years. We have contributed dearly in all

the gains this land has made and suffered disproportionately in all
its failures. . . . I have frequently said and I say now that white
Americans who engage in wishful thinking that we are going to
take them off the hook and solve their problems by all of us collectively moving to separate states or leaving in mass for Africa
should be told loudly and clearly, "Forget it, we are here to
stay. . . ."[25]

Yet Baraka's political liberation workshop adopted the following
resolution:

The Congress of African People recognizes the Republic of New
Africa as an African nation in the western Hemisphere whose
land is subjugated and supports the right of the Republic of New
Africa to organize a peaceful plebiscite among the people living in
the subjugated national territory. The Congress of African Peoples explicitly opposes and condemns any efforts of the United
States or its political subdivisions to interfere with the peaceful
organization of the plebiscite or the peaceful carrying out of its
results.[26]

How unity without uniformity could possibly reconcile these dia-
metrically opposed views on the ultimate outcome of the black freedom struggle was not reconciled at Atlanta nor at the subsequent convention, because of course they are irreconcilable. These kinds of
obvious contradictions were not even discussed or debated at Atlanta in
any effort to reach a meeting of minds or a parting of ways. Instead,
they were simply ignored as if the mere articulation of views in a common forum between Young and Baraka was sufficient to establish unity.
In other words, there was no attempt to debate principled differences
among persons of principle and thereby demarcate lines of principled
opposition within the black political community.[27]
One other contradiction revealed at Atlanta was the lack of clarity
about the nature of a new political party and its relationship to some
other all-inclusive, racially exclusive structure. That is an organization
that might serve as a forum for debate and resolution of issues within
the black community and possibly the development of a minimal consensus agenda that might serve to mobilize the community around a
variety of internal matters and in some of its relationships to the larger
society. These distinct institutions were muddled at Atlanta and
throughout the decade-long convention process. On the one hand, a
political party that would contest elections and seek to participate in

governance of the larger society, whether locally or nationally, to be effective would necessarily have to be a multiethnic coalition, including whites and others who share similar interests or policy preferences. And in the nature of American politics to be effective, the party could not represent the range of ideological tendencies in the black community but rather the community's central tendency of progressive social reform. Certainly, an effective electoral party could not, as Baraka's workshop proposed, do such things as "build schools, housing and hospitals, or fight a war." And for sure Baraka's vision of the party was not shared by those establishment forces in the civil rights community and among elected officials who would be indispensable in building and sustaining it.

On the other hand, a black convention or internal structure of interest, discussion and aggregation might do the kinds of things suggested by Baraka (although not fighting a war) in terms of an internal community infrastructure of hospitals, housing and other communal institutions. But this would not be a party; rather it would be akin to the Jewish "Kahillah" that emerged for a time in the early part of this century, or to the internal philanthropic and communal structure that exists in the Jewish community today in the aftermath of the Kahillah's collapse.[28] Holden called such an internal black structure a "mechanism of collective judgement."[29] It is difficult to create in the United States either of these institutions—a viable third party or an ethnic mechanism of collective judgment and action—but to try to do both simultaneously in a single structure is simply impossible. That this was not understood or even recognized at Atlanta or the subsequent conventions is one key explanation for the failure to date of both institutions and is a major reason the black community in the post–civil rights era has not been mobilized internally or in its external relations with the larger society.

In 1971, the year following the Atlanta CAP meeting, discussion in black leadership circles turned to the 1972 presidential election and the development of a strategy to maximize the influence of the black vote. Throughout the year there were a series of meetings, letters and telephone exchanges that led to the call for a National Black Convention. The central figures in these meetings and discussions were liberal integrationist establishment figures including Jesse Jackson, Cleveland Mayor Carl Stokes, Gary Mayor Richard Hatcher, Detroit Congressman John Conyers, Manhattan Borough President Percy Sutton and Atlanta Representative Julian Bond. Others who participated in at least one of the several meetings held in Chicago, Cleveland and Washington were Michigan Congressman Charles Diggs, Coretta King, the widow of Dr. King, California State legislators Willie Brown and Mervyn

Dymally, Texas State Senator Barbara Jordan, the Urban League's Vernon Jordan, California Congressman Augustus Hawkins (who had been active in the 1930s Negro Congress), District of Columbia Congressional Delegate Walter Fauntroy, Clarence Mitchell of the NAACP Washington bureau and Basil Patterson, the New York politician. To this largely establishment group two prominent nationalist leaders—Roy Innis of CORE and Baraka—frequently attended.

The purpose of these gatherings was to develop a unified strategy to maximize the influence of the growing black electorate in the 1972 election. Several strategies were floated about during this period. Percy Sutton, for example, urged that a well-known black person run for president in order to "nationalize the black vote" and black delegate strength at the Democratic Convention, which he argued might give blacks sufficient strength to determine the outcome of the convention in terms of nominees and platform. This strategy was later endorsed by Congressman Conyers and Mayor Stokes; Conyers went so far as to propose Stokes as the consensus black candidate. Julian Bond proposed what he called a "favorite son" strategy, in which prominent blacks from several states would run in order to amass a bloc of convention delegates that could be used for bargaining purposes. The advantage of Bond's approach in contrast to Sutton's was that it would remove the contentious issue of who should be the single black candidate, and just as importantly, the favorite sons (Bond later added daughters in deference to Congresswoman Shirley Chisholm) would constitute a collective-bargaining mechanism obviating the fears and mistrust of a single individual bargaining behind closed doors for the entire race.

Apart from candidate strategy, the meetings focused on the "black agenda": what issues, policies or proposals should be advanced by blacks in exchange for their support of a party and its nominee. Although there was some discussion of using the Congressional Black Caucus's "Sixty Recommendations to President Nixon" developed and presented to the President earlier in the year, no agreement emerged in the several meetings[30] Some objected that the Caucus recommendations were too broad and far ranging to serve as a bargaining document, while others argued they were too narrow to represent the broad range of interests and concerns of blacks, especially at the "grassroots" (grassroots here to some extent was a euphemism for nationalist concerns) and still others argued that the Caucus document lacked legitimacy because it had not emerged from a broadly based process involving the community as a whole (i.e., a national convention or assembly), but rather from the Washington-based black establishment.[31]

Throughout the series of meetings no consensus emerged on the candidate strategy or agenda.[32] Throughout, however, Baraka argued that these and other issues of black empowerment could only be resolved in a national convention which he called the "absolute sine qua non of black movement—a permanent structure or party."[33] This idea was met initially with skepticism by black establishment leaders, especially senior members of the Black Caucus, but before these matters could be resolved Congresswoman Chisholm's abrupt decision to announce her candidacy for president threw the entire process into turmoil, creating further dissension within the group as well as a degree of anger and bitterness. Chisholm had not participated in any of the year-long series of meetings, claiming "I was not asked to participate and I did not intrude."[34] Chisholm here leaves the reader to infer that the reason she was not invited to the meetings and her subsequent candidacy was not supported by most prominent black leaders was her gender, contending that in all her years in politics she had faced more discrimination because of her gender than her race, and "If anyone thinks white men are sexist, let them check out black men." The implications of Chisholm's remarks are not credible. First, other prominent female leaders did participate in the meetings; and second, her candidacy was not supported by most black leaders (male or female) precisely because it emerged outside of the ongoing consensus-building process involving candidates and strategies that she did not take part in. Participants in these meetings then came to see her candidacy as more feminist than black; a view her remarks about sexism only reinforced. In any event, Chisholm did not attempt to locate her candidacy within the ongoing strategy debates, nor did she consult widely in the black community before she made the decision to run.[35] Thus, her candidacy was not considered "black" but rather an unwarranted effort to get around whatever consensus might emerge as a result of the leadership meetings. Clearly, however, her candidacy was a disruptive factor in the leadership deliberations.

By all accounts—published reports and personal interviews—of the several meetings held during 1971, the one at Northlake on the outskirts of Chicago, cohosted by Hatcher (along with Diggs, Baraka, Jesse Jackson, Coretta King, Willie Brown and Julian Bond) was the most critical.[36] It brought together most of the participants in the several meetings in a single place for a long weekend of discussion, and as a result virtually every major ideological and institutional tendency in black America was represented. (Chisholm did not attend but sent her principal assistant, Thaddus Garrett, as an observer.) Although no final decisions were reached, the meeting was important because it provided an opportunity for frank discussion over an extended period of time of all the varying strategies and approaches by all the principal leaders (the meeting was supposed to be secret but predictably it was leaked to the press). Baraka writes that he again strongly made the case for a national convention:

> Some nationalists . . . rejected the idea [of a convention] because they felt that, in such a diverse setting no real work could be done, the various contradictory ideologies finally neutralizing each other. But we have always felt that the strongest ideology will always carry the day in these kinds of gatherings if the people with the ideology are clear on what they want, provided that the ideology really is the strongest, and not the subjectivism of the group of partisans pushing it. . . . If we feel we are correct, then shouldn't we try to teach and influence rather than retreat to the sanctity of our own partisan gatherings in which no opposition is expected. . . .[37]

Not only were there misgivings about the convention among some of Baraka's nationalist partisans; black establishment leaders were perhaps even more wary of such a mass assembly. Again to quote Baraka's candid account, written shortly after the convention:

> Many moderates and well known civil rights leaders and black elected officials tended to reject the idea of the convention. . . . They felt they would put themselves in a position to be "gori-alled." Julian Bond in a letter to me in effect asked why should he be put in a position to be made responsible for some views with which he might not be in total agreement, feeling that, say a brother like Roy Innis, who does not have to answer to any formal constituency might endanger his, Julian Bond's ability to answer to his constituency. . . .[38]

Baraka's rejoinder to Bond's concern was:

> And the answer is always given by Black Elected Officials—that they have constituencies to be responsive and responsible to, whereas "nationalists, activists, other radicals have no con- stituencies," therefore, they can feel freer in taking wayout posi- tions. Of course I would question the degree and extent to which the average Black Elected Official is totally responsive to his con- stituency. I feel, for instance, where those constituencies are Black,

which most are, there is not nearly enough responsiveness to them by Black Elected Official supposedly representing them. In most instances, Black Elected Official who make statements like this, unless they are in areas where there is a great amount of white voting putting them in office, make these copouts because they are afraid of some national white backlash and the tarnishing of their "image" in white folks' eyes . . .[39]

As will be seen, however, Bond's concerns were well taken in that the Gary convention did take positions—most notably on school busing and the Middle East conflict—that endangered many black elected officials in the eyes of some of their constituents, leading the Congressional Black Caucus to formally repudiate these positions as soon as the convention adjourned.

Nothing was resolved at this Northlake meeting, but at least the various factions had a clear understanding of the lines of cleavages and possible areas of compromise and consensus. Northlake thus prepared the groundwork for more informed communications among the participants in writing and by telephone leading up to the next meeting in Washington.

In November, two months after the Northlake meeting, the key participants gathered again in Washington at a meeting sponsored by the Congressional Black Caucus. The purpose again was to discuss 1972 presidential strategy, but Shirley Chisholm and her candidacy was the focus of much of the discussion. Although the Sutton and Bond strategies of single or multiple black candidacies were discussed, Chisholm, who attended this meeting herself, also advanced her candidacy as worthy of black leadership endorsement; she was supported only by California Congressman Ronald Dellums. Amidst much argument, as a result of the Chisholm candidacy and unable to agree on the Sutton, Bond or any other strategy, Baraka's proposal for a national convention was endorsed by the conferees as a workable compromise, postponing as it did the need to resolve the contentious issues of strategy, agenda and the Chisholm candidacy. Yet the convention idea was embraced reluctantly by black establishment leaders, especially many of the influential members of the Congressional Black Caucus. Some of the reluctance was a result of fears that a mass convention might become a vehicle for the Chisholm candidacy. There was also the perennial concern of some establishment figures that it might be "taken over by radicals" and thus be an embarrassment. Nevertheless, on the evening of November 20th the Congressional Black Caucus issued a press release that in effect became the call of the convention. The next day the *New York*

Times reported an item quoting Caucus Chair Charles Diggs as saying, "The convention is to be held for the purpose of developing a national black agenda and the crystallization of a national black strategy for 1972 and beyond."[40] Thus, the leadership unable to resolve the major issues of strategy and agenda itself threw them into the unpredictable dynamics of a mass-based national convention. The unresolved contradictions were accentuated a month later at a meeting in Gary in which three formal co-conveners were named—Caucus Chair Diggs and Gary Mayor Hatcher representing the establishment forces and Baraka representing the nationalists. At this time it was also agreed that planning and staff work would go forward looking toward holding the convention in Gary within three months.

In retrospect, the March date was probably a mistake. For sure the conveners wished to hold the meeting well in advance of the major party conventions during the summer so that the agenda and strategy would be in place; but three months was probably not enough time to adequately plan a gathering as large and complex as a national convention. This was especially the case given the disparate and loosely organized pattern of staffing involving the Congressional Black Caucus, the Joint Center for Political Studies, the Institute of the Black World, Baraka's CAP and sundry volunteers in Gary, Atlanta and Washington. Consequently, there were the typical logistical problems of inadequate convention meeting rooms, insufficient and poorly allocated floor space for the state delegations and inadequate hotel accommodations and transportation (some delegates had to stay in private homes and others as far away as Chicago, without adequate transportation). But the principal problems that resulted from the time constraints were in terms of committee work and delegate allocation and selection. The four critical committees—Rules and Procedures chaired by former Nixon Administration official Edward Sylvester, Credentials chaired by Colorado State Senator George Brown, Platform chaired by Walter Fauntroy and Resolutions chaired by Barbara Jordan—did not have the time or staff resources to complete their work prior to the opening of the convention, which resulted in more than the usual opening day convention confusion.

These problems were first manifested in the delegate allocation formula and selection procedures. Under the formula adopted, after the call of the convention, delegates were to be credentialed on the following basis: First, each state was allocated a minimum of five delegates based on its percent black population, with approximately one delegate for every 10,000 people. Second, each black elected official in the nation was given an automatic seat; and finally each of the major civil rights organizations were granted ten automatic delegates. This complicated formula sought to assure a mass-based, broadly representative assembly while at the same time guaranteeing the representation of the black establishment of civil rights leaders and elected officials. This led to built-in conflict between these forces in terms of who should speak for a particular delegation. In New York for example, there was constant conflict between the establishment forces and the nationalists, with the former insisting that only elected officials be allowed to speak for the delegation and the latter insisting that the delegation be equally divided between the two camps with cospokespersons.[41] Further, while there was a fairly straightforward formula for delegate allocation, there were no guidelines for delegate selection. As a result the credentials committee had no way to judge the credentials of a given delegation in terms of its representativeness and legitimacy. In some states there were reasonably open, democratic caucuses, in others delegations were constituted by prominent black leaders in a particular state simply contacting persons they wished to be delegates, while in still others the delegations were constituted by a major organized interest in the state (the Michigan delegation, headed by then state Senator Coleman Young, was dominated by persons drawn from the UAW). And in Louisiana, delegates were selected on the basis of arbitrary responses to ads soliciting delegates on black radio stations.[42] While it was probably not possible for the convention (or any private group) to create a democratic mechanism of delegate selection akin to that employed by the government's electoral apparatus, more time to promulgate, distribute and monitor a uniform set of criteria would have facilitated the work of the credentials committee and made for a greater degree of legitimacy of the convention as an assembly broadly representative of the national black community. As it was, however, the credentials committee was forced to certify as valid the credentials of all delegations, no matter how arbitrarily selected.[43]

The second manifestation of this problem of poor planning and inadequate staff support was that the Rules Committee did not prior to the opening of the convention promulgate and distribute rules of order and procedure in terms of the election of the permanent convention officers and the consideration of resolutions and platform items. (Indeed, the committee failed to distinguish between resolutions dealing with statements of principles or philosophy and concrete platform planks, which resulted in confusion during floor debates, and a final agenda that was muddled and confused incorporating platform items and resolutions in a manner in which they could not easily be distinguished.) As a result, the opening session of the convention (which started four hours late) degenerated into a near riot as delegates jeered, shouted and, in the case of the New York delegation, stormed the stage in an attempt to seize the microphone from Congressman Diggs, the presiding officer.[44] After security forces restored order, Diggs recessed the convention in order that the leadership and staff might work out an acceptable set of rules regarding the convention program and the handling of resolutions and platform planks. At an overnight meeting procedures were established to handle these matters and when the convention resumed Baraka replaced Diggs as presiding officer. With less than a day to complete its work, the convention set about debating resolutions, platform planks and the adoption of a continuation structure to follow the convention. By all accounts the key figure in the resolution of these contentious opening day problems (both behind the scenes and as presiding officer) was Baraka, in part because of the sheer force of his personality but also because his CAP organization provided him loyal and competent staff.[45]

The final manifestation of this time constraint and preplanning problem was confusion regarding the adoption of resolutions and planks in the final formal agenda.[46] But even before the floor deliberations on these matters, the draft preamble to the convention agenda presented by Fauntroy's Platform Committee had resulted in the NAACP's widely publicized denunciation of the convention just prior to its opening.[47] Roy Wilkins, the Association's Executive Director, like many figures in the civil rights establishment had been wary of the convention from the outset. (In the 1930s the NAACP had opposed the formation of the National Negro Congress.) In his column, widely circulated in the black press, Wilkins several weeks before the convention warned his establishment colleagues of what he saw as the dangers they, unwittingly perhaps, were courting in calling the convention. Decrying what he called "racial conformity for the sake of racial unity," Wilkins suggested the convention might get beyond the Congressional Black Caucus' control and establish a black political party. He wrote, "of course, the Black Caucus can state that the establishment of a black party is not one of the aims of the March conference. It can declare with perfect truth that a black politician outside the Black Caucus cannot speak for it or those who will gather. Indeed, it is a bit much (but wholly in character with the implied threat) to have the public told a month in advance what 'climate' the 'delegates' are expected to approve."[48] The NAACP objected to what it called the "separatist" and "radical" tone of the document.[49] The NAACP objected specifically to the following language in the preamble:

. . . the American institutions in which we have placed our trust are unable to cope with the crises they have created by their single minded dedication to profits for some and white supremacy above all. . . . They are the natural end-products of a society built on the twin foundations of white racism and capitalism. . . . The American system does not work for the masses of our people, and it cannot be made to work without radical, fundamental change. . . . If we are serious, the Black politics of Gary must accept responsibility for creating both the atmosphere and program for fundamental change in America. . . . We must recognize that no one is going to represent our interests but ourselves . . . we begin with an independent black political movement, an independent agenda. Nothing less will do.[50]

In a memorandum to the NAACP's delegates at the convention John Morsel, the association's assistant executive director, told the delegates that the draft preamble was "unacceptable" because it is "rooted in the concept of separate nationhood for black Americans. It calls for a withdrawal from the American political process. . . . The rhetoric of the platform is revolution not reform."[51] The NAACP was the only group or leader at the convention to publicly criticize the preamble.[52] Most persons questioned at the convention on the contrary indicated they found no difficulty with the document. For example, Samuel Jackson, Assistant HUD Secretary (one of several high-ranking Nixon Administration officials attending the convention as delegates or observers) said, "I have no hangups about the preamble. I think it clearly states the record that black people can unite on."[53] Nevertheless, Fauntroy, the Platform Chair, in a conciliatory gesture to the NAACP suggested that the preamble might be later modified or changed in some way to deal with the organization's concerns. However, the state delegation chairs acting as the convention steering committee voted overwhelmingly to recommend approval of the preamble as drafted, and this was sustained with little debate by the full convention the following day.

While the initial debate centered on the Platform Committee's work on the draft preamble, the principal business—preparing a draft platform—was also a source of conflict. Since there had been no hearings prior to the convention, the Committee decided to hold a full day of hearings in order to solicit the input of the incoming delegations. However, as a result of the first-day turmoil it was further agreed that the state delegations could submit amendments or resolutions from the floor.[54] This procedure of floor amendments resulted in the two most widely publicized, contentious issues of the convention, dealing with busing for purposes of school desegregation and the Middle East conflict.

But before these and other agenda issues could be addressed, two other potentially divisive issues had to be dealt with: whether to endorse a candidate for president, and whether to issue a call for the formation of a political party. Although Mrs. Chisholm did not attend the convention (pleading illness), there was strong support for her in many of the delegations and Percy Sutton strongly urged her endorsement. In addition, there was scattered support for Senators Humphrey and McGovern. The convention leaders (Diggs, Hatcher and Baraka), however, were strongly opposed to any endorsement, including Chisholm's. After lengthy debate the leaders managed to have the convention not endorse any candidate, arguing that it was too divisive.[55]

The issue of a black political party was somewhat more contentious. In his opening keynote address, Mayor Hatcher dealt with the party question by calling for delay, arguing "I, for one, am willing to give the major parties one more chance in the year 1972 to redeem themselves but if they fail us—a not unlikely prospect—we must then seriously probe the possibility of a third party movement."[56] But Jesse Jackson in his plenary address called on the convention to create a black party, exclaiming "Gary is the birth of a new black political party. We can no longer afford to be boys in any major party. We must start believing in ourselves. . . . Damn both white parties. . . . I am a black man. I want a black party. I don't trust white Republicans or white Democrats."[57] Baraka, hitherto the most persistent advocate of a black party as the "sine qua non of the new black politics" did not at Gary advance the idea; rather, he remained publicly silent and served as an honest broker between Jackson and Hatcher.[58] There probably was a majority on the floor to support formation of a party as proposed by Jackson; however, when the matter was taken up, Jackson joined with Ron Daniels (chair of the Ohio delegation and later leader of the convention's Assembly) to argue that the mere "proclamation of a party did not create a party" and that before they took such an important and necessary step, the groundwork in terms of grassroots mobilization should be undertaken and then on that basis the party could be created. The convention adopted this position without serious challenge (although many delegates complained that ample time was not provided for debate), in part because many delegates assumed that the convention's proposed continuing structure would function as a proto-party doing the necessary grassroots work so that the party would eventually evolve.[59]

Except for the issues of school busing and the situation in the Middle East, the adoption of the agenda as proposed by the Platform Committee went reasonably well in spite of the fact that it was unquestionably the most radical set of recommendations and resolutions ever adopted by a black convention or congress. For example, the draft agenda called for the following:

> Proportionate black congressional representation, with a minimum of sixty-six representatives and fifteen senators to be elected at large from the national black community. The same principle should obtain for state and local government.
>
> Proportionate black employment and control at every level of the federal government structure.
>
> Reparations including land, capital and cash to the black community by the white community for slavery and discriminatory treatment in the past.
>
> Enforcement of antitrust legislation, with ownership and control of divested companies going to blacks and other minority groups.
>
> Boosting of estate and gift taxes to 90 percent to end ownership of unearned white fortunes.
>
> Recognition of the Republic of New Africa's right to hold a plebiscite among blacks to determine whether the United States should be divided into separate homelands for blacks and whites.[60]

In addition to this potpourri of radical and nationalist proposals, the agenda also included more traditional liberal reform planks such as welfare reform, national health insurance, federal jobs programs and District of Columbia home rule. Thus, the agenda was internally contradictory, blending elements of reform and revolution. This was by design, since the leadership did not wish to offend any of the ideological factions represented at the convention. This was also irresponsible, since rather than debate, argue and seek some resolution of the differences the convention willy nilly included everyone's pet ideological or institutional position. In this it failed in the major purpose of any convention: to filter, sort, assign priorities and aggregate issues in a consensus agenda.

In this context the two most contentious and highly publicized issues at the convention were trivial—especially the busing resolution—in terms of the internal politics of black America. Court-ordered busing for purposes of school desegregation since its inception had been a con-

troversial issue in American politics and in internal black politics. Overwhelmingly rejected by the white public, polls showed that the black
community was about evenly split. Yet the black establishment of civil
rights leaders and elected officials were overwhelmingly in favor of the
strategy, for legal and political as much as educational reasons. The
busing controversy had fueled the campaigns of George Wallace and
Richard Nixon, and black establishment leaders did not wish to have it
appear that what they perceived as the constitutional rights of black
schoolchildren could be thwarted by popular or political pressures. Yet
busing was never that popular at the mass level or among the non-
establishment black intelligentsia and was actively opposed by organized elements of the nationalist community, most notably CORE under
the leadership of Roy Innis. I discussed earlier the Congressional Black
Caucus's effort at its education hearings to exclude CORE's antibusing
proposals from consideration and its unreserved support of busing in its
agenda presented to President Nixon. Indeed, the black establishment
myopically had sought to stifle dissent on this issue within its own
ranks (see Chapter 6). Thus, it was clear that busing would emerge as an
issue at the convention.

The Platform Committee was evasive on the issue. But throughout
the convention CORE circulated its antibusing, community control proposal and, predictably, when the platform was opened to amendment
from the floor the matter was raised in the form of a resolution offered
by the South Carolina delegation, which "condemned forced racial integration as bankrupt" because "it [was] based on the false notion that
black children are unable to learn unless they are in the same setting as
whites." Instead, as an alternative the resolution proposed "Black community control of our school system and a guarantee of an equal share
of the money."[61]

There was long and acrimonious debate on the floor, with the
opposition led by civil rights leaders and black elected officials (especially Richmond, Virginia's Mayor-to-be Henry Marsh, who at that time
was pressing a busing-based school desegregation suit in his hometown) but the sentiment among the delegates was clear and the resolution was overwhelmingly approved.

The resolution's adoption was widely reported in the national
media and was immediately denounced by the black establishment;
indeed, it was one factor that prompted the Michigan delegation led
by Coleman Young to walk out of the convention in protest.[62] Much of
the criticism did not deal with the substance of the issue of black education but rather with its politics. Typical was Roger Wilkins' column in
the *New York Times*, where he argued that "black separatists such as

Roy Innis and his little band of bitter men had in effect supported Richard Nixon's position that blacks did not want busing."[63] The notion that opposition to busing was to give aid and comfort to enemies of the race was a frequent refrain in criticisms of the resolution. For example, the black weekly *The Michigan Chronicle* opined, "The Black Convention would have been consistent with its debussing position had it invited George Wallace as the keynote speaker."[64] Reacting to this kind of criticism, the convention steering committee (charged with refining the language of the agenda for final printing) several weeks later clarified the resolution's language to "disassociate ourselves from Nixon and Wallace," and concluding, "our politics is that we must have control of our own education, with the option of transportation and any other tools which guarantee superior quality education and also protect all rights guaranteed under the Fourteenth amendment."[65] Since busing had always been ordered by the courts pursuant to the protection of the Fourteenth Amendment's equal protection clause, the compromise language in effect repudiated the substance, if not the spirit, of the resolution adopted by the convention. But to no avail, since this compromise language received little press attention and in the end only served to disappoint both sides in the dispute.

The second resolution that resulted in national controversy dealt with the Israeli-Arab conflict in the Middle East. In 1948 most elements of the black leadership establishment supported the United Nations partitions of Palestine that resulted in the creation of the Jewish state.[66] But by the late 1960s as a result of the growing influence of Pan Africanism with its emphasis on third-world solidarity, the radical and nationalist elements of the leadership community had adopted an antizionist, pro-Palestine position.[67] At the convention the District of Columbia delegation proposed a resolution that labeled the Jewish state "fascist" and "imperialistic" and called for the end of all United States military and economic assistance and the "return of the historical land of the Palestinian and Arab people to them." The adoption of this resolution, like the one on busing, resulted in an outcry from the black and white leadership establishments, and as a result, the steering committee later revised it to eliminate the language on fascism, imperialism, the call for an end to U.S. aid and the return of Arab lands. Instead, it adopted the language of the Organization of African Unity (the umbrella organization of African states), which condemned Israel's occupation of the territories seized in the 1967 war and supported the "struggles of Palestine for self-determination."[68] Like the compromise language on busing, the steering committee's work here received little press attention and satisfied neither side in the conflict (co-conveners Diggs and

Hatcher both repudiated the steering committee language). With the adoption of these two resolutions and the attendant conflict, the convention ended as it began, in controversy and confusion.[69]

The controversy at the end was occasioned by the walkout of the Michigan delegation in protest. Led by Coleman Young, elements of the delegation walked out of the convention amidst great fanfare attacking convention procedures, leadership and the draft agenda. Among the barrage of charges on the convention's last day, Young contended that the convention was planned on too short a notice, that Baraka had presided in an authoritarian manner and reneged on an agreement to postpone adoption of the agenda and that the agenda as adopted was "separatist . . . assuming 95 percent of whites are racists."[70] Reacting to Young's charges, a minority faction of the Michigan delegation denounced him and the majority that went with him as "UAW dominated" and not reflecting the sentiment of the state's blacks.[71] As a result, when Young and his group left, the convention seated a minority delegation headed by Riley Smith.[72]

In the midst of this confusion and acrimony the convention took two final administrative-procedural actions. First, it voted to establish a steering committee of the leadership and state delegation chairs to revise, refine and clarify the draft agenda in time to release the final, official document by May 19, the birthday of Malcolm X. This document was then to constitute the "legitimate" bargaining instrument in negotiations with the two major parties and their nominees. Second, the convention established two "continuation structures" to carry on its work: The National Black Political Assembly (NBPA), constituted by 10 percent of the delegates (about four hundred persons including built-in representation of the civil rights organizations and black elected officials), whose purpose was to conduct the interim business of the convention, endorse candidates, lobby and serve as the "primary broker in dealing with white institutions and black people around the world."[73] The assembly was to meet quarterly. And a National Black Political Council (NBPC) was established as the administrative arm of the assembly. Constituted by fifty-one delegates and the three co-conveners as an executive committee, it was to employ a staff and conduct the day-to-day assembly business. This group was to meet monthly.

In the immediate aftermath of the convention, evaluation in the black press generally fell along two lines. The dominant view in the black press and of black journalists writing in white media was summed up by Thomas Johnson in the title of his *New York Times* essay, "We Met therefore We Won."[74] That is, the convention was a success merely because it was able to bring together such a range of diverse persons, organizations, interests and ideologies in a national assembly. The minority view in the black press, however, was more sober and historically correct. It is best summed up in the *Chicago Defender* editorial, which read "out of the maelstrom of flamboyant, militant rhetoric and the threat of secession from the existing political parties no clear leadership has emerged. The convention was a babel of ideologies, half-baked dilettantism and infantile assumptions. It did not live up to its roseate promise. It had a chance to be a force in the consortium of American politics, it has muffed it."[75]

The *Chicago Defender*'s evaluation was not merely historically accurate; its truth was clearly manifest in the convention's immediate aftermath. A major purpose in the call of the convention was to develop a unified strategy, structure and agenda for effective black mobilization and participation in the 1972 presidential election, especially in terms of the major parties and their nominees and platforms. This strategy within a month of the convention's close degenerated into personality and factional conflicts amidst charges and countercharges of betrayal.

First, as alluded to earlier, the Congressional Black Caucus several weeks after the convention essentially repudiated the agenda adopted at Gary by proposing its alternative, pompously called "The Black Declaration of Independence and Bill of Rights."[76] This document was essentially a repackaging of the caucus's recommendations to President Nixon, involving an extensive program of liberal reform in employment, welfare, health, business development and education. At the press conference releasing the document, the members of the caucus put particular emphasis on its support of busing and for the state of Israel. When queried about the relationship of their agenda to the recently adopted Gary agenda, the members indicated that the caucus agenda was *the* black agenda and its contents were "minimal non-negotiable demands" for black support of any party or nominee in the fall election. This angered Baraka and the other non-congressional leaders of the Gary convention, since all except three caucus members had attended the convention and two had served in leadership capacities. In an effort to secure support for its agenda and the caucus as the principal bargaining or brokerage instrument, the caucus (more specifically Congressmen Clay, Stokes and Hawkins) invited black delegates to the Democratic Convention to a series of meetings to formulate a unified black strategy to influence platform deliberations, although not candidate choice, since the group itself was divided on the choice of the nominee.

This points not only to factional conflict between the establishment forces represented by the Caucus and the assembly but within the Caucus itself. First, Congresswoman Chisholm (with the support of Congressmen Mitchell and Dellums) continued her candidacy. With about a hundred committed delegates (roughly 25 percent of the black delegates at the convention), the Chisholm strategy was to become the black broker by getting the black delegates to support her on the first ballot and thereby deny McGovern, the front runner, the nomination; thereby making room for bargaining between her, McGovern and Humphrey in exchange for support of the "black agenda," leaving aside the question of which black agenda.

But this strategy was opposed by McGovern's principal "black brokers," including Congressmen Clay, Fauntroy and Stokes, Jesse Jackson, cochair of the Illinois delegation and Willie Brown, head of the large California delegation. Each of these individuals, but especially Jackson and Fauntroy, wanted to be seen as the key broker, the kingmaker, at the convention. Prior to the convention Fauntroy attempted to coopt this role by calling a joint press conference with McGovern where they announced that Fauntroy had provided a pledge of sufficient black delegate support (from the District of Columbia and elsewhere) to "put McGovern over the top" with a majority of pledged delegates.[77] Saying he was acting in his capacities as a member of the caucus and the Gary convention steering committee (he had the approval of neither group), Fauntroy said in exchange for his support McGovern had pledged to him that he would appoint blacks to the Supreme Court and other high government posts in rough proportion to their population, provide blacks 10 percent of patronage within the states and provide funds for black voter registration. In addition, McGovern indicated he supported "parts not all of the Gary agenda," taking specific exception only to the planks on busing and the Middle East.[78] When asked what assurances he had that McGovern would live up to his part of the bargain if elected, Fauntroy replied that he had "personal faith" in the man.[79]

Disappointed and angered by this breaking of ranks so soon after Gary, Baraka just prior to the Democratic Convention wrote a bitter essay for *Newsweek* in which he accused black elected officials and other establishment blacks of betraying the hopes of Gary and the masses of blacks for personal political gain, writing that such persons were "colored caucus-ians who were bought and paid for like sleepy eyed . . . hos[whores]."[80] Thus, things had come full circle. The two-year long struggle for a unified black political strategy under the principle of unity without uniformity had not produced unity, but instead it had only exacerbated and made plain for all to see the enormous ideological, institutional and inevitable personality and ego conflicts that characterized post–civil rights era black politics.

At the Democratic Convention in Miami the factionalized black forces were largely irrevelant to the outcome in terms of platform and nominees. Although there was the usual posturing by Fauntroy, Jackson, Chisholm and other black leaders, the central issue at the convention was Humphrey's challenge of the seating of the California delegation on the grounds that the winner-take-all provision that awarded all of the state's large bloc of delegates to Mcgovern was a violation of the party's reform guidelines. Once this issue was resolved in McGovern's favor he was assured of a first-ballot nomination, and all issues of bargaining in terms of nominees and platform were over. In a last-ditch effort to block McGovern's nomination, the Humphrey forces agreed to release their black delegates to vote for Chisholm on the first ballot. This transparent effort to stop McGovern was presented as a show of race solidarity, and Humphrey's black lieutenants led by Arnold Pinkney of Ohio and Charles Evers of Mississippi argued in meetings of the caucus of black delegates that McGovern should do the same thing in deference to Mrs. Chisholm and to create a strategic bargaining environment for blacks. This was easily rejected by the McGovern forces led by his black lieutenants Jackson, Brown, and Fauntroy. Similarly, at the Republican Convention a month later the small delegation of blacks (including many top black appointees of the administration who had been delegates at Gary) argued that there was no need to bargain on the basis of the Gary or any other black agenda since Nixon deserved black support on the basis of his "record"—this was said with what appeared to be straight faces.[81]

In the early fall after the major party conventions, *Black World* published the first of several issues devoted largely to reports and commentary on the black conventions. This first issue included essays by convention participants—Baraka, Missouri Congressman William Clay and activist-intellectuals Ronald Walters and William Strickland. (Both Strickland, then of Atlanta University's Institute of the Black World, and Walters, of Howard University had done staff work both prior to and at the convention.) In his contribution, Baraka presented a detailed and fairly straightforward account of the origins of the convention (but with relatively little on the three-day convention itself); but in what is probably some of the most vitriolic language in recent American political discourse, he attacked his colleagues for their behavior at the Miami convention. Of Chisholm he wrote:

The pity of Miami is that Mrs. Chisholm, though whipped and shaky, did still have the one thing going for her she never used during her campaign, and that is the fact that she is Black. During her campaign, she went into her white woman bag, and her Chi-

cano and Indian, "all the people," watered down Lower East Side
fleabit universalism, which would have been beautiful if she had
merely started by building from a Black base, in the national Black
community. She should have come to Gary. Her absence blew
any chance she had of making a serious campaign.[82]

Of Fauntroy he wrote "[he] is to be looked at closely in this regard. His
moves should be studied for he is truly as slippery as a traditionally
black-eel politician. . . . He has managed to slip back and forth between
the Caucus and the convention wearing both hats. . . ."[83] And of black
leadership behavior at the Democratic Convention in general he wrote:

> But in Miami it was ugly to see how the sellout works. . . . But
> some of the niggers were even more reprehensible. The
> Humphrey niggers led by Arnold Pinkney of Cleveland and
> Charles Evers of Mississippi were lowest of all. They s . . . physi-
> cally! Like old winded rats dizzy from their treadmills they
> bumped into people trying to form the words blacks on their s . . .
> out their mouths. They got Humphrey to release his black dele-
> gates to Mrs. Chisholm . . . to stop McGovern . . . But it didn't
> work. Even though they had this ol' p . . . dressed niggle-o
> preacher from Los Angeles who shouted and wiggled and
> chanted blackness (something they would despise and say was a
> naive concern at any other time and place) all for Hump. But it
> failed. . . . The next day the Hump and Muskie folded up their
> tents and the McGovern negroes caucused in earnest.[84]

This kind of language and worse was to characterize Baraka's
behavior throughout his tenure as a leader of the convention. (In the very
month this article was published Baraka was elected secretary-general of
the convention's Political Council as one of three coleaders of equal status
with Diggs and Hatcher.) It is difficult to understand how he could feel
free to use such language, publicly castigating his colleagues while
expecting to maintain collegial relations and sustain a political organization whose guiding principle was "unity without uniformity."[85] It could
not be done, of course, and though the pretense would go on for several
years, the seeds of the convention's collapse were planted in its first year.

The Little Rock Convention, 1974: The End Begins

The convention at Gary created two "continuation structures" to
carry on its work between its biannual meetings and plan for the next

convention scheduled for 1974. At the first meeting of the assembly held in Chicago, Congressman Diggs was elected its president, Hatcher was elected chairman of the National Political Council and Baraka was elected secretary-general. This cumbersome troika leadership structure continued the pattern of Gary by institutionalizing rather than rationalizing or aggregating the conflicting institutional, ideological and personality conflicts that became ever so clear at Gary and at the Democratic Convention at Miami. There was no clear administrative rationale for such a structure, nor was there a clear demarcation of lines of authority and responsibility between the assembly president, the council chairman and the secretary-general. Rather, this was a political compromise to assure each of the major factions or tendencies (local and national black elected officials and the nationalists) a place in the leadership structure, largely because neither trusted the other to exercise exclusive authority. This mistrust and suspiciousness was reinforced by the provision that each of the three were to function with "equal status" which, ideological and institutional conflicts aside, would make it extremely difficult for the organization to function smoothly administratively or speak with a coherent voice to its various internal constituencies or the external world. For example, rather than grant the power to appoint the assembly's thirteen administrative officers (called "ministers" in such areas as Political Empowerment, International Affairs, Economic Development, etc.) to the president or the secretary-general, as competent administration would require, it was given to an executive committee constituted by the three principal officers. Again, without ideological conflicts between the three leaders this structure was likely to result in management inertia, irresponsibility and the lack of accountability. Given such conflicts, these results were guaranteed.

After its initial organizing meeting in Chicago in 1972 the assembly during 1973 held sessions in Atlanta, Detroit, San Diego and Greenville, Mississippi. In addition to trying to work out the mechanics of establishing and administering a new organization, assembly members devoted attention to the pressing problems of fundraising (which predictably was not going well) and the related problem of establishing a headquarters office and recruiting a paid staff (as at Gary, Baraka's CAP was the most reliable source of volunteer staff support). They also devoted discussion to the role and responsibilities of black elected officials in the assembly and what was described as their "dual loyalty" to the assembly and the Democratic Party. This discussion was exacerbated because although specific provision had been made for the representation of such officials from each state, relatively few attended. Most observers thought the active involvement of these officials was indispensable to the viability of the assembly and the convention.[86] Finally, the group sought to deal with restoring some semblance of the principle of "unity without uniformity" or ideological clarity to the assembly's work, and facilitate planning for the convention planned for the following year.

This latter work was made more difficult as Baraka was at the time moving away from his cultural nationalist qua Pan Africanism ideology toward, first, some eclectic blend of elements of Pan African-ism and socialism and then, finally, toward "scientific socialism" as the correct ideology to guide the post–civil rights era black struggle. Although there were hints of this fundamental change to come in some of Baraka's speeches and contributions to Assembly debates, it was not to become clear until the following year, during the 1974 convention.

Sensing that the pivot of the ideological problem of the assembly was the conflict between or amongst the various schools of nationalist thought and the establishment integrationists, Howard University's Ronald Walters (an active participant in the assembly's work and with good relations with the nationalists and establishment black elected officials) wrote an essay in *Black World* that sought to bridge intra-nationalist and nationalist-integrationist cleavages by defining nation-alism so broadly that it would include virtually all organized forces in the black community. This essay, titled "African-American National-ism—Toward a Unifying Ideology," was published prior to Baraka's abrupt public change of ideology; thus it did not deal with the question of the coming cleavage between orthodox nationalism, integration and Marxism. The purpose of the essay Walters wrote was to "provide an ideological framework for unity without uniformity" by broadening the definition of nationalism, because "in the past it has been defined so narrowly as to make it a dysfunctional code for the masses of black people."[87] Identifying two main divisions in the "objectives" of nation-alism between those who are "land oriented" and those who are "justice oriented," he dismisses the land variety as "substantially a fantasy" that "will distort and confuse the nationalist movement as long as it believes it is operating solely within the classical tradition of other nationalist movements."[88] He then proposed that a mature nationalism that could unify the race would be defined "not as a struggle over land but as a struggle for resources and justice."[89] In other words, national-ism, like integration, was in essence a struggle for parity or equality of black access to the resources of American society. Thus, he concludes:

> For the purpose of this discussion all groups which can be said to
> have adopted a serious program devoted to bettering the spiri-

tual and material conditions of black life are nationalists. . . . What this implies, then, is that the facade of nationalist and anti-nationalist elitism and exclusion must be broken through to form a workable coalition with nationalists and potential nationalists of all types in order that the goals of the black nation are elevated above the squabble over means.[90]

Although a valiant and understandable effort to try to reassert the principle of "operational unity" by focusing on ultimate goals rather than means, Walters's effort failed both as an intellectual and a political proposition. First, the conflict can not be so neatly compartmentalized into goals that all blacks agree on with only minor "squabbles" over means. The two are often, in any ideology, inextricably bound. Thus, the essay begged the question of just what is "a serious program devoted to bettering the spiritual and material conditions of blacks." The Pan Africanists say it is focusing on the liberation of Africa, and the land-based separatists say it is not; the liberal integrationist say liberal reform capitalism is such a program, while the Marxists say it is not—and the list of competing ideological claims goes on and on and on. Walters's analysis is similar to Malcolm X's famous but erroneous formulation in the speech "Ballot or the Bullet," where he argued there were no differences between nationalists and integrationists in objectives since they both wanted "freedom." The difference, Malcolm said, was over means; the civil rights establishment believed that "integration will get you freedom" while he believed that nationalism would, but he argued "we both agree on the goal."[91] If this formulation was viable then there would be no ideological conflict, since all ideologies at this level of abstraction or generality may claim to have the ultimate goal of freedom but differ only over means. Thus, Mao Tse-tung and Ronald Reagan both have the goal of freedom, only Mao thinks communism is the means while Reagan thinks it's capitalism. No mere squabble over means.

In any case, events were in the saddle. While Walters was wrestling with the nationalism and integration cleavages, Baraka was moving toward communism, not nationalism, as "the only serious program of black uplift," and planning was going forward largely under his leadership and staff support for the second convention in 1974—a convention that would show the utter futility of the notion of ideological unity without uniformity.

The 1974 National Black Convention at Little Rock, unlike Gary, was called not to deal with large issues of presidential strategy or the black agenda but rather with the mechanics of organizational development and the nuts and bolts of mass political mobilization. The delegate selection process again varied widely. Despite the adoption of rules requiring community elections, few were held and most delegates reported they were self-selected or selected by others in their state, and observers reported that many of the delegations were heavily weighted toward followers of Baraka, given his more extensive involvement in grassroots organizing prior to the convention.[92] The assembly also reportedly repealed the rule granting automatic delegate slots to black elected officials, which led assembly President Diggs to complain bitterly that what he described as the Baraka-enforced rules changes were "one of the major reasons for the lack of black elected officials at the convention. Here they are people with proven constituencies. They are leaders by their election to public office. The rules were okay two years ago; why aren't they now?"[93]

In fact much discussion at and commentary about the convention dealt with who was there and who was not. Assembly President Diggs did not attend, claiming a scheduling conflict while simultaneously indicating that he would not stand for reelection as president and was thinking about organizing black elected officials in an alternative organization to the convention. Hatcher in his opening address to the convention attacked by name prominent black elected officials and civil rights leaders (including Roy Wilkins, Los Angeles Mayor Thomas Bradley, Detroit's Mayor Young) for their absence, berating them as "political paupers who became political prima donnas."[94] A number of national establishment black leaders did attend, including Congressmen Conyers, Dellums and Mitchell as well as Atlanta Mayor Maynard Jackson and Jesse Jackson. But much press attention and convention gossip focused on the relatively small number of such persons compared to the meeting at Gary, suggesting that their absence undermined the convention's legitimacy.[95] On the other hand, several nationalist leaders suggested that invitations to such persons as Maynard and Jesse Jackson should be withdrawn because, in the words of Owusu Sadaukai, "neo-colonialist, petit bourgeois black elected officials are as much the enemy as their white counterparts."[96] Hatcher, who tried to serve as a bridge between the nationalist and establishment factions, nevertheless was ambivalent about his own role in the convention process, telling reporters at Little Rock, "I will have to reevaluate my future with the convention in light of the unity motto. We need to revive that motto. My future depends on the willingness of some to be tolerant of people when you disagree with them. Part of my reevaluation will be to see if the unity motto is still intact. . . . I don't think we can be effective unless we have an organization in which elected officials, nationalists, conservatives, liberals and civil rights activists can feel comfortable and work within."[97] And in reference to disagreements with Baraka, Hatcher said "I happen to think that the convention is about basic things—political organizing, electing people to office and although we get along personally, Baraka has a grander design in terms of revolution."[98]

Since there was no formal agenda to be considered, much of the debate centered around the role of the convention, the efficacy of electoral politics in the post–civil rights era struggle and whether the convention should formally establish a political party and if so how should such a party be structured in terms of organization and ideology.[99] Hatcher (and most black elected officials), as his comments above indicate, favored a more traditional role for the convention (and any subsequent party) in terms of registration, voting and electing people to office, while the nationalists and Marxist factions favored a less traditional, nonelectoral role.[100] Many nationalists and radicals viewed electoral politics as largely irrelevant to the post–civil rights era black struggle. As Robert Allen, the influential editor of *The Black Scholar* (which with *Black World* was the leading journal for ideological thought and debate), argued "Dabbling in elections on the pretext of organizing and educating is an unnecessary waste of scarce resources. The activity may inflate egos but does little to build a mass based organization."[101] At the convention this view was articulated by Baraka and other nationalist and radicals. For example, Sadaukai, an emerging Pan Africanist leader, in a speech contended "whatever reforms we have achieved have not come from black elected officials . . . we have got to understand that our only salvation is to destroy racism, capitalism and change the world."[102] Rhetorical excess aside, Sadaukai and the forces he represented argued that instead of electoral activism the convention should be a "fighting organization engaged in community struggles involving rent strikes, sit-ins, mass marches, etc. in order to mobilize that half of blacks alienated from voting."[103] These contrasting views were not only reflected in the speech making but in the workshops on political organization. Workshops on political organization or "Political Empowerment" were conducted by Oklahoma State Representative Hanna Atkins and Youngstown, Ohio activists and future assembly President Ron Daniels. Atkins concentrated on registration, voting, campaign finance and management while Daniels focused more on nonelectoral mobilization and grassroots assembly organizing.

The convention at Little Rock formally rejected a resolution to form a political party, ostensibly because the grassroots organizing had not yet gone far enough to prepare the mass base. However, a more basic reason was that deep ideological differences and institutional cleavages precluded common agreement on the nature and purposes of a political party. As Cruse put it in an incisive post–Little Rock analysis, the problem was "whose concept of whose independent party—Conyers' or Baraka's—was to guide the formation."[104] The inability to resolve these differences doomed any progress in party formation during this period and subsequently, including the stillborn National Black Independent Party founded in 1980.

Baraka's view was well known, expressed in the resolution adopted at the 1970 CAP workshop he led and elaborated later in *The Black Scholar* article, "The Pan African Party and the Black Nation."[105] He wanted a party that would combine electoral activism with community organizing and revolutionary action. This multipurpose party formation was described in globalist terms by William Strickland.

> We need a party that can do those things . . . to advance the interests of black people. . . . A party that sees its essential historical task as the challenge to govern this society. That party can not be like the Democratic and Republican parties. It must have some element of the original Peoples Party in Ghana, some elements of the FLN in Algeria, some elements of the PAIGC in Guinea-Bissau, some elements of the LAO Dong Party in Vietnam, some elements of the Chinese Communist party and, indeed, some elements of the Tupamoros.[106]

Black elected officials like Conyers, however, wanted a narrowly focused electoral party whose focus would be to mobilize the black vote as an independent force in American politics that might constitute a balance of power between the major parties in some elections and end the situation where the Democrats took the black vote for granted and the Republicans ignored it altogether.[107] Cruse quotes a Conyer's speech in Newark in early 1974 where he highly commended Baraka for his contributions to black politics and urged the formation of a third party with the Congressional Black Caucus as its starting point:

> It is very important that blacks in the top echelon of political leadership nationalize their constituency. . . . The two party system fails to provide blacks with sufficient representation. Let's go to Little Rock to help promote the third party proposal. Let's get on with it, we have nothing to lose but our chains of loyalty to the Democrats and Republicans and our decades of unrequited votes.[108]

Thus, there was clear sentiment for a party of some kind by leaders of both important factions at Little Rock; but action was deferred because of the absence of consensus on party structure. It is important to examine in some detail this 1970s debate about party formation because it not only sheds important light on post–civil rights era black politics but, equally important, such a party is still needed today, and by understanding what happened during this period black leadership one hopes can move forward in the years ahead to complete this unfinished business of black empowerment.

To anticipate the concluding part of this chapter, the grandiose multipurpose party envisioned by Baraka and Strickland is nothing short of romanticism and even to talk about is a waste of scarce resources. Indeed, the Black Panthers constituted such a formation, and taught us its limits. What is needed is a traditional American third-party coalition of black and other progressive interests in American society, *and* an internal broad-based umbrella black organization that would deal with grassroots mobilization around the myriad of internal problems in the black community. Participation in one of these formations would not necessarily preclude participation in the other depending on ideology, interests or other institutional obligations. But clearly, those who reject electoral activism in principle or because it is viewed as essentially irrelevant would have no place in a political party; nor would persons unwilling to compromise on ideological principle in the give-and-take of a broad progressive coalition find it comfortable in an *electorally* competitive third party.

Finally, nationalists and radicals in black politics take no account of the fact that politicians in the United States, black or white, tend not to be concerned about large questions of ideology or policy but rather about winning. Thus, whatever sentiments they may have in private about nationalist or radical ideas are irrelevant unless they add or detract from the votes necessary to win. As was said by more than one observer of the debate at Little Rock, "nationalists don't scare any politicians because they can not deliver any votes and to them that's what counts."[109] This pragmatic focus on winning by black elected officials and the unwillingness or inability of nationalists and radicals to deliver grassroots voter support is a critical factor in the reluctance of establishment politicians to join in any kind of common political formation. As Congressman Clay bluntly put it in his explanation of why only three of his then sixteen Black Caucus colleagues attended the Little Rock meeting, "my district is 49 percent black and 51 percent white and I get elected every two years. Baraka's district is 65 percent black and they send Peter Rodino, a white man, to Congress. Now tell me, what business do I have letting him tell me about political power and political organization?"[110]

Therefore, at Little Rock the resolution to create a party was rejected because the various factions could not agree on its nature and purpose and because, as Conyers put it, "This is an enormous undertaking. Our primary purpose is to bring together the broad spectrum of black political views to organize grassroots politics. Talk of a third party is still premature."[111] The convention voted formally, as it had two years before at Gary, to defer the party question until more groundwork was undertaken to create the grassroots base. But as Conyers' remarks indicate, this position was based on the fundamentally flawed premise that you need to "bring together the broad spectrum of black views"—flawed because it was this very broad spectrum that made it virtually impossible to reach any kind of consensus about the party or anything else. The convention did adopt a vague set of recommendations urging local assemblies to organize so as to be able to impose sanctions on those black candidates that did not support the Black Agenda. But given the hostility of many local assembly leaders to electoral activism and the nascent state of local assembly organization relative to that of most black candidates, these recommendations were mere words to be safely ignored without fear of peril.

Things Fall Apart: Leadership, Ideology and Organization

In an emotional assembly meeting in Dayton, Ohio in November of 1975, Baraka was ousted as secretary-general. His authoritarian and confrontational leadership style, his rhetorical bombast and vitriol and his unwillingness to abide by the Assembly's recently adopted "Statement of Principles" were all factors in his ouster, but a critical factor was his formal adoption shortly after the Little Rock convention of the ideology of Marxist-Leninism, scientific socialism or communism. As Baraka well knew, the very word communism, amongst Americans black and white, elite and mass, causes alarm, fear and anger because it is viewed as anti-God, freedom and democracy. In other words, "un-American." While some of these reactions are unwarranted, a product of the paranoid style of American political discourse and the misappropriation of the ideology by Soviet-style Marxists, they nevertheless constitute what the Marxists like to refer to as the "really existing situation." And this reality meant that communism as the ideology of the assembly or one of its principal leaders would effectively isolate it from the more pragmatic mindset of the black masses and their establishment leaders. Nevertheless, Baraka, moving with the flow of his fertile

mind and the ideological drift of important segments of the black intelligentsia, moved to forcefully articulate and seek to impose on the
assembly this sectarian, utopian ideology.

At Little Rock, in his speeches, comments to the press and private
meetings Baraka had broadly hinted at his change of ideology. In late
1974 he made his position explicit in an article published in *Black World*
ironically titled (given the confusion it would cause) "Toward Ideological Clarity." In this article, based on a longer position paper he had
written for his organization CAP, Baraka draws on the classical works
of the Marxist-Leninist tradition (as well as such Third World contributors to the tradition as Mao Tse-tung and Africa's Amilcar Cabral) to
develop historically and theoretically the position that blacks everywhere face a dual "race-class" or national (racial and cultural) and class
(capitalism) oppression. Consequently, the nationalist ideology that
focused exclusively on the race or national question was too narrow
and should be broadened to include the class basis of black oppression,
because, Baraka argued, racism could not be eliminated unless capitalism was destroyed. Blacks in the United States, in Africa and throughout the diaspora therefore must wage simultaneous struggles against
racism and capitalism. Thus, he wrote:

> The Black Liberation movement is the vanguard of struggle within
> the U.S. not only against racism but for socialism. . . . Building
> strong disciplined organizations with the correct ideology, based
> on nationalism, Pan Affrickanism and Socialism, and analysis of
> concrete conditions that are able to actively pursue concrete pro-
> grams to help mobilize, organize and politicize the masses of our
> people and to move them effectively to transform this entire soci-
> ety, and in so doing to help alter objective and subjective condi-
> tions throughout the world.[112]

As if the struggling three-year-old convention process did not
have enough to contend with given the institutional and ideological
tensions between liberal integrationist black elected officials and civil
rights leaders and the sundry variety of land-based, cultural and Pan
Africanist nationalists, Baraka now introduced communism into this
volatile mix, undermining even the fragile unity that might have been
possible after Little Rock. As Baraka forcefully (and some participants
say forcibly) articulated his new ideology in assembly meetings and
forums, confusion, anger and bitterness were the inevitable results.
Implicitly in his initial *Black World* essay, Baraka had abandoned the
principle of unity without uniformity, arguing that the civil rights

movement had promoted the creation of a black "neo-colonialism promotes a psuedo-bourgeoisie . . . whose interests more and more coincide with imperialism, thus speeding class formation, or at least providing the illusion of class formation and sharpening class struggle."[113] The implication of this language of class struggle was that there could be no unity with such persons; rather, the black petit bourgeoisie was as much the enemy of black liberation as white racists. Clearly something had to be done if even the illusion of an umbrella black organization was to be maintained.[114] Thus, new Assembly President Ron Daniels called a series of meetings or "ideological forums" to try to develop some real ideological clarity around a statement of principles that would unite and hold accountable all assembly and convention adherents.

During this series of meetings, Baraka wrote a second *Black World* essay directed largely to the nationalist community, in which he sought to clarify the basis of his change of ideology in terms less historical and theoretical but rather more personal and political. First, he explicitly rejected the variety of cultural nationalism that he and Karenga had articulated for the last decade or so, writing that "we thought the African culture reclaimed and projected by black people in the United States or anywhere in the world, would provide the consciousness for us to liberate ourselves. We went so far as to try to impose continental African mores and customs, some out of precapitalist feudalist Afrika [*sic*], upon black people living in North America. . . ."[115] Second, reflecting on his experience in Newark politics and his earlier analysis of the rise in the post–civil rights era of what he called a "black petit bourgeoisie" class, Baraka rejected the traditional nationalist ideological notion of race group unity and solidarity and by extension the convention's guiding principle of unity without uniformity. Of "our middle class grown fat off the gains made by the struggle of the people" he wrote:

> those of us who were still determined to serve the people began to understand that merely putting blackfaces in high places, without changing the fundamental nature of the system itself, simply served to make that system more flexible and dangerous. . . . Increasingly also we found especially in places like Newark— where we have wall to wall black bureaucrats, with Mercedes Benzes, Afros, hip sideburns, cardin suits, humpback high heels, Lincolns who are mayors, superintendents of schools, police chiefs . . . —that it was these very blacks who were now in charge of oppression and exploitation.[116]

Finally, in the orthodox Marxist tradition, Baraka broke with his nationalist colleagues in the assembly and elsewhere by declaring that class had primacy over race in the Afro-American freedom struggle. Noting as he had in his earlier essay that blacks suffered from the double oppression of race and class, he concludes that ". . . it was capitalism that caused national oppression and racism in the first place, and they will only be destroyed after capitalism is destroyed."[117] In conclusion, he rejected affiliation with the Communist Party/USA, dismissing it as "a corporation for collaboration with capitalism." Instead, he argued that his Congress of African People would now constitute the mass-organizing base as "a revolutionary communist organization," but "It is also a black organization which makes it a revolutionary nationalist organization."[118]

Baraka's essay appeared in July of 1975. In October, *Black World* published a remarkable series of candid interviews with the leadership of the assembly, dealing with such issues as the role of ideology, the role of Baraka, the role of black elected officials and the future of the convention in 1976 and beyond. Although invitations to participate in the interview symposia were extended to Mayor Hatcher and to members of the Congressional Black Caucus, they did not respond; thus the symposia includes the responses of Ron Daniels the assembly president, Baraka and Oklahoma Senator Atkins, the former assembly treasurer.

The most important issue on the minds of the editors of *Black World* was the growing conflict occasioned by Baraka's new-found communist ideology and its effect on the assembly and the convention process, especially the participation of black elected officials. Daniels responded by first indicating that the growing number of black elected and appointed officials had been able to produce "no substantial changes" in the conditions of blacks since the 1960s and this had led many in the assembly to reassess the nature of the problem and conclude that the problem was "not simply one of race but in a more pronounced way than was understood in the late sixties one of capitalism."[119] Thus, at one fundamental level of ideology, Daniels indicated broad agreement with Baraka's position on the dual nature of the sources of black oppression and the necessity for a simultaneous struggle against racism and capitalism. However, at another level—the primacy of class or race—he indicated a basic disagreement. This may seem like and indeed was ideological hair splitting or a chicken or egg came first type dispute, but in the charged ideological climate of the period what seems like a minor quibble over detail was, as is often the case among American radicals, elevated far beyond its significance to a matter of profound consequence.[120] Thus, Daniels said, "many of us who are nationalists believe that the race struggle is the primary struggle. . . . By the same token, many of us also understand very clearly that the principle contradiction confronting black people is the question of capitalism, that there cannot really be substantial change in our existence unless capitalism itself is dismantled and replaced by a new society. . . . I remain committed, however, to the idea that the struggle is a race-class, not a class-race struggle."[121]

While separating himself from Baraka on the race-class nature of the struggle, Daniels did not here repudiate communism as an ideology to be included within the broad range of opinion within the assembly. Rather, he indicated that at a recent assembly meeting a resolution was adopted that specifically said, "The NBPA was created to include the broadest possible spectrum of people . . . [who] can agree to our statement of principles, we don't care what your ideology is, and you have a right to express your ideology. . . . What was, in fact, lacking was a statement of principles . . . therefore if we have a statement of principles as they represent the National Black Assembly, to represent their personal or individual notion [sic]. We expect them to project now the notion of the NBPA. Now that does not mean, again, that people cannot advocate their ideology in debates and discussions . . . but once we have adopted a policy, that policy will hold for the NBPA and our officers are expected to speak to it."[122]

Daniels went on to say that while he and Baraka had some ideological differences and some confrontations with each other in the past they were now working quite closely together, and with respect to "scientific socialism" and its critics he said:

> Socialism is a growing force inside the minds of black people across the country and its influence is bound to be felt inside the NBPA. Many people were not really concerned about "scientific socialism" as they were concerned about the communism because people felt that as a matter of practicality communism might be very frightening to some people. But like all political ideas, communism and socialism and various other notions must be heard and understood. In fact, as we look at the broad spectrum of political ideas, certainly communism is far more progressive than anything we might talk about in terms of capitalism at its absolute best. . . . So, scientific socialism I'm sure is going to be heard inside the National Assembly. Amiri Baraka, I'm sure, in his debates and discussions, and as he moves, will be informed by his political ideology, as well as any black elected official might, or myself or others, as we argue policy.[123]

Daniels's remarks here are curious, since in this same issue of *Black World* Atkins quotes from an earlier statement of his that questions not only Baraka's new ideology but his leadership role in the assembly. Atkins wrote, "As Ron Daniels stated in January, 1975,"

> Though I respect Amiri Baraka's right to express his opinions and advocate his ideology, I must express my grave misgivings about the repercussions of having an avowed communist in the leadership of NBPA . . . if in addition to all other problems we confront, we must also constantly be reacting to the fears which communism engenders in the masses of our people. Secondly, I doubt seriously whether the constituency inside the Assembly which adheres to communism is large enough to warrant representation within the leadership of NBPA. . . . Finally, it is my conviction that the tactics of the Secretary-General (both inside and outside of the Assembly) constitute a definite stumbling block to the growth and development of NBPA. His handling of meetings was questioned extensively in Denver. . . . Externally, the Secretary-General's acid tongue," rhetorical bombast and "insults" have served to alienate sizeable segments of organized elements within the national black community.[124]

Atkins also slightly refined her reasons for resigning from the assembly leadership, arguing that while she believed all ideologies should be represented in the organization (including communism), "none should dominate," and that Baraka had sought to impose his ideology on the assembly by "shouting down opposite views, capturing the microphone . . . and generally participating in abusive, verbal assaults." Thus, she wrote, "my resignation as treasurer of NBPA came after months of seeing all efforts at unity deliberately thwarted. Open measures were taken to push out of the organization persons who happened not to express views acceptable to certain 'nationalists.' My discontent and frustration came not from the ideologies being represented but from the brutish tactics employed to dominate the NBPA."[125]

For his part, Baraka reiterated the notion that the assembly should be a broad-based united front of diverse ideologies and philosophies, but also that "only a socialist revolution leading to the seizure of state power led by a revolutionary communist party could bring the ultimate change we seek."[126] He then concluded:

> Only ignorant persons, tools or representatives of imperialism would seek to limit that front or try to put people out of the

Assembly for the reason that they were communists or socialists as some petit bourgeois black elected officials had tried to do (to me). The absurdity of this, of course, was that these questionable patriots belong to political parties that feature George Wallace and James Eastland on one hand or Ronald Reagan and Nelson Rockefeller on the other . . . Black elected officials are not resigning from these parties because of those fascists.[127]

The airing of these sharply conflicting and in some cases contradictory views by the assembly's leaders in the widely read *Black World* suggested that the assembly and the convention process itself faced a severe crisis of leadership, organization and ideology.[128] Although Daniels indicated that he and Baraka were working closely together in moving the assembly's business forward including plans for a 1976 convention that would nominate and run a prominent black leader for president,[129] within two months things had fallen apart and Baraka had been ousted as the secretary-general.

Baraka's removal was decisive because he had brought dedication, hard work and the only semblance of a national cadre of committed, competent organizers who provided much-needed staff support for the fledgling assembly and convention. With his departure the already ailing assembly was mortally wounded. The earlier departure of most black elected officials had injured the organization, and now with the loss of Baraka and his activists cadre, the assembly was in debt, on the verge of collapse, with, according to Manning Marable, perhaps several hundred activists remaining.[130] But paradoxically the wound of Baraka's departure was unavoidable or self-inflicted. As the history of prior efforts at convention building suggest, under any circumstances the 1972 project initiated at Gary faced formidable odds. However, whatever prospects for success it had were substantially undermined by its moving force—Baraka. Thus, in some sense the wound of his departure was beside the point; the process could not survive with him or without him. This is a harsh judgment; but Baraka must share both the praises for the creation of the convention and also the heavy burden of blame for its destruction.

To the extent that this project had any chance to beat the historical odds and endure it was destroyed by the leadership role of Baraka. His authoritarian style of leadership, his taste for rhetorical excess and bombast and his proclivity for ideological oscillation doomed the project from the outset. How could it survive the adoption, by the principal proponent of unity without uniformity, a rigidly exclusive and dogmatic ideology such as scientific socialism, which Baraka sought, by many accounts, to impose in an authoritarian manner on the diverse constituencies of the assembly. This thoroughly utopian ideology predictably would foreclose any possibility of unity with the black establishment but also with large parts of the nationalist community as well. And the very abruptness of this ideological flip-flop suggests a utopian mind-set manifestly unsuited for leadership of all but the most sectarian groups.[131] Remnants of the assembly were to continue for another several years or so, ending eventually in the establishment of the National Black Independent Party, but with the ouster of Baraka in 1975 the essential story line of its epitaph could be safely filed away to await early use.

"Stillborn": The National Black Independent Party, 1976–80

The ouster of Baraka and his communist CAP contingent, while weakening the assembly organizationally and financially, did have the effect of making it a more cohesive body of nationalists, although nationalists of various stripes and sects. In 1975, plans went forward for the group's third convention in 1976 and the nomination of a presidential candidate. The preferred strategy was to have the assembly act as a "pre-party" formation that would nominate a candidate of national stature who might be able to carry a significant share of the black and white progressive vote and thereby act as a balance of power in determining the outcome of the general election between the two major parties.[132] Failing to attract a prominent standardbearer then, the assembly would simply run a symbolic candidacy, in an effort, as Daniels said, "to educate the masses about the contradictions and the vicious nature of monopoly capitalism as it affects their lives."[133]

Throughout the year and into 1976 the assembly held discussions with such prospective candidates as Congressmen Conyers and Dellums and Georgia's Senator Bond. Both Dellums and Bond expressed some interest. In January of 1976 the assembly's executive committee adopted a resolution announcing the selection of Bond as its preferred candidate, indicating, "The nomination shall take the form of a draft movement which will bring together black, Third World and white organizations and persons into a National Committee for Peoples Politics (N.C.P.P.) which shall seek ballot status for the candidate in thirty states." However, when the convention met in Cincinnati in March it was clear that it did not have the organizational or financial wherewithal to mount a credible national presidential campaign. Most glaringly, the assembly had not achieved ballot status in a single state. As a result, Bond withdrew his name from consideration prior to the convention, and although Congressman Dellums briefly flirted with a possible candidacy, he too in a speech to the convention declined to accept the nomination.[134] Given the failure to attract a nationally recognized candidate, the convention reverted to its second strategy by nominating a relatively unknown New York activist, Reverend Frederick Douglas Kirkpatrick, as a symbolic candidate.

The 1976 convention and its candidate had no discernible impact on the year's politics. Its significance was to show the insignificance of the assembly. Reduced to a small cadre of dedicated radicals and nationalists, disillusioned by its inability to have an impact on black politics during the 1976 election, short of money and staff, the assembly was largely moribund until the approach of the 1980 election, declining for example to attempt to put together the off-year 1978 convention. The Carter administration provided a last gasp of life to the dying organization. Elected with overwhelming black support, by the end of his administration black leaders—establishment, radical and nationalist—saw Carter as having betrayed the black vote. A view based on the administration's substantial cuts in the social welfare budget, large increases in military outlays and a refusal to implement provisions of the recently passed Humphrey-Hawkins full employment legislation. To the nationalists and radicals Carter's betrayal was predictable, but it seemed useful as a lesson to once again teach the limits of electoral politics as a vehicle to advance the black agenda. The remaining activists in the assembly in late 1979 thus agreed to hold its fourth convention during the 1980 presidential election year.

Meeting in New Orleans, after the major party conventions, the approximately 750 assembled delegates were largely nationalists and grassroots community organizers with hardly any representation by black establishment civil rights and elected leaders. Given the cohesive ideological and institutional character of the delegates and their strong disenchantment with the major parties and electoral politics, the convention without much debate or dissension voted overwhelmingly in support of a resolution offered by Reverend Benjamin Chavis to establish a black political party.[135] The previous convention position of delaying party formation until the necessary mass base had been established was easily cast aside as most discussion centered around the relationship of the new party to the assembly and to electoral politics. While these issues were debated, resolution of them was put off until the founding convention set for Philadelphia (chosen because it was the site of the first national black convention) in late November after the general elections.[136] For example, on the central question of party structure and purpose the Chavis resolution was a model of muddle, leaving still unresolved the decade-long debate about whose concept of party was to be established at Philadelphia. It read in part:

> The function [of the party] is to advance a politics of transformation for the Black nation and that the party will be a community building, nation building [sic] primarily devoted to infra-structural support, institutional and organizational development within the Black community providing community services, engaging in community struggles and lobbying around private and public issues and electoral politics.[137]

The convention of several hundred delegates met in late November in Philadelphia and formally established the National Black Independent Political Party (NBIPP). In reality, the formation of the party was an illusion, because what really happened at Philadelphia was the death of the convention experiment of the 1970s and its reincarnation in a stillborn infant called NBIPP. As Mack Jones put it in a brief discussion paper shortly after Philadelphia, "The 1972 Gary convention is but the latest stillborn experiment to be entombed in this grave yard of good intentions and the National Black Political Party created in 1980 may be interpreted as the efforts of the pallbearers to deny the grave its victory."[138]

The Philadelphia convention was the last of the several that flowed from the Gary experiment. It was largely a convention of radical nationalists, which should have brought a measure of cohesion. It did not. Its opening debate on the party name degenerated into a rancorous session, with Harlem-based nationalists leading a faction that insisted that the party be called the "African Party." When order was restored the convention leaders (Ronald Walters, Ben Chavis and Manning Marable), after much laborious debate, finally secured formal agreement on party creation but without agreement on its character and structure. A Charter Commission, chaired by Walters, was charged with bringing a draft document to the convention that would deal with the party's relationship to electoral politics, but it could not reach consensus. Thus, a compromise was adopted that called for "an 'Electoral Politics Study Commission' to study the problem and make recommendation on the way in which an electoral organization might associate itself with the party, but that the main body, the National Black Independent Political Party . . . would not be an electoral vehicle but a broad-based organization devoted to community organization and civil rights."[139] Even this compromise language on an electoral role for the party was later dropped. The divisive problem of defining the role and purpose of a black party that defied resolution at Gary and Little Rock could not be settled in the relatively more cohesive environment of Philadelphia. The nature of the dispute may be seen in the views of two of the principal leaders at Philadelphia, Marable and Walters. Walters, in his writings on the party question, views it as both electoral and community action oriented but as largely the former; it would be open to all, would contest elections at all levels, set the black agenda and bargain with the major party candidates with a threat of defeating those who refused to bargain.[140] Marable's views were much more sectarian, arguing that the party should be "a genuine, anti-capitalist party, which rejects fundamental compromise and collaboration with the Democratic party." He also argued that the party should exclude the integrationist black establishment because it "express[es] tendencies toward class collaboration with the state."[141]

The party later adopted a charter with a broad statement of principles defining it as a national, mass-based organization actively opposing "racism, sexism, capitalism and imperialism" and including an elaborate organizational structure of local chapters, executive officers, central and standing committees and a national party congress as the "highest governing body of the party."[142] Yet this was all an elaborate illusion. The third historic effort at a national black congress had failed. Although the NBIPP was successful in establishing several energetic local chapters, notably in Ohio, the District of Columbia, Chicago, Maryland, Manhattan and the San Francisco Bay area, by the next presidential election in 1984 NBIPP's party was over. Walters writes, "the same pattern of ideological in-fighting overcame the organization's forward momentum, and by 1984, it was, ironically, too weak to respond when the Jackson campaign attracted the attention of the national black community as an independent candidacy, albeit within the Democratic party."[143]

Actually, the party did attempt to respond to the Jackson campaign and in the process completed its self-destruction. At both the New Orleans and Philadelphia conventions, black members of the highly sectarian Socialist Workers Party (SWP) constituted a major faction.[144] Well organized and cohesive, the SWP faction insisted that NBIPP define itself rigidly as an "anti-capitalist, anti-imperialist" party opposed to "collaboration and compromise with the Democratic Party and its black petit bourgeois functionaries." When Jackson announced his candidacy Ron Daniels and other more nationalist, less ideologically rigid party members sought to have NBIPP endorse Jackson and actively work in the campaign at the grassroots level. The SWP faction opposed this endorsement, arguing that it was a clear violation of the party charter's prohibition on involvement with either of the two capitalist parties. Rancorous conflict ensued between the nationalist and SWP factions. Eventually, many of the former withdrew from the party to become Jackson campaign activists. Thus, in yet another irony, the NBIPP, which has its roots in a process that in 1972 sought to develop a strategy for mounting a black presidential candidacy, was itself finally destroyed in factional disputes over whether to support the first credible black presidential campaign in the post–civil rights era. Some observers argue that the roots of Jesse Jackson's Rainbow Coalition are to be found in the 1970s convention process initiated at Gary.[145] As Baraka puts it, the Gary convention "was the paradigm for Jesse Jackson's more recent Rainbow Coalition."[146]

While there are some parallels between the convention process and Jackson's Rainbow Coalition, the differences are more striking. Essentially, the Jackson campaigns in 1984 and 1988 emerge out of the failure of the convention process. That is, rather than representing independent black political mobilization in presidential politics, Jackson's campaign represents its antithesis—the further incorporation of blacks into the institutional routines and processes of American politics. This is the ultimate tragedy of the decade-long effort to create and sustain an independent base of black power in the post–civil rights era. In reality, the 1970s have to be seen as a wasted decade in black politics; wasted resources, wasted talent; leaving the African American community less organized, less mobilized and less capable of effective, independent political mobilization than was the case at the time of Dr. King's death. It is important to try to understand why this occurred in order that some lessons might be distilled for the future. For it is still the case that black politics, without some kind of independent structure of political mobilization and representation, is likely to remain an impotent, irrelevant force in American politics.

Can the Lessons of History Be Learned?

History confirms in the convention processes of the 1830s, 1930s and 1970s one simple proposition: The black community is too ideologically diverse to operate for long in a single, all-inclusive organization capable of *representing the interests of the race in its relationships to whites or the larger external political order.* I emphasize representation of the interests of the race in relationship to the external white world because one of the principal problems in the 1970s convention process was that it attempted to blend within one organization or process what structurally are two distinct phenomena. One, an internal mechanism or forum of communal discussion, decision making and action, and two, a mechanism devoted to external relationships of political mobilization, coalition formation and empowerment. I return to this crucial distinction shortly, but first the problem of ideology and organization.

The fundamental error of the conveners of the black congresses of the 1830s, 1930s and 1970s is the assumption that the common condition of race oppression is sufficient to constitute an objective basis for a political unity that would transcend ideological differences. This is not possible, because ideology is important; dealing as it does with fundamental ideas on the nature, causes, strategies and solutions of the black predicament. Differences on these matters between liberal integrationists, nationalists of various sects and radicals give rise to basic differences in political principles, rhetoric, strategy and programs of actions that cannot be preached away with slogans of "unity without uniformity" or "minimum programs of action on which all can agree." Nor can it be dealt with by intellectual exercises that seek to define the differences away by arguing that they are disagreements about means rather than ends since, in this view, all blacks share the common goal of ending race group oppression. Leaving aside the validity of this latter proposition, the question of means is logically interconnected with ends such that in practice, the struggle over means between nationalists, integrationists and Marxists becomes as important and often as rancorous as the struggle over the ultimate ends of a separate black society, integration into a reformed American society or into a radically transformed one. Individuals adhering to ideologies in the sophisticated way that they are defined here tend to be persons of commitment and principle; to ask them to forego principles in pursuit of some all-embracing notion of race unity is neither practical nor principled.

This raises a related problem: the tendency of elements within the nationalist tradition to veer toward utopianism.[147] This is in part a function of the vagueness and imprecision of the ideology. If nationalism is defined as "all those expressions and activities by black Americans that emphasize their common origins, experience and aspirations and that seek to dignify the race," then of course virtually all blacks, from conservatives to revolutionaries, may claim to be nationalists.[148] This is a source of the tradition's enduring appeal, forcing as it does all blacks to think in terms of race-group interests. But it is also a source of its greatest weakness because it has tended to allow the more extreme elements within the tradition to dominate. And this extremist element tends— utopian like—to be opposed to all political organizations and programs that do not seek the "total destruction and transformation of the social structure." This makes common political action problematic if not impossible. Walters, reflecting on the 1970s convention process and the failure of important elements of nationalist leadership to join in system-oriented political processes, concludes that it is a problem of nationalism's "immaturity," writing:

> From this perspective, it can only be concluded that the effort failed basically because Black nationalism contains a strong strain of anti-institutional politics, which is incompatible with the requirements of this system oriented process.... A mature nationalism might have permitted implementation of strategy of independent politics in national elections, but the immature strain emerging from the 1960s may have made such implementation premature.[149]

This immaturity in black nationalism is probably an integral part of the tradition; one that is not likely to mature. It holds, simply stated, that the American political system has not and cannot be made to work in the interests of blacks and therefore participation in it can never constitute a serious program for black liberation, except as a strategy to demonstrate the validity of the foregoing proposition. This "anti-institutionalist" strain in the tradition prevents its leaders and followers from playing the only role that they structurally might play in contemporary black politics, that of an opposition to the one-party dominant black political establishment. As it is, the black political establishment of elected officials today need not fear opposition and once in office are routinely returned with hardly a murmur from the nationalist forces that so forcefully claim to speak for the grassroots or the masses. This is because nationalists are unwilling or unable to act on the simple fact that politicians in the United States, black or white, only understand one thing—winning. A "mature" black nationalism would challenge the black establishment on its own terms and therefore demonstrate a mass base of support for their programs of social transformation, hold black elected officials more accountable for their behavior and gain a measure of legitimacy by demonstrating mass support for an alternative conception of the Afro-American political struggle. This they appear incapable of doing. In addition, the 1970s convention experience suggests that nationalism and radicalism are handicapped further by the fact that in spite of all the rhetoric about mobilization at the grassroots and organizing the masses, the black political establishment is better organized at the grassroots level than are nationalists and radicals. Further, the establishment is more united on ideology and strategy, not bedeviled by the incessant sectarian debates on these matters that characterizes the black nationalist and radical communities. But the basic dilemma of the would-be black opposition is probably once again ideological. That is, the "masses" of blacks probably do not share their interest in separatist programs or fundamental system transformation.

Studies conducted in the late 1960s indicate that the majority of blacks, whatever their gender, age, education or place of residence tend to support the fundamental elements of the integrationist ideology.[150] In addition, black Americans tend to be just about as hostile to communism and socialism as white Americans, manifesting a strong belief in the fundamental elements of the capitalist value structure. Thus, black ideology at the mass level, while substantially more left and reform minded than that of whites, is nevertheless much more pragmatic and utilitarian than the radical leaders of the national black political convention. An important lesson of the 1970s convention process is that the radical and nationalist leaders adopted an ideology and rhetoric that effectively separated them from the grassroots. There is a bit of irony here, since these leaders so often invoked the support of the "masses" and the "grassroots" as a basis of claiming primacy and legitimacy in their conflicts with the black establishment, pointing again to the wishful representations that so frequently distort nationalist and radical thought.

Yet as a sentiment, nationalism is an enduring force in Afro-American politics that is ignored by the integrationist black establishment only at its peril, invoking as it does inchoate consciousness of race oppression, race differences, solidarity and collective race responsibility. This explains to some extent the ambivalent, on-again, off-again relationship between the black leadership establishment and Minister Louis Farrakhan, the most prominent nationalist leader of the post–civil rights era. Given their ties—ideologically, institutionally and financially—to the white establishment, black leaders are reluctant to embrace Farrakhan and other nationalists leaders, but given the salience of the nationalist tradition and ethos among blacks, they cannot follow the wishes of their white patrons and wholly repudiate him or other nationalists. Thus, Jesse Jackson embraces Farrakhan in 1984, denounces him in 1988 and embraces him in 1992, or the Congressional Black Caucus enters a "sacred covenant" with the Nation of Islam but then under pressure from the white liberal establishment the relationship is reassessed or repudiated.[151] This is an enduring aspect of black politics, putting establishment black leadership in a near impossible situation. On the one hand they seek to play leadership roles in mainstream American politics but on the other, they try to lead and not lose touch with the black mainstream, a mainstream in which nationalism and radicalism are integral components.

Aspects of this nationalist sentiment may be observed in the data from the National Black Election Survey reported in Table 2.1. First, there is a relatively high degree of attachment to the race or feelings of closeness (90 percent) but a considerable dropoff in saliency of race identification (50 percent) or its primacy over American identity (10 percent). And while 60 percent of the respondents agreed with the proposition that the "system" was responsible for the black condition, only about a third favor collective over individual action to deal with race problems. In terms of traditional nationalist concerns about Africa, about the impossibility of racial equality in the United States, support

TABLE 2.1

Attitudes of Black Americans Toward Elements of
Black Nationalist Ideology, by Level of Education, 1984

	Total Sample	Some High School	College Graduate
Feel Close to Black People in This Country	93.4%	93.8%	94.9%
Share Common Fate with Blacks	69.3	58.4	83.2
More Important to be Black than American*	11.7	11.3	15.2
System to Blame for Black Subordination	62	63.4	61.6
Blacks Will Never Achieve Equality in U.S.	35.7	30.9	34
Blacks Should Be Active in Black Organization to Improve Conditions	34.2	27.6	42.9
Blacks Should Shop Whenever Possible in Black Stores	55.7	48.2	74.9
Blacks Should Form their Own Party	24.8	32.2	15.6
Blacks Should Always Vote for Black Candidate	18.7	30	15.9
Blacks Should Have Nothing to Do With Whites if They Can Help It	4.2	8.1	3.2
Feel Close to Africans	55.2	58	60.4
Black Children Should Learn an African Language	35.7	43.9	37.3

* The question read, "Which would you say is more important to you—being black or being American, or are both equally important to you? Most respondents indicated equally black and American but a larger percentage of the total sample (13.6 percent) choose American identity first, including 15.8 percent among those not high school graduates and 11.8 percent among college graduates.

Source: Katherine Tate et al., *The 1984 National Black Election Study Sourcebook.* Ann Arbor: University of Michigan, Institute for Social Research, 1988.

for a black political party and support of black business, there is a powerful nationalist strain but it falls off considerably when expressed in
terms of strict black separatism in terms of interracial contacts or exclusive support for black candidates. There is, then, in the post–civil rights
era black community, substantial sentiment and support for economic,
cultural and political elements of black nationalism. And as the data
reported in Table 2.2 suggests, support for the political elements of the
ideology appears to be on the rise. In 1987, 18.7 percent of blacks agreed
that blacks should always vote for the black candidate and 24.8 percent said blacks should form their own political party. By 1994, support for these propositions had increased to 26 and 50 percent, respectively. Ironically, support for the most extreme nationalist sentiment—a
separate black nation—has nearly doubled since the end of the civil
rights era. In 1968 at the peak of black power and black nationalist agitation, Campbell and Schuman found that only 7 percent of blacks supported the idea of a separate black nation.[152] The 1993–94 survey by
Dawson and Brown reported in Table 2.2 shows that this support has
doubled to 14 percent. Indeed, only 29 percent of blacks (not displayed
in the table) in 1994 "strongly" disagreed with this extraordinarily radical proposition. And while most blacks reject the idea of the creation of

TABLE 2.2

Attitudes of Black Americans toward Elements of
Black Nationalist Ideology, 1993–94

	Percent Agreeing
Equality Will Never Be Achieved in America	23
American Society Is Not Fair to Blacks	77
Blacks Should Form Own Political Party	50
Blacks Should Participate in Black-Only Organizations	56
Blacks Should Always Vote for a Black Candidate	26
Blacks Should Support Creation of All-Male Black Public Schools	62
Blacks Should Control the Government in Predominantly Black Communities	68
Blacks Should Control Economy in Predominantly Black Communities	74
Blacks Form a Nation Within a Nation	49
Blacks Should Have Their Own Separate Nation	14

Source: Michael Dawson and Ronald Brown, "Black Discontent: The Preliminary Report of the 1993–94 National Black Politics Study, Report # 1, University
of Chicago.

a separate nation, half (49 percent) embrace the sentiment that blacks in America are a people apart, "a nation within a nation." And, as most black nationalist activists contend, support for most (though not all) nationalist sentiments and programs of action tend to be strongest among the lower classes, as measured in Table 2.1 by differences between those who have been graduated from college and those who have not completed high school. Nationalist activists are thus correct to focus their organizing work at the lower-class grassroots level in terms of building a mass base,[153] although preliminary analysis suggests that the increase in support for black nationalism between 1987 and 1994 comes primarily from a shift among middle class blacks.[154]

The final and in some ways most important practical lesson to be drawn from this survey of the convention experiment of the 1970s is the necessity of structural differentiation between an internal mechanism of black deliberation and action and an external mechanism of political empowerment. The effort to combine, within a single organization or process, a political party that would contest elections within the pragmatic system-oriented election process, along with an autonomous, racially exclusive mechanism of collective expression and action is untenable and renders problematic the success of either.

What is needed in post–civil rights era black politics are two structures. One, an interracial "rainbow"-type third political party, and two, what Holden refers to as a "mechanism of collective judgment, a regular conclave so structured as to represent the widest possible range of opinions and circumstances—a kind of Afro-American general council."[155] Such a mechanism is analogous to what Frederick Douglas and his colleagues had in mind in the 1850s when they proposed a National Afro-American Council to deliberate and develop a nationally supervised "Negro plan for life" that would deal with the internal developmental processes of the race.[156] This type of structure, racially exclusive and autonomous, open to the widest range of ideologies and organizations, would come together on a regular basis to argue, discuss, debate, design and implement a "minimalist" program of action to deal with the internal disabilities of the race in terms of education, drugs, AIDS and any other of the pressing problems that can be addressed with concrete programs. The local councils of the 1930s National Negro Congress are a model for this type of autonomous community action, drawing as they did on preexisting national organizations' local affiliates as the cadre acting under the Congress's national umbrella.

In a sense, such an organization already exists in the National Black Leadership Roundtable, formed in the late 1970s as an establishment alternative to the convention process. Constituted by more than

125 national black organizations—civic, religious, political, fraternal
and economic—the Roundtable is supposed to operate as an
autonomous communal decision-making and action body for the
national black community. Yet it is largely a paper organization; inad-
equately funded and largely ignored by its constituent organizations
and leaders. If the Roundtable had been supported by the leadership of
black America it had the potential to become a force for independent,
collective decision making and action to deal with the internal problems of black America.[157] But although it is an institution of their own
creation, black leaders have ignored the Roundtable and willy nilly
sought to create yet another organization of organizations. In fact, they
have created not one but two such organizations: a so-called national
organization of black organizations organized in 1990 by the NAACP's
Benjamin Hooks and something called the National Organization of
African Americans formed one year later by former Howard University
President James Cheek (see Chapter 3). Predictably, these organizations
will go the same way as the Roundtable, the National Black Political
Assembly and the sundry other efforts of blacks to do what history
teaches is near impossible: to create what Reverend Lewis Woodson in
1838 called "an institution that will . . . unite and harmonize the distant
and discordant parts of our population." One would think that this historical teaching would have been learned by all by now. But no; in 1989,
African American leaders went through yet another exercise in silli-
ness and historical obtuseness: they called the "African American Summit '89."

This ostensible effort to develop an "African-American Agenda"
out of a summit representing "every political persuasion" in black
America,[158] coming so soon after the failure of the Gary experiment, the
1989 summit would be laughable if it did not represent such a serious
misappropriation of the resources of an already resource-poor community that desperately needs rational resource allocation if it is to have
any chance of becoming a force in American politics in the twenty-first
century. Stated simply, blacks today do not need another "black
agenda." Rather than summits and agendas, what is needed is far-
sighted, rational mobilization of resources to achieve implementation of
an agenda that has been reasonably clear and specific for a generation.

The summit at New Orleans came about as a result of a meeting in
Chicago called by Jesse Jackson shortly after the presidential election.
According to accounts of the December meeting, representatives of over
seventy-five organizations decided to issue a call for a national convention in order to develop an agenda of internal community restructuring and cultural revitalization and an agenda of program and policy

to be advanced to external white society. From its origins to its end, the African-American Summit '89 was, pardon the expression, *deja vu* all over again. Indeed, in conversations with participants and in reviewing the clips one might easily confuse the New Orleans summit of 1989 with the Little Rock convention of 1974. The usual suspects were the organizers (Jesse Jackson, Richard Hatcher, Ronald Walters, C. Delores Tucker,); there was the usual meaningless talk about delegate formula and allocation and at the meeting itself the usual babble about who did not show up, who should not be permitted to show up and arguments and resolutions defining the black agenda.

The press release announcing the call of the convention said in part:

The Summit will be open to all African-Americans of every political persuasion . . . , we believe that the greater our diversity, the more representative it is of the entire African-American community; the stronger the mandate which emerges. . . . Unlike some of our earlier meetings, we shall move immediately to put in place a mechanism to implement the conclusions, recommendations and strategies which come out of this summit. As part of the Summit follow-up we shall seek an early meeting with President Bush and the leadership of Congress. The purpose of these meetings will be to discuss our Agenda and enlist their support for specific actions, including a four year legislative agenda. . . . Finally, we shall address ourselves; we shall speak to our own community. The painful process of self-examination is long overdue. We are not a perfect people and those among us who continue to fail to meet the standards necessary to achieve freedom, progress and parity in this country must be exposed, isolated and reeducated.[159]

Needless to say, nothing of the follow-up, in terms of meetings with the president and congressional leaders or mechanisms to "expose, isolate and reeducate" "imperfect" blacks who "fail to meet the necessary standards," resulted from the New Orleans meeting. About eight hundred or so "delegates" showed up for the three-day convention. Organizers had indicated that 4,000 delegates were expected but, again reminiscent of Gary, it was said that the four months planning time was not enough to extend invitations and organize the process of widespread participation and that many establishment blacks did not wish to be associated in convention with nationalists like Farrakhan and radicals like Angela Davis.[160] Thus, there was the usual press speculation about the absence of establishment leaders and the predictable

Hatcher response: "Some people felt that to come to a meeting like this might jeopardize their relationships outside the community."[161]

With the usual series of speeches by the well known (Dellums, Coretta King, Farrakhan, Jackson, etc.), workshops and resolutions (among others, one calling for reparations and the creation of an internal black investment bank for purposes of community economic development), the convention adjourned with the usual talk that it was a success merely because it occurred.

To restate the point, a clear lesson for the learning now and remembering for the future is that black politics in the post–civil rights era does not need any more summits, agendas, conventions and similar exercises in illusions of unity.[162] These conventions or summits tend to be exercises in symbolism, in political theater. Black political leaders, unable to build a sustainable national organization to deal with the internal problems of the race and its relationship to American society, have increasingly in the post–civil rights era resorted to ritual political posturing as a means to cover up or disguise their inability to lead; to develop a realistic program of action to deal with the problems of its core constituency of the inner city poor. Thus, the meaningless rituals of conventions, conferences, sundry new organizations of organizations, caucuses, legislative weekends, ad nauseam.

It is very unlikely that black leaders will be able to overcome the historic ideological and institutional barriers to the formation of an internal mechanism of communal solidarity and action. Similarly, it is not likely that blacks will be able to overcome the institutional, ideological and structural barriers to the formation of a third party. Such a party or parties are sorely needed. The two-party system is increasingly moribund, without programs and policies that prudently and with foresight deal with the problems of the nation in general or its race problem specifically (see Chapter 10). A third party would break the Republican and Democratic monopoly on political debate and discussion. And as indicated in Chapter 10, it would end the untenable status of the post–civil rights era black vote where it is taken for granted by one party and ignored by the other, rendering it usually irrelevant or powerless in national elections.

The impediments to a third party, whether black or multiethnic, are considerable and historically have been difficult to overcome.[163] But by a number of indicators—the decline of partisanship, the decline in voter turnout, the loss of confidence or trust in government and the rise of personalized, protest candidates like Jesse Jackson, Pat Robertson, Pat Buchanan, Ross Perot and Jerry Brown—the two-party system is weak, maintained mainly by election laws, government subsidies and media bias. Structural factors, however, significantly impede the formation of viable third parties that might represent minority (ethnic or ideological) interests because they make it unlikely that such parties can significantly affect election outcomes. The result is that major party leaders can easily ignore minority concerns and minority political leaders are reluctant to embrace the third party because they think they will be ignored.

In addition to these structural and institutional barriers, a black political party faces the dilemmas of ideological conflict discussed throughout this chapter plus the problem of it being black. In the context of American electoral politics, a racially exclusive party is less viable than an inclusive, multiethnic one. Indeed, a racially exclusive party would be, arguably, illegal. Yet, support for a third party is strongest among the more nationalist elements of the black community, who also tend to be those with the least education and income.[164] This means that a third party to be effective in black America would probably have to be racially militant and chauvinistic—led by a Louis Farrakhan rather than a Jesse Jackson for example—which would make it less appealing to the established black leadership, middle-class blacks and the broad progressive mainstream in the United States. It is difficult to see how these impediments might be overcome. It is equally difficult, however, to see how the present situation of black partisanship (discussed in detail in Chapter 10) can go on.

The collapse of the 1970s convention process and the failure of such alternative mechanisms as the Black Leadership Roundtable means that in the post–civil rights era, blacks have to rely essentially on the old-line civil rights era organizations, organizations that have by and large failed to adapt to the new exigencies of post–civil rights era politics and problems. The result is that, twenty-five years after the dawn of the new era, the black community remains organized on the basis of the politics and problems of fifty years ago rather than those of today and the next century.

3

Continuity and Innovation in
Post–Civil Rights Era Black Organization

The black community in the United States has always had an extensive and diversified structure of organization, paralleling that of white America but in some ways much more extensive. Indeed, the problem of hyper black organization has in the past been identified and is today to some extent a problem itself in black society and politics. Amongst this plethora of organizations, however, there were relatively few national or local organizations of an explicitly political nature devoted exclusively to campaign organization, fund raising and electoral activism. Instead, black organizations were generally apolitical— church, fraternal, business, professional—or, when political, have tended to be oriented to civil rights protest or radical or nationalist programs of political change. There were a few exceptions in terms of local political organizations in various cities and states, and the civil rights organizations and the church sometimes engaged in forms of electoral mobilization and lobbying, but in general black organizations were devoted to internal, communal affairs or narrowly focused on civil rights lobbying, litigation and protest. Thus, with the end of the civil rights era the existing organizational structure of black America was not conducive to the new forms of institutional politics. As Charles Hamilton put it, black politicians during the civil rights era were socialized to go to court or the streets rather than the ballot box or the local precinct hall.[1] And in *Black Power* Hamilton and his colleague recognized this problem and asserted that the new black politics would require "searching for new forms of political structure to solve political and economic problems and broadening the base of political participation to include more people in the decision making process."[2] Thus, it was recognized at the outset of the transformation from protest to politics that it would require either transformation in the existing organizational structure of black America and/or the development of new organizational forms.

The National Black Political Convention process was an initial effort to create a new form of organization that would facilitate the black community's participation in institutional politics. Its failure—its grand failure—meant that, with a few notable exceptions, the black community has had to rely in the post–civil rights era on organizations forged in the era of the civil rights movement. Although the National Black Political Convention did not survive as a new institutional formation, several new forms were created in the late 1960s and during the 1970s that have survived and have come to play important roles in the new black politics. They include the Congressional Black Caucus and related organizations of black elected and appointed officials, and the Joint Center for Political Studies. In the second part of this chapter these new organizations are analyzed. What emerges from this analysis of continuity and innovation in black organization is that while there has been some adaptability by black organizations to the new circumstances of the post–civil rights era, there are serious problems in organization that impede effective black participation in the new post–civil rights era politics. Among these problems are a continuing trend toward hyperorganization; a limited capacity for intergroup coordination; resource constraints, including continued dependency on white America for financial support; and the failure to develop any kind of sustained structure to mobilize and discipline the black vote as a truly independent force. Related to this is the fact that in the post–civil rights era, organized money in the form of political action committees has become more important in American politics, and despite several efforts, the black community has been unable to sustain such a group. But probably the most critical shortcoming of post–civil rights era black organization is that it, like its white counterpart, adheres to a top-down, hierarchical, middle-class model of organization and strategy that emphasizes elite "inside the beltway" interaction rather than constituent mobilization. This kind of politics increasingly does not serve the interests of the largely middle class white community, which suggests that it is virtually impossible for it to serve the interests of a black community that is disproportionately poor and increasingly demoralized.

Continuity and Innovation in the
Traditional Structure of Black Organization

Civil Rights Organizations

Of the "big five" organizations of the 1960s civil rights protest era—the NAACP, the Urban League, the Southern Christian Leadership Conference (SCLC), the Congress of Racial Equality (CORE) and the Student Nonviolent Coordinating Committee (SNCC)—one, SNCC, is dead and buried and another, SCLC, is largely a paper organization kept alive on the memory of its founder, Dr. King. CORE too exists largely on paper, with a handful of activists in New York and a couple of other cities. Thus, only the NAACP and the Urban League have persisted into the post–civil rights era in reasonably good, if not robust health. Operation PUSH, although not one of the 1960s era big five did emerge out of one of them—SCLC—and since the departure of Jesse Jackson, its charismatic founder and leader, it too is largely a paper organization that survives only because no one wishes to engage in euthanasia.[3]

SNCC and CORE collapsed for essentially the same reasons.[4] First, their turn toward nationalism and radicalism resulted in factionalism and severe internal conflicts. Second, as a result of this turn toward radicalism, white liberal philanthropic support was lost and these groups were unable to finance their operations on the basis of support generated internally in the black community. As Kenneth Clark has written in a discussion of the continued viability of the NAACP and the Urban League, "One is tempted to hypothesize from these data that the financial success of an organization engaged in the civil rights confrontation is directly related to the perceived respectability of the organization and its nominal head. Correlative to this would be the hypothesis that the relative financial success of a civil rights group is inversely related to the perceived degree of radicalism of the organization and its nominal head."[5] Finally, as noted in Chapter 1, the government's repressive counterintelligence program against SNCC and other radical and nationalist organizations was also a factor in their demise.[6]

SCLC and PUSH remain only barely alive for essentially the same reasons: they were created and maintained by charismatic leaders as their personal organizations and when these leaders departed the organizations inevitably declined. As Clark wrote in 1965, "SCLC is Martin Luther King."[7] Similarly, "PUSH was Jesse Jackson." So, with the death of Dr. King, SCLC itself was mortally wounded. For a time it continued to receive some support, financial and otherwise, as a living memorial to Dr. King but eventually this withered away, in part because the Martin Luther King, Jr., Center for Nonviolent Social Change created by his widow became the repository for those wishing to honor King institutionally. In addition, the organization was quickly wracked by internal conflicts between Ralph Abernathy—King's designated successor—the King family and Reverend Jackson, who eventually left the group to form PUSH. It remains alive today, barely, under the leadership of Joseph Lowry but it is largely a paper organization without a viable mission or vision (given the demise of mass protests, its central organizational innovation), given largely to holding annual conventions, occasional rallies and marches, meetings with the president, testifying before Congress and issuing press releases. Similarly, since Jackson's departure in 1989 from PUSH in order to form yet another organization—the National Rainbow Coalition—PUSH too has declined, including the departure in 1991 of its executive director and the layoff of its entire paid staff.[8] In the post–civil rights era Myrdal's observation of fifty years ago remains generally true: the NAACP and the Urban League are "without question" the most important organizations in the Afro-American freedom struggle.[9] It is important therefore to assess the extent to which they have adapted to the new exigencies of that struggle in the post–civil rights era.

In an insiders' account of the status of civil rights movement organizations in the 1960s Kenneth Clark wrote, "The disturbing question which must be faced is whether or not the present civil rights organizations are equipped in terms of perspective, staff and organizational structure to deal effectively with the present level of civil rights problems. And, if not, whether they are flexible enough in order to be relevant."[10] The answer some twenty-five years later to Clark's questions is, regrettably, no. The major civil rights organizations—Clark's query mainly concerned the NAACP and the Urban League—were not in 1965 equipped in terms of structure and strategy to deal with post–civil rights era problems, and although they have made some changes and adaptations since the 1960s, by and large these two organizations are still only marginally relevant to contemporary politics.[11] The major post–civil rights era problem Clark foresaw in 1965 was the concentrated poverty and what he called the increased "social pathologies" of the ghettos of the northern cities. Thus, the first issue is how the NAACP and especially the Urban League (since it was founded with the specific mission of dealing with the problems of inner-city blacks) have adapted to dealing with what is now called the black underclass. The second issue is how these organizations have adapted to the post–civil rights era transformation from protest politics to the new politics of institutional participation.

In his 1965 article Clark argued that the NAACP and the Urban League had not altered their organizations in any significant way since their founding. He was especially critical of the NAACP, writing, "The techniques, methods and organizational structure of the NAACP in 1965 are essentially the same as they were in the 1920s. If one were to examine the NAACP today and compare it with the NAACP twenty or thirty years ago, the only significant difference one would find is an increase in the number of staff. . . ."[12] Comparing the NAACP in 1990 with the NAACP in 1965, Clark's observations require some modification but by and large they are more correct than not.

In basic organizational structure the NAACP remains essentially unchanged. Formally, ultimate decision-making authority rests with the annual convention and, in the interim, with the sixty-four member board of directors but in fact on most issues decisions are made by the executive director, his staff and increasingly the chairman of the board.[13] The national headquarters tends to exercise tight control over the policy and strategy of its 1700 local branches (organized into seven regions). For example, in 1973 the national office suspended its Atlanta chapter in a dispute over school desegregation, and during the confirmation hearings of Clarence Thomas to succeed Justice Thurgood Marshall on the Supreme Court, the national office threatened to suspend the Compton, California branch because it supported Thomas's confirmation in defiance of the board's contrary decision.

In its eighty-year history the NAACP has had only six executive directors (including Kweisi Mfume, selected in 1995), whose tenures in office have averaged twenty years. The result is that the organization tends to reflect the personality of the leader who dominates the national staff (approximately sixty professionals in 1994). Thus, in its basic organizational structure and its governance, the NAACP of the 1990s continues to resemble the NAACP of the 1960s. One important change in traditional NAACP organization and governance is the decline of interracialism. In contrast to the civil rights era where whites played important roles in leadership and staff, today whites are conspicuous by their absence, reduced largely to token or symbolic roles at both the national and local levels. This change in the racial makeup of the NAACP (and the Urban League) is largely a function of the 1960s black power ideology with its emphasis on racial solidarity and organization.

In every city and town the local chapters of the NAACP are generally recognized as the dominant voice on black affairs and are usually consulted by white economic and political elites on issues related to race. Much of the work of these local chapters is carried out by volunteers and it includes in addition to lobbying on local issues, receiving and processing complaints on the range of civil rights issues: police misconduct and housing and employment discrimination. Like the national leadership, local leaders tend to serve rather long tenures, with the result that it tends to be middle aged to elderly with little opportunity for new, younger and perhaps more aggressive leadership to emerge. It is estimated that 75 percent of the active members in the local branches are 65 or older.[14] And in my personal observations of several NAACP branches around the country, my impression was that their aging leadership not only did not seek to encourage the participation of young people, especially young professionals, in leadership roles, but rather actively discouraged their involvement. It was my sense that the established leaders feared they might be displaced by more aggressive and competent young people.

Nationally, the organization continues its long-time strategy of lobbying and litigation, although with the shift in the 1980s of the judiciary to the right, litigation has declined in importance compared to the civil rights era when going to court was perhaps the group's dominant approach. Going to Congress—to enact new civil rights legislation such as renewal of the Voting Rights Act, the Civil Rights Act of 1991 or the amendments to the Fair Housing Act—has occupied much of the association's attention in the post–civil rights era. In addition, a lion's share of the Washington bureau's time in the Reagan-Bush years was devoted to efforts to block the confirmation of conservative judicial nominations.[15] Although it maintains its own legislative agenda and Washington lobbying operation, increasingly in the post–civil rights era it has relied on the umbrella Leadership Conference on Civil Rights to coordinate a comprehensive civil rights strategy involving labor, Jews, Latinos and women's groups. This from time to time has created tensions and conflicts in terms of issues and strategy, but this coalition effort is more effective than the NAACP acting alone.[16] In addition, with the retirement and subsequent death of Clarence Mitchell—its long time Washington bureau chief known as the "101st senator"—the NAACP's Washington office lacks the experience and ready access to legislators and staff that it had throughout the civil rights era.[17]

In these ways the NAACP's strategy is essentially unchanged in the post–civil rights era. The group has, however, adopted some new approaches. It has negotiated a number of what it calls "Fair Share" agreements with public and private sector entities in terms of hiring black workers and contracts with black businesses. It has also begun to devote attention along with church and fraternal organizations to what it calls "nontraditional civil rights issues": teenage pregnancy, black-on-black crime, drug abuse and other problems associated with the underclass. It is not clear that these efforts are anything more than symbolic, largely because of the magnitude of the problems and the NAACP's lack of resources as well as the absence of a clear strategy to deal with these problems on a massive scale.

What it has not done is develop any kind of structure or strategy to deal with the post–civil rights politics of electoral participation. It does employ a staffperson at the national office to direct voter registration and it encourages the local branches to engage in voter registration campaigns, which some do. However, these efforts have not given the group a viable base, locally or nationally, to consistently and systematically mobilize and discipline the black vote. The organization remains nonpartisan while blacks are largely Democratic, and this inhibits partisan mobilization. Second, the NAACP, like most other civil rights era black organizations, really does not have the capacity to reach its lower-class black constituency in the urban ghettos and in the rural south on a consistent basis. The result is that a major post–civil rights era political resource—the vote—remains only partially mobilized some twenty years after electoral activism became the cutting edge of the new black politics.

Clark in 1965 noted that "In spite of their objective limitations the NAACP and Urban League are [flourishing] [financially]. . . . The success of both might be a reflection at least in part, also of their relative respectability."[18] Clark's point here was that the perceived militancy of SCLC, CORE and SNCC enhanced the respectability of the more moderate or traditionalist NAACP and Urban League and as a result they gained, comparatively, greater legitimacy in the eyes of white philanthropy. This certainly was the case in the late 1960s as philanthropic support for SNCC, CORE and SCLC declined while support for the NAACP and Urban League increased dramatically.[19]

In the post–civil rights era neither the NAACP nor the Urban League are flourishing; rather, both have experienced financial difficulties especially since the 1980s. The NAACP's budget crisis became so severe in the late 1980s that it was forced to move its national headquarters from New York to the less expensive environs of Baltimore (after it could not find cost-efficient facilities in the nation's capital). And this was done only with the help of a grant of more than a million dollars from the state of Maryland and the City of Baltimore plus a half-million dollar grant from the Kresge Foundation.[20] One of the principal limitations of the NAACP as an effective vehicle to advance the interests of blacks is therefore its inability to raise the funds necessary to carry out its work and its continued dependence on the government and white philanthropy for even this inadequate level of financing. This limitation should not be underestimated. If black people cannot or will not financially support their own organizations, then this is an index itself of their relative powerlessness in the struggle for race group advancement, since this struggle frequently requires challenging the major institutions of society.

The NAACP, given its large membership base, has always been more financially self-reliant than the other civil rights organizations. From 1968 to the present it has always received about half its support from membership dues and other internally generated resources.[21] For example, in 1992 more than a third of its general revenues of nine million dollars were derived from membership income alone but more than half of the seven million dollars raised by its Special Contribution Fund was in the form of corporate and foundation donations.[22]

Thus, while the NAACP has adopted some new approaches it remains organizationally, financially and programmatically wedded to the past. It has been unable to adapt itself to the new problems and politics of the present era. It is therefore largely irrelevant insofar as these new problems and the new politics are concerned, whether one is talking about the nation or the local community.

The selection in 1993 of Benjamin Chavis—a man long identified with the nationalist and radical traditions in black politics (he introduced the resolution calling for the founding of the National Black Independent Political Party and was a major figure in its brief existence)—may have represented a groping for a new direction by the NAACP board. However, given the haphazard nature of the selection process, the choice of Chavis (who reportedly mounted a sophisticated campaign for the position including hiring a public relations firm and producing a biographical video) may reflect confusion and disarray rather than deliberation or a shift in strategy.[23] True to his roots, Chavis quickly became embroiled in conflict with elements of the board and the white liberal establishment by first inviting Minister Farrakhan to participate in an NAACP-sponsored leadership summit and then holding a meeting with prominent black nationalists and radicals. According to Chavis's letter of invitation, the purpose of the meeting was to "provide a context for input and access of Pan Africanists, progressives and nationalists into increased levels of membership and active participation within the NAACP at national and local levels."[24] Chavis was immediately criticized by the chair and other members of the board for consorting with extremists and jeopardizing the NAACP's standing with its white patrons.[25] Unless the NAACP board was preparing to chart a new course, which is doubtful, Chavis is likely to have the shortest tenure of any of the association's directors since, unless he abandons his beliefs, he is likely to continue to reach out to nationalists and radicals, which puts in jeopardy the association's historic dependency on white (especially Jewish) liberal political and philanthropic support.[26]

Clark was more generous in assessment of the Urban League than of the NAACP, writing that it was more modern and efficient. However, he noted a paradox that is still true if not more so today than it was in 1965. Clark wrote, "The fascinating paradox is that the very areas in which the Urban League has been most active—the blight of segregated housing and inferior education and persistent and pernicious discrimination in employment—has been those areas in which the virulence of racism has increased in the north. Obviously, one cannot blame the League . . . but it remains a fact, however, that its programs have not been effective."[27] The Urban League, founded a year after the NAACP, emerged out of the same movement of liberal, interracial, integrationist reform, but unlike the NAACP it was not conceived of as a civil rights organization but rather as a social service organization whose primary mission was to facilitate the integration of poor, rural southern black migrants into the urban way of life. It has, therefore, always been less political in the sense of lobbying, litigation, protest and partisanship than other black organizations.[28] This also means that the league has always been more involved with the new post–civil rights issues that now go under the label of the black underclass. Yet as Clark pointed out, one has to conclude that given the magnitude of the problems of inner-city blacks today, the league has been much less successful in its mission than was the NAACP in its civil rights mission. Notwithstanding this paradox, the league should be better prepared to deal with the post–civil rights era dilemmas of the underclass than the NAACP and other black groups, but also less equipped to deal with the new institutional politics. A review of its post–civil rights era work generally confirms the foregoing observations.

Like the NAACP, the Urban League has not changed its basic organizational structure. It remains a nonpartisan, nonmembership organization that relies heavily on white philanthropic sources for financial support. Headquartered in New York (in fairly impressive quarters), the league operates through four regional offices and 118 affiliates in about thirty-five states. Although its national and affiliate staffs are not today dominated by Lester Granger and Whitney Young's social work ethos, it is still a highly professionalized reform organization. Nominally committed to the liberal integrationist ideology of interracialism, the league, like the NAACP, has in the post–civil rights era become much more racially exclusive in its leadership and staff at both the national and affiliate levels, although the tradition that the chair of the board be white has not changed. The league also expresses the tendency of most civil rights organizations to have very infrequent turnover of its leadership, with only five executive directors in its near eighty-year history, including Hugh Price, a former Ford Foundation executive, appointed in 1994.

Toward the end of the civil rights era the Urban League began an important change in its programmatic and financial base of operations. In 1965 it for the first time received modest grants or contracts from the Department of Labor and the Office of Economic Opportunity to conduct various social service outreach and training programs. This represented the league's first involvement with the government as a partner in its urban uplift efforts. This relationship grew modestly until the Nixon administration. In 1970, then league Director Young had an extraordinary meeting with President Nixon and his domestic cabinet. At this meeting it was agreed that the league would in effect become a service delivery agency for the government, relying on special contracts or restricted funds from the government to carry out this work. This for a time allowed the organization to free up its general funds for other purposes and to substantially expand its staff and services.

In 1981, however, the Reagan administration abruptly began to retrench this decade-long relationship. The result was not only a sharp drop in restricted or special project funds and staff but also in the funds for indirect costs of administrative overhead. This forced the organization in 1982 to sharply reduce its national staff and programs. In order to maintain some level of stability in its staff and programs, the league had to return to even greater reliance on its traditional sources of support: corporations and foundations; the Ford Foundation for example provided $1.5 million over two years to the league's general fund to help make up for the sharp cutback in government support.

This represents an enduring dilemma of "black" organizations; they are black in leadership, staff and missions but they are substantially "white" in terms of the money. This enduring weakness of black civil rights organizations has not appreciably changed in the post–civil rights era, in spite of much talk in the 1960s about the need of blacks to control and support their own organizations and sporadic efforts to build a black fund-raising base similar to the United Jewish Appeal.[29] So, for example, in 1991 the league had a budget of about 24 million dollars, 88 percent of which was derived from corporate or government sources.[30] Of this, 26 percent was from corporate contributions (of which 39 percent was restricted to specified projects and programs) and 62 percent from government contracts, all of which was restricted to specific projects.[31] The list of contributors reads like a who's who of the corporate and foundation worlds—Exxon, Ford, Reader's Digest, Henry Luce Foundation, Charles Mott and on and on. . . . In recognition of this dependency problem and the related ups and downs of its staff and programs in accordance with the whims of government and corporate benefactors, the league in 1985 set up what it called a "Fund for a New Era," a permanent development fund with a five-year target of $50 million. This fund was not to be used for operating expenses but rather as a long-term mechanism to stabilize its budget. Yet this fund itself received its largest contribution ($4.5 million) from, alas, the Ford Foundation.[32]

Since the Urban League has historically been dealing with the urban underclass, this has been the area in which it has been most active and innovative, if not effective, in the post–civil rights era. The league is also active in Washington and at the affiliate level in lobbying on civil rights and social welfare issues (like the NAACP, the league in most cities is recognized by local elites as a preeminent representative of the black community and its leaders are routinely consulted on issues of race and civil rights). And like the NAACP, it engages in voter registration. But generally it has made no innovations in organization and strategy in terms of post–civil rights institutional politics. It has, however, made considerable strides in the development of a research and analytic capacity. In his 1965 essay Clark noted that the league was more professionalized, modern and efficient but that it lacked a "research capacity," and in his view this was a critical shortcoming because "major decisions must now reflect painstaking, difficult staff work based on fact finding, intelligence and continuing critical analysis of data and strategies."[33] Under the leadership of Vernon Jordan, the league developed a fairly good research department, which was for a time directed by Robert Hill who did much to get it underway. It has also developed somewhat effective forums for the dissemination of this research to the scholarly and policy communities and the wider public.[34] These forums include its policy research journal the *Urban League Review* and its annual *State of Black America* reports.

Given the heightened attention by the press, academics and politicians to the problems of the black family, the league in the late 1980s began to develop programs to deal with family disintegration and related problems of teenage pregnancy, crime and drug abuse. In 1984 it sponsored, with the NAACP, what was called a "Black Family Summit," which brought representatives of more than one hundred national black organizations to Fisk University to discuss strategies that might address these problems. The basic strategy developed was to focus on the issue of teenage pregnancy through counseling and public relations programs. This focus was chosen because "every single study has found that these two factors [teenage pregnancy and female-headed households] increase vulnerability to poverty."[35] While this is correct, it is also the case that virtually every single study has also shown these problems linked to very high rates of black male joblessness. Thus, without a simultaneous strategy to address this problem (which, as Clark noted, is beyond the capacity of any private organization) the specific focus on counseling and public relations is likely to be of only marginal efficacy. For example, in the mid-1980s the league with a substantial grant from the Charles Mott Foundation developed what it called the "Male Responsibility Project," which involved a national media and poster campaign in conjunction with counseling by local affiliates. The project's aim was to "create in young black males an awareness of their responsibility in sexual relationships and parenting."[36] It included posters and radio and television ads with a song by James Ingram with the lyrics "Be careful, be responsible. Don't make a baby if you can't be a father." Again, while there may be some marginal value to projects of this type, it is difficult to believe that they will have any major effect on the problem. Put bluntly, talk (whether by rock stars, preachers, politicians or social workers) is not likely to change attitudes and behavior that are rooted in structural inequities and in a mass culture where sex is pervasive, from the daily soap operas to the marketing of beer. The best one can say of this project and similar ones is that it is perhaps better than doing nothing and that absent a substantive attack on the problem, symbolism may have to suffice.

This analysis of the structures and strategies of two most important civil rights organizations shows that with a few exceptions they are largely unchanged from what they were in the civil rights era. Times have changed but they have not been able to come up with organizational or strategy changes that would address the new politics and issues of the present era. The basic problem is that while the NAACP and Urban League do good and useful work, they have failed to come up with a new mission, a new vision, a new strategy to mold the mass base of black America into an effective political force. Rather, they continue to speak and act on behalf of a black community that is largely alienated from their middle class, hierarchical model of liberal reformism and civil rights.

The Church

Although the NAACP and the Urban League are wedded to organizational structures and strategies of the past, the church—the largest and potentially most powerful institution in black America—has made some innovations and adaptations to the new circumstances of the post–civil rights era. These changes have marked both the traditional black Baptist church as well as the nationalist-oriented Nation of Islam.

Throughout the civil rights era Dr. King would frequently lament that there were "so many Negro preachers that have not opened their mouths about the freedom movement, and not only that, they haven't done anything about it." In part due to Dr. King's inspirational leadership, this situation began to change during the civil rights era itself; however, these changes have accelerated since Dr. King's death.[37]

The largest organization of African Americans is the National Baptist Convention (NBC). From its inception in the 1880s the organization was a conservative, accommodationist institution in the tradition of Booker T. Washington.[38] During the civil rights era the NBC was under the autocratic leadership of Reverend J. H. Jackson of Chicago. Jackson was one of the few black leaders of national stature to actively oppose the civil rights struggle of the 1960s. And since he dominated the organization, the effect was to further depress church participation in the movement, especially in areas of the rural south. This was so because, as Taylor Branch writes, "Jackson ruled the National Baptist Convention from a power base among rural, unlettered preachers who traditionally avoided politics and all other worldly concerns" under the refrain "leave it to Jesus."[39] This class, regional and ideological conflict between progressive and traditionalist clergy was exacerbated when, at the 1961 National Baptist Convention, Jackson and Dr. King engaged in a nasty personality conflict that eventually led to King's withdrawal from the organization. King's departure and the departure of more highly educated urban clergy to form the Progressive Baptist Convention reinforced Jackson's domination of the NBC and its conservative outlook. Jackson's conservatism continued into the post–civil rights era, as reflected in his 1980 endorsement of Ronald Reagan's presidential candidacy. But two years later Jackson, in an election that surprised most observers, was ousted by Reverend T. J. Jemison, a Baton Rouge preacher who had been an activist during the civil rights era. One of Jemison's first acts was to make it clear that NBC and its constituent churches were going to take a more activist role in politics. First, he pledged to register more than three million blacks in time for the 1984 election, and when Jesse Jackson announced his candidacy for President Jemison quickly endorsed him. This provided Jackson with the principal institutional base for his campaign, raising money and registering and mobilizing voters. Jemison also urged the NBC to become more active in tackling the social problems of the community; many churches (especially the larger urban ones) in the post–civil rights era have become more active in a range of social welfare type projects in housing, drug abuse, teenage pregnancy and recently AIDS.

These changes in the leadership and approach of the NBC represent an important post–civil rights era development. This is not to say that black churches have been transformed into political precincts and social welfare agencies. On the contrary, most are still largely involved in spiritual matters and problems of internal organization.[40] But at least now the largest black organization in the country is no longer under the control of a conservative autocrat preaching the politics of avoidance and accommodation.[41]

Like the traditional black church, the Nation of Islam has also undergone a transformation in the post–civil rights era. Although Islam among African Americans probably can be traced to the slave culture, it was the Nation of Islam under the leadership of the extraordinary Elijah Muhammad that reintroduced Islam to black Americans.[42] During the civil rights era the Nation of Islam grew substantially in size and influence; however, even more than the traditional black church, it was an apolitical organization in terms of institutional politics. Mr. Muhammad's strict dictum of nonparticipation in American institutional politics was one of the factors that precipitated Malcolm X's withdrawal from the organization. As late as the mid-1970s, the Minister of the Nation's District of Columbia Mosque, Dr. Lonnie Shabazz, told me in a personal interview that "We do not vote or lobby in any shape, form or fashion because it would be attempting to advance our interests through the devil's system; it would be mixing two systems (ours and theirs) and there would be inevitable conflict."

If the Nation was not involved in the routines of American politics, it was very much involved in addressing problems of the so-called black underclass, constructing a good part of its mass base on the rehabilitation of the poor with an emphasis on race pride, moral reform, self-help and race solidarity. Although Lincoln probably overstates the matter when he writes that the Nation "has done a better job of rehabilitating the black *declassé* than all the official agencies addressed to the task . . . ,"[43] it is safe to conclude that during the 1960s and 1970s its program of moral reform and internal self-help and economic development was as effective as that of the civil rights organizations and the traditional black church or the social welfare bureaucracies.[44] The Nation was also responsible for helping to foster among blacks a sense of race pride and for keeping the ideology of black nationalism alive. Indeed, the Nation of Islam represents the largest nationalist formation since Garvey's Universal Negro Improvement Association of the 1920s.

All of this was to change with the death of Mr. Muhammad in 1976. Lincoln writes, "the charismatic cult seldom survives the death of its founder."[45] It was, therefore, probably inevitable that Mr. Muhammad's death would result in a fundamental transformation in the organization. The speed and radical nature of the changes, however, surprised both observers and followers of the Nation. Mr. Muhammad had designated his son Wallace as his successor. Almost immediately he begin to repudiate the core principles of black nationalism in the Nation's theology, dismantle and sell the group's business enterprises

and move the organization away from its "proto-Islam" toward orthodoxy and incorporation with the world community of Islam. The name
was changed first to the World Community of Islam in the West and
later the American Muslim Mission; the doctrine of the inherent evil
of whites was dropped as was the notion of a separate black nation.
Finally, the strict dress and moral codes were relaxed and whites were
allowed to become members. As a result, within a year the Nation was
no more; it had been thoroughly Americanized as an integrationist
mainstream orthodox religious institution. In 1978 Saudi Arabia designated Wallace (now referred to as Imman Warith Deen Muhammad) as
the "sole trustee" for the distribution of all funds to all Muslims for the
propagation of the faith in the United States.[46]

At the time of Mr. Muhammad's death, Minister Louis Farrakhan
was by far the best known of the Nation's ministers, far better known
than Wallace. He had inherited Malcolm X's Harlem Mosque (the most
influential outside of the Chicago headquarters) and Malcolm's title as
national spokesman. Farrakhan is also, unlike Wallace, a charismatic
orator in the Malcolm X tradition. As Mamiya writes, "If anyone in the
Muslim movement closely resembles Malcolm X in career and style it is
Minister Louis Farrakhan."[47] It is likely that Farrakhan, like Jesse Jackson, after the death of Dr. King, felt that he rather than Wallace was
better suited to succeed Mr. Muhammad. And like Jackson in SCLC,
Farrakhan was to later act on this belief by forming his own organization or, more precisely, reforming the old Nation of Islam. Unlike Jackson, whose departure from SCLC was largely a matter of personality
conflict and ego, Farrakhan's departure from the Nation was fundamentally ideological. In fact, when he left the group it was no longer the
Nation. When Wallace inaugurated his radical changes in the organization, Farrakhan, while dissatisfied, largely remained publicly silent.
He traveled abroad in Africa and the Islamic world and on returning to
the United States decided he could no longer acquiesce in the Nation's
destruction and thus publicly broke with Wallace. He then set about
to rebuild the Nation on the basis of the original principles of Mr.
Muhammad. This development was probably inevitable given Wallace's radical changes. The result was that Farrakhan and a core of loyalists led a "schismatic counter movement" against Wallace's new
orthodoxy.[48]

Farrakhan based his strategy to revitalize the Nation first on an
appeal to tradition and doctrinal purity among the original followers of
the Nation who were dissatisfied with Wallace's integrationism. Second, he sought to recruit new adherents among the alienated lower middle class and the disaffected young people of all social classes who are

alienated from the traditional church, civil rights and political leadership in the black community. Third, he has sought, while retaining the fundamental tenets of the original doctrines of the Nation, to move toward the mainstream of black political and communal life.[49] He has attempted to form alliances with the traditional black clergy in terms of economic enterprises and activism on social problems. He has also attempted to broaden the social base of the organization to attract middle class blacks and intellectuals by channeling their disaffection into a militant, system-challenging organization. To do this he has to some extent attempted to move away from some of the more controversial tenets of doctrine, such as the ideas of a separate black nation and the genetic basis for white racism as reflected in the white man as devil.[50] Finally, in its clearest break with the traditions of the Nation and the one with the most relevance for post–civil rights era black politics, Farrakhan in 1983 abandoned the doctrine of nonparticipation in institutional politics.

The proximate cause of this change was the candidacies of Harold Washington for mayor in Chicago in 1983 and Jackson for president in 1984. Farrakhan endorsed both men and encouraged his followers for the first time to register and vote. He appeared with Jackson at early campaign rallies, and the Nation provided security for him in the several weeks before he received secret service protection. In Chicago Jackson and Farrakhan had become friends and had worked together on several local projects, and this may have been a factor in his decision to alter the Nation's traditional apolitical stance. But his endorsement of Jackson was not unqualified or unambiguous. Rather, he indicated that he supported Jackson on the assumption that his candidacy would end in failure (perhaps even Jackson's death) and this would demonstrate once and for all to blacks the utter futility of participation in what he called the "wicked" American political system.[51] Blacks then, Farrakhan suggested, would turn to the Nation of Islam as an alternative to institutional politics and integrationism. Thus, Farrakhan's break with the Nation's traditional ban on political participation was at least initially a tactical shift, representing not a change in principle but—through the expected failure of the Jackson campaign—a vindication of principle.

Farrakhan did not support Jackson's candidacy in 1988. As a result of pressures from the media and the Democratic Party establishment Jackson repudiated Farrakhan and his support. This pressure resulted from some ill-advised comments Farrakhan made about Jews and Judaism; comments that had imputations of antisemitism. The rhetorical focus of Farrakhan (and others of his ministers) on Jews is a recent development that has no basis in the nationalist tradition generally or the teachings of Mr. Muhammad specifically (it is after all the white, not the Jewish, "devil" that bears the blame for racial oppression). Malcolm X did not single out Jews for special disapprobation, nor did Farrakhan until 1984. Farrakhan told *Time* magazine that his recent focus on Jews came about as a result of harassment of Jesse Jackson by Jewish militants during the 1984 presidential campaign, and a successful effort by Jewish distributors to block the manufacture and sale of the Nation's line of toiletries, even going so far, he claims, as to pressure Johnson Products, a black-owned company, to renege on agreements to manufacture his products. Thus Farrakhan says, "When I saw that, I recognized that the black man will never be free until we address the relationship between blacks and Jews."[52]

Whatever the reasons, the consequences of Farrakhan's involvement with the Jackson campaign, and his subsequent attack on Jews, were enhanced media attention to him and his ideology. As usual with black nationalism and nationalists, the press reporting was alarmist, painting Farrakhan as an extremist, antisemitic demagogue.[53] However, with black America the results were to increase his visibility and stature as a radical alternative to black establishment leadership.[54] Since 1988 Farrakhan has explicitly sought to make himself the radical alternative to Jackson in a kind of post–civil rights era replay of the civil rights era conflict between Malcolm X and Martin King for leadership and ideological hegemony. Farrakhan's tactical support for electoral participation in 1984 appears to have become, by 1990, a doctrinal shift. The Nation of Islam continues to encourage voter registration and in recent years several Black Muslims have run for local and congressional offices in Maryland, New York and the District of Columbia.

The Nation under Farrakhan is, like it was under Mr. Muhammad and like SCLC under King or PUSH or the Rainbow Coalition under Jackson, an organization that exists on the basis of charismatic authority. Thus, his presence is important to the organization's viability, although it should be pointed out that Farrakhan has several associates who operate effectively in the Malcolm X tradition. But today the Nation is to a considerable degree dependent on a single individual. Farrakhan's approach to building the Nation is to hold large rallies in the Nation's major cities, raise funds and recruit new members, and then once a sizeable following is established, charter a new Mosque (as of the early 1990s the Nation had mosques in about 120 cities).[55] The social base of the organization is not the black underclass but rather the lower middle class and young people and college students who are increasingly attracted to neonationalism by the heroic image of Malcolm X and the music of several rap groups that employ themes from Farrakhan's speeches in their lyrics.

Although Farrakhan and the revitalized Nation may be criticized as authoritarian, demagogic, proto-Islamic leadership formation with tinges of antisemitism, they nevertheless are an important force in post–civil rights era black politics.[56] Farrakhan and the Nation are important because they speak to the other traditions in black politics: nationalism and radicalism. He and the Nation are the only *national* leader and organization that in the post–civil rights era continue to speak in this tradition, a tradition that expresses in a militant way the continued rage that pervades much of black America.[57] The major national radical and nationalist formations of the 1960s—SNCC and the Black Panthers—did not survive into the post civil rights era. They played an important role in black political life by providing an alternative that made the demands of the traditional black leadership seem less militant and therefore much more palatable to whites. For a while it seemed the Nation might go the way of SNCC and the Black Panthers. Farrakhan is therefore to be credited with revitalizing this important alternative to the vacuousness of much post–civil rights era black leadership and politics.

The Nation of Islam and its leader are frequently dismissed as a ministry of rhetoric and rage without programmatic content. This is shortsighted. First, rhetoric is important in leadership, as evidenced in the effectiveness of American presidents from Lincoln to Reagan. Indeed, one influential student of the presidency argues that rhetorical capacity is a defining characteristic of "presidential character."[58] In addition, oratorical skill has always been an important element in Afro-American political culture and its leadership, having its roots in the tradition of black preaching that emerged in the slave culture.[59] And even without programmatic content, a leadership of rhetoric may not be inconsequential. As Bruce Perry concludes in his comprehensive biography, "Malcolm X fathered no legislation. He engineered no stunning Supreme Court victories or political campaigns. He scored no major electoral triumphs. Yet, because of the way he articulated his followers' grievances and anger, the impact he had on the body politics was enormous."[60]

Second, it is shortsighted to suggest that the Nation of Islam lacks a program. Rather, it appears that the Nation has more of a program than the NAACP, the Urban League or the Congressional Black Caucus. It is the only national organization with anything like an indigenous mass base and that operates independently of white philanthropy. The group operates a series of modest small-scale business enterprises and has a somewhat effective social welfare system for its members, and in a number of cities it has recruited a disciplined cadre of young men employed by several cities as security forces in public housing projects. Yet because of its narrow, sectarian religious orientation; its authoritarian leadership and decision-making process; its highly restrictive codes of personal conduct; its traditionalist approach to the role of women; and the tinges of antisemitism that in recent years has characterized the rhetoric of Farrakhan and some of his ministers, the Nation's appeal and influence is likely to remain limited, both within black America and in the larger society. The fact, then, that the Nation as the most important nationalist organization is limited and marginalized in its appeal is but another indicator of the weak state of the internal organizational structure of the post–civil rights era black community. This is most likely a structural dilemma of black politics. Fifty years ago, reflecting on Marcus Garvey and his Universal Negro Improvement Association, Myrdal observed:

> For one thing, it proves that it is possible to reach the Negro masses if they are appealed to in an effective way. It testifies to the basic unrest in the Negro community. It tells of a dissatisfaction so deep that it mounts to hopelessness of ever gaining a full life in America. It suggests that the effective method of lining up the American Negroes into a mass movement is a strongly emotional race—chauvinistic protest appeal. Considering the caste conditions under which Negroes live, this is not surprising. . . . On the other hand, the Garvey movement illustrates . . . that a Negro movement in America is doomed to ultimate dissolution and collapse if it cannot gain white support. This is a real dilemma. For white support will be denied to emotional Negro chauvinism when it takes organizational and political form.[61]

Mass-based black nationalist organizations probably are not, as Myrdal argued, doomed to "dissolution and collapse" but rather to political marginality both in the internal life of the black community and in the larger dynamics of American politics.

The Congressional Black Caucus and the Joint Center for Political Studies

Although some innovations in the organization and strategies of the civil rights organizations and the major black church organization were identified in the foregoing analysis, in general these organizations in the post–civil rights era are fundamentally unchanged from what they were in the 1960s. This failure of organizational innovation by the traditional groups was a factor in the rise of the new structure of black organizations that were designed to meet the requirements of post–civil rights era politics. The most important of these new organizations are the Congressional Black Caucus and related organizations of black elected officials, and the Joint Center for Political Studies (since 1990, Political and Economic Studies). Both of these organizations emerged in the late 1960s out of a perceived need to develop new organizational forms to deal with post–civil rights era problems. There has in fact from the outset been a symbiotic relationship between the Joint Center and the caucuses of black elected officials, with the former encouraging the formation of the latter and providing their initial administrative infrastructure. This relationship may be seen in the person of Kenneth Clark, who played a major intellectual and bureaucratic role in the formation of both new organizational forms.

In his 1965 essay on the civil rights organizations, Clark was skeptical about their ability to adapt to post–civil rights era concerns. He also wrote, "one obvious difference is that civil rights leaders have not been elected by any substantial number of Negroes. Either they are essentially hired executives, holding their office at the pleasure of the board of directors or else they emerge as leaders by charismatic power, later creating an organization which they in effect control."[62] The implication here is that civil rights leadership lacks the legitimacy and accountability that comes from election by large numbers of blacks. In 1965 the leadership of black America was still largely in the hands of the civil rights establishment, since there were only a handful of black elected officials (only five members of Congress, for example). This was to change in 1965 with the passage of the Voting Rights Act, which facilitated the rapid growth in the number of black elected officials. In 1967, 1968 and 1969, Clark convened a series of meetings of leading black Americans to discuss the future of the civil rights movement. Of particular note is that of the twelve at the 1967 meeting, none were from the traditional civil rights organizations but seven were involved in electoral politics.[63] It was out of this meeting that the idea of the Joint Center was formulated, at the urging of the black elected officials, who argued that the new era of electoral politics required an "institutionalized approach." Later, in the first issue of the Center's newsletter Clark wrote, "Negro elected officials have, in a significant sense, become the new leadership of the civil rights movement."[64] Clearly then, the formation of the Center and the caucuses of black elected officials were in part a conscious effort to displace the traditional civil rights leadership with a new leadership of elected officeholders, who it was thought were more adaptable to post–civil rights era politics.

In 1969 the Congressional Black Caucus was organized. And in subsequent years six other national organizations of black elected and appointed officials were organized, these being the National Conference of Black Mayors, the National Association of Black County Officials, the Judicial Council of the National Bar Association (an organization of black judges), the National Black Caucus of State Legislators, the National Black Caucus of Local Elected Officials and the National Association of Black School Board Members.[65] These organizations, with the collapse of the National Black Political Convention, are the major new post–civil rights era political formations. Although they are new forms, the question is, How effectively have they adapted to post–civil rights era exigencies? Since most of the research is on the Congressional Black Caucus and since it is the most important of the caucuses of elected officials, I focus the analysis on it. However, in general these organizations are a product of the 1960s black power movement with its emphasis on racial solidarity and separatism. This relatively mild form of black nationalism, what Holden calls "caucus separatism," does not, as he writes, "propose much genuine institutional separation between black and white, but . . . does propose to reallocate decision making in such a way that some specific members of the black bourgeoisie gain a larger role."[66] In other words, caucus separatism was a way for middle-class blacks to embrace the principles of black power while simultaneously pursuing their narrow professional or political interests. The civil rights era resulted in the integration of blacks into a variety of institutions from which they had been previously excluded or admitted in only token numbers. Once integrated, blacks then began to pursue race group interests. This caucus separatism is thus one of the enduring organizational innovations of the post–civil rights era; organizations not only by elected officials but by blacks in virtually all American institutions—universities, professional associations, trade unions, industry and federal, state and local bureaucracies. Again, these are mechanisms for pursuing largely middle class or professional interests in the context or under the umbrella of race interests.

The caucuses of elected officials follow the familiar model of hierarchical, top-down organization, having hardly any direct linkages or interactions with the grassroots or mass base of the community. Rather, their linkages are to fellow elites—black and white—within the establishment. As such their influence is at best modest, limited to annual conventions and workshops, press releases, legislative testimony and the assorted meetings with other politicians and bureaucrats. For example, a major activity of the six caucuses of elected officials is to cosponsor with the Joint Center a quadrennial National Policy Institute, a nonpartisan gathering of elected officials during the presidential election year to develop black policy priorities and discuss election year strategies. Except for the printing of yet another agenda of black policy priorities and the chance for persons from around the country to get together and talk, these meetings have little consequence. Rather, they are political rituals having more in common with a convention of the Elks than effective political mobilization. Indeed, since the Congressional Black Caucus sponsors on an annual basis its "Legislative Weekend" which also brings several thousand blacks to Washington to discuss policy priorities and political strategies, it is difficult to see any useful purposes in the duplicative and repetitive quadrennial policy institutes.

The Congressional Black Caucus is the model for this form of caucus separatism among elected and appointed black politicians, and in its prominence at the national level it is the most important of the six groups. In the post–civil rights era the black congressional delegation has grown from five in 1968 to thirty-nine in 1992. This growth is a function of several factors. The concentration of blacks in highly segregated inner-city neighborhoods, the Supreme Court's one person, one vote decision in *Baker v. Carr* and its progeny, and the implementation of the 1965 amended Voting Rights Act with its prohibition on racial gerrymandering and its requirements that congressional district lines be drawn in such a way that blacks and other minorities have the "opportunity to elect the candidate of their choice." The size of the black House delegation at thirty-nine after the 1990 redistricting process constitutes 9 percent of the House (about 17 percent of the Democratic Caucus), and unless the Supreme Court radically changes the way it deals with race and redistricting, this number is not likely to change very much in the foreseeable future. In *Shaw v. Reno*, a five-person Court majority suggested that it might radically change its approach of more than two decades of allowing state legislatures great discretion in drawing district lines to facilitate the election of blacks.[67] In her opinion for the majority, Justice O'Connor suggested that the irregular shapes of the twelve new majority black districts created in 1992 might violate the equal protection rights of white voters. At this writing the Court has not rendered a final judgment but if it was to follow through on its logic in *Shaw*, virtually all of the new districts drawn in 1992 could be invalidated.[68]

Blacks now hold all of the majority black district seats except one, and it is not likely that even in the best of circumstances more than two or three more can be drawn. This is important because, of the blacks serving in the House, only three (Dellums of Berkeley, Watt of Oklahoma and Frank of suburban Connecticut) are from white majority dis-

tricts. It is possible that a handful of blacks may be elected from majority white districts in the future but it is likely to be just that—a handful.
Until the 1992 redistricting, most black congresspersons represented
northern urban constituencies. Now all of the southern states except
Arkansas elect at least one black to Congress and several elect two, and
also for the first time, several represent the large population of rural
blacks in the south, which may help to shift the focus of the Caucus
away from its preoccupation with urban poverty to include the neglect
of its rural counterpart.

Except for their race, black congresspersons resemble their white
colleagues in terms of social background. They are largely middle-aged,
middle-class men (although women constitute 20 percent of the black
congressional delegation compared with 9 percent of the House as a
whole), with considerable educational and occupational attainments.
Although disproportionately liberal compared to the House as a whole,
in terms of routine voting behavior the group is not unlike the typical
Democratic congressperson representing urban constituencies. Nor are
they unlike the typical congresspersons in the financing of their campaigns and their capacity to retain their offices once elected. They rely
heavily on PAC contributions, largely from trade unions although corporate connected PACs contribute substantially to several caucus members.[69] This points to an important constraint in post–civil rights era
black politics. In an era when PACs have become increasingly important in financing increasingly expensive campaigns, blacks, despite several efforts, have been unable to develop a viable PAC to finance their
own campaigns and equally important to contribute to the campaigns
(and thereby exercise some influence) of others. The new black politicians at all levels—city, state and local—like the traditional civil rights
organizations are heavily dependent on white people and institutions to
sustain themselves.

Blacks in Congress, like their white counterparts, usually do not
face serious opposition after their first or at most second election to the
House.[70] In any given year after the first election, about half the members run unopposed in either the primary or general election or both,
and the average margin of victory for the delegation is 80 percent in
both primary and general elections. As is the case for most members of
the House, the financial and other advantages of incumbency, the relatively small stratum of politically active citizens in the districts, the tendency toward extremely low voter turnout, the one-party dominance in
the districts and the disproportionate dependence of black congressional campaigns on externally generated PAC money all operate to
create a near permanency of tenure for the black congressional delega-

tion. This is on the one hand a serious problem in the new black politics. Serious because it narrows the political discourse in the black community and because the accountability and responsiveness of representatives to their constituents is usually thought to require some degree of electoral competition, with the prospect of unresponsive officials being turned out of office. This prospect rarely exists in black electoral politics (or nonelectoral politics, noting the arbitrarily long tenure of the national and local heads of the NAACP and Urban League) at the congressional or any level of government—raising, at least theoretically, the problem of the lack of accountability of black leaders to the black community.

On the other hand, this near-permanent tenure, whatever its consequences in terms of democratic accountability and responsiveness, has the effect of enhancing the aggregate influence of blacks in the House, since formal influence is largely based on seniority. Some observers have argued that for this reason alone, factors that might facilitate more competitive elections and frequent turnover should be discouraged. Holden, for example, at the outset of post–civil rights era black politics, wrote, "Activity in black politics should be directed not only to the initial election of congressmen but to . . . minimizing those effects which would lead to a great deal of turnover in black congressmen . . . to the extent that black congressmen are sacrificed/replaced on some ritual of 'blackness,' to that extent the whole group of black congressmen will be relatively unexperienced and ineffectual."[71] Notwithstanding that what Holden calls some "ritual of blackness" might in fact involve principled, ideological or policy differences, in the post–civil rights era the small black congressional delegation has amassed considerable aggregate seniority. The result is that its members formerly chaired and, after 1994, are the senior or ranking member of several important committees and subcommittees in the House; and in the next century there is the possibility that blacks will chair such critical committees as Judiciary, Ways and Means and Appropriations.

This rise of blacks to positions of influence in the House is not necessarily the unambiguous plus for the advancement of black interests that Holden implies. First, as blacks rise in the institutional power structure, they may be required to put the interests of the committee, the party or the House before the interests of their constituents. This was the stance taken by Congressman Gray during his tenure as Budget Committee Chairman when he opposed the Caucus budget in favor of the more conservative Democratic Party budget (see Chapter 8). In addition, since the reforms of the 1970s requiring the election or ratification of committee and subcommittee chairs instead of strict adherence to seniority, committee chairs do not exercise the kind of autocratic power they once did. They are now much more responsive to the wishes of the Democratic Party majority, since if are not they may be removed, seniority notwithstanding. It is also possible that institutional versus race loyalties may not be the problem, in that as some blacks advance in the House hierarchy, they may take on the values of the institution, even when these conflict with the interests of the race. This, of course, is a central meaning of the notion of the institutionalization of the movement. In any event, while blacks in power in the House may be able to use their positions to marginally affect legislation in a way that advances black interests, in terms of advancing the fundamental black or progressive agenda these positions in and of themselves are inconsequential (see Chapter 8).

The Black Caucus

The Congressional Black Caucus emerged out of the black power movement's call for racial solidarity and independent black organization. In 1968 the first post–black power group of congresspersons was elected. Younger and more activist and movement oriented than their colleagues, this new group in 1969 sparked the formation of the Caucus as a racially exclusive organization that would represent the collective interests of blacks in Congress. The more senior members of the black congressional delegation were apprehensive and reluctant to form a *black* caucus because of concern about the reactions of their white colleagues and because of its separatist or nationalist implications. Congressman Hawkins, for example, consistently argued that the group should not be racially exclusive but open to all who shared its objectives. Congressman Charles Rangel described the reaction of the House leadership as "somewhat leery" and noted that among most House members, "There is no question there was a great deal of resentment. Some people felt that color should not be something that binds a group; that we are all Americans and there was no need for one ethnic group to bind."[72] In general, however, the leadership took a wait-and-see attitude toward the group, after assurances from Congressman Diggs and other senior members that the group was "responsible" and not some militant black power clique that would subvert the decorum and integrity of the House.

The Caucus first came to national attention as a result of its boycott of President Nixon's 1971 State of the Union address. The boycott was undertaken to protest the president's refusal to meet with the group. Throughout 1970 the group repeatedly requested an audience with the president, but Nixon refused. The official White House explanation for the refusal was "scheduling problems"; however, presidential aides privately characterized the Caucus as "a bunch of extremists running around the country stirring up trouble" and argued "no rule requires a president to set down with a militant band of his opponents."[73] Nevertheless, the president reluctantly agreed to the meeting, informing the Caucus through Senator Edward Brooke that he would see members after a face-saving period of a couple of months so as not to appear to be reacting to the boycott.

The boycott and subsequent meeting with the president were important for two reasons. First, they brought the heretofore obscure group to the attention of the press and public. There were scores of generally laudatory articles in the black press and considerable attention in the national press (the *New York Times* suggested the group was assuming the leadership of blacks nationally, filling the void left by the deaths of Martin Luther King and Whitney Young), including a *Newsweek* cover story and an invitation to appear on the prestigious "Meet the Press" television interview program. Second, by granting the audience the president, reluctantly to be sure, conferred legitimacy on the Caucus as a black power group in the Congress. As Congressman Clay said after the meeting, "I think the mere fact that the president responded pleases us because he says once and for all here is a group to be reckoned with in our political system."[74]

As a black power organization the Caucus fairly quickly gained legitimacy and respectability in Congress and the broader policy process, but its organization on a racially exclusive basis continues to pose, as Congressman Hawkins warned from the outset, a series of dilemmas in terms of racial solidarity as an organizing principle in American politics. As demonstrated at the Gary convention, race per se does not form a basis for collective political interests and action, rather ideology, interests and partisanship may and frequently do transcend the superficial commonality of race. This may be seen in the case of the Caucus in terms of its handling of issues of race and ideology with respect to members.

In 1975 Congressman Fortney Stark of California applied for Caucus membership. A white liberal Democrat with a voting record indistinguishable from the Caucus aggregate, Stark said he wished to join the Caucus because it "represents the problems and struggles not only of blacks but of all poor and underprivileged people." After what then–Caucus Chairman Rangel described as a long and agonizing discussion, the Caucus rejected Stark's application. The Caucus explained its rejection in symbolic terms, saying in a press release, "Essentially, the Caucus symbolizes black political development in this country. We feel maintaining this symbolism is critical at this juncture."[75] Yet in 1990 the Caucus accepted for membership Congressman Gary Franks, an extremely conservative black Republican elected from suburban Connecticut who, judged by his voting record, is hostile to the aspirations of blacks and poor people.[76] Indeed, several of his colleagues in the Caucus have publicly denounced Franks as a "traitor to the race" and an "Uncle Tom." Obviously, there is no solidarity or bond here based on race. Yet fidelity to the principle of an all-embracing racialism prevents the Caucus from acting on principle and excluding Franks, or Franks himself from resigning, which would be consistent with conservative principles which clearly postulate that race has no place as a basis of political organization and action in the United States.[77] As was pointed out frequently by the Caucus and others during the debate on the confirmation of Supreme Court Justice Clarence Thomas, "blackness" in politics is a matter of principle, not mere skin color.[78] While the Caucus could articulate and act on this principle and reject the symbolism of a conservative black on the Supreme Court, it cannot act on this principle in its own organization, adhering instead to a superficial racial symbolism that allows the excluding of a progressive like Stark and the welcoming of a reactionary like Franks because he is a "brother."[79]

When the Caucus was formed, its members and some observers saw it not as just another organization of legislators but as an institution that would organize and represent in Washington the interests of the national black community. The death of Dr. King, the shift of movement strategy from protest to electoral politics and the perception that organizations like the NAACP and the Urban League had lost their viability led members of the Caucus to argue that as the "highest body of black elected officials," they had both the experience and the legitimacy to act as the principal spokesgroup for blacks in national politics. Through a series of hearings and conferences in the early 1970s the Caucus sought to develop a new post–civil rights era black agenda and gain recognition (from the president, the Congress and the media) for itself and its agenda as representing the basic demands of black America. This role of the Caucus was never accepted by all members of the group (senior members such as Congressmen Nix and Hawkins were particularly wary of the Caucus attempting to function beyond a narrow legislative role) and was rejected outright by the traditional civil rights organizations, as well as the still-influential radical and nationalist elements of the leadership in the community. Rejection of this national leadership role for the Caucus was one of the factors that led to the calling of the National Black Political Convention in 1972: it was argued that the Caucus was too narrowly based to legitimately represent the range of interests and ideologies in the black community. By the mid-1970s the Caucus had abandoned its pretensions of exercising this kind of national leadership role, to concentrate on the internal mechanics of the legislative process and to act as the symbolic collective voice of blacks in Congress.[80]

It is this symbolic representational role that distinguishes the Caucus from the scores of other informal legislative groups in the House. This symbolic role involves such activities as formal recommendations and testimony on matters such as judicial nominations, the presentation in floor debates of various black agendas and state of black America reports, the development and presentation of its alternative budgets, occasional meetings with the president, and its annual legislative weekend.

The legislative weekend, held in the fall of each year, usually brings several thousand people to Washington to participate in panels and workshops with academics and government officials on the range of domestic and foreign policy issues of interest to blacks. The weekend is also the Caucus's principal fundraising mechanism: there is a $200 per person awards dinner, a spouses benefit luncheon and fashion show, a midnight champagne fashion show and a prayer breakfast. These events generate the half-billion dollars that sustains the Caucus Foundation's annual budget. Its small staff is limited to routine administrative work, running a modest research operation, a graduate intern program and planning the annual legislative weekend and fund-raising activities.[81]

Like most of the civil rights organizations, the Caucus is essentially an inside-the-beltway Washington establishment organization employing the traditional hierarchical model of top-down politics without a mass base to sustain it. The Caucus early on attempted to establish such a base in order to bring pressure on the Congress to support its legislative agenda. Although within the traditions of the House it is considered improper to intervene in the politics of another's district, the Caucus attempted to do this when in 1979 it created what it called an "action alert communications network." It was designed to bring pressure on those congressmen with at least a 15 percent black constituency. The network was to include regional, state and local coordinators who would be responsible for mobilizing blacks in the targeted districts to lobby congressmen to support Caucus legislation. In addition, the network was to be linked with the caucuses of other black elected officials and the National Black Leadership Roundtable. Although this network was given some credit for the defeat of South Carolina Congressman Walter MacMillan in 1978 (MacMillan was the autocratic Chairman of the House Committee on the District of Columbia who opposed home rule for the city), it generally has been ineffective. The most careful academic study of the network concludes that it may even have been counterproductive in that, rather than reducing the level of opposition to Caucus policy goals, it increased it among the targeted legislators.[82] A number of factors explain the network's failure, including lack of financial and staff resources and countervailing pressures by other constituent groups within the targeted congressman's district. However, without such a grassroots, mass mobilization base the Caucus in Washington, given its relatively small size, can engage in no more than symbolic politics. This of course was a key factor in the calling of the National Black Political Convention and another reason that its failure in the 1970s was such an important development.

The Joint Center for Political Studies

In her projected authorized history of the Joint Center Darlene Clark Hines writes, "The twenty year history of the Joint Center for Political and Economic Studies is as much an overview of the transition from protest to politics as a chronicle of the creation and evolution of a unique institution."[83] Professor Hines is correct; to trace the Center's history is a good case study of the institutionalization of the Afro-American freedom movement. In fact, the Center was founded and funded specifically to encourage and facilitate the shift in black politics from movement-style protest to institutionalized political participation.

The idea of a black think tank or research institution devoted to strategic and policy-relevant research on the black condition has a longer history than the 1960s movement transition. It may be traced at least to 1897 when DuBois at Atlanta University began a series of conferences that eventually evolved into a large-scale scientific project devoted to study of the Negro problem.[84] As the civil rights era drew to a close, black leaders of all stripes—integrationist, nationalists and radicals—began to call for an institutionalized approach to research on race and racism. I noted earlier Kenneth Clark's 1965 lament about the inadequate research capacity of the civil rights organizations and his call for the development of such capacity. As is shown below, Clark played a key role in the eventual creation of the Center but others were involved as well. For example, at the first national black power conference in 1967 in Newark, one of the resolutions adopted called for the establishment of a "national clearinghouse for information, research and reports on all activities of all black people." The National Conference of Black Political Scientists, founded in 1969, in 1970 held a conference to explore the idea of a black think tank. In 1973 James Farmer,

the former Director of CORE and for a time thereafter an assistant secretary at HEW in the Nixon administration, received a $150,000 grant
from the Office of Education to establish a black think tank to be called
the "Council on Minority Planning and Strategy."[85] Thus, in the late
1960s and early 1970s there was considerable ferment among the black
intelligentsia about the need to develop some institutionalized capacity
to deal with the post–civil rights era situation. As Holden wrote, "black
politics urgently requires its own think tank," because "it is urgent to
develop some institutional capacity which brings more penetrating
analysis and knowledge into alliance with political purpose."[86] Two
organizations emerged out of this ferment—the Institute of the Black
World (IBW) associated with Atlanta University and the Joint Center for
Political Studies, initially associated with Howard—but only one of
them, the Center, survives.

The collapse of IBW and the flourishing of the Center have important implications for understanding the nature of the institutionalization of the movement. Black civil rights organizations and black politicians depend disproportionately on white corporations and foundations
to survive. And as Henry writes in his analysis of white philanthropy
and black organizations, "American foundations are creatures of capitalism and as such are cautious reformers and strong supporters of the
status quo."[87] This is as true, perhaps more so, for think tanks as for civil
rights organizations or black congressional or mayoral candidates. As
Weaver writes, in funding think tanks, corporations and foundations
are usually buying an institution's image and reputation, and as a consequence, "Ideology in these institutions has generally involved exclusion of radicals or extremes. . . ."[88] Weaver is only half correct. American
corporations and foundations do not fund *radical left* think tanks; however, they routinely fund a number of radical right think tanks such as
the Heritage Foundation, the Hoover Institution, the CATO Institute
and the Manhattan Institute. The Joint Center is a resolutely centrist
organization in terms of mainstream American politics, while IBW was
ideologically eclectic, including on its board of directors, advisory council and among its resident fellows and guest scholars, the full range of
ideologies in black America: nationalists, radicals and integrationists.[89]

IBW was founded and initially led by Vincent Harding, the distinguished historian, theologian and advisor to Dr. King.[90] It was
founded in 1969 as part of the Martin Luther King, Jr., Center for Social
Change at Atlanta as a community of black scholars, artists, teachers,
students and organizers. Its purpose was to develop what Professor
Harding called a "usable history, one that could inform the liberation
struggle."[91] The relationship with the King Center was severed after a

year but the Institute continued its work until 1976, when it was closed due to a lack of financial support. Initially supported by modest foundation grants and a substantial grant from Wesleyan University, in its several years the Institute in its newsletter, occasional papers and monographs published material by black thinkers of all ideological stripes—Marxists, nationalists, integrationists—from throughout the black world including Africa and the Caribbean. While the Institute saw itself as an independent center of research and analysis, it was also an advocacy organization committed to engagement in the struggle for African and African American liberation. Although there are other reasons for IBW's failure to sustain itself financially, one factor is that its image and ideology did not conform to that preferred by American corporations and foundations. Thus, the radical wing of the black movement was unable to sustain what it critically needed and needs, a gathering place for critical research and thinking.

Kenneth Clark and the Ford Foundation played a major role in the organization of the Joint Center. Ford and the other major foundations had contributed a relatively small proportion of their total grants to civil rights and other black organizations during the civil rights era. However, given the dearth of funds available to these organizations, even these relatively small amounts played a crucial role in maintaining their viability. This began to change toward the end of the civil rights era. The Ford Foundation made its first major commitment to the black struggle in 1967, the first year after the black power revolt and the onset of widespread ghetto rebellions. Under the leadership of McGeorge Bundy, the former national security advisor to Presidents Kennedy and Johnson, Ford created a new national affairs decision and began to increase substantially its support of the black movement. The foundation in the late 1960s and through the 1970s played a major role in financing the movement's transition from civil rights protest to participation in institutional politics, funding both traditional civil rights as well as the new black power groups. In 1967, for example, Ford awarded a controversial grant to CORE to conduct a voter registration campaign in Cleveland, which was credited (and blamed) for helping to elect Carl Stokes as the first black mayor of a major American city. In 1971 Ford pledged grants of $100 million over six years to Howard and other selected black universities. A clearly stated purpose of these grants was to enhance graduate education in the social sciences in order to create a new cadre of black scholars who might contribute their perspectives to research, analysis and policy development and evaluation. It is in this overall context that Ford came to play a pivotal role in the creation of the Joint Center.

In 1967 the Ford Foundation provided a grant to Clark so that he might create a research organization to carry on his work. Clark, because of his research on the school desegregation cases (work which was cited in the *Brown* decision) was recognized as perhaps the nation's most eminent black social scientist. In addition, he had written an important book on urban black poverty, *Dark Ghetto*, and he was (and is) a radical, almost fanatical integrationist and was an unrelenting foe of the new black power movement. In a sense then, as Henry writes, the Ford grant was designed to "institutionalize Clark."[92] With the grant, Clark formed the Metropolitan Applied Research Center (MARC), not as a pure think tank or research organization but rather as an activist, advocacy organization. As its first annual report stated, the purpose of MARC was ". . . to mobilize the skills, the techniques and methods of the social sciences as an effective form of power to influence policy decisions and actions by government agencies on behalf of neglected and deprived groups of the city."[93]

MARC was a biracial organization in governance and staffing and in its several years held forums and conferences with the participation of the major civil rights leaders and black and white students of race and poverty. MARC (with another Ford grant) also sponsored a national conference of more than six hundred black elected officials. This was the first national meeting of the nation's black elected officials and at this conference, once again, the need for some kind of research and technical support organization for the emerging black elected leadership group was high on the agenda. Such an organization was thought especially needed to provide information, training and technical assistance to blacks holding office in the rural south. Out of this conference a proposal was developed and submitted to Ford to create a Center for Minority Group Affairs.

As originally submitted, the proposal, drafted by Howard Law Professor Frank Reeves, envisioned an activist, advocacy role for the center similar to Clark's MARC; however, it was subsequently revised by Clark to limit its activities to research and educational and technical assistance for black elected officials. The reference to race or minority was also dropped and the new organization, with an $820,000 grant, became the Joint Center (joint because the institution was to be administered jointly by MARC and Howard University).[94] It began operation in late 1970 as an interracial, bipartisan organization directed by Howard's Reeves. The initial board of directors was largely black and included black academicians and political leaders. Chaired by long-time Democratic party activist Louis Martin, the other members included Massachusetts Republican Senator Ed Brooke, Sam Jackson, an assistant HUD secretary in the Nixon administration, Eleanor Farrar, MARC's vice president for Washington operations and the only white member, James Cheek and Andrew Billingsly, president and academic vice president, respectively, at Howard and Kenneth Clark. The organization thus had a decidedly establishment, centrist cast. Its staff of thirteen included two senior research associates—one white, one black—and Sharon Pratt Dixon as staff lawyer.

The proposal originally envisioned close cooperation between the Joint Center and Howard University (especially its political science department) in terms of research and program development. However, this relationship never materialized except on an ad hoc basis. This was in part because of more or less inconsequential personality differences between Center staff and Howard political scientists, but also because the perceived radicalism of some of the latter did not fit well with the Center's centrist orientation. There was also a sense on the board that Howard and its faculty lacked the prestige of black faculty at the leading white universities.

This early tension between the Joint Center and black political scientists has continued throughout the Center's twenty-year history. Not only was it reflected in the lack of systematic cooperation between the Howard faculty and the Center but also in the lack of collaboration between it and the organized black political science community. In 1969, a year before the Joint Center was founded, black political scientists had organized the National Conference of Black Political Scientists (NCOBPS). And it was envisioned that the Joint Center and NCOBPS would work together in research and program development. This relationship, however, was stillborn. The ostensible reason was a dispute over appointments to the Center's research advisory board. Reeves invited NCOBPS to submit the names of three of its members to serve. Three names were submitted (including the NCOBPS president as ex officio), all on the faculty at historically black universities. The Center's board rejected all three names, requesting that the names of more eminent political scientists be submitted, specifically mentioning black faculty at two of the ivy league universities. NCOBPS rejected the request and withdrew from any further institutional cooperation with the Center, although individual NCOBPS members continued to serve from time to time on the Center's staff and to conduct research for it on an ad hoc basis.

Again, this tension continued throughout the Joint Center's history. It has two interrelated sources. First, as Weaver writes, funders of think tanks "are usually buying an institution's image and reputation."[95] Consequently, the Center from the outset sought to enhance its image and reputation by relying on the more prestigious ivy league white universities rather than scholars from traditional black universities. An institution's image and reputation is based not just on the reputations of its researchers or staff; it is also ideological. NCOBPS was committed institutionally (although its individual members share the range of ideologies in the black community) to the black power ideology and a radical analysis and interpretation of the black condition. Thus, the Center in seeking to please its funders, unlike IBW, sought to avoid any tinge of radicalism or black power nationalism.

The Joint Center's early projects included the collection and dissemination of data on the rapidly growing number of black elected officials (eventually this became its annual *Roster of Black Elected Officials*), the publication of a monthly newsletter and the provision of technical training, workshops and publications to black elected officials on electoral strategy, implementation of the Voting Rights Act, local government personnel and budgeting practices as well as information on the preparation of proposals for various federal grants. Most of these workshops and publications were directed at the new group of blacks being elected to office in the rural south. The Center also from the outset encouraged black elected officials to form caucuses and was instrumental in creation of the National Coalition on Black Voter Participation.

In 1972 Reeves was succeeded as the Joint Center's President by Eddie Williams, a former foreign service officer and academic administrator at the University of Chicago. Williams set about to broaden the Center's work beyond educational and technical assistance and research support for black elected officials. Williams also sought to diversify the Center's board and staff and to broaden the base of its financial support. In 1976 the Center dissolved its relationship with Howard University and became an independent, tax-exempt entity. And in 1981 the Center, with grants from the Rockefeller and Hewlett Foundations, began what it described as an intensive review of its mission and plans and projects for the future. As part of this process, several conferences of individuals from the corporate and foundation communities, journalist, academics and government officials met to help the Center plan its future agenda. The result was an announcement that the Center would become a "national research organization in the tradition of Brookings and the American Enterprise Institute," rather than simply a "technical and institutional support resource for black elected officials."[96]

If a chronicle of the Joint Center's history is, as Professor Hines suggests, a chronicle of the institutionalization of black politics, then in it we can see in a more careful analysis of its work what has happened to black politics in the last twenty years as it has lost its social change potential and become coopted into systemic political routines. In its leadership, staff and board, the Joint Center is probably the only truly interracial "black" organization to endure twenty years after black power. Its twenty-one member board usually includes six or so whites including two or three persons from the corporate sector. Its administrative and research staff as well as its guest scholars in residence and those independent scholars commissioned to conduct research are also interracial. This stands in sharp contrast to other major national black civil rights and political organizations, where the inclusion of whites is either nonexistent or at best token. The Center also continues to rely largely on scholars affiliated with the nation's prestige white universities, giving only token representation to historically black colleges and universities, and these chosen scholars, black and white, tend to be resolutely centrist, avoiding both the extremes of left and right in American and African American politics. This staffing pattern (about fifty resident staff and fellows) is consistent with the pattern of funding by large corporations and foundations who seek to purchase respectability and moderation. Since its inception, the Ford Foundation has provided unrestricted general support to the Center, and generally more than 90 percent of the center's budget comes from corporate and foundation contributors, a list of which reads like a who's who of corporate America. The Center is much more dependent on such sources, drawing very little of its support from endowments, as does Brookings, Heritage Foundation or the Hoover Institution. Its 1991 budget of $4.4 million is modest compared to the Brookings Institute's $77 million or the more than $10 million of Heritage, the American Enterprise Institute or the Urban Institute.[97] With this modest budget the Center has done a remarkable job in facilitating the institutionalization of black politics. Its studies of the growth and development of black elected officials, its work on the implementation of the Voting Rights Act, its work on the development of a consensus black agenda and its monthly newsletter (*Focus*) has made the Joint Center the recognized, authoritative source on black politics in the post–civil rights era.[98]

If the observation that a successful think tank is "an arrangement by which millions of dollars are removed from the accounts of willing corporations, the government and the eccentric wealthy and given to researchers who spend much of their time competing to get their names in the paper" is correct, then the Center is a very successful institution, in that the national news media routinely quotes it as an authoritative source on black politics and race policy issues in the United States.[99] The modern process of policy making in the United States involves an interlocking relationship between the nation's corporate and financial elites, politicians, interest groups and, increasingly, nongovernmental think tanks or policy research institutions.[100] The Joint Center was created to "ease the transition" of blacks into this process and away from movement-style politics. It has done this and in doing so has, in spite of its generally competent research and technical studies, helped to render post–civil rights era black politics largely an elite, hierarchical phenomenon that is largely irrelevant to the internal problems of the black community or to the mobilization of the resources that might result in system responsiveness to the post–civil rights era black agenda.[101]

Conclusion

The purpose of this chapter was to review post–civil rights era organizational developments in order to assess how well black organizations have adapted to the requirements of the new institutional politics and the new post–civil rights era issues captured in the term *black underclass*. There have been some innovations in the structures and strategies of the traditional civil rights groups, the black church and the revitalized Nation of Islam along lines that make them somewhat more relevant to the new politics and the new issues, and the Congressional Black Caucus and the cognate caucuses of black elected officials and the Joint Center for Political Studies represent new organizational forms that have some relevance to the new politics. However, these changes have not been enough and consequently, twenty-five years after the civil rights era, the black community remains organizationally ill prepared to take part effectively in institutional politics or to address the problems of the underclass.[102] Effective participation in institutional politics requires a national capacity to mobilize and use in a disciplined fashion the limited resources of the black community; some mechanism to address the internal disabilities of the black community in a way that will transform it into an effective pressure group; a *critical* research and analytic capacity; and an independent fund-raising and financing capacity to sustain these institutions. At best today the black community has only the most rudimentary elements of these organizational requisites. The collapse of the National Black Political Convention process in the 1970s reflected and resulted in the further fragmentation, ideologically and institutionally, of the black community. This fragmentation has been exacerbated in the 1980s by the rise of a vocal and well-financed group of black conservative spokespeople who, while lacking an ideological or organizational base in the community, have nevertheless, because of their access to white elites, money and media, constituted yet another force for centrifugalism. After the collapse of the Convention as a national institution of mass mobilization and organization, more establishment-type black leaders sought to create an alternative in the form of the National Black Leadership Roundtable. It, however, is largely a paper organization, ignored by black leaders and invisible to the masses. So, rather than try to revitalize it and make it an effective force, black leaders have sought to create yet another organization. In August of 1990 the NAACP and reportedly one hundred other leaders of national black organizations gathered in Washington to form the National Organization of Black Organizations. Its purposes, as stated by Benjamin Hooks, are familiar to any passing observer of post–civil rights era black politics. They include plans for a "communications network to share information, development of a brain trust to research and make recommendations on social and economic concerns affecting blacks and developing strategies . . . to take responsibility for our destiny."[103] Again, this reads like the 1967 resolution of the Newark black power conference or any of the sundry summits or meetings of black elected officials or leaders that have been routinely held in the last twenty-five years. Needless to say, nothing has been heard of the National Association of Black Organizations since its initial press release.

Another goal of the Convention was to mobilize and discipline the black vote as an independent force in American elections. Again, with its collapse, nothing has come along to replace it; the result is that the black vote has never been fully mobilized (with voting in national elections hardly ever exceeding 50 percent) and remains today largely a captive of the Democratic Party, a party which has in the last twenty-five years moved increasingly away from blacks and their progressive policy concerns (see Chapter 10). The Joint Center represents an institutionalized research capacity that virtually everyone in the late 1960s identified as an important resource for the post–civil rights era. It, however, is so tied to the parochial concerns of black elected officials and so dependent on white corporations and foundations that it is unable to provide a critical perspective on the internal problems of the race or render a sustained critique of post–civil rights era racism and the political economy. (The Humphrey-Hawkins debate discussed in Chapter 7 cried out for a sustained critique of modern capitalism from the perspective of the employability of African Americans.) In a memorable phrase, California Assembly Speaker Jesse Unruh remarked that money was the mother's milk of American politics. Given the rise of PACs and expensive media-based electoral and lobbying campaigns, this is even more the case today, and to carry the analogy to black politics, one

might say it is an infant desperately in need of nutrition.[104] Black organizations and leaders are largely dependent on white corporations and
their philanthropic progenies to support their work. This makes it
nearly impossible for them to challenge the prerogatives or privileged
position of business in American society, even though it is arguably in
the interests of their constituents to do so. Some efforts have been made
in the last twenty-five years to create some black equivalent to the
United Jewish Appeal or the United Way; these efforts for reasons not
entirely clear to me have failed.[105] Similarly, efforts in the 1970s and
1980s to create an effective black PAC have also failed. The result is a
kind of policy research and political rhetoric more relevant to gaining
and maintaining funding or winning and holding office than mobilizing
and advancing the interests of a dispossessed people. Thus, blacks, who
probably have more organizations (at least on paper) per capita than
any other ethnic group in the United States, are nevertheless not effectively organized. Many are mere paper organizations and those that
are not are devoted mainly to the routines of Washington or city hall
politics, with limited resources and little of an effective strategy or programs to organize the black community into a cohesive pressure group.
Meanwhile a kind of nihilism grows among the black downtrodden,
who have little faith or hope in a system that neglects them and in a
leadership that does not lead them.

PART III

Because of the structure of American politics as well as the nature of the Negro community, Negro politics will accomplish only limited objectives. This does not mean that Negroes will be content with those accomplishments or resigned to that political style. If Negroes do not make radical gains, radical sentiments may grow. How these sentiments will find expression is perhaps the most perplexing and troubling question of all.

—James Q. Wilson (1967)

When we talk about black politics we are not talking about ordinary politics. And we are not talking about ordinary politics because the American political system has not created a single social community in which the reciprocal rules of politics would apply. Conventional politics cannot solve this problem because conventional politics is a part of the problem. It is part of the problem because the political system is the major bulwark of racism in America. It is part of the problem in the sense that the political system is structured to repel fundamental social and economic change. We hear a great deal about the deficiencies, real or imagined, of certain black leaders, but not enough attention, it seems to me, is paid to the framework within which they operate. That framework prevents radical growth and innovation—as it was designed to prevent radical growth and innovation.

—Congressman Mervyn Dymally (1971)

4

Black Incorporation and Institutionalization in the Post–Civil Rights Era: Leading America and Leading Blacks

In his enduringly fascinating and still controversial study of the organization of power in American society, C. Wright Mills makes the point that there are three levels of power in the United States: (1) a power elite of top-level economic, military and political decision makers which in an overlapping, intricate set of cliques share decisions of national consequence in economic and foreign policy; (2) a diversified and relatively balanced pluralist structure of power at the middle level represented in the Congress, the two parties, state governments and local politics; and (3) the mass of unorganized people who have relatively little power over those at the middle level or the elite.[1]

Building on the work of Mills and others, Thomas Dye and his colleagues in the early 1970s sought to specify empirically the individuals who constitute the nation's power elite. Mills argued that power in the United States was largely institutional because "no one . . . can be truly powerful unless he has access to the command of major institutions, for it is over these institutional means of power that the truly powerful are, in the first instance, powerful."[2] Employing this institutional approach to the study of the elite Dye developed an operational definition that includes those "individuals who occupy the top positions in the institutional structure of American society. These are the individuals who possess the formal authority to formulate, direct and manage programs, policies and activities of the major corporate, governmental, legal, educational, civic and cultural institutions in the nation."[3] This definition of the institutional elite resulted in the identification of 7,314 elite positions in three interlocking sectors, including the corporate sector (major corporations, financial institution, utilities, insurance and transportation), the public interest sector (the major national media, educational and philanthropic institutions, and the leading law firms and civic and cultural organizations) and the government sector (the top federal executive, legislative, judicial and mili-

tary leaders).[4] By far the largest number of these positions are in the
nongovernmental sectors, 4,325 (59 percent) in the corporate sector,
2,705 (37 percent) in the public interest sector and in the governmental
sector only 284, or 3 percent. Thus, incorporation into the American
structure of power at the elite level rarely involves holding elected or
appointed office.

Of the 7,314 positions identified by Dye, blacks occupied only 20.
And like their white counterparts, most blacks in the power elite were in
the nongovernmental sector, most often as members of the boards of
directors of major corporations or cultural institutions. Among such
individuals identified during the early Bush years were William Coleman, Andrew Brimmer, Franklin Thomas (member of several boards
and head of the Ford Foundation), Clifton Wharton, Patricia Harris and
Samuel Pierce. In the government sector four blacks were identified,
William Gray, the House Majority Whip, Louis Sullivan, the Health
and Human Services Secretary, Justice Thurgood Marshall and General Colin Powell, Chairman of the Joint Chiefs of Staff. As with the
typical white member of the elite, one sees an interlocking relationship
between the sectors as several of the persons now in the corporate sector formerly held important positions in the government sector. Institutional positions of power do not necessarily translate into the effective
exercise of power, rather they provide a base for that exercise, giving the
individual the formal access to the institutions that in some circumstances may result in the effective use of this institutional base. That is,
individuals in these institutions may or may not use their positions to
exercise power; however, the point is that individuals outside of these
institutions are much more limited in most circumstances in their capacities to effect the course of national decision making. Overall, then, to
talk of black empowerment in the post–civil rights era is just that, talk,
if one analyzes the higher circles of power. To the extent that blacks
are integrated or incorporated into the structure of power in America it
is at what Mills described as the noisy spectator sport of "the semi-
organized stalemate of the middle levels of national power."[5]

Black Incorporation at the Middle Level of Power

For Mills the Congress is the "prime seat" of the middle level of
power,[6] but this level also includes most executive branch officials, state
and local government officials and persons in the hierarchy of the party
system. These institutions deal with routine interest-based politics and
those issues that do not impinge on the fundamentals of preservation of
capital and the maintenance of the national security state. Except for

the party system one might argue that individuals in these middle-level institutions are charged with the responsibility of managing the consequences at the state and local levels of the decisions made by the power elite.

This is especially the case for the big-city mayors. Throughout the post–civil rights era blacks have controlled several big city governments—Newark, Gary, Detroit and Atlanta—including the mayor's office and a majority of city council seats. In these cities the conditions of the black underclass have not improved in the last twenty years; if anything they have grown worse. This is because big-city black governments have generally pursued policies and programs of minority appointments and employment, contracts to minority businesses and efforts to restrain police misconduct in minority communities, but little in the way of policies that might effect the underlying problems of ghetto poverty and dispossession. At this middle level of urban government the limited authority of their charters, the fiscal constraints and the privileged position of business in the local economy are usually so great that local governments find it all but impossible to undertake programs that would deal with the problems of ghetto joblessness and poverty.[7] The paradigmatic case of the impotence of black power in the cities is Atlanta, first, because it is the most thoroughly researched case, and second, because Atlanta is admirably suited of all places for the potential effective exercise of urban black power. It has a large, fairly prosperous black middle class; it is an important center of black intellectual activity centered around the Atlanta University complex; it was the headquarters city of the civil rights movement; and as the birth and burial place of Dr. King, it remains a place where the ethos of the movement ought to have some continuing impact, especially since many of the city's leaders are veterans of the movement. Yet the research on Atlanta shows that Mayors Maynard Jackson and Andrew Young and other black officials in the city, rather than bringing a new progressive agenda to the city's politics have on the contrary allowed Atlanta's business establishment to continue to do business as usual albeit on a nonsegregated basis.[8]

Since 1970 the Joint Center for Political Studies in its annual *Roster of Black Elected Officials* has compiled data on the number of black elected officials and their distribution by category of office and region of the country.[9] At the peak of the civil rights struggle when the Voting Rights Act was passed in 1965, it is estimated there were about five hundred black elected officials in the United States. Today that number has increased to 7,552, approximately 1.5 percent of the estimated 500,000 elected officeholders in the United States.[10] This number is thought to be very near the outer limits of projections for such officials in the near future. That is, no one projects that this number, for example, is likely to double by the end of the century.[11] Thus, the most basic conclusion that emerges from statistical analysis of black incorporation in the post–civil rights era is that after more than two decades it remains partial, incipient incorporation and that full incorporation (at about 12 percent of the total) is not likely to occur. A variety of explanations may be advanced for the failure after twenty years of an almost single-minded focus by black elites on electoral office for this strikingly low level of incorporation of blacks in elective office. They include lower black registration and voting, usually attributed to blacks' lower socioeconomic status; white racial bloc voting (the failure of whites except in rare instances to vote for blacks); certain structural features of the American electoral systems, such as single-member congressional districting, the apportionment of Senate seats by states rather than population and at the local level at large elections and multimember districts; the failure of many blacks in rural southern constituencies to elect blacks, even where they constitute a majority of the voting age population; and racial gerrymandering and other techniques that may operate to dilute the black vote. It is remarkable that so few blacks have been elected to office, since the impression from the media is that blacks are fully incorporated in the system. In addition, most (more than 75 percent) of those blacks holding elected office are concentrated in relatively insignificant city council and local school board offices, mainly in the rural south. In 1992, for example, only seven blacks held statewide elected executive or administrative office. Put simply, black incorporation into elected office is incipient.[12]

We know less about the number and distribution of black appointed officials, in part because there is no systematic standardized data source (akin to the Joint Center's annual rosters of black elected officials) and because there have been relatively few systematic studies. Representation of blacks in appointive office will vary by level of government, the size of the black population in a state or locality, systemic racism and black political mobilization in a given jurisdiction and which of the two major parties are in power. I expect, however, that at the level of policy-making cabinet, subcabinet and agency heads, the aggregate level of black representation in state and local government is low.

Systematic data are available on the appointment of blacks to federal executive positions.[13] Prior to the Kennedy administration blacks were not appointed to high-level positions in the executive branch of government (before 1960 only two blacks had held subcabinet posts in the federal government: an assistant attorney general in the Taft administration and an assistant secretary of labor in the Eisenhower administration), although informal "racial advisers" were assigned to various agencies and departments under both Taft and Franklin Roosevelt. Thus, statistical measurement of black incorporation at this level of power begins in 1960. In the face of considerable delay and obstruction from southern racists in the Senate, President Kennedy appointed several blacks to high-level posts in the executive and judiciary. And President Johnson made a number of historic "first Negro who" appointments to the cabinet, the subcabinet, the independent regulatory commissions, the judiciary and the diplomatic service. These appointments coming near the peak of the black power rebellion were important symbolic manifestations of the formal cooptation of blacks. Yet at the end of the Johnson Administration blacks constituted less than 2 percent of executive branch appointees (but about 4 percent of the judiciary). In the post–civil rights era a fairly steady increase in such appointments is observed, 4 percent in the Nixon-Ford administrations (most by President Nixon), 12 percent under President Carter, about 5 percent under President Reagan, 6 percent under President Bush, and 13 percent by President Clinton.[14] If one uses proportion of population as the measure of equitable incorporation, then by the end of the Carter administration one may conclude that statistically blacks had been fully incorporated. Yet, given that a traditional criteria for such appointments is the rewarding of loyal constituency groups, some blacks argue that in Democratic administrations blacks should receive 20 percent of party patronage, since they constitute roughly that percentage of the Democratic Party national vote.[15] Similarly employing this criteria, 4 to 5 percent black appointments in Republican administrations may be viewed as equitable, given the minuscule contribution of blacks to the party vote and the paucity of competent Republican loyalists (especially as in the case of the Reagan administration when a conservative ideological litmus test was also employed).

Until the Reagan and Bush administrations, black executive branch appointees tended to be concentrated in the civil rights and social welfare bureaucracies (HUD, HEW, EEOC, the Civil Rights Commission) rather than in the inner or elite bureaucracies dealing with economic and internal and national security affairs (State, Treasury, Defense and Justice). More than 75 percent of the appointees in the period 1960–84 served in one or more of these agencies or in civil rights enforcement positions in other agencies. Presidents Reagan and Bush broke this pattern of traditional black jobs by appointing several blacks to middle- and high-level posts in the foreign policy and national security area, including national security advisor and chair of the joint chiefs of staff. President Clinton's initial appointments continue this trend of nontraditional appointments, including cabinet secretaries of Energy, Commerce and Agriculture, staff positions at the White House and national security council and subcabinet posts at the State and Defense Departments. The only area of elite policy making in the executive where blacks have not yet penetrated is the senior White House staff and the economic policy-making apparatus, although this too may change by the end of the Clinton administration. These nontraditional appointments are another indicator of the institutionalization process at work as blacks increasingly occupy positions involving management of institutions of general rather than narrowly race-related concerns.

Of all the institutions of American society, blacks are most thoroughly incorporated into the party system or, more precisely, the Democratic Party, since the black presence in the Republican Party is miniscule.[16] In 1972 the Democratic Party adopted fundamental reforms in delegate selection rules and procedures designed to eliminate racial discrimination in the process. These reforms also required each state to adopt an affirmative action plan to assure the representation of blacks, women and other minorities in rough proportion to their presence in the population.[17] And at its 1974 midterm convention the party, threatened by a black boycott, adopted a charter that called for the representation of blacks and minorities at the conventions and in all party organs as "indicated by their presence in the Democratic electorate."[18] As a result of these reforms, between 1976 and 1988, black delegates at the party conventions increased from 11 to 23 percent. Similarly with other party organs, in 1988 blacks constituted 20 percent of the Platform Committee (cochaired by Congressman William Gray), 31 percent of the Credentials Committee (also chaired by a black, Pennsylvania House Speaker K. Leroy Irvis) and 26 percent of the Rules Committee, also chaired by a black, Little Rock Mayor Lottie Shackleford. Following the negotiations between Jesse Jackson and Michael Dukakis at the 1988 convention, the percentage of blacks on the Democratic National Committee was increased from 17 to 22 percent, providing a critical bloc of votes in the election in 1989 of Ronald Brown, Jackson's 1988 convention manager, as party chairman. In his largely insider's account of the 1974 midterm party convention, Walters writes that its results meant that blacks had developed "a sustained institutional base of power within the party" and the Black Caucus had "matured into a new force within the party." Yet, he concludes, "In the final analysis, racism, lack of political influence and other tangible and intangible factors often limit real influence within actual decision making organs of the party institution, and certainly within presidential campaigns, even though blacks may have impressive titles."[19]

The Changing Structure of Post–Civil Rights Era Leadership

Although the incorporation of blacks into middle level elected and appointed office is incipient and has had only a modest effect on the composition of these institutions (except for the executive in Democratic administrations), it has had a major effect on the nature and work of the leadership of black America; divorcing it from internal, communal institutions and processes. This recruitment and socialization process results in a hierarchical, institutional model of black leadership that threatens to render the indigenous mass base of the black community leaderless or, in the worst case, the creation of a leadership group opportunistically working against the collective interests of the race in pursuit of narrow personal or political advantage. Something of the nature of this post–civil rights era transformation in black leadership may be seen in the changing composition of *Ebony*'s list of the one hundred most influential black Americans. Since 1963 *Ebony* has published this list annually.[20] The most striking change in black leadership composition revealed in the *Ebony* lists is the decline between 1963 and 1990 in the percentage of civil rights leaders and "glamour personalities" (famous athletes and entertainers) and a sharp increase in the percentage of persons who are elected and appointed officials of government.[21] In 1963, 18 percent of the *Ebony* leadership group were leaders of local or national civil rights organization and 10 percent were glamour personalities. By 1990 the list included only 6 percent civil rights leaders (all national leaders) and 3 percent glamour personalities. In 1963 only nine elected officials were listed; by 1990 the number was thirty-eight. If one combines here appointed officials and judges, then more than half of the leadership of the race today is a part of the official structure of government. This represents a radical transformation in race leadership; in 1944, similar surveys of "leading Negroes" found politicians "conspicuous by their absence."[22] This transformation in race leadership may be an inevitable consequence of the logic of the civil rights revolution and the processes of cooptation and institutionalization that accompanied it, but like the decline of the indigenous black community institutions that also accompanied the civil rights revolution, this kind of integration has its advantages and disadvantages. Blacks of all social classes and ideological labels are often heard to lament that integration in all too many instances has resulted in the decline or destruction of a number of important institutions that thrived under segregation, including neighborhoods where all social classes lived in relative proximity, as well as independent businesses, schools and cultural institutions. Although not as frequently heard—indeed rarely heard -one might also lament the consequences for communal leadership of the logic of integration as increasingly the best and brightest in the community are drawn into systemic institutions and processes and away from the community and its needs. This of course has its advantages, but its disadvantages should not be overlooked.

Systemic institutions and processes have their own logic of recruitment and socialization which may not correspond to the interests of the race. In addition, their tendency to draw away indigenous, communal leaders has resulted in many young black people in the ghettos feeling leaderless in the post–civil rights era, disconnected from civil rights, church and elected officials, either not knowing who these are or if they do, viewing them as distant celebrities.[23] Finally, black civil rights and other communal institutions may find it difficult to compete for the talent to lead and staff their organizations, given the lure of money and prestige of mainstream institutions.

These problems have to an extent been exacerbated by the ascendancy of the conservative movement in the 1980s. This movement has literally sought to create and sustain a new alternative black leadership group molded in its own image. This has been done in part through the funding of the research of selected black conservative intellectuals, journals and "spokespeople," and the widespread dissemination in the mainstream media of their ideas.[24] This has also been done through the appointment of conservative blacks to highly visible positions in the Reagan and Bush administrations. Prior to the 1980s, blacks who identified with the Republican Party and served in Republican administrations were identified with the party's more liberal Rockefeller wing and were recruited from or had long association with mainstream institutions of the black community. Men like Samuel Jackson, Arthur Fletcher and William Coleman—all persons who held high-level positions in the Nixon and Ford administrations—were identified with the civil rights movement and were socialized in mainstream black institutions, churches, colleges, fraternities and civic and civil rights organizations. For example, of the twenty black appointees I interviewed during the Nixon and Ford administrations, most had some mainstream black socialization experience and only two identified with the Goldwater-Reagan right wing of the party. And during the Nixon administration, black appointees, instead of supporting or remaining silent in the face of Nixon's anti–civil rights rhetoric and proposals, actively and aggressively opposed the president, at one point even hinting at mass resignations (see Chapter 5). All of this changed with the Reagan administration.

Unlike Nixon and Ford, Reagan sought to bypass traditional black Republicans (Samuel Pierce's appointment as HUD secretary was a notable exception) and create his own alternative, not only through the appointment process but also by skillful use of the prestige of the White House. First, Reagan ignored establishment black leaders and occasionally even openly scorned them. And as outlined in White House internal memoranda the administration sought to create a new leadership by inviting conservative blacks to the White House for highly publicized meetings with the president, thereby conferring legitimacy and publicity. As one White House aide wrote, "One thing the White House can do is bestow publicity on people. If you have credible people, they can be alternative leaders."[25] This was the approach followed when Robert Woodson and a small group of conservative activists and intellectuals were invited to the White House to meet with the president (the group called itself the "Council for a Black Economic Agenda"). After the meeting and the attendant publicity, the leaders of the traditional civil rights groups requested a meeting; the White House refused, consistent with its strategy of avoiding "established black leadership" as one White House aide put it.[26] Sure enough, Woodson by the end of the 1980s had become in the eyes of the national press a black leader and was routinely called on to comment on race issues from a black conservative perspective. (Another example is Allan Keyes, a former high-level State Department official and Republican Senate candidate from Maryland.)[27]

Apart from using the White House to confer publicity and prestige, the Reagan and Bush administrations recruited their appointees from a new generation of young, highly educated blacks whose backgrounds show little identification with traditional black institutions. Frequently educated at white universities, they have aggressively defended the Goldwater-Reagan approach to race and social policy, both publicly and in internal administration deliberations.

The paradigmatic case of this new, alternative black leadership is Supreme Court Justice Clarence Thomas. Educated at predominantly white institutions and then immediately recruited by conservative politicians and business institutions, Thomas has had hardly any contact with traditional black institutions.[28] Appointed at a relatively early age as an assistant secretary of education (in charge of civil rights enforcement) and then Chairman of EEOC, Thomas embraced almost completely the right-wing agenda on issues of civil rights and social and economic policy. Thus, when nominated at age forty-three to succeed the legendary Thurgood Marshall on the Supreme Court, Thomas was opposed by virtually the entire black leadership establishment, which argued, in effect, that a black who was conservative was unfit to sit on the Court. Thomas was attacked by black academics and politicians in unusually strong language as an "Uncle Tom" and a "hustler" and as "unworthy to shine the shoes of the hero he would replace."[29] Yet this was not the view of ordinary blacks, who apparently saw only Thomas's color, not his ideology. In polls conducted on the eve of the Judiciary Committee's hearings blacks, like most whites, indicated they did not know enough to form an opinion as to whether he should be confirmed; this in spite of a full summer of intensive media coverage of the nomination focusing on his race, ideology and the opposition of the black establishment. Among blacks, 23 percent supported the nomination and 10 percent were opposed while among whites 25 percent favored confirmation and 10 percent were opposed.[30] After the charges of sexual harassment by Anita Hill, a former Thomas aide, riveted the nation's attention on the nomination, blacks, like most Americans, favored the nomination by a margin of two to one. The overwhelming support of blacks (and women) played a major role in persuading wavering senators (especially southern Democrats) to support confirmation.

The Thomas appointment demonstrated starkly the dilemma for the race created by the transformation of post–civil rights era black leadership. Thomas at a relatively young age fully embraced the right-wing agenda (whether sincerely or opportunistically is not clear) and thereby put himself on the fast track for a high-level systemic position, ultimately a seat on the Supreme Court, which makes him not only one of *Ebony*'s elite but one of the handful of blacks in the nation's power elite.[31] Yet during his confirmation hearings Thomas sought to win confirmation not on the basis of his conservative ideology but rather on the basis of his race and his inspiring struggle to overcome the handicaps of racism and poverty; up from slavery in the tradition of Booker T. Washington or from the ghetto in the tradition of Malcolm X. This created a dilemma for the traditional black leadership in arousing mass opposition to Thomas, since many blacks and a number of whites apparently supported Thomas on the basis of his racial background alone, notwithstanding his often-stated philosophical stance that race or affirmative action should not play a part in decisions of this sort.[32] Thus, by a skillful appeal to white racial guilt and black solidarity, blacks with views adverse to the interest of the race are able to advance in the system on the basis of race.

Yet, there is another aspect to this leadership dilemma. Unless traditional black leaders are prepared to argue that no self-respecting black should serve in right-wing administrations; that such administrations are so repugnant to the interests of blacks that black appointees could only be functionaries in the betrayal of the race; unless one is prepared to make this case—an arguable one that no one in the black leadership has argued—then it seems that their case against Thomas was inconsistent and contradictory. If right-wing presidents did not appoint blacks to high-level positions in the government then this too would be a cause for criticism from black leaders. Yet such appointments are not likely to be made unless the individuals are or at least act as if they are ideologically compatible with the appointing president. Thus, to call for a black successor to Justice Marshall and then criticize President Bush for choosing a black conservative is to fly in the face of the right's decision to use its powers to cultivate a new black leadership in its own image. Indeed, one can make the case (see Chapter 5) that Bush's HHS Secretary Louis Sullivan, who is a product of the traditional black establishment and the Republican Party's more moderate wing, nevertheless in the course of his work in the cabinet faithfully articulated and executed Bush's agenda on social policy. Yet, one rarely heard any criticism of his tenure, at least not from blacks.

Overall, then, the incipient incorporation of black leadership into systemic institutions and processes has had the perhaps predictable consequence of further isolating black leadership from the community it would purport to lead. And perhaps most ominously, this process of incorporation has encouraged the creation of a new cadre of authentically white-created black leaders. These consequences while perhaps predictable are nevertheless sad; sad because they can only bode conflict and confusion in the future and the further eroding of the much talked of leadership solidarity in the Afro-American freedom struggle as its enters its fourth century.

5

Blacks and Presidential Policy Making: Neglect, Policy, Symbols, and Cooptation

What differences has it made that in the last twenty years blacks have become routine participants in the presidential and congressional decision-making processes? An important assumption by proponents of black incorporation is that blacks will become advocates of black interests in the policy-making process; that where they have the capacity to make or influence decisions they will reflect the values of the group. The theoretical discussion in Chapter 1 suggests an alternative hypothesis about the consequences of incorporation, namely that rather than advancing the interests or values of the race, the consequence of institutionalization will instead be the adoption by individuals of the interests and values of the institutions; and the more powerful a person becomes within an institution the more likely he or she is to hold its values. It is essentially these alternative assumptions that we examine empirically in this and later chapters dealing with black participation during the last twenty years in presidential, congressional and Democratic Party institutional processes.

In this chapter the focus is on the presidency and executive branch decision making.[1] What can be said of the institutional legacy left behind by those blacks who have held high-level appointments in the executive branch? Did they work toward solving the problems of race? Did they have the president's ear? Were they effective? These are the questions examined in this chapter. The focus is on the post–civil rights era administrations—Nixon-Ford, Carter, Reagan and to an extent Bush—first because this period is the focus of the book as a whole but also because the phenomenon itself is largely a post–civil rights era one. Prior to the 1960s blacks simply were not a part of the executive branch of government. Black participation in executive policy making was generally limited to the occasional advice a president might seek informally from one or more blacks in whom he had personal confidence (Frederick Douglas's counsel to President Lincoln and Booker Washington's to Theodore Roosevelt are perhaps the best known instances of this practice), or to advice on racial matters from the so-called black cabinets that emerged in the administrations of William Taft and Franklin Roosevelt.[2] In the Kennedy and Johnson administrations the handful of black appointees would occasionally gather informally to discuss civil rights and related issues but overall blacks in the executive branch were by and large uninvolved in the formulation of the civil rights and Great Society initiatives of the 1960s.[3] Essentially, then, black participation in decisions of the executive on more than an occasional or ad hoc basis is a post–civil rights era phenomenon beginning with the Nixon administration.

The Nixon Administrations

As the first post–civil rights era president, Nixon appointed about thirty blacks to subcabinet positions in his administration. This represented at that time the largest number of African Americans ever to serve in the government, nearly three times the number appointed by President Johnson. Nixon had campaigned for office on a vaguely antiblack or anti–civil rights platform, with antibusing and law-and-order rhetoric designed to appeal to the unreconstructed white south and the Wallace vote. Consequently, unlike in 1960 when he received roughly a quarter of the black vote, in 1968 he received less than 10 percent. Nevertheless, consistent with the logic of incorporation or systemic integration ongoing when he took office, Nixon did not, indeed by 1969 could not, revert to the practice of the Eisenhower administration of excluding blacks from the government. Although probably in deference to his white southern constituency Nixon did not appoint a black to a highly visible cabinet post, he did make subcabinet appointments as well as appointments at the independent agencies and regulatory commissions.[4] The process of black incorporation by the late 1960s had become irreversible, party and ideology notwithstanding.

The Nixon administration came to power at about the same time that the black power principles of race solidarity and organization were being adopted by the black leadership establishment. This had an important effect on this new group of government officials, leading them early in the administration to form a separatist race group caucus called the Council of Black Appointees.[5] The significance of the group's formation was not in terms of its impact on policy but rather that in the late 1960s and early 1970s blacks in the administration felt they had a responsibility to try to advance the interests of the race in the councils of government. They did not see themselves as simply officials who merely happened to be black; rather, their sense of race consciousness and solidarity was such that they felt compelled to try to organize collectively to advance what they understood to be the interests of the race, even when these ran counter to the publicly stated position of the President. In all likelihood their sensitivity to their roles as race advocates was influenced by the salience of the ethos of black power during this period. This interpretation is supported to some extent by the fact that the kind of race solidarity and organization exhibited by blacks in the Nixon administration is not observed in subsequent administrations. In the Reagan administration in fact, the contrary is observed; black appointees, rather than challenging policies generally thought to be adverse to black interests, became instead their enthusiastic advocates. The Council of Black Appointees *as a group* sought to influence administration decision making on only one issue, school busing. This, however, was the most controversial race-specific issue during Nixon's tenure. This issue not only was a source of black-white tensions but it also divided the black community at both the elite and mass levels. Yet the black leadership establishment (from whence the leading blacks in the administration were drawn) was, publicly at least, united in support of court-ordered busing as one option to desegregate the schools, while the president was just as firmly committed to an antibusing policy as a strategic calculus to shore up his support among southern whites and among those northern blue-collar white voters who had supported George Wallace in the 1968 election. Thus, the issue throughout the late 1960s and early 1970s pitted the black establishment against the policy and political interests of the president. Black appointees in this conflict sided with the leadership of black America rather than their president.

During its first year the Nixon administration in an unprecedented act asked the federal courts to delay the desegregation of certain southern school systems. Although a unanimous Supreme Court rejected the request, this was the first time the federal government had intervened in court in opposition to school desegregation. This action sparked a revolt in the government's civil rights bureaucracy; attorneys in the Justice Department's Civil Rights Division filed a written protest, and several resigned. Leon Panetta, director of HEW's Office of Civil Rights, resigned in protest, and James Allen, the Commissioner of Education, was fired, in part for his strong opposition to administration policy. Later, in a nationwide television address the president proposed declaring a "moratorium" on all school busing for purposes of school desegregation until passage of his Equal Educational Opportunity Act, a bill which in effect nullified the right of the courts to order busing for purposes of school desegregation. Finally, Vice President Agnew suggested that the administration, if all else failed, would consider a constitu-

tional amendment to ban all busing for purposes of school desegregation. In response to these developments the Council of Black Appointees
prepared and sent to the president a detailed, formal position paper
setting forth its objections to the administration's proposals, particularly the idea raised by the vice president of a constitutional amendment. The president ignored the council's missive. A second paper was
sent and again no acknowledgement by the president or his senior staff.
Finally, feeling that the president (or his staff) was seeking to ignore
the group's statement, the council sent a third copy, and this time issued
a press release indicating that the group had sent a position paper to the
president relative to his school desegregation policy. The group emphasized that it was not its intention to publicly oppose the president, that
it remained loyal to the administration but felt the press attention was
the only way "to get around Nixon's palace guard and make sure he got
the statement and also to some extent to let the public know our position."[6] Asked what was the impact on the president's school desegregation policy of the council's efforts, Constance Newman, then chair-
person, replied, "Well, he did not support the constitutional
amendment and we would like to think we played some role in that, yet
we were of course disappointed by his support of antibusing legislation." Yet the president had never publicly supported a constitutional
amendment, and many Washington observers felt the Agnew statement was only a "trial balloon" floated to make the president's legislative proposals seem more responsible. Thus, on an issue perceived as of
signal importance to blacks, black appointees found it difficult to gain
even an audience with the president to present their position and on the
record had no impact on the eventual policy.

Feeling increasingly frustrated about their inability to have an
effect on the president's decision, and with black leaders attacking the
administration in increasingly harsh language (the NAACP's board
chairman called the administration the first openly antiblack administration since Woodrow Wilson's), black appointees decided to make
public their internal policy disagreements with the president. This was
done through a series of not-for-attribution interviews by several black
appointees with Paul Delaney, a black correspondent for the *New York
Times*. In the published story, the appointees urged the president to,
among other things, issue a "major policy statement" committing his
administration to equality of rights and an improvement in the enforcement of civil rights law. Otherwise, they implied, they might resign in
protest, raising the possibility that all senior-level blacks might leave the
government.[7] In spite of these efforts the administration continued to
pursue its antibusing rhetoric and policy proposals, and the black

appointees were powerless despite a year-long effort to affect the decision-making process. At least, however, the record shows that they tried, and on an issue of paramount political importance to the president.

If busing was the most controversial race issue during the late 1960s and early 1970s, by the end of the decade it had been replaced by affirmative action, the series of policies and programs designed to take race into account as means to overcome past patterns and practices of racism, to diversify educational institutions and the workplace and to enforce relevant provisions of the Civil Rights Act of 1964. Like busing, affirmative action is an issue that divides the nation on race lines, divides the black community but nevertheless is overwhelmingly supported by the black leadership establishment. Black appointees have been intimately involved in the shaping of national policy on affirmative action, going back to the Kennedy and Johnson administrations. The roles they have played during this thirty-year period provide interesting contrasts on the part played by black appointees in advancing the interests of the race. In the conservative Republican Nixon administration black appointees played an important role in developing affirmative action policy as we know it today, while in the Democratic Carter administration other black appointees sought to effectively destroy it.

The government developed and began to implement affirmative action in the Kennedy and Johnson administrations, but the process reached its full doctrinal and practical application in the Nixon administration in the form of its Philadelphia Plan.[8] The Philadelphia Plan began to take shape originally in the Johnson administration. Although the logic and procedures of the Philadelphia Plan have become the model for affirmative action programs in government, the academy and business, in areas such as university admissions, private and public employment and government contracting, it was originally designed to deal with the peculiar problems of discrimination in the construction industry.

In 1966 Labor Secretary Willard Wirtz created the Office of Federal Contract Compliance as the administrative unit to enforce Executive Order 11246.[9] As its first director he appointed Edward Sylvester, who was then a relatively low-level staff person in the department's international bureau. Graham writes that Sylvester had a reputation as a "tough, competent and dedicated administrator" and that "By 1967 the OFCC, like the EEOC but on a smaller scale, was accumulating a staff of activist blacks and white liberal reformers, whose zeal for enforcement mirrored that of their young, attractive and aggressive leaders—Edward Sylvester at OFCC and Clifford Alexander at the EEOC."[10] Sylvester shortly after taking office began to develop a plan to deal with discrimination in the construction trades. What he proposed was the "Cleveland Plan." Under its provisions local compliance committees were established. These committees, while not setting firm target numbers for black contractors, would require that before a final contract could be signed the winning bidder would be required to submit detailed reports that listed by trade or craft in all phases of the work the specific number of black workers to be hired. This plan resulted in protests from the AFL-CIO, business groups, the construction companies, conservative Republicans and liberal (labor-connected) Democrats in the Congress, who all charged that the Cleveland and later Philadelphia Plans in effect established de facto racial hiring quotas in violation of the 1964 Civil Rights Act. Because of this opposition in the Congress and elsewhere, the comptroller general (head of the Congress's independent General Accounting Office) was asked by members of Congress to review the plans in order to determine if they were consistent with government bidding and contracting procedures. The comptroller general ruled that Sylvester's plan was illegal not because of its alleged racial quotas but because it violated standard government bidding and contracting procedures which require that contracts be awarded "only on the basis of the lowest bid, with all specifications or requirements spelled out before the bidding." In other words, if a contractor were to be required to employ a targeted number of blacks this would have to be spelled out in advance in the invitation to bid. As Graham notes, this created for Sylvester a dilemma; if the plan required explicit numbers prior to the award of the contract then it would be called an illegal quota; but if the numbers remained vague then they would violate the comptroller general's ruling that bidders be specifically informed in advance of all requirements. Given the comptroller general's ruling and the widespread opposition, Sylvester was forced to rescind the plan.

In spite of his skillful and dedicated work, Sylvester left office in 1969 without having put into effect an effective plan to enforce nondiscrimination in employment by government contractors. This was in part because time ran out in the last year of Johnson's lame duck presidency and because of the opposition not only from business and congressional conservatives but liberals and labor, key constituent groups along with blacks in the Democratic party coalition.[11] One would have thought that any hope for the Sylvester Plan would have died with the election of the conservative, Republican business-oriented Nixon administration, especially given Nixon's election year anti–civil rights rhetoric. However, Sylvester's plan was revived, strengthened and implemented, and again this was in part a result of the skillful and dedicated work of two Nixon administration black appointees.

Nixon selected as his Labor Secretary George Schultz, an economist at the University of Chicago with a reputation as a moderate on civil rights and race issues. Shultz, for reasons that are not entirely clear from the records reviewed by Graham and Hood, apparently decided to revive the Sylvester Plan and was able to persuade the president to go along. Whatever the reasons, the Nixon administration, in spite of the opposition of business and congressional conservatives, embraced the Johnson administration's affirmative action strategy. Shultz reorganized the Department and created a new assistant secretary for Wage and Labor Standards, with the head of OFCC reporting to him rather than directly to the secretary. For this new position he choose Arthur Fletcher, a black Republican who had run for Lieutenant Governor in Washington. Fletcher said when asked to take the job, he insisted on two things: one, that he be allowed to make equal employment a "labor standard" and two, that he be allowed to pick his own deputy who would head OFCC. In fact, Fletcher in a personal interview told me, "The Philadelphia Plan was my baby. When I came in there was no specific standard for equal opportunity. It was viewed as social engineering and not as labor standard enforceable at law. So, one of my conditions for accepting the job was that I could make equal opportunity a labor standard. When Shultz asked me to take the job this is what I told him." Fletcher overstates his role, overlooking, for example, the origins of the Philadelphia Plan in the Johnson administration and Shultz's leadership. It is probably more accurate to say as Graham writes that "Fletcher presided with Shultz's blessings over the redesign of the Philadelphia Plan."[12]

With his deputy John Wilks (also black) at OFCC, Fletcher set about immediately to revise the Sylvester Plan in a way that would overcome the objections of GAO. The revised plan issued six months after he took office avoided the quota issue by establishing target goals for minority employment which bidders would agree to try to meet. The GAO objection was met by the plan's prohibition on any negotiations after contracts were awarded. In announcing the plan Fletcher indicated that it would eventually apply not only to Philadelphia but to all cities across the country "as soon as possible" and he forthrightly defended goals or targets for black employment as "necessary because of historic segregation and discrimination."[13] The comptroller general ruled that Fletcher's revised plan was still illegal, this time because it used race or national origin as a determinative factor in employment decisions which, he held, was a violation of Title VII of the Civil Rights Act.[14] Opponents said then, as they do now, that the notion of targets or goals were simply euphemisms for racial quotas. After a series of congressional hearings, opponents of the plan in the Senate passed an amendment to an appropriations bill that prohibited the expenditure of any federal funds on any contract which the comptroller general holds to be in contravention of any federal stature. After intense lobbying by Shultz and the president, the House rejected this amendment by a vote of 208 to 156. A majority of House Democrats (including many northern liberals) voted for the amendment while Republicans opposed it by a margin of 124 to 41. The irony here of course is that affirmative action received its initial legislative ratification over the objections of the Democratic majority in Congress and only with the support of the conservative Republican president and legislative majorities.[15] Twenty years later this ideological and partisan alignment on affirmative action is completely reversed, as indicated by the debate and vote on the Civil Rights Act of 1991 (see Chapter 6).

Given the amendment's defeat, Fletcher and Wilks shortly thereafter issued a revised order applying principles and procedures of the Philadelphia Plan to *all* government contractors. This was a radical change in policy, since Sylvester's original affirmative action plan was ostensibly narrowly designed to address the unique problems of racism in the craft unions, where there were ample empirical findings to establish employment discrimination. This new order simply assumed historical racism or discrimination and applied the Philadelphia Plan nationwide, covering by Fletcher's estimate from one third to one half of the national workforce. This new order led to renewed attacks from congressional opponents, but to no avail, and the order in its final form was issued in February 1970. It required government contractors (with contracts of at least $50,000 and fifty or more employees) to file an acceptable affirmative action plan that would include (1) an analysis of all job categories to determine the underutilization of minorities (underutilization was defined as having fewer minorities in a particular job category than would reasonably be expected by their availability in the relevant labor force) and (2) a specific plan with goals and timetables to correct any identified underutilization.

This revised and extended Philadelphia Plan subsequently became the model for voluntary affirmative action programs throughout American society. It is today the source of bitter partisan, ideological and race conflict. The key point for purposes of this analysis is that the policy is substantially the result of the work of black appointees—Sylvester in Johnson's administration and Fletcher and Wilks in Nixon's—who used their positions in government to advance a policy that they perceived to be in the interests of blacks. This case shows that black appointees did make a difference. As Graham writes, "what was new by 1970 was the growing insider role of the civil rights lobby within the executive establishment. . . ."[16] This insider role of blacks in the executive branch has grown substantially in numbers since 1970. However, the policy impact or consequence has not been commensurate. Indeed, the early years of the Nixon administration in many ways represents the high point of black attempts to shape executive branch decision making.

The Carter Administration

President Carter appointed three times more blacks to high-level office than did President Nixon. Yet, a review of the record of the Carter presidency on issues of concern to blacks shows this relatively large number of persons had only a marginal effect on decision making. Although blacks in the Carter administration did not form a separatist caucus or council, black appointees did meet on an ad hoc, informal basis on several occasions in order to discuss race-related issues. Several respondents to the mail questionnaire said that a formal organization was unnecessary because of their larger number and the greater power and prestige of Carter appointees compared to those in the Nixon administration. One respondent put it this way:

> I do not see the need for a Black coalition of executive branch officials to address policy issues in this administration since there are adequate numbers in high positions in the various agencies. Each of these officials is in a position to effect policy changes in his or her own agency and to achieve coordination with other agencies. Meetings of Blacks are important for purposes of education and communication rather than for purposes of unified action.

Yet there was widespread support for the idea of race solidarity and collective responsibility. For example, 85 percent (seventeen out of twenty) of the respondents answered affirmatively the question: "In general, do you think it useful for blacks in the administration to get together and discuss common problems and seek to influence administration policies of special relevance to blacks?" One subcabinet officer explained:

> I believe there is a need for Blacks in this administration to work collectively as a group as well as individually in their respective positions in order to see that policies and programs are developed to address the needs of Black people. And I think it is very

necessary for Black leaders, both in and out of this administration to discuss common problems and seek ways to influence the
needed change. In addition, I believe there should be a focus upon
organizing support bases in the Black community so there will be
an even greater coalition which can influence the political process and the formulation of policy. I see this kind of involvement
of Blacks in this administration as part of the contribution they
can make to enlarge the role of blacks in the nation's economy. We
are in the same cause and therefore we must work together to create opportunities and greater accomplishments of Blacks.

Thus, whatever the record shows in terms of the actual effect of these
individuals on race-related policy decisions, it is clear that most were
inclined to try to use their positions to advance the interests of the race.

Andrew Young, President Carter's fellow Georgian and his principal supporter among black leaders during the campaign, was the
most prominent black appointee in the administration. In the scores of
books and memoirs reviewed, he is by far the most frequently mentioned black official in the administration. Most of the references, however, are to the role he played in Carter's 1976 campaign, the significance of a black as the first United Nations ambassador, his often
controversial remarks and to his firing as a result of an unauthorized
meeting with representatives of the Palestine Liberation Organization.
Gaddis Smith's observations are typical: "President Carter's appointment of Andrew Young as United States Ambassador to the United
Nations, the first black to hold such a high diplomatic position, was a
signal to both Africans and to a domestic constituency. He immediately became an uninhibited spokesman who won acclaim among black
African leaders and caused consternation among South African whites
and some conservative Americans because he belittled the Soviet
threat."[17] Young clearly thought he had a special mandate to participate in shaping U.S. foreign policy toward Africa, especially southern
Africa. And, as Smith points out, he had a view (consistent with that of
most black leaders) that U.S. policy in the region reflected too much
concern with the Soviet threat and not enough with African issues on
their merits. In this view, Young in Carter policy deliberations was
allied with his nominal superior, Cyrus Vance, the secretary of state,
while Zbigniew Brzezinski, the national security advisor, took the traditional cold war view that the major threat to American interests in the
region was the Soviet-Cuban presence.[18] Abernathy writes that the
administration eventually established as its goal in the region to "set in
motion a peaceful and progressive transformation of South Africa

toward a biracial democracy . . . while forging elsewhere a coalition of moderate black leaders in order to stem continual radicalization and eliminate the Soviet-Cuban presence from the continent."[19] And he writes, "Andrew Young played a key role."[20] Other sources, however, are less clear on the goals of U.S. policy in the region or Young's role in shaping it. Mollenhoff writes that it is unclear what Young's influence on the president was in terms of African policy;[21] and Smith concluded that it was inconsequential. In fact he argues that "Young was fired because of his unauthorized conversations with a Palestinian leader, but more generally because his philosophy was contrary to the administration's new direction. African policy now reflected more concern with meeting Soviet influence and less with African issues per se."[22] Overall, then, the evidence of Ambassador Young's influence on administration decision making in his area of special interests and concern is ambiguous.[23] He certainly made an effort to turn U.S. policy away from its cold war mentality in southern Africa; what is ambiguous is how effective he was in his efforts.

Aside from Young, HUD Secretary Harris is the most frequently mentioned appointee. Shull writes that she had good rapport with Carter and frequently sent him memos with recommendations on housing and welfare policy.[24] Several sources indicate that she played a major role in shaping Carter's welfare reform and urban policy proposals.[25] The urban policy proposal was the first attempt by a president to develop a comprehensive approach to the nation's urban problems.[26] It therefore resulted in a range of jurisdictional disputes between HUD, HEW and the Departments of Commerce, Labor and Agriculture. Early in 1977 Carter appointed Harris to chair an interagency task force—the Urban and Regional Policy Group—to manage these jurisdictional disputes and to develop the administration's urban policy.

Harris's task force proceeded slowly until the Urban League's Vernon Jordan in a July 1977 speech attacked the administration for its inattention to urban and minority problems. Jordan's attack angered the president but resulted in instructions to his staff and to Harris's task force to speed up development of the urban policy proposals.[27] With the active involvement of Stuart Eizenstat, the president's principal domestic policy advisor, Harris's task force in late October prepared a draft report recommending to the president that the administration's urban policy focus exclusively on the nation's largest, most distressed central cities and that all existing federal programs be targeted toward these cities in a comprehensive strategy. The task force also proposed additional targeted programs at a cost of ten to twenty billion dollars. After this document was leaked to the press, conserva-

tives and rural and suburban members of congress criticized the proposed policy because of its central city focus and its cost. President
Carter then directed Harris to revise the proposal to remove its exclusive focus on central cities and drastically scale back its costs. At this
point, Eizenstadt and the White House staff increased their role in the
policy formulation process and Harris's role in the development of the
final policy apparently diminished.[28] The final Carter urban policy submitted to the Congress was a scaled-down version of Harris's original
recommendations, focusing less on the largely black central cities and
with no additional money for targeted programs.

In the case of urban policy, then, Harris developed a fairly bold
program to deal with the problems of the cities but in the end was
unable to persuade the president to embrace it as administration policy.
It is also useful to point out here that the spark for early movement on
urban policy came not from Harris but from Vernon Jordan's speech.
Wolman and Merget write that Jordan's "remarks, as a highly respected
spokesman from a core of the President's constituency galvanized the
Administration into action and constituted a turning point in the urban
policy process."[29] The policy developed by Harris generated opposition from other important elements of Carter's constituency—conservatives and rural and suburban interests—and this plus the president's
own fiscal conservatism meant that in the end Harris could not carry the
day in the final decisions of the administration.

Carter's fiscal conservatism also affected the development of comprehensive welfare reform. The administration's welfare reform proposals contemplated consolidating a number of in-kind welfare grants
into a comprehensive reform program that would increase welfare benefits and provide more than a million jobs for welfare recipients, without any outlay of additional funds. As part of this strategy HEW Secretary Califano proposed that HUD's housing subsidies be "cashed out"
to pay for welfare reform. Harris objected to this approach to financing,
writing in a memorandum to the president that Califano's proposal
"robbed the poor to pay the poor."[30] In the end, while Carter rejected the
idea of a total cash-out of rent supplements, he did agree over what
Califano calls Harris's "intense objections" to transfer part of HUD's
rent subsidies to finance higher welfare benefits.[31]

If the Young and Harris records reveal some attempts on their
parts to advance race interests in administration decision making on
issues within their scopes of responsibility,[32] the records of the next two
persons—Drew Days and Wade McCree at the Department of Justice—
show the opposite. During the Johnson and Nixon administrations,
black appointees played important roles in the development and imple-

mentation of affirmative action as national policy. Ironically, in the
Carter administration Days and McCree sought to destroy their work
by taking the now familiar right-wing view that it is impermissible
under the Constitution for the government to take race into account in
order to remedy historical or institutional racism or to diversify the
nation's workplace or institutions of higher education. McCree, the
solicitor general, and Days, the assistant attorney general for civil rights,
were both men with distinguished legal credentials, both card-carrying
members of the liberal black establishment. They were also appointed
largely because they were black. Carter's nomination for attorney gen-
deral of his friend, Georgia appeals court judge Griffin Bell, resulted
in criticism from blacks, who alleged thatBell had a record of insensitivity if not hostility to civil rights. In part to appease his critics, Bell
selected McCree and Days to run the department's two divisions most
responsible for civil rights decision making.

Early in their tenure, Days and McCree were confronted with the
case of *Regents of the University of California v. Bakke* (438, U.S. 265, 1978).
Bakke was the first case to reach the Court in which the issue of racial
preferences and quotas were unambiguously raised in terms of their
legality under Title VII of the Civil Rights Act and/or the equal protection clause of the Fourteenth Amendment. The case generated enormous press coverage and controversy and was widely viewed by civil
rights leaders as the most important case on race to reach the Court
since the *Brown* school desegregation cases. Days and McCree worked
closely on the case in terms of its policy, legal and constitutional implications.[33] The case was, as then EEOC Chair Eleanor Holmes Norton
put it later, "not without difficulty, raising novel constitutional and
statutory questions,"[34] but blacks in the civil rights community, in
Congress and in the executive branch undoubtedly felt that a way
would be found by Days and McCree to resolve the issues in a manner
that would uphold the principles of affirmative action. This feeling was
surely reinforced when Attorney General Bell said he would go along
with whatever decisions Days and McCree made. This assumption was
quickly laid to rest when it was learned that Days and McCree had
declined a request by Archibald Cox, counsel for the University of California, to support his brief that upheld the legality and constitutionality of the University's special admissions program setting aside sixteen
of one hundred slots for minority students.

The first draft of the brief prepared by McCree's office took the
position that the very principle of affirmative action—not the issue of
quotas, but the very principle itself—violated the equal protection
clause of the Constitution. The brief said "we doubt that it is *ever* proper

to use race to close any portion of the class for competition by members of all races" and that "racial classifications favorable to minority groups are presumptively unconstitutional."[35] This draft was leaked to the press and immediately caused a firestorm of criticism in the civil rights and black leadership community. President Carter had early on queried McCree about the direction of the brief but was politely told that the traditional independence and deference due to the solicitor's office made it inappropriate to respond. Stuart Eizenstadt insisted that the president not only had a right to see the brief but also the right to have his views expressed in it. Reluctantly McCree transmitted through the attorney general a copy of the brief to the White House. On reviewing the draft, Eizenstadt told Carter that it was "analytically flawed" but more importantly that politically it was a "disaster" because it would put the administration on record as opposing affirmative action and would damage relations with blacks, a core Democratic constituency. The Congressional Black Caucus and other senior blacks in the administration were holding meetings and attempting to arrange conferences with the president and McCree in order to force a change in the brief.[36] They were joined by Vice President Mondale and HEW Secretary Califano in memorandum and at a cabinet meeting in urging the president to direct the attorney general to request the solicitor to rewrite the brief. Although McCree was reportedly outraged by what he considered unseemly political pressure, eventually the draft was revised and the final brief filed with the Court asked that the principle of affirmative action and the use of race-conscious admission procedures be upheld, while urging that the instant case be returned to the California courts for further consideration.[37]

This case study shows in perhaps the starkest way the limits of institutional incorporation, integration or cooptation. Even when drawn from the mainstream of the black establishment, blacks do not necessarily see their responsibilities once in government in the same way they might have in their noninstitutional positions. Days, the former NAACP Legal Defense Fund Counsel, told the *New York Times* prior to his confirmation:

> I have been in a position at the Legal Defense Fund in which I could advocate a specific view—one that was primarily black though it has benefitted whites as well. If confirmed, I expect the same opportunity to work for the vindication of constitutional rights; but because I will be responsible for formulating policy that affects the entire government, there will be more considerations I will have to weigh.[38]

Similarly, Dreyfuss and Lawrence describe McCree during *Bakke* as struggling with "conflicting roles as representative of the United States and President Carter's spokesman" but "His color made him spokesman for blacks and other minority groups whether he liked it or not."[39] And Sindler writes that at one point during the debate about the brief, McCree rejected suggestions that he be "true to the black community," arguing that "I have to be true to myself."[40] This notion of conflicting loyalties, race interests versus personal convictions, institutional roles versus race group solidarity is examined more closely in the concluding part of this chapter; but here follows an examination of the Reagan and Bush administrations where this problem of institutional loyalties and conflicts among black appointees took on a new and more ominous dimension.[41]

The Reagan and Bush Administrations

Forty-nine books or memoirs on the Reagan administration were reviewed and the indices were searched for information about twelve senior-level black appointees and on eleven race-related issues including the renewal of the Voting Rights Act, the Bob Jones case, Executive Order 11246, South Africa and welfare reform. In these sources, entries were found on only four senior level officials—HUD Secretary Samuel Pierce, National Security Advisor Colin Powell, EEOC Chair Clarence Thomas and Clarence Pendleton, Chair of the Civil Rights Commission. In addition, two low-level black White House staff aides were mentioned in connection with the Bob Jones tuition tax exemption controversy.

Of the four senior level black officials, most of the material is on Pierce (except for Powell; there is considerable material on his role in national security decision making, which I do not include here given my focus on issues of race). References to Thomas and Pendleton are limited largely to discussion of the circumstances of their appointments. For example, in an essay by Robert Thompson in Tinsley Yarbourgh's edited volume *The Reagan Administration and Human Rights*, Pendleton's appointment is described in terms of his long-time association with Reagan aide Edwin Meese. Thompson writes, "Pendleton's principal [qualification] . . . seems to have been his association with Ed Meese whose views on civil rights were consistent with those of the administration."[42] Thompson also quotes Pendleton as telling a reporter that his views on affirmative action were consistent with Reagan's because "whatever the administration's policy is in this respect, I have no choice but to support that policy."[43] And several sources refer to

Pendleton's dissent in a 1982 Civil Rights Commission report endorsing busing for purposes of school desegregation. In one case the sources differ as to Pendleton's role. Early in the administration the Civil Rights Commission requested that executive departments and agencies submit information on their civil rights enforcement activities and affirmative action. The Departments of Labor and Education refused. The commission then threatened to issue a subpoena. Thompson indicates that Pendleton voted against the subpoena,[44] while Dugger reports that he joined with his fellow commissioners in the threat to issue the subpoena if needed to obtain the information (the subpoena was not issued as the two departments voluntarily supplied the material).[45] Most of the sources, however, deal with Pierce's role in administration decision making on issues relevant to his department and on race issues generally.

Before turning to Pierce's impact on presidential policy making it should be noted that not only did Reagan administration blacks not form a formal organization, most came into office determined not to follow the traditional pattern of black appointees focusing on "black issues." Rather they (and the president) argued that blacks in the administration would carry out their official responsibilities and would not as blacks seek to shape administration policies on race issues unless such issues came within the purview of their official duties. In other words, there was to be no collective action by blacks in the Reagan administration in behalf of black interests. As Edwin Meese told a pre-inaugural meeting of black conservatives "[black appointees] are not going to be ambassadors to black people. They're going to be there because they have a substantive role to fulfill."[46] However, by 1982 as a result of attacks by black civil rights and political leaders on administration budget and race policies, the administration reversed course. The president formally designated Melvin Bradley, the senior black on the White House staff, as special assistant with responsibility for "continuously monitoring the impact of all administration policies on minorities and the disadvantaged," and several senior-level black appointees indicated that they would begin to meet occasionally to discuss administration policies on blacks and propose recommendations to the president and his senior advisors.[47]

Samuel Pierce as the only black cabinet member dealt not only with issues relevant to his department but with the full range of race-related or civil rights issues. Unlike Pendleton, Thomas and most other senior black appointees, Pierce was not a new right conservative or "Reaganut," rather he was a product of the eastern, liberal Republican tradition. Evans and Novak describe Pierce as the "only bona fide liberal" in the cabinet.[48] Liberal is an exaggeration here, since except for civil rights Pierce described himself as a "true believer" in the Reagan revolution, arguing, "I really believe his programs are grounded on solid economic principles. . . . The one area where I might differ—and this applies more to several top aides than to the president—is in the area of civil rights. I've spoken to the president about civil rights on several occasions. He has assured me that he's committed to racial justice. And I believe that."[49] Pierce did play an important role in administration deliberations on civil rights issues during his tenure but before turning to this, his role at HUD is examined.

Evans and Novak describe Pierce as a liberal because, they write, he was Reagan's "only constant adversary" who "constantly defended HUD programs that had been growing since the days of LBJ's Great Society."[50] Other accounts differ on Pierce's role in defending his department's programs. Dugger describes the massive cuts in the HUD budget and concludes that Pierce was not much different from the rest of the administration except for being black.[51] Similarly, Brownstein refers to Pierce's "steady dismantling of Johnson's Great Society programs."[52] What seems to distinguish evaluation of Pierce's tenure at HUD is effort versus results. Stockman, Evans and Novak and even Brownstein seem to agree that in internal administration discussions Pierce made an effort to defend some of HUD's programs from the massive budget cuts proposed by the White House budget office but that he generally failed. One exception, noted by several sources, is Pierce's successful defense of HUD's Urban Development Action Grants (UDAG), which provided for local economic development projects. Stockman writes that he wanted to eliminate the program. "But Secretary of Housing and Urban Development Sam Pierce launched a noisy campaign to spare this turkey, and soon the White House switch board was flooded with HUD orchestrated distress calls from local Republican mayors and businessmen who happened to be in the redevelopment and construction business."[53] With this exception, the sources indicate that Stockman won every budget battle with Pierce, with the results that in his tenure Pierce presided over the near total decimation of government support for low and moderate income housing, seeing budget authority drop from $35 billion in 1980 to $10 billion by 1988, representing the largest decline in budget authority and appropriations than in any other domestic program category.[54] His private misgivings notwithstanding, Pierce before Congress and in the press ardently defended these massive cuts.[55] Thus, the record here is one of effort, *perhaps*, but little effectiveness in defending programs that disproportionately benefitted low income Americans, particularly blacks. Therefore Pierce's effectiveness as an advocate of black interests cannot be established on the basis of his record at HUD. And to some extent even his dedication to the preservation of HUD programs might be questioned, given his "true believer" commitment to Reaganomics. Pierce, for example, said that while the cuts hurt blacks they were necessary to turn the economy around.[56]

On civil rights issues the available studies indicate that Pierce was both more active and effective. Pierce departed from the administration's civil rights stance, and he argued that he felt "a special responsibility to tell the administration what's on the minds of black Americans."[57] Pierce was involved in administration decision making on all the major civil rights issues. In his own area of responsibility—the implementation of antidiscrimination in the sale and rental of housing—Pierce is credited with persuading Reagan to support strengthening the enforcement provisions of the Fair Housing Act of 1968.[58] The Fair Housing Amendments of 1988 were introduced during the Carter administration and by the 1980s enjoyed widespread congressional support; however, the law as Lamb writes "was plainly inconsistent" with Reagan's previous record on civil rights. Enforcement of antidiscrimination in housing under the 1968 act was limited to expensive and time-consuming pattern or practice litigation by the Justice Department or through "conference, conciliation and persuasion" by HUD. Given the well-documented continuation of pervasive housing discrimination since passage of the 1968 act, most authorities were agreed that the enforcement provisions were inadequate.[59] Under the 1988 amendments, when HUD conciliation fails, the department may issue a "discrimination charge" and the Justice Department is then obligated to pursue the matter as a civil suit, if the parties agree to choose federal court resolution of the charges. If the parties do not choose to go to court, the HUD Secretary may refer the case to an administrative law judge within the department. If the law judge finds that the discrimination charge is valid he may provide relief in the form of damages, attorney's fees and civil penalties of up to $50,000. These provisions in the minds of most observers added "teeth to fair housing policy for the first time."[60]

Outside of his responsibilities at HUD, Pierce was also involved in administration decision making on renewal of the Voting Rights Act in 1982, on maintenance of the affirmative action Executive Order 11246 and on the Bob Jones tax exemption controversy. On each of these issues he appears to have had some moderating effect on the anti–civil rights posture of Reagan and his more conservative cabinet secretaries and White House aides. Although Pierce was attacked in the press for supporting a provision that would have allowed states to "bail out" from the Voting Rights Act's preclearance provision (which requires covered jurisdictions to clear any proposed changes in their election processes with the Justice Department on a showing that they had ended discrimination), he argues that in cabinet deliberations he only did this as a means of laying before the president all of his options but that he from the outset strongly urged the president to support a straightforward extension of the Act for twenty-five years, including the controversial effects rather intent standard of proof.[61] Reagan initially rejected the effects test and supported the bail-out provisions, positions which Pierce says "disappointed" him. In the end, however, under pressure from moderate congressional Republicans, Reagan reluctantly signed the 1982 Voting Rights Act which included the effects test as supported by Pierce and the civil rights lobby.

Similarly, in White House deliberations on Executive Order 11246, Pierce supported the position of the civil rights lobby. Going back to its origins with the Philadelphia Plan, conservatives had inveighed against the order, arguing that it mandated quotas. During his campaigns for president, Reagan had implied that he would use his "stroke of the pen" authority to revoke or at least substantially modify the order. In the end he refused to do either. Administration conservatives including Edwin Meese, Education Secretary William Bennett and White House aide Patrick Buchhann in meetings urged the president to directly revoke the order. They were joined by two leading blacks with civil rights responsibilities—EEOC Chair Thomas and Pendleton of the Civil Rights Commission. Pierce by contrast joined with cabinet "moderates," including Secretary of State Shultz (who of course had proposed the order as Nixon's Labor Secretary), Labor Secretary William Brock and Transportation Secretary Elizabeth Dole, in arguing that the order on its merits was a necessary tool to fight job discrimination and that it did not require quotas; and the merits aside they argued that to revoke the order or substantially revise it would lead to great controversy and in all likelihood would be reversed by congressional action.[62] Pierce's support for the order may have been crucial, given the views of Thomas and Pendleton and their civil rights policy responsibilities. Put another way, if he had joined Thomas and Pendleton in opposing the order this may have tipped the scales for the president, given his long-time hostility to affirmative action and his campaign promise.[63]

In 1980 the Republican platform pledged that the party would "halt the unconstitutional regulatory vendetta launched by Mr. Carter's IRS against independent schools."[64] The reference was to a twelve-year order issued by Nixon, not Carter, denying tax exemptions to schools

practicing racial segregation. It was issued as a means to stop the prolif-
eration of segregated private schools in the south after implementation of
the *Brown* school desegregation decree. It, like executive order 11246,
had long rankled conservatives and fundamentalist Christians who
argued that it interfered with religious freedom. This was the case with
Bob Jones University which, although it had a few black students, prohibited on religious grounds interracial dating. In this context, Reagan in
early 1982 approved an order by the Treasury Department revoking the
IRS order. Barrett writes, "none of the black staff members was consulted in any way and no one suggested that it would have deep reso-
nance among blacks."[65] It did, however, create heated criticisms not only
by blacks but also in the Congress and the press. And public opinion
polls indicated that three-fourths of the public opposed tax exemptions
for schools practicing racial segregation. As a result of these criticisms
Reagan, who claimed to be surprised by the reaction, called on Melvin
Bradley and Thaddus Garrett, a black aide to Vice President Bush, to
get their reactions. Bradley, who had worked for Reagan while he was
Governor and was the only black on the White House staff, was not
consulted prior to Reagan's decision because as Barrett writes, "he was
too far down the pecking order and rarely saw the President."[66] Bradley
and Garrett told Reagan they were dissatisfied with his decision and
that the blacks they had talked to were also unhappy. Then Reagan is
said to have said, "We can't let this stand. We have to do something."
and called Pierce over to discuss the best way to get out of the situation.[67] Pierce urged Reagan to simply admit a bureaucratic error and
revoke the Treasury Department's order. After further high-level review,
Reagan partially reversed the decision by agreeing to submit legislation
to Congress that would by stature reverse his decision and codify the
executive order. However, pending congressional action, he allowed
the IRS to continue to grant tax exemptions to Bob Jones and similarly
situated schools. In a sense he could have it both ways, satisfying to
some extent both his white southern conservative constituency and his
critics. Reagan's decision and proposed legislation were rendered moot
by the Supreme Court's decision in the Bob Jones case in which it held
(eight to one) that exemptions for discriminatory schools violated the
nondiscrimination policy embodied in the 1964 Civil Rights Act.[68]

This case illustrates in an interesting way the role that blacks may
play in the decision-making processes of the executive. First, on an
issue of obvious (except perhaps to Reagan) interest to blacks, they
were completely left out of the process until it became politically dam-
aging to the president. Then their advice was sought but it was only
partially heeded. At least it might be said that these persons once con-

sulted did the right thing. This shows perhaps that it is useful to have even invisible blacks around, although one wonders what the situation might have been if the individuals consulted by Reagan had been Clarence Thomas and Pendleton rather than Bradley and Garrett.

It is too early to do a detailed analysis of the Bush administration; there are as yet no books or memoirs documenting its decision-making processes.[69] Thus, this brief analysis relies largely on press accounts of decision making on race-related issues and the activities of black appointees. The administration's most controversial race-related decision—apart from its machinations about the Civil Rights Act of 1990–91—involved a proposal to abolish race-based scholarship in colleges and universities. This surprise decision was announced by a black man, Michael Williams, the assistant secretary of education in charge of civil rights. Williams claimed that he was prompted to make the policy change in response to the decision by the University of Arizona's Fiesta Bowl to contribute $100,000 to each participant school in the 1991 game in order to establish a scholarship for minority students in the memory of Martin Luther King, Jr.[70] Such scholarships are widespread throughout the academy, including the National Science Foundation's doctoral and postdoctoral awards to minority students. They have been viewed as a critical component of programs to diversify the nation's college and university student bodies. Williams claimed, however, that such scholarships violated Title VII of the 1964 Civil Rights Act, which prohibits discrimination on the grounds of race in any program receiving federal assistance. Williams's announcement led to widespread criticisms from nearly all quarters except right-wing conservatives. As a result President Bush, claiming that he and his staff had not been informed beforehand of Williams's decision, ordered it suspended while a comprehensive review of the issue was undertaken by the White House staff and the Department of Education.[71] In doing so, Bush praised Williams as an "extraordinary, sensitive, very intelligent person," noting that because of his race no one could accuse him of making the decision on a racist basis.[72] Bush's argument here points to the dilemma for the black community in the post–civil rights era of having blacks in high places taking actions adverse to the black community and then having their white bosses say "Oh, the decision cannot be racist because the decision maker is black." Historically, blacks are familiar with this kind of racial manipulation, as it goes back to what Malcolm X referred to as the field negro and the house negro, or simply, the notion of the Uncle Tom. However, Bush's remark probably resonates well among some white Americans; and it is a skillful way to advance policies adverse to black interests.

Williams claimed he did not act on instructions from the White House, although he said he consulted with what he called "lower-level White House aides who were friends and acquaintances."[73] Nevertheless, his actions were not inconsistent with Bush's veto of the Civil Rights Act of 1990 and the conservative movement's general hostility to affirmative action. It is possible therefore to interpret the whole incident as simply the use by whites of a pliable black man to advance their policy agenda on race. This interpretation is strengthened by several other facts about the incident. First, in testimony before a House subcommittee it was revealed that Williams in fact did not originate the letter to the Fiesta Bowl but that the idea was developed by Williams's white deputy, Richard Kramer, who was advised by the rabidly conservative Washington Legal Foundation.[74] Second, the Department of Education really did not alter the Williams decision; rather, in essence the new rule it proposed said that scholarships granted exclusively to minorities did violate Title VII but that race could be used as a factor in such awards, if it was not an obligatory criteria.[75] Finally, the administration's flip-flop on the issue and its deliberately ambiguous revised rule sent a signal to conservative opponents of affirmative action to challenge minority-based scholarships in the courts. At this writing the Washington Legal Foundation has two cases working their way through the courts on the basis of Williams's reasoning in the Fiesta Bowl letter.[76]

A final aspect of this two-sided nature of black appointees was raised in an interesting way by the comments of California Congressman Fortney Stark regarding Health and Human Services Secretary Louis Sullivan, the only black member of the Bush cabinet. Stark caused a stir by calling Sullivan a "disgrace to his race" because of his failure to support a comprehensive national health insurance program.[77] In the early years of the Bush administration, national health care became a major policy and political issue; however, the idea of national health insurance has long been a major item on the post–civil rights era black agenda, usually ranking number two just behind full employment. Stark, Chairman of the House Ways & Means Subcommittee on Health, argued that as a black man it was Sullivan's moral responsibility to support national health insurance, particularly because a disproportionately large number of those without health insurance are black.[78] In opposing such a program Stark said Sullivan had "turned his back on the poor, most of whom are minorities. . . . Louis Sullivan comes as close to being a disgrace to his profession and his race as anybody I have seen in the cabinet. . . . He came here suggesting he wanted to help the impoverished, now he wants to help the health companies and private enterprise."[79] Sullivan responded with anger to Stark's remarks saying "I wish he had the guts to say that to my face. It's too bad ultra liberals like Pete Stark haven't progressed to the point that they can accept the independent thinking of a black man that does not conform to their own stereotypical views."[80] Yet Stark's "stereotypical" view of Sullivan is simply the view of most blacks; that blacks in power ought to use their positions of power to advance the interests of the race and not simply to go along to get along. With respect to national health insurance, as Stark suggests, Sullivan became a loyal front man to advance policies not of his own making, and arguably adverse to the interests of his race.[81] Stark, the first white to seek membership in the Congressional Black Caucus, was strongly criticized in the press and by his Republican colleagues in the House and later apologized for injecting race into the debate, but nevertheless repeated his criticism of Sullivan for supporting Bush administration policies that he argues are hostile to minorities and the poor.[82]

In its second year the White House Office of Policy Development and its director William Roper convened a series of meetings of domestic subcabinet officials and outside experts on poverty and urban policy to discuss possible new strategies to attack problems of poverty and the urban underclass. Several promising options were discussed, including (1) large-scale community intervention in high poverty areas to include expanded family planning services, expansion of tax credits for the working poor, block grants for investment in poor children, national minimum child support benefits supported by federal funds to supplement income; (2) uniform national welfare benefits; (3) consolidation of all federal benefits in a single office for ease of access; and (4) an increase in welfare benefits in states with the highest poverty rates.[83] All of these proposals were rejected because they were thought to be too expensive or because they were thought to be too liberal for a conservative Republican administration.[84] In the discussion within the administration of these proposals so important to black people, blacks were invisible; not a part of the subcabinet group or among the outside experts who reached the decision that the administration should continue to neglect the problems of poverty and the ghetto underclass.

Conclusion

Until the advent of the Reagan and Bush administrations it may be generally said that black appointees did try to represent the interests of the race as these are conventionally understood. On the range of race-related issues of the last twenty-five years—school desegregation, affirmative action, voting rights, housing discrimination and South Africa policy—the evidence reviewed here, while not definitive, suggests that they brought into the government the perspectives of the black community.[85] Yet, as Holden writes:

> No executive appointee, no senior bureaucrat, automatically represents the "interest" with which he has in the past been most identified merely because of past identification. The bureaucratic enterprise contains its own incentives which impose directions and constraints upon the functionary. Thus, it is fatuous to expect that a Black functionary will automatically "represent Black interests" or that if he attempts to do this he will automatically be effective, without some external relationships. The bureaucracy, like Congress, depends on constituency relationship.[86]

The evidence reviewed here shows how the incentives or imperatives of the "bureaucratic enterprise" or the logic of institutionalization shaped the behavior of black appointees in several administrations, perhaps most dramatically in the cases of Days and McCree on affirmative action in the Carter administration and Sullivan on national health insurance in the Bush administration. Holden's observation also calls attention to the fact that even when appointees might try to represent the interests of the race they will not necessarily be effective. They might not have the president's ear or the interests of blacks may conflict with an administration's ideological or partisan needs or with the interests of other groups in the president's electoral or governing coalitions. This is particularly the case for blacks serving in Republican administrations, since blacks are an insignificant part of the party's electoral coalition. And although no post–civil rights era president, whatever his party or ideology, has thought it prudent to try to govern the country without including blacks in his administration, this itself poses a problem when the administration is hostile to the interests and aspirations of blacks, as has been the case with post–civil rights era Republican presidents. The result has been, in the Reagan and Bush administrations (although not Nixon's), the recruitment of blacks with little relationship to the internal institutions and processes of the black community and ideological and policy views at variance with those of the community's established leadership and Afro-American mass opinion. In this situation the incorporation of blacks into decision-making processes may actually work against the interests of the race, allowing presidents hostile to black interests to pursue those policies and then to say (as President Bush in effect said with reference to Clarence Williams and the minority scholarship issue), "Oh, it can't be antiblack or racist, because look, he is black." This raises the question of whether in right-wing administrations the interests of the black community would be better served if there were no black appointees at all, a position some critics took with respect to the Thomas Supreme Court appointment, arguing that it would be better to have an all-white Supreme Court than one with a black right-wing conservative ideologue. In any event, this study of twenty-five years of black involvement in presidential policy making suggests that more than mere statistical incorporation is required if the causes advanced by blacks are to become public policy. What is needed is a powerful constituency outside of government so that any president and his appointees, black or white, will feel the pressure to act on the needs of the race. Without such a powerful constituency, the incorporation of blacks into the executive branch will remain largely symbolic.

6

Blacks in Congressional Decision Making:
A Policy Consensus on Civil Rights, 1970–1994

Throughout the post–civil rights era black leaders—integrationists, nationalists and radicals—have held near countless conferences, conventions and meetings devoted to the development of the black agenda. In Part II I traced the twists and turns in this agenda-building process from the early black power conferences through the National Black Political Conventions and the Joint Center's quadrennial Institutes of Black Public Officials. These agendas focused largely on non–civil rights issues, issues of social and economic reform in areas such as employment, welfare reform and national health insurance. Except for the long struggle over busing and school desegregation in the late 1960s and 1970s and the more recent conflicts over affirmative action, civil rights has not been a major priority on the various black agendas. This is because by the late 1960s the traditional civil rights agenda had been enacted and to a large extent institutionalized. This process of institutionalization of the traditional civil rights agenda has been thoroughly documented by Hanes Walton, Jr., and Hugh Davis Graham in their books on the civil rights policy process.[1] Graham labels this process of institutionalization "quadrilateralism," the routinization of the civil rights regulatory process as a consequence of the "capture" of the relevant congressional committees, executive agencies and the judiciary by the civil rights lobby.[2] This process has historically characterized policy making in the United States. First, there is the initial controversy and debate about the law itself, then a period of consolidation and finally institutionalization, as interest groups, the bureaucracy, congressional committees and the courts work out a modus operandi in the day-to-day conduct of business. As this process unfolded in the early 1970s, black leaders began to shift attention from civil rights to broader issues of social and economic reform.

Blacks in the United States at least since the New Deal have always had a "dual agenda" which focused on narrow race-specific civil rights reforms as well as broader non-race-specific social and eco-

nomic reforms.[3] Until the 1960s, however, the civil rights part of the
dual agenda took priority, for obvious reasons given the overt and odious forms of race discrimination in education, housing, public facilities and access to the political process. With the removal of these overt
racist barriers, the issues of social and economic reform could now take
priority. And they did, as most post–civil rights era black agendas
focused on non–civil rights issues. It should be clear, however, that the
civil rights issues did not go away, they simply became less of a priority.
Throughout this twenty-five year period blacks have had to work in
the executive branch, the courts, the bureaucracy and the Congress in
order to maintain and modestly extend the gains of the 1960s. The last
twenty-five years of conflict over civil rights suggest first that there is a
consensus on the broad principles and policies of civil rights, and second, that black participation in systemic institutions and processes—
elections, lobbying, coalition building, litigation—was sufficient to
maintain and modestly extend the civil rights agenda, in contrast to its
impotence in advancing the social and economic reform agenda. In this
chapter I trace the emergence and consolidation of the civil rights consensus by analyzing the legislative struggles of the late 1960s through
the 1990s. In the next two chapters I trace the legislative struggles over
the issues on the social and economic agenda, which in contrast to civil
rights shows that routine, systemic political participation is not enough
to advance the post–civil rights era black agenda.

My procedure is to examine in some detail the legislative struggles
over busing for purposes of school desegregation, and the civil rights
bills of 1990 and 1991. These two cases are examined in detail because of
their substantive importance and because they show the power of
blacks in the legislative process. Throughout this period in general and
in reference to these two cases specifically, blacks have confronted hostile presidents and yet nevertheless have prevailed. This is no easy task
for a relatively resource-poor group such as African Americans.
Matthew Holden's observation about the possibilities of what he called
"an exposed minority" leveraging the legislative process to advance its
interests against a hostile president sets a theoretical context for the
analysis in this chapter. He writes:

> *The necessary implication is that a racial minority, that is also a political
> minority, is notably exposed if it can not discover means of leveraging
> within the legislative process.* It is apparent that no group in Ameri-
> can society can withstand steady, recurrent hostility from the pres-
> idency. The reason simply is that there are too many forms of dis-
> cretion within the scope of the executive. But a group that

possesses a significant position in the legislative process has means by which to exact from an administration a high price for adverse action.[4]

This is precisely the situation that blacks confronted during most of the post–civil rights era; a hostile president but a "significant position in the legislative process" that has allowed them to leverage it on civil rights issues so that presidents have found, in Holden's phrase, the "game is not worth the candle."[5]

While I focus in detail on these two cases to show this process of leveraging and coalition development on civil rights, other cases should be noted here that provide further evidence of the viability of the civil rights consensus and the effectiveness of the civil rights coalition. In the last chapter I discussed the defeat in 1970 in the House of Representatives of an amendment which would have rendered illegal the administration's Philadelphia Plan. In 1972 the Congress adopted amendments to Title VII of the 1964 Civil Rights Act granting the EEOC the right to institute class action suits in employment discrimination cases. In doing so it rejected amendments that would have prohibited federal courts or executive agencies from using numerical goals and timetables under Title VII or executive orders. Early in the Nixon administration the Senate rejected two nominees to the Supreme Court—Clement Haynsworth and Harold Carswell—in part because of their perceived hostility to civil rights. In 1974 the Congress, after a long struggle spearheaded by the Congressional Black Caucus, repealed the Byrd amendment, which had permitted the importation of chrome from Rhodesia in violation of UN sanctions imposed on the colonial Ian Smith regime. Further evidence of the civil rights coalition's effectiveness in Congress during the last twenty-five years include the renewal and strengthening of the Voting Rights Act in 1970, 1975 and again in 1982 (all passed in spite of opposition to key provisions by the Justice Department and Presidents Nixon, Ford and Reagan); the negative congressional, press and public reaction to President Reagan's attempt to provide tax exemptions to educational institutions practicing racial discrimination; the passage of the Civil Rights Restoration Act by a more than two-thirds vote overriding President Reagan's veto;[6] the passage, again over the objections of President Reagan, of the Martin Luther King, Jr., holiday act; the passage, once again over Reagan's objections, of legislation imposing sanctions on South Africa; and the defeat of Robert Bork's Supreme Court nomination, in part because of his perceived hostility to civil rights and affirmative action. Each of these legislative acts alone represented a substantial, and not necessarily predictable victory, but taken together they make the case that on the civil rights part of the black agenda blacks had amassed considerable leverage in the legislative process and have made hostile presidents at a minimum pay a cost for their opposition. The two cases below illustrate the nature of this leverage and the partisan and ideological contours of the post–civil rights era coalition and consensus.

Busing and School Desegregation

Court-ordered busing as a means to implement the 1954 Supreme Court decree requiring desegregation of the nation's public schools emerged as a controversial issue in the late 1960s, fueling the presidential campaigns of George Wallace and Richard Nixon. Especially after the courts ordered busing in several northern school districts, the issue became highly controversial, sparking mass white protests, boycotts and violence. Black public opinion throughout the controversy was about equally divided but white opinion was overwhelmingly hostile (in the range of 75 to 80 percent).[7] In this climate liberal and conservative members of Congress, north and south, introduced a series of bills to restrict or bar altogether the right of the courts to order busing for purposes of school desegregation. In addition, Presidents Nixon and Ford proposed similar legislation and sought to mobilize public pressure in order to secure passage, but to no avail. Several bills and amendments restricting busing were passed in the House usually by large margins but were either defeated or significantly watered down in the Senate. For example, in 1974 the House passed by a vote of 281 to 128 a bill, vigorously supported by President Nixon, that flatly forbade the courts to order busing for purposes of school desegregation beyond the school nearest or next nearest the student's home. It also required the courts to reopen any existing cases, regardless of how long they had been settled, which did not comply with the next nearest school rule.[8] The Senate in a narrow 47 to 46 vote rejected the House version of the legislation and instead adopted 56 to 36 an amendment restricting court-ordered cross-district busing unless the courts find that it is "needed to guarantee a black child his constitutional rights," a prohibition which in effect transformed the Senate legislation into a nonbinding suggestion to the courts.[9] On similar votes during this period 1969–74 the civil rights lobby led by Clarence Mitchell of the Leadership Conference on Civil Rights prevailed either in committee or in the Senate through filibusters or narrow floor votes.[10] These victories on busing represented a significant achievement for the civil rights coalition, given the overwhelming hostility of white opinion, the disaffection of many northern liberals and vigorous lobbying by the president. These legislative victories turned out to be short lived, however, and ultimately hollow, because within a month of the Senate's vote discussed above, the Supreme Court in *Miliken v. Bradley* began the process of dismantling court-ordered busing for purposes of school desegregation; a process that was virtually complete by 1980 such that during Reagan's tenure the issue was no longer a matter of political or legislative controversy.[11]

There is an ironic quality to the outcome of the busing debate that has implications for black politics today, especially the issue of affirmative action discussed later in this chapter. Throughout the controversy several black members of Congress sought to fashion a compromise with white liberal and centrist congressmen to restrict court-ordered busing in exchange for enhanced financial support for urban black school districts and increased black control of the educational process.[12] All such efforts were blocked by the NAACP and other traditional civil rights leaders (especially influential was Kenneth Clark) on the grounds that (as one NAACP official told me in a 1973 interview) while well-meaning, such compromises should not be pursued in Congress; the NAACP would rather rely on the courts than Congress to protect the rights of blacks because:

We do not want to establish a precedent whereby the political branches of government, reacting to political pressure, interfere with the courts' constitutional mandate to enforce the provisions of the Fourteenth Amendment because such a precedent could be used to undermine other rights of blacks not popular with the white majority.[13]

Yet it was the Supreme Court, not the "political branches," that finally brought an end to busing as a desegregation tool. This should have been clear to the NAACP and the civil rights lobby, since the Court itself is a political institution; and it was unlikely that it would continue to enforce, in the face of overwhelming mass and elite opposition, a policy as dubious as school busing. As William Raspberry, the black columnist, wrote at the time, "It has been clear for some time that busing for purposes of integration was in its terminal stages, the question was whether Congress or the courts would administer the *coup de grace.*"[14] By passing up the opportunity to strike a bargain in Congress to enhance black educational resources and control on a national basis, the civil rights establishment made an enormous error.[15] Indeed, it is probably safe to conclude that this busing strategy fueled by the civil rights legal fraternity is the most important political miscalculation by black leadership in the entire post–civil rights era; the Vietnam of black politics. This is because enormous political capital was expended for near a decade on this issue contributing to (1) increased racial cleavage and conflict, (2) cleavage and conflict within the black leadership (busing was one of the issues that rancorously divided the integrationist and nationalist factions at the 1972 Gary Convention) and (3) providing a ready symbolic issue that right-wing forces (represented initially by George Wallace and later by Agnew, Nixon and Reagan) could use to rally a national majority in presidential elections. This all for a policy of marginal if any effect on black educational attainment and one that predictably would end in the outcome we see today.[16]

The fundamental problem was that the civil rights legal fraternity, given its important victories during the litigation phase of the movement, lost sight of two important historical facts: (1) the Supreme Court is a political institution that responds on most issues slowly but surely to the fundamental currents of national election majorities, and (2) in its two-hundred-year history the Court, excepting the brief era of the Warren Court, has either been indifferent or hostile to black concerns, usually more so than the explicitly political branches of the national government.[17] These historical facts were demonstrated most acutely in the Court's 1988–89 term, in which it in sledge hammer fashion rendered a series of opinions, all by narrow majorities, that undermined fundamentally the basic structure for enforcing civil rights era antidiscrimination statutes.[18] What these decisions represented was the final coming to power for the first time in the post–civil rights era of a conservative court majority on race—a result of sixteen years of appointments by conservative Republican Presidents.[19] Thus, if civil rights are to be secure in the post–civil rights era, blacks will have to rely at least in the short term on the political process rather than the Court.[20] I return to this issue later in the chapter when I take up the civil rights bills of 1990 and 1991 and the problem of affirmative action. However, for the theoretical purposes of this chapter, the busing issue provides further evidence of the effectiveness of the civil rights legislative coalition in an almost worst case scenario: overwhelming opposition in public opinion and the active opposition of two presidents who made antibusing legislation a top priority.

The Civil Rights Act of 1991

In its 1988–89 term the Supreme Court's conservative anti–civil rights majority clearly defined and consolidated itself, leading Justice Marshall to remark in a speech after the term's close that "It is difficult to characterize the [1988–89] term's decisions as anything other than a deliberate retrenching of the civil rights agenda."[21] Throughout the Nixon and most of the Reagan administration there was never a clear, decisive anticivil rights majority. For example, in the *Bakke* case only four of the nine justices took a clear anti–affirmative action position, holding that it was legally and constitutionally impermissible to take race into account in admissions decisions while four justices held that race and even a racial quota were permissible under both Title VII and the Fourteenth Amendment. Justice Powell then split the difference holding that race was a permissible consideration but a strict quota was not. In subsequent cases the Court usually oscillated between approval and disapproval of various affirmative action programs in narrow five-to-four or six-to-three rulings. The replacement of Justice Powell by Anthony Kennedy finally gave the conservatives their long-awaited reliable fifth vote. And in 1988–89 they began to use it to undermine or retrench two decades of antidiscrimination jurisprudence.

In six decisions rendered one after another, the Court significantly narrowed the whole structure of enforcement of antidiscrimination law in the area of employment: In *Ward Cove v. Atonio* (490 U.S. 642, 1989) the Court set new standards for suits challenging discrimination in hiring and promotions under Title VII, holding that plaintiffs in a "disparate impact" case had to identify the specific practice that caused the discriminatory effect and show that the employer had no "business need" for it. In addition, the majority held that some discriminatory practices could be justified if they served in a significant way an employer's "legitimate employment goals." The dissenting justices and attorneys specializing in employment discrimination law argued that these new standards, which reversed two decades of law going back to *Griggs v. Duke Power* (401 U.S. 424, 1971), would establish a near insurmountable burden of proof for victims of employment discrimination. In the second case, *Martin v. Wilks* (490 U.S. 755, 1989), the Court ruled that long-settled consent decrees involving job discrimination could be open to subsequent attack by individuals who had not been party to the original settlement. The effect of this decision was to make it difficult to reach agreement in such cases and to threaten costly, near endless litigation by victims of discrimination. In *Patterson v. McClain* (491 U.S. 164, 1989) the Court ruled that the right to sue for job discrimination under an 1866 Reconstruction era law applied only to initial hiring and not to racial harassment or discrimination on the job. In *Jett v. Dallas Independent School District* (491 U.S. 701, 1989) the Court further weakened the 1866 law by holding that it did not provide a basis for suits challenging local governments for acts of discrimination. In *Lorrance v.*

AT&T Technologies (490 U.S. 900, 1989) the Court held that the statute of limitations for challenging a discriminatory seniority plan begins to run when the plan is adopted rather than when it is applied to an individual in an actual employment situation. The effect here would make it virtually impossible to challenge such plans since most individuals would not likely know of the plan or its adverse effects until it was applied, and then, the Court said, it would be too late. Finally in *Price Waterhouse v. Hopkins* (490 U.S. 228, 1989) the Court held that in cases where there was evidence that a business made an employment decision for both legitimate and illegal reasons it could avoid liability for discriminatory conduct if it could show simply that the decision was justified on the legitimate grounds, notwithstanding its unlawful dimension.

These decisions are largely technical, involving matters of burden or standards of proof, statutes of limitation and so on; but taken together or in their cumulative effects they represented a substantial weakening of the capacity of individuals to obtain relief for illegal job discrimination.[22] In the speech by Justice Marshall cited above, he argued that given the Court's now evident hostility to civil rights, the civil rights community would now have to turn to Congress to preserve and extend the civil rights agenda. This the civil rights lobby begin to do immediately after the end of the Court's 1989 term, calling on the President and Congress to pass legislation that would reverse what it called the Court's erroneous interpretation of the 1866 and 1964 statues. This set in motion a two-year-long battle that resulted in enactment of the omnibus Civil Rights Act of 1991, which reversed or substantially modified each of the six decisions. The eventual passage of the 1991 Act after much partisan bickering was further evidence of the power or leverage of the civil rights coalition, and the partisan and ideological nature of the congressional civil rights coalition.

The first and perhaps most significant piece of evidence of the consensus on civil rights is that President Bush and his attorney general agreed that a new civil rights act was needed to reverse or modify each of the six decisions, and in a series of meetings with the civil rights leadership the president pledged to work together on the appropriate legislative language to achieve this result. Several conservative commentators and legislators pointed to the irony of a conservative administration seeking to overturn (rather than praising) the decisions of a court of its own making. In general, the Bush administration's position reflects what I call this broad civil rights consensus shared by all except the Republican party's right wing. In addition, under the leadership of party Chairman Lee Atwater, the Republicans had set a goal for the

1992 election of getting 15 to 20 percent of the black vote, doubling its 1988 share. Atwater argued that if this could be done the Republicans could be well on their way to becoming the majority party in Congress as well as at the presidential level. To do this Atwater argued that the party had to maintain at least a moderate stance on civil rights while appealing to young and middle-class blacks on the basis of traditional conservative principles on economic and social policies. The political feasibility of this strategy was encouraged by the fact that early in his tenure, Bush's approval rating among blacks was 51 percent, roughly the same as the 52 percent among whites. This was more than three times as high as Reagan's initial approval rating among blacks and even in the spring of 1990 with the prospect of a Bush veto his approval rating among blacks still stood at 52 percent, compared with 14 percent for Reagan at the comparable point in his first term.[23] This high black approval rating and the prospect for chipping away at the Democrats' core constituency thus provided a partisan reason for administration support of some kind of civil rights bill. On the other hand, to give this support threatened to weaken Bush's position in his own core right-wing constituency. Thus, the administration was faced with a classic case of political cross pressure. Its resolution of the conflict was also classic: the president tried throughout the two-year legislative struggle to have it both ways—thereby pleasing neither blacks or the right wing.

The administration early on agreed on most of the provisions of the 1990 bill as drafted by congressional leaders and the civil rights lobby, agreeing to overrule all but two of the six decisions of the Court. The administration supported the Court's holding in *Martin v. Wilks* concerning the reopening of consent decrees, while the congressional leadership would have substantially modified it. The major difference— largely technical but highly partisan—dealt with the *Wards Cove* case and the issues of the burden and standards of proof. First, both sides agreed to reverse the Court's holding on the burden of proof. The Court had held that once a "disparate impact" had been established, it was up to the employee to show that the practice causing this impact was not required by "business necessity." Both sides agreed to reverse this on grounds that the employer was in a better position to know why a particular practice was necessary to conduct business. The issue in conflict became the "standard" of proof. The Court had held that plaintiffs in employment discrimination cases must not only identify specific discriminatory practices but also show that they did not serve the employer's "legitimate employment goals" or business needs in a "significant way." The Democratic Party bill changed this language to require that the alleged discriminatory practice be "essential to effective job performance." The Bush administration argued that this would be difficult for employers to prove and that in order to avoid costly litigation they would resort to quotas. Weeks of debate and negotiations ensued. Finally, Senator John Danforth of Missouri and Senator Edward Kennedy fashioned compromise language that they thought would be acceptable to the administration. Instead of "essential to effective job performance," the employer would have to show that the practice "bears a substantial and demonstrable relationship to effective job performance."[24]

This version passed the Senate 62-34, with the support of fifty-three Democrats and nine Republicans. In the House it was approved by 273 to 154, 239 Democrats and 34 Republicans supported it while it was opposed by 139 Republicans and 15 Democrats. Thus, while the vote reflected a clear majority, it was (especially in the House) a largely partisan majority. Bush, who had strongly encouraged the Danforth-Kenneth compromise, was now caught in the middle. He seemed initially inclined to sign the bill, was privately urged to do so by senior blacks in the administration (including HHS Secretary Sullivan and Constance Newman of the Office of Personal Administration) and publicly by Arthur Fletcher, the Chairman of the Civil Rights Commission. Yet, the bill clearly did not have the support of a congressional Republican majority, and conservative columnists and administration officials (including the vice president, the attorney general, HUD Secretary Jack Kemp and C. Boyden Gray, the White House counsel and the principal White House staffperson on civil rights) urged a veto. With the civil rights leaders demonstrating outside the White House gates, the *New York Times* headline (May 15, 1990) "Trying to Head Off His Own Veto, Bush Holds Meeting on Rights Bill" aptly summarized Bush's dilemma. In the end the president bowed to the pressures of his party majority and his right-wing base and vetoed the bill. The override vote in the Senate shows the partisan, ideological and regional bases of the post–civil rights era coalition.

In the civil rights era, in spite of the opposition of Barry Goldwater—the Republican nominee in 1964—the Civil Rights Acts of 1964 and 1965 were passed with the support of House and Senate Republican majorities, while the partisan, ideological and regional bases of opposition were rooted in the south among conservative Democrats. This all began to change in 1964 as the post-Goldwater Republican Party began to move to the right on racial issues.[25] The 1972 Nixon campaign accelerated this rightward drift on race, and Reagan consolidated it in 1980. In every year before 1959, House and Senate Republicans were more liberal on race issues than were the Democrats. For example, in 1958 two-thirds of all "racial liberals" in the Senate were Republicans, but by 1966 the number was down to 18 percent.[26] This decline in Republican racial liberalism is a result of three factors. First, the defeat of moderate midwestern, western and border-state Republicans (especially senators) by liberal Democrats. Second, the growing racial liberalism of southern Democrats (again especially in the Senate) as a result of the enfranchisement of blacks. Third, the election in the South and West of an increasingly hard core of right-wing Republicans, who in spite of the large bloc of black voters in the south are nevertheless able to win by appealing to whites only, moderates as well as hard-core unreconstructed racists. (This group includes Gramm of Texas, Mack of Florida, Helms of North Carolina and Lott and Cochran of Mississippi). As a result, in the post–civil rights era, support for civil rights is now overwhelmingly Democratic.[27] This may be seen in the Senate override vote on the bill in 1990 and the final passage of the Act in 1991. The Senate vote to override was 66-34, one short of the consensus two-thirds majority. All Democrats supported the override. In addition, it was supported by eleven Republicans. These Republican "racial liberals" tend to some extent to correspond to the party's traditional civil rights era regional base. Five were from New England and the Northeast (Chafee, Cohen, Jeffords, Heinz and Specter), two were from the Pacific Northwest (Hatfield and Packwood of Oregon) plus Danforth of Missouri and Bosohwitz and Durenburger of Minnesota. While the civil rights coalition approaches the consensus two-thirds majority,[28] it is also tenuous, depending on an effective southern black vote that moderates to an extent the behavior of Democratic senators on civil rights. When this vote is not effective and Republican senators are elected, then the South reverts to its civil rights era pattern of racial conservatism. Although more than half of the Republican racial liberals in the Senate are from the Northeast and New England, this may be idiosyncratic to the individual senators, since there are instances where senators from these regions (D'Amato from New York, Smith of New Hampshire and Roth of Delaware) identify with the party's racial right.

With the sustaining of the veto of the 1990 bill, the partisan cleavage on the issue became more intense. Democratic partisans charged the president with being racialist, of playing the "race card" and of using the quota issue as code word to appeal to antiblack sentiments in the electorate. The president continued to invoke the specter of quotas (widely opposed by whites and although not to the same degree by blacks as well) and charged the Democrats with trying to embarrass him and undermine his support among blacks. Given the widespread agreement by both parties on most provisions of the bill, the highly ambiguous and technical nature of the differences on the *Wards Cove* language and the eventual 1991 compromise, it does appear that there was an element of partisan posturing on both sides. That is, in all likelihood if both parties were not seeking narrow partisan advantage, the 1991 compromise could have been reached in 1990. In any event, there was little attention to the issue beyond the Washington beltway. For example, during the most intense period of the debate on the 1991 bill, polls indicated that most Americans, black and white, had little awareness of the debate or knowledge of the issues involved and that there was hardly any public opinion for or against the bill.[29] And if the Democrats thought that the Bush veto would significantly undermine his approval among blacks they were wrong, as Gallup approval rating in the months immediately after the veto remained relatively high, dropping from 51 to 25 percent in the month after the veto but rising to 44 percent the next month and staying at about this level throughout the months of the debate on the 1991 Act.[30]

Debate on the 1991 legislation was nevertheless highly partisan, involving several issues and groups that did not play a part in the 1990 debate. In a speech before the Congressional Black Caucus's informal swearing in ceremony, the House Speaker announced that the civil rights bill of 1991 would be HR 1 in the new Congress, indicating symbolically that it was the Democratic Party's number one priority. Meanwhile the president and his partisans continued to inveigh against quotas. Again, most of the dispute centered on the standard of proof argument emanating from *Wards Cove*. But new actors and issues also emerged in this second debate.

First, the issue of "race norming" emerged as part of the quota debate, with conservatives arguing that the practice should be outlawed. Race norming or, more precisely "within-group score conversion" is a practice implemented by the Labor Department in 1980. It encouraged state employment agencies and some federal agencies to adjust scores on employment examinations by race so that the scores of black applicants would be ranked only with blacks, Hispanics with Hispanics and whites with whites. Thus, a black who scored in the 85th percentile of black test takers would be placed on the same footing with white applicants who scored in the 85th percentile among whites, although the black applicant's raw score would have ranked her much lower when compared to all applicants. The effects of this process, labeled by the press "race norming," was to eliminate the disparate impact of the test and thus qualify more blacks for entry level employment. Again, this practice was quietly introduced in the first year of the Reagan administration by the Labor Department and was implemented with little public knowledge or controversy. However, during the debate on the 1991 bill the practice became known (as the result of a letter to the editor of the *New York Times* from a University of Delaware sociologist). Conservatives immediately attacked the procedure as a perfect example of the kind of quota Bush had talked about in his veto of the 1990 legislation.

Second, the issue of damages for women victimized by overt or intentional discrimination divided the administration and congressional Democrats. Under the 1964 Civil Rights Act, victims of such discrimination are entitled only to back pay and reinstatement; however, under the 1866 statute, which covers only race discrimination, blacks in intentional discrimination cases are entitled to sue for compensatory and punitive damages. Women's groups and congressional Democrats argued that this was unfair and sought to amend either the 1964 Act to permit suits for punitive damages as well as back pay, or to change the 1866 law so that it would cover gender as well as race discrimination. These issues brought new groups into the 1991 legislative debate. Women's groups and legislators in the House played a more activist role in the negotiations to fashion a final compromise that would deal with the issues of damages in intentional discrimination cases. The result was in the final debate in the House, and in the press the bill was presented not as a civil rights bill for blacks but as a women's rights bill, even by leaders of the civil rights organizations and the Congressional Black Caucus. This strategy shift from the rights of blacks to the rights of women was thought to be more likely to gain public support and perhaps the votes needed to override another veto. Congressman Jack Brooks, Chairman of the Judiciary Committee and lead sponsor of the bill, argued quite explicitly that the bill was about "rights for white women": If they flagrantly harass you and mistreat you in your job, a white woman, there is no compensation. . . . Even if you are upset and your boyfriend or husband is upset, you get nothing for it. But, if you are black, you could get punitive damage for harassment.[31]

Getting enough public support and votes to override a possible second veto was a key element in the strategy of the House leadership. As a result, the bill produced by House leaders involved a number of compromises with conservative Democrats and moderate Republicans, compromises (including an explicit ban on race norming and quotas) which eventually led the Congressional Black Caucus to reject it in favor of what was described as a "pure" bill. Finally, each side tried to enlist the support of the business community. Early in 1991 Robert Allen, the Chief executive officer of AT&T and Chairman of the Busi-

ness Roundtable's Human Relations Task Force, initiated discussion
with the civil rights lobby, looking toward the development of compromise language that could lead to the Roundtable's support of the
bill. The major corporations represented in the Business Roundtable
were inclined to support the bill because in the years since the *Griggs*
decision and the Philadelphia Plan, affirmative action goals and timetables had become part of routine business practices; as one observer
noted they are as "familiar to American businesses as tally sheets and
bottom lines."[32] The small-business community represented by the
Chamber of Commerce and the National Small Business Federation
was strongly opposed to the bill's proposed revision of *Wards Cove* and
the proposed punitive and compensatory damages, arguing these
would result either in costly litigation and damage awards or, alterna-
tively, quotas. This split in the business community eventually led to a
breakdown in the negotiations between the civil rights lobby and the
Business Roundtable, with various large corporations taking independent positions while small business owners engaged in an intensive
letter-writing campaign urging a vote against the bill.[33]

In the House, three bills were considered: the administration's,
the Democratic leadership bill and one offered by the Congressional
Black Caucus. On the contentious *Wards Cove* issues all sides agreed
once again that once a finding of discrimination was established the
burden of proof would be on the employer, not the employee, to prove
its legitimacy. There was disagreement on the nature of the proof
required. The Court had held that a specific employer practice had to
be cited to prove discrimination. The Caucus bill rejected this in favor
of allowing employees to show that a group of practices cumulatively
had a discriminatory effect. The administration accepted the Court's
position on this issue, while the Democratic bill also called for citing a
specific practice or practices unless a Court found that despite a "diligent effort" this could not be done. And on the issue that had resulted
in the Bush veto—what kind of business necessity would justify a disparate impact practice—the administration used the *Wards Cove* "legitimate employment goals" or the stricter "manifest relationship" standard. The Democrats' language called for a "significant and manifest
relationship to the requirements for effective job performance" while
the Caucus said the practice must "bear a substantial and demonstrable relationship to effective job performance."[34] Although these differences in language may make some differences to specialists in
employment discrimination law, to most observers they rather seemed
like distinctions without "manifest," "significant," "substantial" or
"legitimate" differences.

On the issue of punitive and compensatory damages for women, the administration bill allowed such damages only in cases of harassment, limited awards to $150,000 and required the case to be tried by a judge rather than a jury. The Democratic compromise amended the 1964 Act to allow punitive and compensatory damages in all cases of job discrimination, but the amount was limited to $150,000 or the total of back pay, whichever was greater. It also provided that either side could request a trial by jury. The Democratic compromise did not satisfy the women's groups because it did not, like the 1866 Act on race discrimination, provide for unlimited damages. Thus, the Black Caucus bill simply amended the 1866 Act to cover sex and the 1964 Act to provide for unlimited damages. Finally, the Democratic majority bill included language banning race norming but at the same time it also banned tests that are "culturally biased," defined as those that do not "validly and fairly predict a person's ability to perform the job for which the test is based as a qualification, without regard to test taker's race, religion, sex or national origin." Finally, the Democratic version included language stating explicitly that the bill did not "require or encourage or permit quotas." In fact, the bill makes quota hiring an illegal employment practice under the 1964 Act, allowing individuals to sue for damages if they can prove they lost a job or promotion because of a quota.[35] These provisions on race norming and quotas were added by the Democratic leadership in order to blunt the attacks of congressional conservatives and the administration on the quota issue and to attract a veto proof majority. The Caucus bill was silent on both these provisions while the administration bill only included the language barring race norming.

The various Democratic Party compromises were not enough to produce a two-thirds, veto-proof majority. The Democratic bill passed 273 to 158, seventeen short of the needed two-thirds, and just one vote more than the vote on the somewhat more liberal 1990 bill.[36] The more sharply focused partisan character of the 1991 debate resulted in intense lobbying by the president and the Republican party leadership in order to get members to support the president and the party line. Consequently, nine Republicans who had voted for the bill in 1990 switched in 1991 and voted no.[37] Overall, the 1991 bill was supported on final passage by 250 Democrats, 22 Republicans and independent Congressman Bernie Sanders of Vermont.[38] It was opposed by 143 Republicans and 15 Democrats. The pattern of Democratic opposition is clear: eleven of the fifteen Democratic no-votes were cast by southerners, three by suburban Chicago area Democrats and one by a Utah Democrat. In most cases the southern Democrats had relatively small black populations, although in three of the eleven cases the districts' black populations were near one-fourth.[39] No particular regional pattern is discernable in Republican support for the bill except no southern Republicans supported the bill, confirming once again that southern Republicanism has become the hard core of racial conservatism.[40] Otherwise, support for the bill scattered across all regions of the country, although seven of the twenty-two votes came from the relatively large New York Republican delegation.

After the passage of the bill in the House in June, partisan charges and countercharges of racial quotas and racial insensitivity went on throughout much of the summer while moderate Republicans, led once again by Senator Danforth, sought to fashion compromise language that would gain administration support. Danforth's role was pivotal this time because he was also the principal Senate sponsor of the Clarence Thomas Supreme Court nomination, which was being considered at the same time as the civil rights bill. This gave him some additional leverage in the White House negotiations; however, the discussions (largely between Danforth and White House counsel Gray) dragged on throughout the summer, Danforth finally saying the negotiations were fruitless and that he was prepared to work alone with his Senate colleagues to fashion a compromise that could attract enough votes to override a veto. The issue that led to the breakdown was a letter from Bush to Danforth that in effect not only supported the Supreme Court's *Wards Cove* position, but went further and repudiated wholly the principles and procedures of the *Griggs* decision, a decision all sides had previously agreed had to be restored. Danforth's compromise language, consistent with *Griggs*, forbade any employer to impose a qualification for a job not necessary for its performance, if such qualification had a disparate impact on minorities or women. This is the heart of *Griggs* which struck down a high school diploma as a job qualification because it was not related to job performance and it had a discriminatory effect on black workers. In his letter to Danforth the president rejected this principle because he said it would "seriously if not fatally undermine the renewal of our educational system by discouraging employers from relying on educational effort and achievement."[41] In the letter the president cited a letter to him from the education secretary where this point was made in explicit racial terms, as the secretary argued that the bill would take away incentives from inner-city kids to complete high school. Thus, the administration argued that allowing irrelevant educational requirements to deny blacks jobs was in fact doing them a favor by encouraging them to stay in school. This was obviously a sham, a sham which outraged Danforth and led him to break off the talks, declaring that the Bush position was "ridiculous" because it would deny an otherwise qualified fifty-year-old black man a job simply because he had failed a generation ago to graduate from high school.[42] Clearly, this was an effort by Gray at the White House to forestall any compromise. Danforth recognized it as such and immediately sought to develop a veto-proof majority.

It is likely that at least in the Senate Danforth would have been successful. Reportedly, the president was told by Senator Robert Dole, the Republican leader, that there were probably enough votes to override his veto with at least the minimum dozen Republicans needed.[43] This is said to have caused the president to direct Gray and his staff to seek a final compromise. In the final compromise the key issues were largely on the terms proposed by Senator Danforth throughout the summer.[44] On the central issue of *Wards Cove* the compromise essentially repudiated the Court and reimposed the *Griggs* standard. The final bill required that employer qualifications be "job related for the position in question and consistent with business necessity."[45] On the issue of damages for gender discrimination, the *New York Times* described the compromise as a "major Bush defeat."[46] Bush had wanted to limit damages to cases of sexual harassment, wanted the amount not to exceed $150,000 and trial by judge rather than jury. The compromise provided for damages in all types of gender discrimination, not just harassment, provided for punitive and compensatory damage awards of up to $300,000 for employers of five hundred or more and provided for trial by jury.[47] The final issue in contention was the *Martin v. Wilks* case, involving the rights of third parties to later challenge consent decrees in employment discrimination cases. The administration supported the Court's decision fully but the final compromise rejected it. The language said, "People could not sue to reopen employment cases if they had 'actual notice' of the decree at the time it was entered and a 'reasonable opportunity' to object or if their 'interests' were adequately represented in the original case. Challenges would also not be allowed 'if reasonable efforts were made to provide notice to interested persons.'"[48]

This version was quickly approved by the Senate in a vote of 77 to 22. This was not the end of this particular legislative dance, however. In yet another indicator of the administration's ambivalence on the legislation and its wish to have it both ways, just eighteen hours before the president was to sign the bill in a White House ceremony with the congressional and civil rights leadership, Boyden Gray circulated a draft executive order to all cabinet officers which called for the abolition of all government affirmative action programs.[49] The draft order (which removed all references to racial preferences and goals and timetables) was to be announced at the signing ceremony for the civil rights act. It was leaked to the press and predictably resulted in widespread criticism in Congress, the media and from the civil rights lobby. It was never issued, with the White House press office contending the idea was Gray's alone and had not been cleared by the president or his chief of staff.[50] In signing the bill, the president affirmed his support of the Act and of civil rights, but in what the *New York Times* called editorially a "sneak attack," the president issued an executive order directing the civil rights enforcement agencies to use as the "authoritative" interpretation of the new law a memorandum by Gray. Gray's memorandum, which was read into the *Congressional Record* by Senator Dole as well as by several Republican opponents of the bill, in effect argued that the new law was an "affirmation of existing law," including *Wards Cove*, the decision it was clearly designed to overturn. Senator Danforth said the Gray memorandum was "plainly wrong."[51]

The dance of legislation was finished, for now. But only for now, because, given the ambiguity of the statute's language, its conflicting interpretations, tortured legislative history and the evident hostility of the Supreme Court, the dance of litigation must now be watched—it may likely lead to another legislative dance on civil rights, as the Court could effectively undermine the 1991 Act.[52]

Conclusion

Although the partisan and regional bases have shifted, the civil rights coalition that enacted the civil rights reforms of the 1960s remained intact until the election of 1994.[53] In the twenty-five years since the end of the civil rights revolution more than a dozen major civil rights or race-specific bills or amendments have come before the Congress, and blacks and the civil rights community prevailed on each of them. In addition, race and civil rights were key factors in the defeat of three Supreme Court nominees during this period. These successes of blacks on civil rights were all the more remarkable because in a couple of instances they were achieved in the face of overwhelming opposition from public opinion, and on virtually all of them the legislation was passed in spite of hostility from the president. This suggests that on civil rights, narrowly construed, blacks had significant leverage in Congress and that there was a bipartisan consensus in support of the maintenance and even a modest extension of the civil rights gains of the 1960s. There remains a substantial anti–civil rights constituency in the United States today, centered now in the Republican right wing, especially its southern and western bases. However, there is also a small but significant body of Republican racial liberals in the Congress, especially the Senate. The Democratic party in Congress including its influential southern bloc is overwhelmingly committed to civil rights, either in principle or because of the leverage of the black vote. The result has been a bipartisan consensus and coalition.

Yet, there is a sense that these post–civil rights era victories are to an extent irrelevant, symbolic as much as substantive insofar as the life chances of blacks in the United States today. This has been the view of black conservative critics of the black leadership establishment throughout most of the post–civil rights era.[54] The conservative critics in their blanket indictment of civil rights overstate their case; the several renewals of the Voting Rights Act since 1965 have been substantively important in securing the enfranchisement of southern blacks, in a fairer and more racially equitable reapportionment process and in the election of more minorities to local, state and federal legislative offices.[55] Yet certainly the decade-long legislative struggle in the 1960s and 1970s over school busing was largely a pyrrhic victory, predicted and predictable. The victory of the black lobby in the 1990–91 struggle to enact the Civil Rights Act may also be largely symbolic, if not pyrrhic.

The detailed study of the passage of the Civil Rights Act of 1991, while demonstrating the leverage of the civil rights coalition in Congress, also shows—in its twists and turns, its technical disputes over burdens and standard proofs, its packaging as a women's rights bill and its contradictory language on quotas, race norming and culturally biased tests—that the logic of civil rights legislation, like the logic of school busing litigation earlier, may have about run its course as a remedy for racial injustice. President Bush's consistent inconsistency on the legislation, Boyden Gray's attempt to revoke the whole body of affirmative action at the same time the president was signing the bill and the president's technical directive that the 1991 Act was to be interpreted as a reaffirmation of existing law further suggests that despite the legislative victories of the past decade, the issues of civil rights and affirmative action are becoming increasingly irrelevant. The two-year-long struggle to enact yet another civil rights bill has for example resulted in a law that employment discrimination attorneys describe as so riddled with confusing, contradictory and ambiguous provisions that it will take years for the courts to sort it out.[56] Yet it was the Supreme Court in its narrow, crabbed reading of existing law that made the 1991 Act necessary in the first place. It is therefore unlikely that it will read the deeply flawed 1991 Act with little more than the hostility that now appears to be the conservative majority's approach to race cases. This is especially so now that the federal judiciary at all levels is now firmly in the hands of Reagan-Bush appointees. The 1991 Act's statutory ban on race norming may also result in the substantial loss of jobs in the public sector, a traditional source of black employment in the white-collar sector.[57]

Beyond the specifics of the 1991 Act, the larger question is the continued viability of affirmative action. In its various forms, affirmative action is entrenched in the larger corporations, universities and many state and local governments. However, in small businesses (where many new jobs are created) it is not; and the available evidence suggests that racial discrimination in these sectors persists. It is not likely that the Civil Rights Act of 1991 or government affirmative action programs will be effective in altering these racist practices.[58] This suggests to me that, as in the busing struggle of a decade ago, blacks may be investing too many resources, symbolic and material (both of which are limited) in what may be a futile endeavor. Thus, I should like to argue that civil rights affirmative action issues must be rethought with an eye toward making them less of a priority item on the black agenda. It should be clear that my reservations about affirmative action are not of the same cloth as those critics, black and white, who argue that affirmative action is unfair reverse discrimination against whites; that it only benefits middle-class blacks; that it stigmatizes blacks and undermines their sense of achievement or self-esteem; or that it should be illegal or unconstitutional to consider race in allocative decisions so as to achieve diversity in the workplace and educational institutions or to remedy historical and institutional racism. On the contrary, I believe that on each of these points the critics are wrong or they vastly overstate the claims. Rather, my concern with affirmative action as a post–civil rights era issue is that for blacks, the benefits are probably not commensurate with the costs in terms of resources invested and that such a focus diverts resources away from the more urgently needed focus on the internal reorganization of the black community and the development of a long-term strategy of mobilization for social change.

One problem with affirmative action, like busing, is that there is much more talk about it than there is actual action.[59] This fuels the popular sentiment among whites that somehow whenever they fail to get a job, promotion or place in school it is because of an affirmative action quota for blacks. This of course is not the case, as a cursory review of the data on black joblessness at all educational levels and the evidence on continuing race discrimination would show; indeed, the available research tends to suggest that the principal beneficiaries of two decades of affirmative action have been white women.[60] Thus, as in the transformation of the 1991 Act into a women's rights bill, blacks devote substantial resources to a cause whose disproportionate beneficiaries are whites, gender notwithstanding. The effect, however, of this painting of affirmative action as widespread and as largely for the benefit of blacks is, like busing, to provide fuel for the campaigns of right-wing politicians such as Reagan, Jesse Helms, David Duke, George Bush and Patrick Buchanan, who cynically use the issue to exploit the ignorance and fears of working-class whites. Again, if the benefits were significant, then these political costs would be worth paying. But since they are marginal,[61] than the economic benefits may not balance the political costs, particularly since the focus by white liberals and the right also tends to divert attention away from the real remedies—internal and external—to the problems of the black community. There is, too, the tendency to lump all affirmative action programs together, from specialized minority scholarship programs to the admission programs at elite universities to those ordered by the courts or executive bureaucracies as a means to enforce relevant antidiscrimination statutes. Those of the latter type may necessarily be race specific and as the Supreme Court has held may even require quotas,[62] while those such as admission policies at elite universities may very well be administered on a flexible basis to benefit disadvantaged students of all races.[63] And while I am not overly bothered by the problem of racial stigmatization involved in most of these programs, some of them (such as the National Science Foundation's Minority Doctoral Program) may have that effect and might just as effectively be administered in a non–race-specific way.[64] My final reason, however, for suggesting a rethinking of affirmative action is that in the American democracy it probably cannot in the long run be sustained. Thus, like busing, the struggle may not only be symbolic but futile.[65]

7

Blacks in Congressional Decision Making:
The Humphrey-Hawkins Act as Symbolic Politics

Undoubtedly, persistent, widespread unemployment is the central problem confronting the post–civil rights era black community. The causes of this widespread joblessness are still the subject of debate among social scientists, but its debilitating effects on family and community life are not. Nor is its persistence—in good times and bad, in war and peace and in the civil rights and post–civil rights eras. Indeed, blacks are often heard to say, "The only time we have had full employment was during slavery." Thus, it would be virtually impossible for the leadership of a community wracked throughout its post-emancipation sojourn by recession- and depression-level joblessness not to make employment a central concern. One need only recall the cries of alarm and the calls for emergency action by white leaders during the 1982 recession when the unemployment rate reached near 10 percent. What more then for the leaders of the black community, where in the last twenty-five years an unemployment rate at or near 10 percent has been an abiding feature. Thus, the Humphrey-Hawkins full employment act is a natural result of post–civil rights era black politics. Concern with this issue is as old as the post–civil war era quest for forty acres and a mule as a means to provide an economic underpinning for the freedmen. However, until the great depression and the New Deal, blacks, like most Americans, tended not to look to the government for solutions to the employment problem. The New Deal changed this, as the federal government for the first time assumed responsibility for managing the economy so as to assure all citizens employment and economic security. Blacks were not much involved in New Deal economic policy making, except to try to assure nondiscrimination in the implementation of the relief and work programs. This concern with nondiscrimination early on led the NAACP, for example, to focus on race-based allocation of jobs. Even then, however, some blacks saw this approach as misguided because it did not address the more fundamental, systemic problem of the failure of the capitalist economy to produce sufficient jobs for all willing and able to work. Ralph Bunche in a 1939 article made this point as part of his overall critique of the programs of the black civil rights leadership. He wrote:

> It [the civil rights leadership] appears unable to realize that there is an economic system, as well as a race problem in America and that when a Negro is unemployed, it is not just because he is a Negro, but more seriously, because of the defective operation of the economy under which we live—an economy that finds it impossible to provide adequate numbers of jobs and economic security for the population. More seriously still this movement tends to widen the menacing gap between white and black workers, by insisting that jobs be distributed on a racial basis.[1]

This focus on the systemic basis of the problem and its interrelationship with racism was not explicitly addressed by the civil rights leadership until the end of the civil rights era, but from the New Deal on, the leaders of black America had as one of their priorities the implementation by the federal government of programs and policies that would address the problem of black joblessness.

Even as attention in the early 1960s was focused on the civil rights agenda, black leaders and national policy elites were concerned about the unemployment situation. The leaders of the major civil rights organization were well aware that blacks had not shared in America's postwar economic prosperity. On the contrary, the economic situation of blacks seemed to be deteriorating, with the unemployment rate rising to double that of whites, and Secretary of Labor Willard Wirtz warning that black workers were increasingly vulnerable in an economy that was rapidly shifting from industrial manufacturing to a more technical, service sector.[2] Awareness of this problem, however, did not make it the priority concern of the civil rights leadership or national policy elites, in part because the odious forms of segregation in the south seemed more pressing. Although the 1963 March on Washington was billed as a march for "jobs and freedom," the unemployment problem, as Graham writes, "lacked the gripping symbol of nationwide economic discrimination that was provided in the south by the black martyrs in the fight against Jim Crow."[3] In 1963 the Urban League did propose its comprehensive "Marshall Plan" to combat ghetto joblessness and poverty,[4] and black leaders were early supporters of Lyndon Johnson's war on poverty, although they were not participants in its design and from the outset complained that it was substantially underfunded. Nevertheless it required the achievement of "freedom" in the form of the civil rights laws of the 1960s before the focus of the civil rights leaders could turn to "jobs." Martin Luther King symbolized this shift from freedom to jobs in his last year as he joined the striking garbage workers in Memphis in their protracted struggle for a livable wage and decent working conditions while simultaneously planning a massive poor peoples march on Washington whose principal goal was to secure a federal commitment to a guaranteed job or income for all Americans. The strategic debate within King's inner circle about the efficacy of the poor peoples march has important implications for the theoretical concerns of this study. On one side of the debate were those who argued that by 1968, protest was not enough; that it had lost its effectiveness as a means to advance the post–civil rights era black agenda and that blacks had to turn to institutional politics and coalitions in order to advance the movement's economic agenda. Dr. King's view to the contrary was that the radical social and economic reforms required to address the problems of poverty could not be realized unless there was a radical movement of social protest.

Full Employment and the Transformation From Protest to Politics

In *Bearing the Cross*, David Garrow recounts in great detail the near year-long debate between Dr. King and Bayard Rustin over the wisdom of the poor peoples march.[5] Rustin did not oppose the goals of the poor peoples campaign; rather, he argued that they should be pursued through conventional, institutional politics. Rustin had outlined the logic of this shift from "protest to politics" in his 1965 *Commentary* article discussed in Chapter 1. In addition, Rustin argued that the protests at Birmingham and Selma which helped to secure passage of the civil rights and voting rights acts were successful for a unique set of reasons that could not be duplicated by the poor peoples campaign. First, unlike the issues of employment and poverty, the issue of civil rights was within the American tradition morally unambiguous. Second, the issue of civil rights was localized in the southern region of the country, while the issue of joblessness was national. The strategic implication of this was that blacks could draw on allies from nonsouthern groups and politicians who could join in the cause at relatively little cost. The brutal violence of the southern authorities, which did so much to galvanize elite and mass support for civil rights, was not likely to be replicated by federal authorities in Washington. Finally, in the poor peoples campaign the federal government itself would be the target of the protests—the enemy, so to speak—while in the civil rights protests the government in Washington was part of the audience to be mobilized. Once mobilized it became a powerful ally that could alter the structure of southern race relations. Given these limitations, Rustin contended that protest had simply outlived its usefulness in the black freedom struggle.

King's response to Rustin's analysis was essentially to argue that the kind of "radical restructuring" envisioned by the poor peoples campaign could only come about as a result of a mass movement of the poor (of all colors) who could appeal not only to the moral conscience of the nation but bring such pressure to bear that the federal government would have no alternative except to act. Although King was in private and occasionally in some of his speeches flirting with the notion of a restructuring of American society along democratic socialist lines, this was not an explicit focus of the campaign; but this radical implication was implicit in the notion of a government guaranteed job or income.[6] A program of radical change therefore required a movement of radical action. At the time of his murder King, without the assistance of Rustin and with the tepid support of many of his top aides (including the young Jesse Jackson), was going forward with plans for the march. After his death the poor peoples campaign, under the leadership of his successor Ralph Abernathy, was carried out in Washington. But King's death had demoralized the organizers and participants, and the campaign turned into more of a final tribute to King than a well-organized protest along the lines of Selma or Birmingham.[7] Except for the promise of a few minor changes in food stamp and welfare regulations, the campaign had little impact on the increasingly conservative Congress or on the president's support for fundamental reform in welfare policy or full employment.[8] The 1968 poor peoples march was the last major movement protest of the era. Its failure appeared to vindicate Rustin's critique of the continuing efficacy of protest and gave further impetus to the ongoing black leadership establishment's strategy shift from movement to institutional politics.

Whether the poor peoples campaign would have followed the same course if Dr. King had lived to lead it cannot be known. Reverend Abernathy was no Dr. King, either in strategic and tactical skills or in his charismatic authority. But, given the increasingly rancorous state of American race relations in 1968 and the growing conservative backlash in Congress and public opinion resulting from the black power revolt, the ghetto rebellions and the Vietnam protests, it is probable that even if Dr. King had lived, the poor peoples campaign would not have resulted in federal full employment legislation or fundamental reforms in the welfare system.[9] The logic of social movement outcomes as discussed in Chapter 1 also suggests that black politics, the outcome of the poor peo-

ples campaign notwithstanding, was moving in an increasingly institutional direction. Whether Dr. King would have followed this logic as
did most of his associates (he was being urged at the time of his death to
run for president) or whether he would have continued to press for
movement activism is not clear. In any event, King's death was symbolic of the end of the era of protest in the Afro-American freedom
struggle and the beginnings of its incipient institutionalization.

The theoretical and substantive bases of this transformation were
discussed in Chapter 1. To review here briefly for purposes of analysis
of the Humphrey-Hawkins, case I return to the strategic analysis of
Rustin, and the more academic discussion of Browning, Marshall and
Tabb. Both Rustin and Browning and his colleagues agree that by the
late 1960s protest was not enough to advance the black agenda. Browning, Marshall and Tabb did not seek to specify that agenda; however,
Rustin in his *Commentary* article clearly envisioned it as one of radical
economic and social reform (including full employment and reconstruction of the ghettos) that would in his words result in the "qualita-
tive transformation of fundamental institutions, more or less rapidly, to
the point where the social and economic structures which they comprised can no longer be said to be the same."[10] Rustin's strategy to
achieve this far-reaching agenda of reform was the development of a
multiracial coalition of minorities, liberals and labor that would come
together to become the governing majority. Browning, Marshall and
Tabb advance the same argument. As an alternative to protest, they
argue that policy responsiveness to black demands requires incorporation into systemic institutions and processes. Such incorporation to be
effective requires (1) the mobilization of the resources of the black community, (2) the development and maintenance of an interracial, multiethnic coalition of other progressive constituencies and (3) the transla-
tion of this coalition into an electoral majority that becomes the
government. The Humphrey-Hawkins Act may be seen as an application of Rustin's strategy or as limiting case study in the incorporationist
theory of Browning, Marshall and Tabb. Humphrey-Hawkins is a textbook case. Everything was done right, according to theory: There was
the effort to develop a consensus, deracialized issue—full employment—that appealed across lines of class and color. There was the effort
made at both the mass and elite level to mobilize the black community
in support of the bill, and the effort to construct a broad multiethnic
coalition. Finally, in the Carter administration, blacks and this broad
coalition constituted the governing majority in the executive branch as
well as the Congress. Yet, in spite of this textbook case in institutional
politics, the outcome of this legislative struggle for full employment

was no more successful than the ill-fated struggle of the poor peoples campaign. To tell the tale of the Humphrey-Hawkins Act is therefore to tell a story on the limitations of the fundamental strategy of post–civil rights era black politics.

The Humphrey-Hawkins Case: Deja Vu All Over Again[11]

As indicated in Chapter 1, at the Urban League's first national conference to consider post–civil rights era issues, Charles Hamilton presented a paper that articulated the analytic and strategic basis for the full employment priority, arguing that the issue was ideal for consensus building in the black community, the mobilization of a multiracial progressive coalition and the shift from movement-style protest politics to the new institutional politics. Full employment was central among the Congressional Black Caucus's 1969 recommendations to President Nixon and in its subsequent issue agendas for black America. It was also adopted as the number one priority by the Joint Center's first National Institute of Black Public Officials. The Humphrey-Hawkins bill thus emerges out of this broad post–civil rights era black leadership consensus.[12]

Origins of the Bill

The task of translating this broad consensus into a concrete legislative proposal became the responsibility of the Congressional Black Caucus. Early on, the Caucus divided itself into a series of committees or "brain trusts" to deal with domestic and foreign policy issues. These so-called brain trusts, corresponding roughly to the members' House Committee assignments, were designed to solicit the research and advice of scholars and other policy experts within a specific issue area. Workshops or hearings were then held at the Caucus's annual legislative weekends, where persons from across the country could be informed and an informal national issue network could develop. Once an issue was put in the form of a bill, it became the responsibility of the brain trust to mobilize support for its enactment.

Given this division of labor within the Caucus, it fell to Congressman Augustus Hawkins of the Watts district in Los Angeles, a member of the House Education and Labor Committee and chair of its subcommittee on Equal Employment Opportunities, to take responsibility for the employment issue. Hawkins, a senior member of the Caucus first elected in 1962, was a traditional, New Deal/Great Society liberal integrationist. In the context of the internal politics of the Caucus, Hawkins was (he retired from Congress in 1990) among the more conservative members. In demeanor he was quiet and reserved. As a traditional liberal he was reluctant to embrace the philosophy of black power and as such was leery of the formation of the race-exclusive Caucus of blacks in the House. He was the most outspoken Caucus member in opposing the 1972 National Black Political Convention and the notion of a black political party. In a sense, then, Hawkins's leadership on the employment issue was fortuitous, for in background, philosophy and temperament he was ideally suited to lead the legislative struggle on a non-race-specific bill like full employment that required the formation of a multiracial coalition. Hawkins as chair of the Employment Opportunities Subcommittee and the Caucus brain trust on employment was the pivotal actor in holding hearings, drafting the legislation, negotiating its many revisions, getting it out of committee and managing the House floor debate. In addition, his subcommittee played an important role in developing public awareness of the issue and mobilizing interest group support.

According to Essie Seck, all indications are that Congressman Hawkins began working on a draft of the legislation as early as 1973.[13] In that year a symposium was held at UCLA on full employment policy, and Hawkins circulated a preliminary draft of his bill for discussion purposes.[14] And in June of 1974 the first version of the bill, the Equal Opportunity and Full Employment Act, was introduced in the House.[15] This bill, like its 1946 counterpart, represented a fundamental change in the operations of the market economy. First, it returned to the principles and language of the 1946 Act by declaring in its opening section that all adult Americans able and willing to work have the right to equal opportunities for useful paid employment; that the federal government is responsible for guaranteeing this right and for assuring that national full employment is attained and maintained; and that other national economic goals shall be pursued without limiting the rights established by the act. This is the language borrowed from the 1946 Act, with the important addition of the language specifying "equal opportunities." This addition, of course, was designed to address the concern of the framers with the problem of racial discrimination. This first draft also sought to make clear that the nation's other economic goals—low inflation and a balanced budget—were not to be pursued at the expense of the full employment goal. In addition to these broad declarations of policy the bill required the following: (1) the president must submit to the Congress the estimated level of expenditures necessary to reach full employment; (2) the Congress must act on his recommendations within thirty days; (3) the creation of a Job Guarantee Office and a stand-by Job Corps to provide jobs for registered job seekers, including public service projects, as a part of community public service work projects; (4) the understanding that any person who presents him or herself in person shall be considered willing and able to work; (5) the authorization of such sums as needed to carry out the provisions of the act for the fiscal year 1975 and for each succeeding fiscal year; and (6) provision of the federal district courts with jurisdiction over actions seeking relief pursuant to the act. Finally, like the 1946 act, this first draft did not include a numerical goal or percentage that would constitute full employment because it was thought that such a number would be meaningless. (In 1975 the bill was modified to establish a numerical goal of 3 percent unemployment to be achieved within three years of enactment. Later this was changed to 4 percent within five years).

During the discussions of the crafting of the 1946 act, Bailey quotes one of the participants as arguing that the government could tinker with the economy through changes in the tax laws, interest rates and antitrust laws, but "the only real guarantee of full employment was government spending, so why not call a spade a spade."[16] The 1974 version of the bill did just this. Whatever one thinks of the merits of the legislation, one thing is clear: it would have—through the automatic spending provision and the provision of judicial relief—provided jobs for all who sought them. It called a spade a spade.

It is not clear whether Hawkins saw this 1974 bill as a realistic measure that could be enacted or as simply the opening bid in the long process of legislative bargaining. It turned out, of course, to be the latter. The 1946 Act went through seven revisions in six months before it reached the Senate floor. The 1978 Act went through three major revisions in four years before it reached the House floor for debate. The first major change came about as part of the effort to build a broad coalition of interests in support of the legislation, while the second came about in negotiations to obtain the support of President Carter. When the final revised bill reached the House floor in 1978 it, like the 1946 bill, bore little resemblance to the original bill. It had been weakened in four significant ways: First, the stand-by Jobs Corp and the Job Guarantee Office had been eliminated. Second, the automatic spending authorization provision was dropped. Third, the right to sue was deleted. And finally, although the broad language and principles of "full" employment guaranteed by the federal government were maintained, these goals were given parity with maintaining low inflation and a balanced budget. Thus, as in 1946, the bill was transformed into a discretionary planning and goal-setting act, without even the new institutional mechanisms—the Council of Economic Advisors and the Joint Economic Committee—created by the 1946 legislation.

The Mobilization of Support:
The Full Employment Action Council

The first major revision occurred in 1976 as a result of consulta-
tions by Hawkins and his staff with leading economists (Bertram Gross
who had worked on the 1946 act and Leon Keryersling were principal
consultants) and representatives of liberal and labor interest groups.
In 1946 the "lib-lab" coalition organized what it called a continuation
group to develop strategy and mobilize support for the bill.[17] Similarly,
in 1976 the Full Employment Action Council (FEAC), a broad umbrella
group of liberal, labor, civil rights, religious and political groups was
organized. Except for the more influential role played by the black
groups this coalition was very much like the one in 1946. Cochaired by
Dr. King's widow Coretta and Murray Finley, president of the Amal-
gamated Clothing Workers of America, the FEAC's board of directors,
according to Seck, was a "Who's Who of labor, liberal, civil rights and
women groups."[18] A price was paid for labor's participation in the coalition. Because of the historic hostility of the courts in labor relations
cases, the AFL-CIO was wary of giving the courts jurisdiction in
employment cases and insisted that the individual right to sue be
deleted. Most other groups in the FEAC disagreed, arguing that
removal of the judicial enforcement mechanism in effect eliminated the
right to a job. Hawkins and Mrs. King argued that without labor's support there would be no bill; as a result the FEAC board reluctantly
agreed to delete the provision.[19] The second major change eliminated the
bill's automatic spending provisions. This was done largely to satisfy
those members of the coalition and congressional supporters who
argued that this provision would undermine the bill's credibility in the
eyes of those concerned with a balanced budget and inflation.

Hawkins and the coalition then sought to mobilize interest group
and mass, grassroots support for the revised bill. Hawkins continued to
use his Employment Opportunities Subcommittee as a forum to build
public and congressional support for the bill, including a series of
regional hearings in several large cities. Congressman Hawkins and
Senator Humphrey also prepared articles explaining the nature and
purpose of the legislation and helped to persuade colleagues on the
Banking, Housing and Urban Affairs Committees and the Joint Economic Committee to give the bill a sympathetic hearing.[20] But the main
task of lobbying and mobilization of support fell to the FEAC. Early
on, Jesse Jackson and groups of black ministers sought to mobilize the
jobless in several cities in demonstrations and rallies in support of the
bill.[21] The leaders of fifteen major black civil rights and political organi-

zations agreed to coordinate a national lobbying campaign. Local FEACs were established in more than one hundred cities and many constituent groups within the coalition (the National Farmers Union, the National Council of Churches and the American Jewish Committee) took actions independent of FEAC, including passing resolutions of support, writing members of Congress and sending representatives to testify before congressional committees. The FEAC sponsored what it called Full Employment Week during the first week of September, 1977. Across the country rallies, workshops and seminars were held, commercials were broadcast on local television stations and the CBS radio network. During the week, more than five thousand pieces of literature were distributed and 300,000 signatures were collected on petitions to Congress.[22] It is difficult to assess the impact of the coalition's efforts on the legislative outcome; however, it is clear that the supporters of Humphrey-Hawkins assembled a broad coalition and engaged in a well-organized lobbying campaign.

Compared to the well-organized lobbying efforts of the bill's supporters, the opposition to the bill involved only a few groups and was limited to informal contacts with administration officials, congressional leaders and congressional testimony by leading business groups, principally the National Association of Manufacturers, the Chamber of Commerce and the Business Roundtable. Business did not mobilize extensively on the bill as it has on other controversial economic legislation—common situs picketing for example during the Carter administration—because it guessed that the bill as originally drafted would be watered down by administration and congressional leaders sufficiently to satisfy its interests before it even came close to final passage. Once this was done, although the major business organizations continued to oppose the legislation, the opposition appeared largely perfunctory since the bill's threat to the privileged position of business had been removed in its several revisions. Reading the testimony of business representatives on the revised bill, one finds the same arguments used against the 1946 act: that the notion of full employment threatened unacceptable government intrusion in the free enterprise system; that it would involve costly "make work" public service jobs; that it would lead to large budget deficits; that the 4 percent target would lead to run-away inflation; and that with lower taxes and less government spending and regulation the market itself would move the nation toward full employment.[23] Organized business opposition on an issue of this sort is clearly going to influence Washington politicians, whether or not their opposition is expressed informally or in a well-orchestrated pressure campaign.

One such form of pressure, which pluralist "group theorists" tend to ignore, is more important and effective than any other, and business is uniquely placed to exercise it without the need of organization, campaigns, and lobbying. This is the pervasive and permanent pressure upon governments and the state generated by the private control of concentrated industrial, commercial and financial resources. The existence of this area of independent economic power is a fact no government, whatever its inclination, can ignore in the determination of its policies, not only in regard to economic matters but to other matters as well. . . . It is implicit testimony to the power of business that all governments, not least reforming ones, have always been profoundly concerned to gain and retain its "confidence." Nor certainly is there any other interest whose "confidence" is deemed so precious, or whose "loss of confidence" is so feared.[24]

Apart from business, the other major opposition to the bill came from academic economists, particularly John Kenneth Galbraith and Charles Shultz. Galbraith and Shultz were not only important academic economists but also long-time functionaries in Democratic administrations (Shultz was to become Chairman of Carter's Council of Economic Advisors). Their views, therefore, carried considerable weight especially among liberal Democrats in Congress. Throughout the congressional debate, for example, reference was made to Galbraith's testimony in which he told the Senate Banking Committee:

At a four percent unemployment rate, there is no question the American economy can be dangerously inflationary. . . . I must specifically and deliberately warn my liberal friends not to engage in the wishful economics that causes them to hope that there is still some undiscovered fiscal or monetary magic which will combine low unemployment with low inflation.[25]

Schultz's opposition was probably more influential than Galbraith's. Seck writes, "It is widely agreed that Charles Shultz's early criticism of the bill helped to side track it in 1976."[26] In his role as Carter's chief economic advisor he was principally responsible for the negotiation of the final revised version of the bill. In testimony before a Senate subcommittee Shultz said, "The chief obstacle . . . is inflation. I believe S.50 does not sufficiently recognize that fact, and hence needs to be changed in a number of important respects. Moreover, the combination of 'employer of last resort' provision in this bill and the wage standards that go with it threatens to make the inflation problem worse."[27] During the 1976 campaign Shultz was among the several persons consulted by Jimmy Carter on economic policy. Whatever chances a substantive Humphrey-Hawkins bill might have had in the Carter administration were undermined by Shultz's roles before, during and after the 1976 election.

Blacks, the 1976 Election and Full Employment

    In the theory I am pursuing here, blacks in the Humphrey-Hawkins case fulfilled two of the three key elements of effective institutional politics: they developed a broad-based, non-race-specific issue that would have benefitted whites as well as blacks, mobilized the black community (at least its leadership) behind the issue and put together a fairly broad-based coalition of liberals, labor, Jews and other groups in support of a specific legislative proposal. The final requirement of the theory is the election of a president who becomes the leader of a governing coalition that would enact and implement the legislation. Blacks were an important part—in the primaries an indispensable part—of the coalition that elected President Carter. And during the campaign black leaders sought, with some success, to get the Democratic Party and its nominee to commit themselves to the Humphrey-Hawkins bill.

    Jimmy Carter received 94 percent of the black vote. Without this support he could not have defeated President Ford. The 1976 election was so close that to say this, however, is to say very little. President Carter could not have defeated President Ford without the support of labor, the Hispanics or the Hawaiians. In the general election, the key component of the Carter victory was his ability as a native son to bring the traditionally Democratic South back to the party coalition. The black vote turned out to be decisive in the election because Carter could not have won without the South and he could not have won the South without overwhelming black support (Ford carried 55 percent of the southern white vote). It is important, then, not to overstate the significance of the black vote in Carter's election. Carter received only 7 percent more of the black vote than Humphrey in the 1968 election and roughly the same vote as George McGovern in 1972. Carter won because he could carry a significant proportion of the southern white vote and Humphrey and McGovern could not. Thus it was not the magnitude of black support that was decisive but that support in conjunction with significant support from Carter's fellow white southerners. It is this 45 percent white southern support, and not the 94 percent black support, that made the difference between Democratic defeat in 1968 and 1972 and victory in 1976. If blacks cannot be said to have made the difference in Carter's victory in the general election, such can be said for their role in the primaries. Charles McCamey's analysis is essentially correct:

> Black voters were responsible for several of Carter's key victories. In Florida, for example, Carter's first place finish over Alabama Governor George Wallace and Senator Henry Jackson established him as a major contender. In Michigan, Carter won a narrow 2,000 vote victory over Rep. Morris Udall on the same day he was he was losing badly in Maryland to California Governor Jerry Brown. Without strong black support, neither his Florida or Michigan victory would have been possible, and Carter's road to the nomination might well have been blocked. In other states—North Carolina and Illinois to name two—black voters helped swell Carter victories to impressive levels.[28]

Black support for Carter in the early primaries was important for another reason: it gave Carter, the one-time Georgia governor, legitimacy in the eyes of northern white liberals. If blacks had not supported Carter or indeed had opposed him, then his candidacy would have inevitably been tainted with racism and this would have given liberals in the North, suspicious of his antiestablishment candidacy from the beginning, a legitimate basis to deny him the nomination. This is the significance of the support of then Georgia Congressman Andrew Young and the King family (one need only consider the impact on Carter's campaign if Young and Reverend King had taken the position of Georgia State Senator Julian Bond and denounced Carter as a "Georgia cracker" or worse). In this sense, it is accurate to say that black support was absolutely indispensable in Carter's eventual election, because he could not have become the Democratic nominee without black support.

During the course of the campaign, black leaders sought to get Carter to endorse the revised bill, which had restricted (although not eliminated) government last-resort jobs, the right to sue and the automatic spending provisions. This new version of the bill was introduced in both the House and Senate in 1976. Both Andrew Young and especially Mrs. King urged Carter to endorse this new version of the bill. He refused. In April of 1976 Carter in an offhand remark created a brief media flap that resulted in his endorsement of Humphrey-Hawkins. What Carter said was, "I see nothing wrong with ethnic purity. I would not force integration of a neighborhood by government action." The remarks were made in response to a question about scatter-site housing in the suburbs. Black leaders and the press interpreted Carter's statement as racist in that it seemed to support segregated housing and the exclusion of blacks from the suburbs.[29] Because of his southern background, the possible racist implications of these remarks were perhaps more salient among blacks and northern liberals. Thus Carter and his aides in consultation with Young and Reverend Martin Luther King, Sr., sought to reestablish his civil rights bona fides. The result was a statement endorsing the Humphrey-Hawkins bill. Carter said "I support and as president would sign the Humphrey-Hawkins bill as amended, given my current understanding of it."[30] But several weeks later in an interview with two business magazines, he backed away from this support, saying that the bill's unemployment targets would create double-digit inflation.[31] Thus, from the 1976 campaign through the legislative debates to the final signing of the Act, Carter's record on Humphrey-Hawkins could be described as "inconsistent and contradictory."

The party platform endorsed the principles of the bill without mentioning it by name. It said, "The Democratic party is committed to the right of all adult Americans willing, able and seeking work to have opportunities for useful paid jobs at living wages. To make this commitment meaningful, we pledge ourselves to the support of legislation that will make every responsible effort to reduce adult unemployment to 3 percent within four years."[32] However, Carter's principal representative to the platform committee, Stuart Eizenstadt, said that neither this platform plank, nor any other for that matter, was binding on the nominee because "Governor Carter realized from the beginning that this was to be the party's platform, not his platform."[33]

Once elected, Carter said and did nothing about the bill. As discussed earlier, Carter appointed a large number of blacks to highly visible positions in his administration. But in substantive policy areas of concern to blacks—full employment, national urban policy and health insurance—he hesitated. Early in the administration Vernon Jordan, President of the Urban League, drew widespread press attention when he attacked the president for ignoring the concerns of the one group responsible for his election.[34] Relationships between Carter and the black leadership community in general were becoming strained. In May of 1977 the Congressional Black Caucus requested a meeting with the president to discuss the Humphrey-Hawkins bill, among other things. He refused.[35] In the fall of the year Carter finally agreed to the meeting with the Caucus to discuss the bill. At the meeting he agreed to make a revised version of the bill among his legislative priorities for the following year and instructed Charles Shultz to meet with Senator Humphrey and Congressman Hawkins to negotiate a final bill the administration could support.[36] Since Shultz had done so much the year before to scuttle the bill, his appointment to lead the administration's team was not a good sign. Of the others involved in the administration's team of negotiators—White House domestic policy aide Eizenstadt, Federal Reserve Chairman William Miller and Labor Secretary Ray Marshall—only Marshall supported the bill's principles.[37] In the negotiations, Shultz sought to delete all language relating to a *right* to a job and elimination or modification of the 4 percent target goal. Although he was not successful, "during the negotiations he was said to have used stalling tactics such as claiming, as Carter did, to be unfamiliar with the provisions; playing around with the unemployment goals, suggesting 7% in five years or 6% in eight years, etc."[38]

The delay in reaching an acceptable compromise resulted in further tensions and conflict between the president and the Black Caucus. As the time for the Caucus' annual legislative weekend approached Carter once again met with the group to discuss the bill. To break the deadlock in the talks, the Caucus urged the president to call a Camp David Summit with the Caucus, House and Senate leaders and the FEAC to provide a sense of urgency for the bill's passage.[39] Carter refused, and as a result, Congressman John Conyers walked out of the meeting in protest.[40] Later, several members of the Caucus led a large group of persons attending its legislative weekend in protest demonstrations at the capitol urging support for the bill. Carter addressed the Caucus dinner and received what was described as a "rousing, jubilant reception," and in the call and response style of black preachers he said "we can never stop moving toward full employment until every man and every woman has a job and I am determined to see this bill passed this year. . . . [We] can never be satisfied until the hundreds and thousands of young black men walking the streets looking for a job can find one."[41]

The final version of the bill endorsed by Carter retained the language guaranteeing full employment as a right and a 4 percent target goal for adults; but in exchange Carter got language included that put controlling inflation on an equal footing with reducing unemployment, and authority for the president to modify the bill's goals or timetables in the third year after passage. It also removed any language dealing with direct authorization of expenditures. Thus, like the 1946 Act, by the time the bill reached the floor of the House for debate it was largely symbolic. As Massachusetts Senator Edward Brooke, the Senate's only black member and a ranking member of the Banking Committee that had been instrumental in crafting language to make the bill acceptable to his Republican colleagues, said, "the bill was somewhat emasculated, if not totally emasculated."[42]

The revised bill was widely criticized within the FEAC, with numerous groups arguing that the compromise was unacceptable; that it had rendered the bill meaningless and unworthy of coalition support. Coretta King said she was not completely satisfied with the Carter compromise but thought it was better than nothing. A statement released by her and FEAC cochair Finley said, "We are practical people. . . . We know that without the President's support this legislation would have great difficulty in Congress. . . . We would urge those who are evaluating this proposal to compare it with what now exists, rather than naively comparing it to the ideal without regard for political or economic realities."[43] The FEAC finally endorsed the passage of the Carter compromise; however, several groups dissented.[44] The compromise bill was also dismissed by the national press. The *Washington Post* called it a "hollow promise," and in an editorial that was quoted by conservative opponents of the bill throughout the congressional debate, the *New York Times* said:

> The bill is deeply flawed. An earlier version which set unattainable target goals for the unemployment rate and promised too much. Now, it promises too little. It would legislate wishful thinking, not a reduction in unemployment. It deserves a harder look from its boosters and rejection by Congress. It would play a cruel hoax on the hard core unemployed holding before them hope— but not the reality—of a job. For that reason alone Humphrey-Hawkins should be rejected.[45]

Again, to draw a parallel with the 1946 Act, by the time the bill reached the floors of Congress the substantive debate was over. The real deals and compromises were made in committee and in the administration negotiations with the Caucus and the FEAC. The floor debates in a sense were anticlimactic. Again, however, as in 1946, the opponents who had successfully emasculated the bill substantively now sought to undermine its psychological and symbolic significance, and as in 1946, they were successful.

The Congressional Debates

The House debated the bill for several days in early March, 1978. Those who favored the bill, mostly Democrats, argued that the legislation provided a useful planning mechanism to fulfill the goals of the original 1946 Act.[46] As Congressman Hawkins put it, "This simply suggests that we return to a lawful observation of what is already the law of the land."[47] While conceding that the legislation did not create a single job, proponents argued that it committed in specific language the federal government to *full* employment with specific numerical goals and established a planning mechanism and process for the president, the Congress and the Federal Reserve to achieve those goals within a five-year time frame. Opponents, mostly Republicans and conservative Democrats, attacked the bill on several grounds. First, it was argued that it was meaningless, a cruel hoax, as the *New York Times* said. Congressman Sikes said, "it has been so diluted as to be meaningless . . . it would offer the unemployed a promise as hollow as the one made thirty years ago. The bill would not create a single job and would have no impact on the unemployment rate."[48] Several Republican members argued that while the bill's substantive provisions were meaningless, that it was, as Congressman Latta said, "A blue print for a planned economy, most of the details of which could have been lifted out of any socialist handbook," or Congressman Hyde, "This will delight the Fabian socialists. It is a giant step toward central economic planning."[49] A number of conservative Democrats opposed the bill on the grounds that the 4 percent unemployment goal would be inflationary. Said Congressman Jones of Oklahoma, "I rise with disappointment and reluctance to oppose this bill. . . . A 1976 CBO study indicates that in an effort to reach the 4 percent unemployment goal, we would risk a 1.25 percent increase in inflation the first year. The safeguards against inflation in the bill are too vague and unspecific to be of real value."[50] Republicans during the debate rejected the Jones notion of the unemployment-inflation trade-off arguing as did then Congressman David Stockman, "The unemployment-inflation trade off . . . did not arise on our side of the aisle. It has never been argued by conservative economists. The whole notion that there is a trade off between full employment and maintenance of price stability is an artifact of Keynsians; the 'Phillips curve' in fact was conceived, hatched and projected from the Brookings Institute by the same people who are making the administration's economic policy."[51] The final theme that runs through the House debate is that the bill was being passed or should be passed as memorial or tribute to Senator Hubert Humphrey, who had died the year before. Congressman Long noted that the bill is "a fitting memorial to our dear friend and colleague, Hubert Humphrey," and Congressman Perkins observed that "passage of it will be a fitting tribute to the memory of the late Senator Humphrey, whose legislative accomplishments stand second to none."[52]

Although the debate was extensive in the House, as the foregoing shows it was largely without substance or passion since its passage was a foregone conclusion and the participants were simply going through the ideological rituals. For example, Congressman LaFalce noted that "Business interests have been virtually silent on this bill, because they really do not object that strenuously to it at all. . . . Indeed, the Business Roundtable has not only not come out in opposition but it has come to the brink of endorsing it."[53] Thus, apart from ritualistic ideological rhetoric about socialist blueprints, the Phillips curve and empty symbols and hollow promises, opponents of the legislation tried to offer a series of amendments that would undermine whatever symbolic value the legislation might have. As one Congressman said, since the bill is a "Sears Wishbook," we can add anything to it that we wish. Thus, amendments to balance the budget were offered by several congressmen; Congressman Kemp offered an amendment for across-the-board tax cuts; and there were amendments to establish a 3 percent inflation target; to require a budget surplus and to establish 100 percent parity in farm support. Again, the strategy here in part was to make the bill's 4 percent unemployment goal look foolish by linking it to what was viewed as other unrealistic or unattainable goals. Except for the 100 percent farm parity (which was adopted over the objections of Congressman Hawkins and the Black Caucus by a vote of 264 to 180), all of the amendments were rejected. The only amendment of consequence and controversy was offered by Majority Leader Jim Wright requiring the president to establish annual and five-year goals for inflation as well as unemployment. This amendment, supported by the president and the Business Roundtable was adopted as an alternative to a specific 3 percent inflation goal. It passed 277 to 143. With that, everything was over except the voting. On final passage the bill was approved overwhelmingly, with the opposition coming mainly from Republicans and conservative Democrats.

The Senate took up the bill in October near the session's end. Some Caucus members suggested that Senate Majority Leader Robert Byrd deliberately delayed scheduling the legislation until late in the session because he really did not favor it. Although Senate Minority Leader Howard Baker did not like the bill, he agreed to work out a scheduling agreement in negotiations with Senators Byrd, Cranston, Brooke and Muriel Humphrey. Without Baker's cooperation the bill would have died in the end-of-session rush to adjourn prior to the fall election. Baker noted that his willingness to allow consideration of the bill was out of respect and veneration for Muriel and Hubert Humphrey, noting that this was the only legislation that would bear Humphrey's name.[54] Senate debate focused largely on amendments that would establish numerical goals for inflation (the Senate Banking Committee on a close vote had added an amendment that set a zero percent inflation goal), a

balanced budget and limitations on government spending to 20 percent of the gross national product. Although these amendments had
been rejected by the House and were opposed by the administration,
they were adopted as part of a bipartisan leadership compromise.[55] Otherwise, the Senate debate followed the lines of the House debate; Senators who favored the bill argued that while the legislation was more
symbolic than substantive, it represented nevertheless a "useful statement of principles" and provided a "planning" and "process" framework to achieve the goal of full employment. Senator Javits said, "It is
essentially a planning bill, a bill of concept and intention."[56] Opponents
argued that the law was innocuous, a cruel hoax, or that it was the
beginning, the first step in the process of a planned economy.[57] The Senate passed the bill 70 to 19 (eleven senators not voting). The opponents
were largely right-wing Republicans, along with two southern conservatives (Stennis and Eastland of Mississippi) and liberals Biden, Weiker
and Hatfield.[58]

President Carter signed the Humphrey-Hawkins Act on October
27 at a White House ceremony with leading members of the FEAC and
the Black Caucus. In his remarks the president said the Act was a "first
step," not a "panacea," and that he intended to make inflation not jobs
his priority, saying "But I warn you that our fight against inflation must
succeed if we are to maintain the steady economic growth necessary to
avoid an *increase* in unemployment and to achieve the goals in the
Humphrey-Hawkins bill" (emphasis in text).[59] Mrs. King in her remarks
recalled that her husband had started the drive for full employment in
1968 with the Poor Peoples Campaign and thus the Act was a tribute to
him, and in effusive language Congressman Hawkins described Carter,
who had so consistently worked to emasculate his original bill, as a
"magnificent President" and the Act itself as a "modern day magna
carta of economic rights."[60]

Conclusion

Politicians exaggerate, and it is perhaps understandable that after
years of labor Congressman Hawkins, like any parent with a newborn
baby, would see a beautiful offspring; but the child was ugly. It was a
meaningless piece of legislation, not a cruel hoax on the unemployed,
only because they were either unaware of the law or, if aware, knew it
as more Washington lies. The Act—Public Law 95-523—amended the
1946 Employment Act by inserting the word "full"; by establishing
quantitative goals for reaching full employment in a specified time
period, and a process whereby the President, the Congress and the Fed-

eral Reserve Board would develop coordinated, integrated policies to meet the goals of the Act. The Act also provided that policies be developed to eliminate the disparities in unemployment rates between minorities, but also women, youth and others in the labor force. While acknowledging that the Act did not require the president, the Congress or the Federal Reserve to do anything (except for reports and analysis) that they were not already authorized to do, the Act's proponents satisfied themselves with the notion that if these institutions wished to act, the legislation provided a planning framework to move toward a full employment economy.[61] But in the decade and more since the bill was passed, neither the president, the Congress or the Federal Reserve have sought to use the planning processes in the Act to move toward a 4 percent unemployed rate. As Congressman Hawkins woefully wrote in a 1986 article, "Since the passage of the Act, we have yet to see an economic report from the President, a Federal Reserve report or a Joint Economic Committee report that constructs the actual programmatic means for achieving full employment."[62] On the contrary, economic policy makers today generally consider 5 to 6 percent unemployment as the so-called natural rate of unemployment, or full employment. This natural rate of unemployment, which translates into 10 to 12 percent for blacks, is accepted by Republicans and Democrats and liberals and conservatives. (Lawrence Summers, Democratic nominee Michael Dukakis's chief economic advisor in 1988, defined 6 percent as full employment).[63] Thus, in the years since Humphrey-Hawkins was enacted, not only have no programmatic means to reach its goals been implemented, but the 4 percent goal itself has in effect been repealed. So, as Congressman Hawkins asks, "What happened to full employment?" Why did this priority item on the post–civil rights agenda end up as an empty symbol? Why did the Full Employment Act of 1978 fail?

As a first answer one may turn to history. The Full Employment Act of 1978 failed for essentially the same reasons that the 1946 act failed. The 1946 act was proposed at a time when there was a fear of a post-war return to depression levels of joblessness. When this did not materialize, much of the political momentum for the bill disappeared. When the Humphrey-Hawkins Act was first proposed in 1974 there was no fear of massive unemployment. Thus, there was little political pressure for the legislation from the beginning. Rather, the bill was viewed throughout the legislative struggle as a "black" bill pushed by the Congressional Black Caucus in response to the persistent recession level unemployment rates in the black community. Thus, despite of all the talk about the deracialized nature of the employment issue (i.e., that more whites are unemployed than blacks and therefore whites would benefit more from the bill than blacks) and the effort to construct a multiracial coalition in the Washington community, the bill was viewed as race-specific legislation—a black bill.

The perception of the bill in the Washington community is the critical variable, since, as in 1946, the bill probably had little salience beyond the beltway. As far as I could learn, no polls were conducted on public support for Humphrey-Hawkins (which is itself an indicator of the press's lack of interest in the legislation) but it is very likely that if such polls had been conducted they would have shown what the 1946 polls showed: very little public knowledge of the legislation.[64] This again points to the limits of the hierarchical, middle-class model of mobilization employed by the bill's supporters. As in 1946, an impressive coalition of liberals, labor, church and civic groups was brought together in the FEAC to support the legislation. Yet, this was a mobilization of the "lib-lab" elite of Washington interest groups rather than a grassroots mobilization of the jobless. Sporadic efforts were made by the coalition's black elements to mobilize the ghetto jobless but they were sporadic and certainly did not create anything like movement-style mass pressure. The struggle was fought in the narrow confines of routine Washington interest group politics, where the coalition's resources were no match for the disproportionate influence of business. In this context, if a meaningful Humphrey-Hawkins bill was to have any chance, the full support and resources of the presidency was imperative. Yet, again as in 1946, the president was a reluctant and inconsistent warrior in the battle. Carter did not like the legislation, endorsed it only as a campaign ploy and once elected only moved to fulfill his campaign promise as a result of persistent pressure from the Black Caucus and other black leaders. His economic and domestic policy advisors with the exception of Labor Secretary Marshall were also hostile to the legislation and worked to effectively emasculate it. The imperative of presidential support in this case became ashes in the mouth of the bill's supporters. With friends like Carter, the bill did not need enemies.

The principal enemy of the legislation—the business community—did not mobilize as extensively as the bill's supporters because it knew it could depend on its privileged position in the structure of power to effectively undermine the bill. Business opposition was predictable on a bill like the original legislation, and so, then, was the predictable opposition of key leaders of Congress and the administration interested in maintaining "business confidence." If this powerful structural nexus between business and government is to be broken and legislation touching the prerogatives of capital is to be enacted, more than routine Washington interest group politics is required.

To restate this historical explanation in theoretical terms, routine politics is not enough; not enough because even when the black leadership is mobilized on an issue of transracial significance, develops a broad-based multiracial coalition and elects a nominally sympathetic president, the result is not substantive policy responsiveness but either neglect or symbolism. In this case, although blacks were an important part of the coalition that elected the president and the Democratic congressional majority, when push came to shove, the governing coalition was more attentive to the interests of business—a group not a part of the voter coalition that elected it—than it was to its most loyal coalition constituency group.[65]

So what is to be done about the desperate unemployment problem in black America? I have focused here on the legislative struggle—the process rather than the substance of full employment. Is full employment attainable in a capitalist economy? I do not know. And if it is attainable, what would be its effects on ghetto joblessness? During the congressional debate on Humphrey-Hawkins the consensus view seemed to be that full employment (defined as 4 percent of the adult labor force) could not be achieved in the U.S. economy without unacceptably high levels of inflation or some permanent system of government restraint on wages and prices.[66] It was frequently pointed out during the debate in Congress that while only a small part of the population was affected by unemployment, everyone is hurt by inflation, and the idea of wage and price controls was almost universally rejected, in particular by organized labor. Thus, it is not clear that full employment and reasonable price stability are possible in the United States, except in times of war. During the Humphrey-Hawkins debate, Senator Harry Byrd, an opponent of the bill, inserted the following into the record:

> It was not until 1943 at the very peak of World War II that unemployment fell below 4 percent. The rate for that year was 1.9 percent. The rate remained very low for the rest of the war. . . . Then came the Korean War, and another mobilization effort pushed unemployment down to the 3 percent range for 1951 through 1953. From 1954 through 1965 the unemployment rate did not once drop to 4 percent. It was not until 1966, with yet another war being fought, that the United States experienced unemployment of less than four percent. The rates for 1966 through 1969 were 3.5 percent and 3.8 percent. . . . Looking over these data for the past 38 years, we see that our nation has not known unemploy-

ment of 4 percent or less in a single, normal peace time year. . . .
Every decline in the rate to 4 percent or less has been associated
with war.[67]

Thus, there may be something to the "Phillips curve," the notion of a
tradeoff between maximum employment and inflation. And this relationship may have worsened since the 1960s, as is suggested by those
who argue that the so-called natural rate of unemployment has
increased from 4 to 6 or 6.5 percent.[68] On this substantive issue I am an
agnostic. During the hearings and debate on Humphrey-Hawkins it
was pointed out that since the 1960s the German and Japanese
economies have functioned with average rates of unemployment of 1.5
percent or less, and a number of scholars have developed innovative
and thoughtful analyses that suggest the feasibility of using public sector jobs to create full employment.[69]

But even if the unemployment rate was driven down to 4 percent
and maintained at that level, it is not clear that this would touch the
depths of black joblessness in the ghettos or the rural south. The underlying assumption of the full employment strategy as developed by
post–civil rights era black leaders is that the only way to secure jobs
for blacks is to force the unemployment rate down so low for whites
that the rate for blacks will necessarily fall to acceptable levels. That is,
if virtually all able-bodied and willing whites are employed, the
employers will be forced to turn to black workers. But this may not be
the case. Employers, for example, may rather than turning to blacks for
labor simply bid up the price of white workers to attract more into the
labor force (with wage inflation as the predictable consequence), either
because they are perceived to be more skilled or because of individual
or institutional racism. There is some evidence for this in the data on the
economic recovery after the 1982 recession. At the peak of the recession the unemployment rate was near 10 percent overall and near twice
that for blacks. By the late 1980s the rate for the country as a whole had
been reduced to 4.9 percent and in the northeast and middle Atlantic
regions it had fallen to within the Humphrey-Hawkins target of 4 percent. The results in the black community, however, even in the northeast and middle Atlantic areas, were still at the recession level, 10 percent or more.[70] Although employers did begin to draw on blacks for
new workers, they also began to bid up the price for white suburban
workers. Thus, throughout the sustained economic recovery of the
1980s the black community remained in recession. It is likely that this
will always be the case in the American economy. That is, full employment is not enough to penetrate the depths of ghetto joblessness. What

is needed is not a deracialized strategy of full employment but rather a race-specific strategy that goes hunting where the ducks are. The unemployment problem is this country is disproportionately a black problem; therefore, policies should be directed at creating jobs where they are needed. This would ideally take the form of a multiyear, multibillion dollar, long-term attack on concentrated poverty. It will be argued that this race-specific approach cannot garner the kind of transracial support necessary to be enacted. But the lesson of Humphrey-Hawkins is that neither can non-race-specific approaches. This means that the leadership of black America needs to direct its attention more to mobilization of its ghetto constituents and less to building coalitions from the top in Washington. *If* effective government actions are to be taken to deal with the problems of ghetto joblessness and poverty, the black community itself must be mobilized into a sustained movement of internal redevelopment and external protest and politics. A movement that would be so powerful in its pressure that the system would have to go beyond its now routines of neglect and symbolism.

8

Blacks in Congressional Decision Making: Neglect and Invisibility on Social and Economic Reform

In the terminology of the modified systems model developed in Chapter 1, the response of the system in the last twenty-five years to the black demand for civil rights has been substantive in terms of policies and programs that to some extent deal with problems of discrimination in employment, voting and housing. The response to the demand for full employment may be characterized as symbolic. The Humphrey-Hawkins Act provided an image or legislative symbol of change but had no effect on the unemployment situation in black America. In this chapter I examine the broader "black" agenda of social and economic reform as embodied in a series of alternative budgets debated in the House since 1981.[1] In systems terminology, the output or response to this broader reform agenda is best characterized as neglect—essentially, acting as if there was no demand, no input. The Congressional Black Caucus's budgets have been invisible, ignored by the Congress and the national media, leaving black members of the House frustrated, and isolated from the mainstream of American politics.

In another sense, however, the Caucus's budgets themselves may be seen as symbolic inputs or demands. While the system's response to the black demand for full employment was symbolic, the demand itself was substantive. Black leaders sincerely believed, perhaps naively, that a legislative means could be found to guarantee a job to all persons willing and able to work. With the alternative budgets, this is not the case. No member of the Caucus thought that there was a realistic chance to enact their alternative budgets. Edelman, the leading student of symbolic politics in the United States, reminds us that "Basic to the recognition of symbolic forms in the political process is a distinction between politics as a spectator sport and political activity as utilized by organized groups to get quite specific, tangible benefit for themselves."[2] In pressing for civil rights and full employment legislation blacks were seeking concrete, specific benefits for the group. By contrast, the budget proposals presented over the last ten years were rituals, presented to give the folks back home an image of action; a reassurance that their representatives were representing them. The budgets were also a symbolic representation to the Washington establishment, black and white, that there was an alternative to the mainstream consensus on social and economic policy. Although they were symbolic, an analysis of the House debate and voting on these budgets provides a tool to further sharpen our understanding of the black predicament in the post–civil rights era. This is because, although symbolic or ritualistic in impact, the budget documents themselves do represent a kind of mainstream consensus approach on the part of blacks to the nation's problems. The budgets therefore are examples of not a black budget, not a black agenda but an agenda for the nation developed from the perspective and condition of blacks. To analyze the system's response to them provides important insights into the nature of the racial divide in the post–civil rights era; that one must not simply talk about *the* mainstream in American politics, but instead, about streams of thought in American politics that diverge sharply along lines of race. Analysis of these budgets in terms of House voting patterns also shows how isolated blacks are in national politics, and the minuscule size of the liberal-progressive coalition in the Congress. Finally, analysis of Congressman William Gray's role as Chairman of the House Budget Committee during deliberations on the Caucus's alternative budgets constitute a case study on the constraints of institutional politics on the post–civil rights era Afro-American leadership.

The Caucus first presented an alternative budget in 1981 in response to a challenge by President Reagan to critics of his first budget to come up with a viable alternative of their own. In response the Democratic Party majority in the House developed a diluted version of the Reagan budget that largely accepted prevailing conservative economic assumptions, but with somewhat higher social welfare expenditures and somewhat fewer tax breaks for corporations and the wealthy. Thus, the Caucus set about to fashion the only real alternative to the conservative economic and social policies of the Reagan administration and the Democratic majority in Congress;[3] in the words of the *Washington Post*, "the only proposal that could be described as liberal."[4] With relatively few resources compared to the president's Office of Management and Budget or the Democratic majority's Congressional Budget Office, and in 1981 with no black serving on the House Budget committee, the Caucus developed a budget document that was widely viewed as a comprehensive, economically sophisticated alternative to the administration and congressional proposals.[5] In preparing its budget the Caucus

relied on staff from the offices of its individual members and the exper-
tise of their various committee roles as well as the assistance of outside
experts and advisors. Prior to introducing its first budget in April of
1981 the Caucus sought to develop a broad coalition of support by con-
sulting with the leaders of more than one hundred labor, environmen-
tal, civil rights, social welfare and peace groups.

The Caucus budget adopted the principles and planning framework of the Humphrey-Hawkins Full Employment and Balanced
Growth Act. President Carter repudiated the basic principles and planning design of this legislation almost as soon as he signed it. Moreover,
toward the end of his administration, Carter adopted a mini-Reagan
agenda that included cuts in domestic spending programs and
increased military outlays. The Caucus and other Democratic liberals
opposed Carter's drift to the right, but any hope of reversing this conservative policy direction was shattered with Reagan's election. Carter
sought to move policy in a conservative direction incrementally. Reagan
sought (with considerable success) to bring about a revolution in the
contextual basis of political and policy debate in the United States. The
first objective of the Reagan revolution was to discredit liberalism and
delegitimatize the role of the government in the society and economy,
and through its economic program, cripple the state's capacity to act by
destroying its revenue base. This general attack on liberalism had a
specifically racial component. First, to delegitimatize the black quest
for racial and social justice through recurrent attacks on affirmative
action, the welfare state and the "failed" Great Society spending programs of the 1960s. Second, to change the context of the policy debate
on the so-called black underclass from an emphasis on the responsibilities of government toward a focus on the shortcomings of blacks themselves in terms of the absence of individual responsibility, "family values" and community "self-help." It is within this drastically altered
political and policy context—the most inhospitable for liberal/left policy initiatives in the post–civil rights era—that the Caucus presented
its budget alternatives.[6]

Consistent with the Humphrey-Hawkins planning framework,
the centerpiece of each Caucus budget has been a major jobs program
that would "address the problem of structural unemployment which
affects such a large segment of the Black population in America."[7] Thus,
in addition to a multi-billion-dollar direct job creation program, the
Caucus budget in 1981 included a $4 billion urban infrastructure pro-
gram, a $4 billion increase in mass transit and highway spending and
substantial increases in Aid to Families with Dependent Children ($3.2
billion), food stamps ($5 billion), medicare ($3 billion) and $1.2 billion

for a variety of health programs serving low-income citizens.[8] The Caucus proposals on tax reform were structured with an eye toward a balanced budget in the context of full employment and stable economic growth. To pay for these expenditures the budget proposed fundamental changes in the tax code that shifted the burden more toward large corporations and individuals of substantial wealth (including withholding income tax on interest, repeal of dividend exclusion, limitations on some mortgage interest deductions and repeal of tax subsidies for oil companies and other allowances for large corporations that resulted in their paying relatively little or in a few cases no taxes).

Finally, and perhaps most controversial, the Caucus proposed substantial reductions in military outlays (in 1981 from $264 billion to $196 billion), including the elimination of Reagan's entire strategic weapons buildup (the MX missile, the Trident-2 submarine, the Trident-2 missile, the sea and ground launched cruise missile, the Pershing 2 missile and the B1 bomber). In addition, substantial cuts were proposed in the Navy's 650 ship program, NATO, and the Rapid Deployment Force. As a result of these expenditure cuts in the military and the tax proposals, the Caucus alternative budget despite relatively large increases in social expenditures projected a balanced budget by 1985, earlier than that of the administration or the Democratic majority.[9]

In 1981 the Caucus budget was defeated 356 to 69, in 1983, 322 to 86, in 1985, 333 to 76, in 1986, 361 to 54 and in 1987, 362 to 52.[10] Using the 1983 vote (because it received the largest support of the five) shows the limits of the progressive coalition in Congress. Table 8.1 shows the pattern of support for the Caucus budget in the House, revealing substantial support among the relatively small cadre of House liberals (in any given year liberals constitute about a quarter of the House), 53 percent among the group as a whole and 32 percent excluding blacks. In the House as a whole not counting blacks, support drops to 15 percent and among Democrats (excluding blacks), support is at 27 percent. An analysis of the voting patterns is consistent with what we know about congressional roll call votes on non–civil rights issues of concern to blacks: no support from Republicans, relatively little support from rural and southern districts with large black populations and modest support from urban Democrats from elsewhere.[11] The data here reveal that on the fundamental social and economic priorities of black America there is support in Congress from only about 15 percent of the members, far from anything like a dominant or majority coalition. And this level of support is deceptive, since perhaps more than half of the whites voting for the budget in any given year did so while harboring strong reservations either about the tax proposals or the military cuts or both. Essen-

TABLE 8.1

Distribution of Support on Roll Call Votes (in percentages) for the
Congressional Black Caucus's Alternative Budget, 1983

Members of the House	Percent Support for 1983 Caucus Budget
All House Members	20%
All House Members (excluding blacks)	15%
All House Democrats	33%
All House Democrats (excluding blacks)	27%
All House Liberals*	53%
All House Liberals (excluding blacks)	32%

* Liberalism determined on the basis of members' score of 75 or more on the rating scale of the Americans for Democratic Action. By this measure there were 159 liberals in the House in 1983. Liberalism rating scores were calculated from Michael Barone and Grant Ujifusa, *The Almanac of American Politics, 1986* (Washington, National Journal, 1985).

tially, what many House liberals said during the debates was that they supported the Caucus proposals to increase social welfare spending but were opposed to the mechanisms to finance them through tax reform and cuts in military expenditures.[12] Relatively few members outside of the Caucus supported the alternative budgets without significant reservation, most notably former Congresswoman Rose Mary Oakar of Ohio and Congressman David Bonior of Michigan. For example, the following remarks by Congressman Bonior are rare throughout the years of House debate on the Caucus budgets:

Mr. Chairman, I rise in support of the Dixon amendment. The amendment we have before us now more closely mirrors my values and I believe the values of the district that I represent. I think if you were to present to the people of this country the numbers that have been laid out here in terms of the deficit, in terms of tax equity, in terms of domestic programs and in terms of needs to cut defense, and took away all the labels, conservative caucus, Black Caucus, or freeze, and had them pick, I think you would be very surprised at the number of people in this country that would identify themselves with this particular program. I would like to suggest to my colleagues that my constituents in 1972 voted 65 percent for George Wallace. I have maybe 1½ percent black population but I think this resolution fits very closely with the needs of the people I represent. While I might not agree with all the revenue assumptions in the amendment, I believe they take a great step toward fiscal responsibility.[13]

Thus, if one strips away the votes of "commendation" and "faint praise" and those cast with strong reservations, then coalition support for the Caucus budget in the House is even less than 10 percent of the House as a whole, 15 percent of House Democrats and no more than a third of House liberals.

Indeed, what is more revealing about the status of the black agenda in the House than the outcome of the roll call votes on the budgets is the sense of isolation, frustration, anger and bitterness by blacks in the House as they are routinely ignored by party colleagues and leaders.[14] For example, during the 1982 debate, Congressman Conyers remarked:

Finally, Mr. Chairman the most painful part of my remarks is reserved for those whom I love and respect and have worked for the most. The Democratic leadership, whom I have supported and voted for, worked with, cooperated with for every single year of which I have had the high privilege to serve in this Congress. The Democratic leadership has now for the second year in a row chosen to ignore this work product. It did not criticize it, leaders of the party will not praise it, they just do not see that it exists. It is the invisible document . . . but the time has come—as a matter of fact long overdue—where we must address the critical underlying questions of why we cannot get more than 69 votes. . . . And it is about time we get a little bit of respect or criticism for the nature of our work product. We bring you millions of Democratic votes to the Halls of the Congress and to the national ticket, more than anybody else on this side of the aisle, excluding nobody. And they are watching us and you. And I want to say that time is running out. You are not going to explain in a long hot summer why 70 people out of a majority Democratic body could not do anything but give us a nodding tip of the hat.[15]

Similarly, Congresswoman Chisholm observed:

Why? Is it because of the terminology "black"? What would happen if we removed the term "black"? The fact is that months were spent putting this budget together. . . . Why? Here we come again today, everybody wants to get rid of us, get us off the floor, we are taking up their time. Well, we are going to take up time because it is important to recognize that 18 members of the House of Representatives have been responsive in terms of accepting certain challenges. But because of inherent racism in the bloodstream of America, it becomes increasingly difficult to get beyond the color of one's skin. . . . I know when the Congressional Black Caucus budget was coming forth I heard some remarks around here, "They are coming up again this year." "We'll give them their time because, after all, they are members like the rest of us here in the House of Representatives."[16]

In response to Chisholm's remarks, Ohio Congresswoman Oakar said:

"Unfortunately, I happen to believe it is because it is presented by the Black Caucus. I really feel very badly that I have to say that on the floor of the House of Representatives but I personally feel that is why it is not getting more support because, in my view, in many ways and I cited earlier the fact that it was the only budget resolution that did not deprive the elderly of their health insurance, and yet we know what a volatile and important issue it is. . . . I really commend you and I am glad you said what you said. It is about time that we openly acknowledged that there is that subtle form of prejudice that exists.[17]

And finally on this point of isolation and invisibility Congressman Dellums during the 1985 debate:

Mr. Chairman, it is with some sense of sadness and pain that I rise this evening because as I look around this body including even to the press gallery, that at the time the Congressional Black Caucus offers its budget it's break time, time to chat, time for the press to get a cup of coffee, read a newspaper, engage in conversation.[18]

The budget debates show not just the absence of a progressive coalition in Congress or the Democratic Party that would support the black agenda of social reform, but more profoundly, the irrelevancy of that agenda and the Black Caucus itself in the congressional process. As David Broder wrote of the 1982 debate (Broder was one of the few Washington correspondents to discuss the Caucus budget in a nationally syndicated column), "There is a perfectly good case to be made that it deserved to be defeated. A lot of people—myself included— would have gagged on the elimination of all new strategic weapons that it proposed. But this budget was not just defeated by the House of Representatives. It was ignored."[19]

As black power has nominally increased in the House in terms of seniority and important committee and subcommittee and party leadership posts (evidenced, for example, by the elevation of Congressman William Gray to Majority Whip—the third-ranking post in the Democratic leadership hierarchy), black substantive power is no greater now than it was twenty years ago when the Caucus was formed. On the fundamental policy preferences of the black community in spite of two decades of agenda building and efforts at black voter mobilization and coalition formation, the system's response has been neglect. This is not to say the Caucus is not effective on incremental issues of importance to blacks. For example, the Caucus has been effective in getting minority set-asides included in federal public works appropriations; in exempting basic welfare programs from the Gramm-Rudman budget reduction process; in welfare reform that established spouse eligibility for AFDC in every state (but with what Congressman Augustus Hawkins, one of its principal authors and chairman of the Committee on Labor and Education, called work provisions so restrictive that they constituted "slavefare," "conjuring up images of Victorian work houses"); and race-specific support for black colleges in the form of the Black College and University Act of 1986.[20] Incremental changes, however, are not enough. Indeed, the so-called radical reforms embodied in the Caucus budget alternatives are only good first steps in the direction needed to reconstruct black America and start to put a stop to growing emisseration and dispossession. As Congressman Dymally candidly noted in his presentation of the 1987 budget:

> It adopts instead a Humphrey-Hawkins target in compliance with the Full Employment and Balanced Growth Act of 1978 of a level of 4 percent unemployment in the civilian labor force through fiscal year 1990. . . . But I would dare say that no budget, even the budget of the Congressional Black Caucus adequately addresses the issues of economic policy, although I would hasten to argue that the Congressional Black Caucus budget goes further in this respect in attempting to trigger employment, move toward reindustrialization and embrace the concept of reconversion away from a heavy reliance on militarism and military might as a way of propping up the nature of our economic system.[21]

One of the dangers of formal cooptation with the trappings of power rather than its substance is that over time it tends in a subordinate community to reinforce interpersonal and political alienation, cynicism and despair at the mass level and tension and conflict among the group's elite. This is well illustrated by the tenure of Congressman Gray as Chairman of the Budget Committee. Despite his pledge to "do the right thing" as chairman and not "tolerate the vicious attacks we've seen over the past four years on those programs aimed at the least fortunate," as Chairman he consistently produced and defended on the House floor budgets that reflected the neo-Reagan consensus of majority House Democrats, sparking on one occasion an open revolt by committee liberals.[22] The irony, of course, is compelling, since under circumstances other than his leadership role Gray would have been among the committee rebels but instead he found himself defending the status quo, a status quo all his power as chairman found him helpless to alter.

Gray's tenure as Budget chairman sparked considerable backroom bickering and tension within the Caucus, which occasionally spilled over into the national press. Once he became chair, Gray declined to support the Caucus budgets even with a symbolic "vote of commendation" as cast by Majority Leader Foley. Rather, he voted "present."[23] Gray explained this "paradox of power" by saying:

> It's not an issue of being black. The issue is I'm Chairman of the Budget Committee, a Democrat. I build a consensus. I walk out with budget. Now, do I vote against my own budget? . . . That doesn't make a lot of sense. It's not a problem of race. It's a problem of what happens to any member of Congress who gets elevated to a position of leadership. I am not here to do the bidding of somebody just because they happen to be black. If I agree with you, I agree with you. I set my policy. I think it's a fair policy but that policy has nothing to do with being black. It has to do with the position I have institutionally as Chairman of the Budget Committee.[24]

To which Congressman Conyers responded that he "took exception" to Gray's failure to cast a symbolic vote of solidarity with the Caucus. "I draw the line where he actively campaigns against the Black Caucus resolution," stated Conyers.[25] Yet Gray's behavior was a predictable consequence of his position, almost inevitable in the post–civil rights era institutionalized black politics. Institutionalization, as Stinchcombe tells us, occurs "when a value or practice is distributed in such a way as to exert a continuous force in favor of the value or practice. . . . Thus, the institutionalization of a value or practice can be fruitfully defined as the correlation of power with commitment to that value or practice, so that the more powerful a man is, the more likely he is to hold the value."[26] In other words, it is highly unlikely that a woman or man will rise to the top of the party hierarchy in Congress or any other institution unless he has come to share its basic values and practices. Congressman Gray is thus correct: "It's a problem of what happens to any member of Congress who gets elevated to a position of leadership."[27] The problem for the black community is that since its problems are unlike those of just any other community, it requires representatives that don't act like just any other member of Congress who just happens to be black.

Conclusion

In 1993 the size of the black congressional delegation increased by near half, from 25 to 39. This led many in the press and in the Black Caucus itself to engage in myopic talk of the enhanced status of the Caucus as a powerful clique in the House.[28] Representative Dellums remarked, "I think the Congressional Black Caucus has moved to a whole other level. . . . We can win now. We've gone beyond just being 'the conscience of the House.'" Similarly, Congressman Rangel said, "Thirty-nine [Caucus members] in the House is a big count. Thirty-nine votes is a lot of votes to ignore and take for granted." And finally, Caucus Chair Kweisi Mfume exclaimed "I believe our best days are in front of us. Because of the sheer and awesome increase in numbers, we are given a great opportunity to effectuate real and meaningful change."[29] However, despite its increased size in the 103rd Congress its influence in the body, arguably, was unchanged.

During negotiations on the 1993 Clinton budget, blacks in the House Democratic Caucus were an important force in insisting that the $21 billion increase in the earned income tax credit (which supplements the income of workers whose pay falls below the poverty line) remain in the final budget resolution. The Caucus as a bloc threatened to oppose the budget unless it included this important anti-poverty initiative. Since the budget resolution passed by a single vote in the House, the Caucus's stance may have been critical in retention of this progressive item in an otherwise moderate, neoconservative budget. Although the 1992 Democratic platform pledged increased funding for infrastructure, urban aid, education and welfare reform, the first budget submitted by a Democratic president in a dozen years gave primacy to deficit reduction per se rather than as part of an overall program of investment in human capital and urban revitalization. The Caucus, consequently, once again presented an alternative budget to reflect its liberal priorities of higher taxes on corporations and the wealthy, much larger defense cuts and increased domestic spending.[30] This budget—cosponsored by the newly formed House Progressive Caucus—was defeated by a vote of 335 to 87. Thus, even with twelve new members the Caucus budget received *one* more vote in 1993 than it did in 1983, when it was supported by 86 members (the highest vote for any of its budgets).

Similarly, in 1994 the House passed a harshly punitive crime bill that included increased spending on police and prisons but also mandatory sentencing for a variety of crimes including first-time drug offenses, the punishment of young people as adults, life in prison for persons convicted of three felonies (the so-called "three strikes and you're out" provision) and expansion of the death penalty to cover more than fifty federal crimes. At the insistence of the Caucus and other House liberals, the Democratic Caucus also included in the bill several so-called crime prevention measures, including funds for community schools, youth employment, community economic development, drug treatment and antigang grants for arts, sports and other after-school activities. Congressman Conyers—the senior black member on the Judiciary Committee—was also instrumental in getting his Democratic colleagues on the committee and in the party caucus to include a provision called the Racial Justice Act, requiring the courts to consider evidence of racial discrimination prior to imposition of the death penalty. Because of its highly punitive nature and the expansion of the death penalty, the leadership of the Caucus opposed the legislation. At its crime "brain trust" hearings on the bill, Caucus Chair Mfume said in order to prevent its passage the Caucus would, if necessary, "bring the government to a stop," and Congressman Craig Washington, who chaired the hearings, said the bill would pass only over the Caucus' "political dead bodies."[31] Yet, in the end the bill (supported by the House leadership and the president) passed

The bill passed the House 235 to 195, with the support of twelve of the thirty-nine black representatives. This in spite of the fact that the racial justice provision was deleted in the House-Senate Conference. While a united Caucus might have defeated the legislation, most members were apparently persuaded that the so-called prevention funding included in the bill outweighed its punitive measures, especially since the Caucus was urged to support the bill by most big city black mayors.[32]

The votes on the Caucus's alternative budgets, the fate of the Humphrey-Hawkins bill and the initiatives of the Democratic party leadership on issues that disproportionately affect black Americans (crime and welfare) show the Congressional Black Caucus has relatively little leverage or influence in congressional decision making. On the contrary, except for civil rights issues, blacks in Congress are frequently an isolated, invisible, inconsequential minority unable to enact (or often even get serious debate and deliberation on) proposals it deems minimally necessary to meliorate the problems of joblessness, crime and dispossession that plague its core constituency.

The Caucus's status in the post–civil rights era as an isolated, frustrated, relatively inconsequential force in the House is exacerbated by the election in 1994 of a Republican majority for the first time since the Caucus's formation. As part of the Democratic majority, Caucus members were able to exercise some leverage at the margins on House decision making as committee and subcommittee chairs (in the 103rd Congress, 1992–94, blacks chaired four full committees and seventeen subcommittees). As the tenure of Congressman Gray as chair of the Budget and Congressman Dellums as Armed Services chair shows, this leverage is at best marginal; it nevertheless carried some weight in shaping the internal House agenda. More important, however, than the loss of formal positions of committee leadership,[33] the Republican House majority deprives the Caucus of its principal source of influence in congressional decision making—its capacity as a minority faction within the majority party caucus to develop legislative packages that balance liberal and conservative elements in bills that can command a House majority. As pointed out earlier, by threatening to withhold its vote on final passage the Caucus was able to get the Democratic Caucus to exempt welfare from the Gramm-Rudman budget-cutting regime, to get a less punitive welfare reform bill in 1988; a more expansive civil rights bill in 1991; the retention of the earned income tax credit in the 1992 budget; and the inclusion of social welfare programs in what otherwise may have been a strictly punitive 1994 crime bill. While these are incremental changes, even they were only possible because the Caucus was a significant minority within a majority. With a Republican majority, the Caucus becomes a minority within a minority with little leverage, since the Republicans will, like the Democrats, shape legislation in their Caucus to conform with their conservative agenda and coalition. As members of the dominant party coalition, the Black Caucus throughout the post–civil rights era has been able to have some influence, however modest, on congressional decision making, given their size as a House voting bloc and the importance of the black vote in the party's electoral coalition. The control of the Congress by the conservative Republican coalition—to the extent it endures—means that blacks in the House, more so than at any time in the last twenty-five years, are a mere presence in a legislative body dominated by a hostile majority faction.

This is the paradox of black power in the post–civil rights era addressed by Professor Lani Guinier, the University of Pennsylvania law professor nominated by President Clinton to be an assistant attorney general. In the controversy about her law review articles that led the president to label her "antidemocratic" and withdraw her nomination, the emphasis in the press coverage and by Professor Guinier herself was on her notions of cumulative voting as a remedy to problems in drawing single-member majority black districts. However, the truly radical idea in Guinier's work is her proposed "restructuring of the electoral and legislative process based on a model of proportionate interest representation for self-identified communities of interest . . . [b]y changing *both* the way representatives are elected and the rules under which legislative decisions are made" (emphasis added).[34] Guinier's theory thus deals with two problems. First, the problem of the electoral system gerrymander in which the relatively innocuous remedy of cumulative voting is proposed. The second problem is what she calls the "legislative gerrymander" in which she proposes the notion of "proportionate interest representation" to deal with domination of a legislature by a "permanent hostile, majority faction."[35] The legislative gerrymander reflects the post–civil rights era "paradox" that blacks elected from single-member districts may enjoy minority presence but not influence. A part of the problem, Guinier notes, may be racism, writing that "Since prejudice affects the deliberative and collective decision making process within the legislature as well as the electorate, blacks elected from single member districts are simply less empowered to influence their white colleagues, whose single member district base enables them to ignore black interests without fear of electoral consequence."[36] Whatever the reason, she argues that "it is not enough that a representation system gives everyone an equal chance of having their political preferences *represented*. A fair system of political representation should consider mechanisms to insure that a disadvantaged and stigmatized group also have a fair chance of having its policy preferences *satisfied*" (emphasis in original).[37] As a remedy to this situation, Guinier proposed that courts might consider ordering unanimity or supermajority requirements to pass certain types of legislation, "thereby forcing everyone into indispensable coalitions and providing real power to minority representatives."[38]

Guinier's theorizing about the paradox of black power in the post–civil rights era applies to the states and localities covered by the Voting Rights Act, but its logic applies with equal force to the situation of blacks in Congress who, as the budget debates show, face a legislature dominated by a "permanent, hostile majority faction" unwilling to seriously consider policies and programs to meet the needs of their constituents. The fate of Guinier's nomination suggests there is no institutional or judicial remedy to this problem at the local, state or federal level. The question then becomes, What does a permanent minority do when its fundamental interests and policy preferences are ignored by an indifferent, hostile or even racist majority? Frequently, the recourse has been various forms of protest and civil disobedience.

When the Black Caucus was formed, there was concern among House leaders that its members might violate the norms and decorum of the House and disrupt its proceedings. It has not. It should. There are a variety of ways that blacks in the House might protest congressional and presidential neglect of them and their constituents. For example, they might stand with backs turned in protest during the president's annual State of the Union addresses or they might engage in an ongoing series of filibusters to disrupt and delay the work of the House. Although the rules of the House do not permit filibusters in the classic sense, there are ample opportunities for a determined minority to frustrate and delay action by the majority.[39] To quote Jesse B. Simple, Langston Hughes's wise Harlem street corner man of the 1940s:

> Now you take for instant, we got two colored congressman down in Washington. But they can't even stop a filibuster. Every time them civil rights bills come up, them old white southerners filibuster them to hell and gone. Why don't them colored congressman start a filibuster. . . . If I was down yonder in Congress representing the colored race, I would start a filibuster all my own. In fact, I would filibuster to keep them filibusters from starting a filibuster. With the fate of my race at stake, you ask how would I hold out! Why, for my people I would talk until I could talk no more! Then, I would use sign language. When I got through with that, I would get down on my knees and pray in silence. And nobody better not strike no gavel while I am communing with my maker. While I am on my knees I would get some sleep. When I riz up, it would be the next day, so I would start all over again. I would be the greatest one man filibuster of all time.[40]

An ongoing filibuster by the Caucus or the simple act of standing in silent protest at every State of the Union address would send a powerful signal of discontent across America and the world and might help to arouse in the black community a new spirit of militant mobilization. But, alas, this is not likely to occur. Black congressmen are likely to continue to express their frustrations in militant rhetoric on the House floor but refrain from militant action. Again, this is the nature of institutional politics. The institutional norms and folkways of the House encourage exaggerated courtesy, compromise, deference and above all loyalty to the institution. And the black members of Congress are probably more loyal to the House and their roles in it than they are to blacks.

Part IV

The Negro demands less by his ballot, not only in actual results but even in mere respect for himself as a voter than any of all the groups that go to make up the American citizenry; although some of these groups are far smaller in numbers and even weaker economically.

—James Weldon Johnson (1924)

You're the one who sent Kennedy to Washington. You're the one that put the present Democratic Administration in Washington, D.C. The whites were evenly divided. It was the fact that you threw 80 percent of your votes behind the Democrats that put the Democrats in the White House. . . . And despite the fact that you are in a position to be a determining factor, what do you get out of it? The Democrats have been in Washington, D.C. only because of the Negro vote. They have been down there four years and all other legislation they wanted to bring up, they have brought up and gotten it out of the way and now they bring up you. And now they bring up you! You put them first and they put you last. Because you're a chump, a political chump. . . ! The party that you backed controls two-thirds of the House of Representatives and the Senate; and still they can't keep their promises to you. Because you're a chump! Anytime you throw your weight behind a political party that controls two-thirds of the government and that party can't keep the promises it made to you during election time; and you're dumb enough to walk around continuing to identify yourself with that party, you are not only a chump; but you are a traitor to your race!

—Malcolm X (1964)

9

Symbolic Politics at High Tide:
Jesse Jackson and the Rainbow Coalition

This book is devoted in good part to the study of the transformation of black politics from protest to systemic political participation. The campaigns of Jesse Jackson for president are emblematic of this transformation, in a sense the symbolic peak of this twenty-year transformation in the nature of the black freedom struggle. Jackson is a fitting embodiment of this process. He began his career as a protégé of Dr. King, the preeminent 1960s protest leader; in the decade of the 1970s he transformed himself into Dr. King's successor as the preeminent race leader and then in the 1980s made an effective transformation from protest and race leader to presidential candidate and party leader. The successes and failures of his campaigns test the limits of post–civil rights era black politics.

The idea of a black running for president is as old as the post–civil rights era.[1] The notion of a black presidential candidacy was one of the reasons for the calling of the National Black Political Convention in 1972. Indeed, the strategy and rainbow symbolism of the 1984 and 1988 campaigns have their origins in the 1972 Gary convention. Jackson was a major actor at Gary, calling for the formation of an independent black political party that would include progressive whites and that would field a candidate in the 1972 election.[2] The idea of a black presidential candidate and/or a black political party was aborted throughout the 1970s as a result of the ideological and factional disputes that eventually led to the convention's collapse. But the point here is that the original idea of a black running for president did not emerge full-blown out of Jackson's mind in 1983. It had been on the black agenda since the end of the civil rights movement.[3]

Given that the idea of a black candidacy has been around since 1970, what are the factors that precipitated the Jackson candidacy in 1984? The Reagan administration was an important one. Its overt hostility to civil rights and its regressive social and economic policies threatened to reverse the gains of the 1960s civil rights revolution and retard

whatever prospects there were for continued growth of the black middle class and to leave to fester the increasingly desperate conditions of
the black poor. The Reagan administration thus exacerbated a decade-
long sense of fatalism and cynicism about the prospects for progress on
the problems of racism and poverty in the United States. There was
indeed a sense that not only was progress not being made but that the
race was falling behind, that things were getting worse. The Reagan
administration's attitudes and policies were perceived as bad enough
but perhaps to be expected, given the president's long-standing hostility to the aspirations of blacks; but the Democratic Party's response
seemed not much better. In Congress the Democrats had capitulated to
the Reagan revolution in social and economic policies and there was
increasing talk amongst party leaders that if the Democratic Party was
to be successful in presidential elections it would have to adopt a more
conservative stance. More ominously, a number of party leaders, newspaper and television commentators and Washington pollsters and consultants were directly or indirectly blaming blacks for the party's failure
to elect a president (see Chapter 10). This was the special interest canard
heard so often after the 1980 election; the Democrats had lost the support of whites in the south and among lower-middle class European
ethnic groups because they were too closely identified with special
interest groups, especially blacks. This argument was forcefully stated
in a series of speeches and post mortems on the 1980 election by Hamilton Jordan and Bert Lance, aides to former President Carter, who
seemed to blame Carter's defeat on blacks and other special interests.
Jordan, for example, wrote in the *New Republic* that the Democratic
Party was "too liberal" because it was the "captive" of special interest
groups (blacks, feminists and labor) and that in order to win the party
nominee and platform in 1984 it should take a public stand in opposition to issue stances or policy interests of one or more of these groups.[4]

Thus, the situation in 1983 was this: blacks, the group that had
been Carter's most loyal supporters both in the primary contest with
Senator Kennedy and in the general election (in spite of his turn to the
right in the last two years of his administration), were now being
blamed for his defeat because their support presumably drove away
too many whites. To blacks this was an almost classic blame-the-victim
syndrome that so frequently characterizes discussions by whites of
problems of race in this country. It angered and disillusioned the black
establishment, demonstrating the race's vulnerability in the electoral
process after more than twenty years of struggle for inclusion in the
Democratic Party. This situation to some blacks bordered on the absurd.
While they were accused of "capturing" the Democratic Party and mak-

ing it an instrument of their special interests, many blacks knew the opposite was the case. In spite of all the talk, blacks knew they were relatively powerless inside the party and they, not the party, were the captives. As Howard Professor Ronald Walters wrote in a 1983 paper, "The major candidates and the party apparatus have believed that the Black vote is a captured vote, unable to mount credible strategies of leverage, so the tendency increasingly has been to ignore the importance of the vote and the policy interests it represents."[5] Blacks in 1983 thus felt trapped, cornered; taken for granted by the Democrats, ignored by the Republicans and with no other alternatives. By all accounts these feelings of disillusionment, despair and cynicism all congealed in the Chicago mayoral election of 1983. Jackson claims this election was the proverbial straw that broke the camel's back, leading him to think about a black candidacy in 1984. Jackson told *Playboy*:

> Before the election, Walter Mondale came to town to support Richard Daley's son while Ted Kennedy came to support then Mayor Jane Byrne. In other words, the progressive wing of the Democratic party was moving to the right. What could we do? Most people got upset. I said we've got to figure a way out of this.[6]

Jackson's way out was to mount a challenge for the Democratic nomination, arguing that "Blacks will never again be taken for granted."[7] How this would end the captive status of the black vote or slow the rightward drift of the party was not clear, and therefore the idea of a black presidential candidate in 1984 became the subject of intensive analysis and debate in the black leadership community.

The idea divided the black leadership community along lines similar to those observed at the National Black Political Conventions of the 1970s. The established, institutional, relatively more conservative or traditional black leadership generally opposed the idea in general or a Jackson candidacy specifically, while the more insurgent, grassroots, radical and nationalist leaders tended to support it generally or a Jackson candidacy specifically. In a background paper prepared for distribution and discussion among black leaders, the Joint Center for Political Studies outlined the costs and benefits of the strategy. The benefits included (1) giving prominence to issues of concern to blacks, (2) encouraging black voter registration, (3) assembling a cohesive black delegate bloc that might play a role in adoption of the platform or picking the nominee in the case of a brokered convention and (4) gaining experience and developing a national organization for future presidential campaigns by blacks.[8] The risks or costs according to the Joint Center paper included (1) taking votes and delegates away from the more liberal or progressive candidates, (2) diverting support from the eventual nominee with the result that he might feel less committed to black policy and patronage concerns, (3) failure of the black candidate to attract black voter support resulting in relatively few delegates, (4) intensification of racial polarization in the electorate as the result of a highly visible black candidate, (5) fragmentation of the black leadership community and (6) a black candidacy might make the eventual nominee appear the "captive of blacks and other special interest groups."[9] The Joint Center's paper became the basis of private discussion and argument within the leadership group and in the pages of the national press. Joseph Madison of the NAACP called the idea of a black presidential candidate "the biggest hoax that's been pulled on blacks that I can think of."[10] John Jacobs of the Urban League wrote that after discussion with black leaders around the country he had concluded that a "black candidacy would be a counterproductive retreat into emotionalism." On the other side, Ronald Walters argued in the pages of the *Los Angeles Times*, the *Washington Afro-American* and the *Washington Post* that the candidacy was "no joke" but "a tough strategy to end the hat in hand tradition of black politics" and Congressman Conyers argued that it would end "the twiddle dee and twiddle dum politics practiced by both Democrats and Republicans [that] has ceased to furnish real answers to real problems of jobs, justice and peace that affects so many citizens." Finally, Jackson himself weighed in with a *Washington Post* essay that claimed that the strategy would enhance black self-esteem and the role of blacks in shaping party policy and programs, as well as help the party win in the fall as a result of a more conscious and mobilized constituency of minorities and the poor.[11]

Although rarely mentioned in the public debate amongst blacks, another factor for those opposed to the candidacy of a black had nothing to do with the relative costs or benefits of the idea abstractly but rather with the presumptive candidate: Jackson. Although other names—DC Delegate Walter Fauntroy and Georgia legislator Julian Bond—were discussed, as well as the notion of multiple candidates along the favorite son model, it was clear by late spring of 1983 that Jackson had seized the moment and if there was a candidate it would be Jackson. Clearly, the best known and the most popular national black leader and running third behind Mondale and John Glenn in the early opinion polls, Jackson was not so popular among his peers in the leadership community. He was especially disliked and distrusted among the black establishment's influential Atlanta wing—Andrew Young, Ralph

Abernathy, Joseph Lowry and the King family—because of his behavior in the immediate aftermath of Dr. King's murder and because of the manner in which he left SCLC and created his own organization. Others viewed him as an overly ego-driven opportunist with an authoritarian style of decision making and little organizational capacity or willingness to follow through on initiatives once set in motion. Undoubtedly, as among any group of politicians, there was also some jealousy that Jackson had become the preeminent post–civil rights era black leader and that he, rather than they, mayors and members of Congress who claimed the legitimacy of elected office, would be the candidate. As Reed put it, many in the black establishment saw "Jackson's presidential maneuvering as an impertinent attempt to assert a brokerage position through the electoral realm. In this sense then reaction to Jackson had the makings of a turf dispute."[12]

Throughout the spring of 1983 an ad hoc group of black establishment leaders—mayors, members of Congress, and leaders of civil rights organizations—calling themselves the "Black Leadership Family" met to deliberate the pros and cons of the "concept" of a black running for president.[13] At its third meeting in Chicago a group of twenty of this group endorsed the idea of a black running for president and agreed to form an exploratory committee to decide who should be the candidate.[14] In many ways this was a rump group.[15] Many of the persons who attended the earlier meetings and were opponents of the idea (such as Mayors Coleman Young, and Andrew Young and CBC Chair Julian Dixon) were not present, and the idea of an exploratory committee to select the candidate was simply window dressing, since by the time of the meeting it was clear that if there was to be a black candidate it would be Jackson. Indeed, Jackson, although he denied it at the time, had indicated that he was prepared to run independently of the wishes of the "family." Thus, the meeting only served to provide a thin veneer of collective legitimacy to what in fact was a foregone conclusion, at least in the mind of Jackson. In any event, in the fall of the year Jackson announced his candidacy on the CBS news program "60 Minutes," the most widely watched prime time television news program.

The Strategic Objectives of the Jackson Campaigns

While there are some important differences between Jackson's first and second campaigns, in broad theoretical and strategic terms the 1984 and 1988 campaigns may be analyzed as one.[16] In the remainder of this chapter I focus on the strategic objectives of the campaigns, the class and ethnic character of their voter coalitions and the limitations of the Rainbow Coalition as a personalized political movement.

From the outset of the debate about the efficacy of a black presidential candidacy it was argued that one of its contributions would be to raise progressive ideas and issues that would otherwise be ignored. To a degree, but only to a degree, the campaigns were somewhat successful in this regard. To raise issues in a national presidential campaign is not easy, given the tendency of the media to focus on trivia, personality and the horse race aspects of the campaign. This normal issueless focus of press coverage of presidential campaigns was exacerbated in the Jackson case because of his race, racism and the tendency of the press to view his campaign through the prism of his unelectability, which, in terms of the horse race aspect of coverage, made Jackson as one writer put it, "A horse of a different color," who could not win and therefore should not be taken seriously in terms of ideas and issues.[17] As a result, although the Jackson campaigns in both 1984 and 1988 developed fairly distinctive left of center or progressive issue stances in scores of position papers, speeches and platform presentations, these tended to get lost in the fog of media attention to the horse race, to "Hymie" and "Hymie town" (Jackson's unflattering reference to Jews and New York City), to the fulminations of Farrakhan and the perennial question, "What does Jesse want?" as *Time* magazine put it in a cover story. Reed, for example, quotes approvingly a column by James Reston in the *New York Times* that said Jackson's policy proposals were so superficial that they could "fit on a bumper stick."[18] This is simply not the case: so manifestly incorrect that it borders on a deliberate non-reading or misreading of the campaign record. Jackson developed progressive foreign policy positions on Latin America, East-West relations and NATO, South Africa and the Middle East disputes.[19] Many in the press ignored or dismissed Jackson's views on these issues precisely because they were different, outside the establishment orthodoxy, a "Third World" perspective as one critic called them. To some extent Jackson's views on foreign policy were also probably discounted by the Washington press establishment because of the view that while blacks could discuss welfare, civil rights and food stamps, foreign policy (except perhaps Africa) was beyond their competence. Whatever the case, it cannot be said that Jackson had nothing new or distinctive to say about foreign policy.

In domestic policy Jackson also had a distinct perspective and contribution that located him to the left of his principal opponents in both 1984 and 1988. For example, Jackson developed a comprehensive economic policy dealing with tax reform, deficit reduction, industrial policy and employment. Very much like the Congressional Black Caucus's alternative budgets, its centerpiece was a $50 billion "Rebuild America" infrastructure program and a national planning mechanism to coordinate government, capital and labor in a national industrial policy. While it is true as critics on the left point out that Jackson's economic policy was well within the tradition of American liberal reform,[20] it was much more progressive than anything proposed by Mondale, Hart, Gore or Dukakis. In fact, it was sufficiently progressive that it earned the endorsement of Michael Harrington, the nation's best-known democratic socialist as well as the Democratic Socialists of America. There was some reluctance by the Democratic Socialists to endorse Jackson, first because of worries and concerns about his alleged antisemitism but also because he consistently resisted the advice of a number of persons who wished him to speak openly in democratic socialist language. Jackson's failure to abandon the rhetoric of free enterprise and openly embrace democratic socialist principles and rhetoric was a political calculus, believing (probably correctly) that he would lose more votes by doing so than he would gain, and would be further isolated and ostracized by the party establishment and the media. Thus, he coyly feigned ignorance on the subject. For example, when asked by *Playboy*, "Do you identify with the European social democratic tradition?" he replied, "I don't know enough about it to say I identify with it."[21] This is disingenuous, and historic—it was probably the first time Jackson had ever said he did not know enough about anything to comment.

Yet, the Jackson economic agenda got lost in the campaign's fog. Robert Browne, Jackson's principal economic advisor in 1984, offers a revealing account of why this may have occurred. It is worth quoting at length:

> This inability to distinguish candidate Jackson's race from his program was nowhere more dramatically demonstrated than when the Sunday *New York Times* presented the economic program of the three major candidates at the height of the primary. The prestigious Business Section of the Sunday *New York Times* requested each of the three candidates to submit a 700 to 800 word statement that would summarize their economic programs, with the understanding that these statements would be printed on consecutive Sundays, along with an appropriate response by a prominent economist. Rev. Jackson's statement appeared on April 22, 1984, and just below it, on the same page, was the response to it, written by George Gilder. The headline on the Jackson statement read, "Jackson: Tax Reform and Jobs" and the statement focused on these topics, plus deficit reduction, an anti-inflation plan,

industrial policy, and reducing dangers posed by the Third World debt problem. Mr. Gilder's response was entitled "But What About Welfare's Grim Side?" and opened with a statement: "America desperately needs a radical black leader who will tell the truth about the devastation of his people by the patronizing social-ism of the welfare state." Later he asserted "Jesse Jackson seems to imagine that blacks cannot make it without help from the gov-ernment." In fact, the Jackson statement did not contain the words *black*, *welfare*, nor any of the synonyms or code words for them. Indeed, Jackson risked the possible alienation of black voters pre-cisely because his economic program was devoid of any specific pleading for the black community or any recognition that it mer-ited special consideration. One would not have guessed this from Gilder's response, however. The racism permeating the white community effectively precluded most whites from perceiving Jackson other than as a black candidate focusing on black issues. He did not, but they were incapable of hearing otherwise.[22]

Browne's point is useful. But another reason for the lack of atten-tion to Jackson's agenda beyond media myopia and racialism is that Jackson himself in his press conferences, debate appearances and stump speeches deflected attention away from his substantive agenda by emphasizing reform of party rules and electoral procedures. As Christo-pher Edley wrote during the 1984 campaign, "Reading the recent press reports one might be led to believe that Jackson is running for president in order to reform the Democratic Party, rather than to preach and teach. Yet for me, at least, the chief attraction of his candidacy was the promise of adding color to the policy debate. A brawl over the rules is dangerously diverting."[23] Jackson's focus on the party rules regarding delegate allocation was to some extent understandable, since he believed, correctly, that the party's rules unfairly deprived his con-stituency of fair and equitable convention representation. (In 1984 Jack-son won 18 percent of the primary vote but was allocated only 9 percent of the delegates). Jackson's focus on the second primary issue, an issue that in 1984 he frequently labeled a "litmus test" for his eventual sup-port of the nominee and party, however, was less understandable.[24] It was less understandable first because there is much debate among scholars and politicians, black and white, about the origins and conse-quences of the second primary, and about the probable consequences of its abolition on southern and national politics and on the election of blacks to office. It is also less understandable because the National Democratic Party and a presidential campaign are probably not appropriate forums to seek resolution of the second primary and other complex vote dilution techniques.[25] Finally, and most critically, elevating the second primary to the status of a litmus test had the predictable effect of shifting media and public attention away from the substantive items of the campaign agenda. A similar situation existed with the planks presented by the Jackson forces at the San Francisco convention. The four issues presented—cuts in military spending, the second primary, no first use of nuclear weapons and affirmative action— emerged not from any overarching strategic vision or from the issue priorities of the campaign, but from the minutiae of platform drafting politics.[26] The effect of the convention debate and vote on these issues (they were all defeated) was, therefore, to leave the campaign without a sharp ideological edge or policy purpose.

The substance of Jackson's domestic and foreign policy stances in 1988 did not differ much from 1984. They were somewhat more refined but still placed Jackson in a distinctive left of center ideological position when compared to his opponents.[27] Issue and ideological continuity between 1984 and 1988 campaigns notwithstanding, there were two themes of the 1988 campaign that distinguished it from the 1984 effort and suggest further its more institutional or less insurgent nature. First, in 1988, Jackson through most of the campaign dropped his challenge to the party's delegate allocation rules and to the second primary and related voting rights violations. The delegate allocation rule on the threshold vote required to get any delegates was altered slightly (from 20 to 15 percent) but Jackson's demand in 1984 for a proportional "one person, one vote" delegate allocation formula was rejected by the party's Fairness Commission (created in 1984 in response to Jackson's challenge of the party rules). In addition, the number of unelected, unaccountable "super delegates" drawn from the party's office-holding establishment was increased. And although the second primary issue was not dealt with in the four-year interval, in 1988 Jackson ignored it, choosing for the most part to "play by the rules of the game," rules that he vigorously protested in 1984 and rules that to some extent still deprived him of a fair share of delegates based on his popular vote.

Second, Jackson in 1988 chose to emphasize what political scientists call valence issues, issues on which candidates compete by claiming to stand for the same universally desired values. Although valence issues do not realign voters or divide the candidates, parties or constituent groups, they may have a powerful effect on voter support of the candidate who most effectively articulates them.[28] Such was the case with two issues in 1988: drug use and the personal responsibility of the young for teenage sex and pregnancy.[29] Jackson was almost universally acclaimed by the press and his opponents (in both parties) as the most effective advocate on these issues. Although valence issues tend to be ones where there is little the government can do effectively to manage (this is certainly the case with drug use and teenage sex), they resonate well with an aroused and dispirited public and they are in their nature inclusive, not insurgent. However, it must be said that on the issue or ideological objectives of his campaign Jackson was only partially successful. He did develop, and try to inject into the campaign debate, new perspectives on domestic and foreign policies but because of the structural and racial biases in press coverage as well as his own tactical miscalculations during the campaign and at the conventions, he was only marginally successful in shaping the policy debate. Thus, in neither 1984 or 1988 were either of the major party candidates in the general election required to address issues raised by the Jackson candidacy.

An examination of the platforms confirm this conclusion. Although it is popular among journalists and citizens to discount party platforms as empty symbols that have no bearing on the behavior of candidates or their subsequent administrations, available research suggests that platforms are not inconsequential and looked at over time do bear some relationship to public policy.[30] Platforms not only have some relationship, however modest, to the subsequent actions of the administration but they may also serve as crude indicators of the relative balance of power of constituent interest groups within a party's coalition and of the broad ideological direction of the party. Looked at this way, the outcome of the 1984 and 1988 party platforms may be analyzed in terms of the effectiveness of the Jackson campaigns in their objective of moving the party in a progressive direction and the relative influence of blacks in the party. Both the *Washington Post* and the *New York Times* described the 1984 Democratic Party platform as the most conservative in a generation.[31] My analysis of post-war platforms show that this characterization is exaggerated. The platform in 1984 was no more conservative in either domestic or foreign policy than those adopted in 1980 and 1976. It was, however, considerably more moderate or centrist than the platforms adopted in 1968 and 1972. In those years the party moved in a fairly sharp liberal or progressive direction; however, this leftist tendency was reversed in 1976 to reflect the pressures after McGovern's defeat to move the party toward the center. The 1984 and 1988 platforms reflect this centrist tendency, although the 1988 platform is brief and vague, characterized more by its long catalogue of criticism of Reagan administration policies than by specific platform commitments of its own. This brevity and vagueness was a deliberate strategy choice on the part of Party Chair Paul Kirk and the Dukakis campaign as a means to avoid a rancorous conflict with the Jackson forces over specific policy planks. The fundamental point here is that in 1984 and 1988, when blacks had achieved their highest levels of mobilization in the party with delegate representation, and representation on the platform committee at historically high levels, the substantive results in terms of platform language were less than in 1968 when black representation on the platform committee and at the convention were minuscule. Thus, as in Congress and in the executive, as nominal black influence has increased (measured by the number of office holders and delegates), substantive black influence has remained the same or declined. Analysis of the platform language on full employment—the centerpiece of the post–civil rights era black agenda and of Jackson's economic proposals—serves to make this point.

Since the adoption in 1944 of language embracing the principle of a full employment economy, the planks dealing with the issue have varied in their commitments to use government intervention to achieve the goal, with the strongest commitments in 1968 and 1972. The Appendix compares the language on the full employment issue from Democratic Party platforms from 1944 to 1992. In 1968 the platform included specific programmatic language to achieve full employment and to deal with ghetto joblessness. The 1968 language is almost exactly what the Congressional Black Caucus or Jackson would propose twenty years later. Not only did the platform commit itself to specific programs to achieve the goal of full employment including the government as employer of last resort, it also specifically pledged to undertake programs to deal directly with the problem of ghetto joblessness. The 1968 platform language here was quite specific and parallels what blacks still seek some twenty years later:

> Some of the most urgent jobs in the revival of the inner city remain undone because the hazards are too great and the rewards are too limited to attract sufficient private capital. To meet this problem, *we will charter a new federal banking structure to provide capital and investment guarantees for urban projects planned and implemented through local initiative*—neighborhood development corporations, minority programs for self-employment, housing development corporations, and other urban construction and planning operations. We will also enact legislation providing tax incentives for new business and industrial enterprises in the inner city. Our experience with aid to small business demonstrates the importance of increased local ownership of business enterprises in the inner city (emphasis in text).

Yet, in 1968 blacks were a bare 6.7 percent of convention delegates with few persons on the platform committee, while in 1984 and 1988 blacks constituted 17.7 percent and 23 percent respectively, were amply represented on the platform committees and, in 1988, the committee was cochaired by a black man and the black community had been mobilized in an unprecedented way.

The second strategic objective of a black presidential candidacy was to create an environment at the conventions where blacks would be in a "balance of power" position with respect to choice of the party nominee. This approach to be effective requires that the convention be deadlocked, no candidate having enough delegates to win the nomination on the first ballot. The flaw in this strategy is that this strategic environment at a Democratic convention has not existed in decades. And with the more recent rules changes, tilting the nominating process toward an early, consensus nominee, it is less likely to occur. On the contrary, the structure and process of the nomination is such that the nominee is usually determined early in the primary season; since 1976 usually by the time of the April vote in the New York primary. This was the case in both 1984 and 1988; consequently, Jackson was not in a balance of power position that would permit bargaining on the nominee or anything else.

However, there is a more basic flaw in the strategy. If one assumes a deadlocked convention with several candidates, and none having the capacity initially to command a majority, could a black candidate with, say, a quarter to a third of the delegates effectively bargain so as to determine the nominee? Probably not. First, the white candidates would still control two-thirds of the delegates and it is probable that for ideological, strategic (with the goal of victory in the fall election) and racial reasons they would see it in their interests to coalesce among themselves and isolate the black candidate and his or her delegates. Second, assuming the best strategic situation, where blacks could pick the nominee, presumably in exchange for his or her commitments on policy and patronage, s/he would then be labeled the blacks' candidate, which would of course be exploited by the Republicans in the fall election to the nominee's possible disadvantage. Thus, even if a candidate received the nomination as a result of black support s/he would be inclined to quickly move toward the views of the white majority in order to win the general election. To some extent this occurred with Jimmy Carter after he won the nomination in 1976 with critical black elite and mass support. The Carter administration case illustrates the final flaw in this strategy. Even if a candidate won the nomination and the presidency, like Carter, he would not be bound to keep his promises to blacks.

Rather, to be reelected he would in all likelihood move away from his commitments to blacks to the extent he thought necessary to win. Carter did this in 1980 and black approval of his job performance fell to the same low level as among whites.[32] Yet unlike whites, who could and did express their dissatisfaction with Carter by voting for the Republican, blacks had nowhere to go, no means (except not voting) to impose sanctions on Carter and the Democrats. Thus, they were trapped; the black vote was a captive vote. And the willingness of black leaders and those blacks who voted to close ranks behind a Carter (or a Mondale, Dukakis or Clinton) despite their conservative leanings only serves to reinforce this tendency: it is assumed that the party's most liberal voting bloc will remain loyal because they have no choice.

Walters, perhaps the most tireless advocate in the last two decades of a strategy of black independence in electoral politics and an advisor to Jackson in both 1984 and 1988, has consistently argued that in order for a bargaining strategy to be credible in presidential politics, blacks must be in a position to have someplace else to go, in case the Democratic nominee or president fails to bargain or repudiates his commitments.[33] That someplace else can only be a third, progressive party of the left. The failure of blacks to create such a party since 1972 thus looms large in the failures of black leadership in the post–civil rights era. I return to this problem in the next chapter. But first, all of the objectives of Jackson's campaigns ultimately depended on the extent to which the black vote was mobilized and the extent to which a multiethnic coalition could be created and sustained. Thus, I conclude this analysis of the campaigns in terms of their effectiveness in mobilization of the black vote and the development of a rainbow coalition.

The Myth of the Rainbow Coalition

The idea of a progressive multiethnic coalition of voters that might become the majority in national politics is based on two distinct but interrelated assumptions. First, the mobilization of the black vote. Since 1972 blacks have constituted roughly 20 percent of the Democratic Party voter coalition, and they are homogeneously liberal; thus, if they could be mobilized in significant numbers they could become the core or the base for the transformation of the Democratic Party, or failing that, the core of a new progressive party coalition. The second assumption is that enough nonblacks (whites, Latinos and Asian Americans) could be mobilized in a coalition with blacks to form a multiethnic "rainbow" majority.[34]

The 1984 campaign data from a variety of sources indicate that there was a significant increase in black registration and voting during the primaries and caucuses. It is probable that in 1984 for the first time in the history of the Democratic Party's nomination process, black Americans voted at a greater rate than whites. An analysis by the Joint Center of the turnout in twelve 1984 Democratic Primary states showed that in every state, voting was greater in "black areas" than in the state as a whole.[35] Increased black turnout from 1980 to 1984 ranged from 14 percent in Georgia to 127 percent in New York state. This compares to an overall increase in 1984 Democratic Primary voting of 4 percent between 1980 and 1984. This large increase in black participation is attributable to the enthusiasm generated by Jackson's campaigns. Blacks comprised 18 percent of primary voters in 1984 and 21 percent in 1988.[36] Jackson received nearly all of this vote. Exit poll data in 1984 showed that Jackson carried about 85 percent of the overall black vote. In the early primaries in Alabama and Georgia, Jackson had received 50 and 60 percent of the black vote, Mondale receiving the majority of the remaining vote. However, as the primary season developed, Jackson's percentage of the black vote steadily increased until he was receiving 85 to 90 percent of the total. Jackson's support in the black community cut across all demographic categories. In the early southern primaries, young and rural blacks were slightly more favorable to Jackson than older and urban blacks. But by the end of the primary season Jackson was receiving about the same level of support from all strata of the black community. In 1988 Jackson increased his share of the black vote from the 80 to 85 percent range to 90 to 95 percent. In fact, unlike in 1984, in 1988 the black vote was conceded to Jackson by all candidates. For example, at the 1988 Congressional Black Caucus dinner Dukakis asked plaintively "Let me be your second choice." The Jackson campaign, therefore, was reasonably successful in both elections in mobilizing its core constituency. (Although Jackson was successful in mobilizing a larger than usual black turnout in the primaries and caucuses, his successes here do not compare with the massive turnout in the Chicago mayoral election of 1983 or the 1991 Louisiana governor's race between Edwin Edwards and David Duke. In both those elections black turnout is estimated at more than 75 percent. Turnout at these levels might have allowed Jackson to actually win the New York and Illinois primaries.)

However, in an important sense, the first requirement of an effective progressive coalition was met: the black community was mobilized to the extent that it represented its approximate proportion of the national Democratic electorate, and it was essentially a cohesive vote for Jackson. The second requirement—the mobilization of whites and other minorities in numbers sufficient in combination with the black vote to constitute a majority—was not fulfilled, despite an all-out effort on Jackson's part to appeal to these groups in terms of issues and campaign scheduling. Jackson's idea of a rainbow coalition included (in addition to blacks), Hispanics, Asian and Native Americans, poor whites, women and youth, what Congressman Conyers called a "coalition of the rejected." With a few exceptions here and there, this coalition did not materialize at either the mass or elite level.

Jackson's issue appeal to whites was to the poor and the working class rather than the middle income, well educated. There are basically two lines of thinking among scholars about voter coalitions across racial lines. The first contends that, given white working-class hostility to blacks, "the ally for the Negro for the foreseeable future is the cosmopolitan white bourgeoisie."[37] On the other hand, Carmichael and Hamilton in their chapter "The Myth of Coalition" in *Black Power* wrote, "It is hoped that eventually there will be a coalition of poor blacks and poor whites. This is the only coalition which seems acceptable to us and we see such a coalition as the major instrument of change in American society."[38] The evidence from the Jackson campaigns supports the first of these theories of black-white coalitions since Jackson received the bulk of his support from upper-income, well-educated "cosmopolitan" whites rather than the working class, a pattern also found in the election of black mayors and blacks in other biracial constituencies. Thus, in attempting to build a biracial coalition on the basis of the working class, Jackson was going against not only a good body of social science theory but also the post–civil rights era experience of black candidates running across racial lines. Williams's analysis of white perceptions of a black candidate suggests that "slightly more than three quarters of the white electorate might automatically oppose a black candidate for president or, even in the best possible scenario, take a lot of convincing."[39] This is because in 1988 approximately 25 percent of whites said they would automatically vote against any black candidate and of the three-fourths who said they might support a black, only 26 percent said that any black currently on the scene was qualified to be president.[40] This meant that Jackson in effect was appealing to only about one-fourth of the white electorate and it was disproportionately middle and upper class, not poor and working class.

Perhaps only a small proportion of this white opposition to Jackson was based on racism, with the remainder involving reservations about his character, ideology and lack of experience in government. Nevertheless, as Schelling contends, even a moderate level of racism at the individual level can foster extreme levels at the aggregate level.[41] This evidence suggests that the strategy of appealing to lower-class whites was bound to fail, which of course it did. This is shown not only in the survey data on white working-class attitudes but also in depth studies of their beliefs and values. In a series of interviews specifically designed to explore the prospects for a biracial coalition of working-class Americans Bostch concludes that working-class white men:

> exhibit enough racial prejudice so that they could be separated from their black working class peers on a number of issues. The most important of these issues evolves from the negative stereotype of the "lazy, shiftless" black apparently held by most of these white men. Blacks are seen as threatening because they wish to use the powers of the national government to change the rules of meritocracy to gain an unfair advantage in jobs and promotions. This stereotype embitters white workers toward all governmental power and threatens to alienate whites from blacks, who generally feel they are discriminated against.[42]

A principal problem here is that with the decline of organized labor the American working class is essentially without organization or leadership. Indeed, a history of working people in the last twenty-five years could also be titled "We Have No Leaders." The labor movement, like the civil rights movement, has been coopted into the Democratic Party and the routines of system politics and labor-management relations, rendering it largely irrelevant as a force in American politics.[43] First, labor's membership has declined to less than 15 percent from its post-war high of about 35 percent. Second, the AFL-CIO is characterized by an entrenched, aging, autocratic white male leadership (the AFL has had only four presidents in its hundred year history), although its membership is increasingly composed of minorities and women. Finally, the leadership of labor has been reluctant to confront white working-class racism with organizing strategies and programs that seek to develop a transracial worker solidarity. Related to this in the post–civil rights era, trade union members increasingly have moved away from labor's broadly progressive social welfare agenda toward an embrace of Reagan-style conservatism.

With the exception of William Winspisinger of the International Association of Machinists, Jackson received little support from leaders of trade unions. Yet Jackson frequently sought to take his campaign to the communities of the working class, and his speeches made eloquent appeals to the interests of poor whites and the cause of transracial class solidarity.[44] This did not translate into votes. In 1984 Jackson received about 10 percent of the aggregate white vote cast in the primaries, not enough to analyze its class composition on the basis of the exit polls. In 1988 he doubled his aggregate support among whites to approximately 20 percent, ranging from 10 percent in the southern primaries to about 25 percent in Connecticut and Wisconsin. This is sufficient to make some inferences about the class basis of Jackson's white support. The evidence from the *New York Times* exit polls from the several states where Jackson received significant white support unambiguously shows that it came from well-educated affluent voters rather than the poor and working class. In 1972 McGovern tried to assemble a "rainbow" of the rejected: a progressive coalition of minorities, the poor and the young. He failed; poor and working class whites tended to support Nixon while more educated whites supported McGovern, leading one wag to quip that McGovern had carried "Harlem and Harvard." This is a nice way to characterize the nature of Jackson's biracial coalition in 1988.

Apart from the absence of white working-class support, Jackson received little support from Jews, the most progressive white ethnic voting bloc. Jews are indispensable to a progressive electoral and governing coalition in the United States, because of their historic commitment to civil rights and progressive causes;[45] their disproportionate financial support of national political campaigns;[46] and their integration and active participation in influential U.S. institutions, especially publishing, the press, universities and civic organizations.[47] Although there has been movement in a conservative direction in recent years, American Jews still score disproportionately high on most measures of liberalism, and in 1980, 1984 and 1988, Jews were the only white ethnic group to cast a majority of their votes for the Democratic nominee.[48] Also, in big city mayoral elections, Jews among whites have been disproportionate supporters of black candidates, as even in Chicago in 1983 when the opposing candidate was Jewish.[49] Jews therefore should be a natural constituency in the rainbow coalition. However, in 1988, when Jackson was receiving about 20 percent of the white vote, he may have got 7 percent of the Jewish vote (a figure within the margin of error in the exit polls). A part of this dissatisfaction has to do with Jackson's controversial past—his alleged antisemitic remarks and relationships with Palestinian leader Yasser Arafat and the Nation of Islam's Minister Farrakhan. However, the root of the problem is the black position on the Middle East conflict, specifically support of the Palestinian quest for self-determination. More generally, it is what Raab and Lipset call a "third world" approach to U.S. foreign policy.[50] This approach is no mere Jesse Jackson phenomenon; rather it is a consensus view in black America, shared by its intelligentsia and leadership establishment. This third world approach is anchored in black identification with all oppressed peoples, especially the world's oppressed colored peoples. This identification with the oppressed is rooted in a shared historical experience and perhaps in the Afro-American religious tradition.[51] This means that until there is a just resolution of the Palestinian conflict, it is unlikely that Jews will take their natural place in the rainbow coalition or any other black-led progressive coalition.[52]

Eighty percent of whites voted against Jackson in 1988 and ninety percent in 1984. Jackson explained his low white voter support in terms of racism; as he put it, "whites have developed over their history a lack of regard for the intelligence and hard work of black people."[53] Racism was clearly a factor; however, Jackson's lack of government experience, his controversial past and his left-liberal ideology were also factors in his relatively low level of support among whites.

White women were also to be a part of the rainbow coalition of the "rejected." This was really a silly assumption. Silly, because it assumes that women identify with their subordinate gender status rather than their race, religion or social class. Although there has emerged in recent years a modest gender gap of 5 to 7 percent between white males and females with the latter more likely to vote for liberal or Democratic candidates, it is not sufficient to suggest that women would constitute any kind of distinct voting bloc for a broad ideological coalition of the left. It was not women as a group, then, that Jackson sought to mobilize; it was rather an ideological category—feminists—that was the coalition's target. Jackson embraced the entire feminist agenda in both 1984 and 1988, even on the issue of abortion, which he in the past had equated with slavery and genocide. At the 1972 Gary convention Jackson led the opposition to the proposal by a group of women to include in the platform a plank affirming a woman's right to an abortion, equating the Supreme Court's decision in *Roe v. Wade* to the Dred Scott decision sanctioning slavery. Later, in an essay published in the National Right to Life's bulletin and in an open letter to the Congress, he eloquently condemned abortion as a "policy of killing infants" because he said "human life begins when the sperm and egg join. . . ." Rejecting the argument that abortion involved a right to privacy, Jackson wrote, "If one accepts the position that life is private, and therefore you have the right to do with it as you please, one must also accept the conclusion of that logic. That was the premise of slavery. You could not protest the existence or treatment of slaves on the plantation because that was private and therefore outside your right to be concerned."[54] Jackson also consistently argued in 1984 that the party should choose a woman as the vice presidential nominee (in 1988 he argued that he should be the vice presidential nominee). Yet, this embrace was not reciprocated. He was not supported by a single national white feminist organization or leader, nor do the exit polls indicate that he benefitted from the gender gap, except that black men in 1984 were somewhat more likely to vote for him than black women.

Jackson also made a consistent effort to include in the coalition other racial minorities, including Hispanics, Arabs and Asian Americans.[55] He fully embraced the Hispanic agenda on immigration and bilingualism.[56] His support of the Arab American leadership position on recognition of the PLO and Palestinian self-determination was well publicized throughout both campaigns and was at least one of the factors in his loss of support among Jewish Americans. At the elite level, Jackson was supported by several Hispanic leaders including former New Mexico governor Tony Anaya and former and current presidents of the League of United Latin American Citizens, the largest Mexican-American civil rights organization, and he was supported politically and financially by Arab American leaders including James Zogby of the Arab Anti-Defamation League.

Yet, at the mass level, Jackson received relatively little support from Latinos (except Puerto Ricans in New York) and Asian Americans. The idea of a rainbow coalition of people of color is probably as much of a myth as the idea of a working-class coalition. Color discrimination and social class in the United States tend to overlap, providing an objective basis for a coalition of color. That is, people of color in general (*in general* is to be emphasized, since Japanese Americans, Cuban Americans and immigrants from India, for example, have somewhat higher class status than other members of the Hispanic and Asian American communities) tend to be lower class and to face discrimination from whites, and this is thought to provide a basis for coalition with blacks in terms of support for civil rights and social welfare programs. Yet, while majorities of both Latinos and Asian Americans feel they face discrimination from a hostile white majority, they feel they have more in common with whites than they do with blacks.[57] And Latinos and Asian Americans are just as likely as whites, if not more so, to embrace negative stereotypes about blacks. For example, the most recent survey report shows that 51 percent of Latinos, 53 percent of Asians but 45 percent of whites said they believed blacks were prone to crime and violence; and 40 percent of whites, 33 percent of Latinos and 48 percent of Asians said they believed blacks "care less about family." As the authors of this report write, these negative stereotypes regarding blacks constitute a "serious barrier" to cooperation and coalitions between blacks and other people of color.[58] In addition, the Cuban

American community is a reliable part of the Republican coalition and Mexican Americans are increasingly leaning in a conservative direction,[59] while in the 1992 election President Bush received 65 percent of the Asian American vote (higher than that from any other discrete ethno-religious group including white born-again Christians). Thus, it appears that despite commonalities in social class and real and perceived discrimination, the basis for a rainbow coalition of color is at best tenuous.

It is difficult to get reliable data on the extent of minority group support for the rainbow coalition, except for that of Hispanics. On the basis of analysis of 1984 exit poll data, Morris and Williams estimate that Jackson received 33 percent of the Puerto Rican vote, 17 percent of the Mexican vote and 20 percent of California's Asian American vote. In 1988 Jackson won the Puerto Rican vote (61 percent) in New York but in Texas and California the large Mexican American population voted two to one for Dukakis.[60] Overall, then, with the exception of the Puerto Rican vote in New York and perhaps the Arab American vote, the rainbow coalition was not able to get majority support from any group other than its core black base. This result is not for lack of effort on Jackson's part. In terms of issues, campaign organization and staff, and campaign scheduling and speeches, Jackson made an all out effort to reach out to feminists, low income whites and other minority groups— in the case of the feminists and the abortion issue, even going so far as to repudiate long-held religious and moral views. Yet in the end, the coalition at the end of the rainbow remained largely black.

Jackson: The Man, the Movement, the Coalition

In his *Cycles of History*, Schlesinger argues that the absence of effective political parties tends to result in the rise of personalized political movements whose stability tend to depend on the vagaries of individual personality and character.[61] Students of politics of all ideological stripes view this as an unhealthy development for the polity and especially for the interests of low-income or working-class people because it leaves them subject to exploitation by the inevitable "opportunism of politicians."[62] This is why political scientists are so strongly committed to political parties as requisite institutions for democratic governance.[63] Yet with the ongoing decline of political parties in the United States, personalized political movements have become almost a defining feature of American politics, at virtually all levels of government and from all ideological points on the spectrum. The politics of the 1980s has seen the rise of what one scholar calls "candidate centered" presidential elections that operate relatively free of the constraints of party.⁶⁴ The Jesse Jackson phenomenon is therefore not unique; rather, it appears to be a structural characteristic of modern American politics.

The recognition of the need for some kind of institutional constraints on personalized politics was one of the principal reasons that the National Black Political Convention convened in 1972. The failure of this project left a vacuum that Jesse Jackson filled in the 1980s. As indicated earlier, when the idea of a black running for president began to circulate in black leadership circles, a number of ad hoc meetings were held to discuss the idea and eventually a decision was taken to support the idea, although not Jackson, as the candidate. But this decision was largely symbolic, as the group was not representative of the community and it acted only to give a cloak of collective legitimacy to a decision Jackson had already made. Thus, the problem of a personalized candidacy remained, especially given Jackson's well-known reputation for acting opportunistically and egotistically. The problem was how to develop a mechanism that would give the campaign not only the symbolic cloak of collective legitimacy but its substance as well. The Black Leadership Roundtable and the Black Leadership Forum—the structures created in the aftermath of the collapse of the convention to engage in collective decision making—were ignored by Jackson precisely because their decision on the idea itself might have been negative or, if not, they might have looked to another candidate or sought to impose some constraints on Jackson's campaign. During the ad hoc meetings, Ronald Walters prepared a discussion paper that proposed the establishment of a broadly representative national campaign committee of thirty to fifty members whose purpose would be to "move from the tradition of a *personal* candidacy to one which is representative of the black community, or which has the potential of such representation. . . ." (emphasis in text).⁶⁵ Walters proposed that the candidate have the right to select 51 percent of the committee's membership (which of course made it something less than democratically accountable) and that its principal purpose be to hold the candidate "accountable" in the bargaining process and provide the campaign "legitimacy." Specifically, Walters proposed that the "candidate should not be empowered to bargain alone (bargaining here means all phases of the process—presenting the issues, evaluating the counter-offers, and passing judgment on the result). The candidate should have the right to meet alone with the other candidates, but should not conduct the entire bargaining procedure without the participation of members of the national committee. This means the national committee should be convened at regular intervals such as monthly or at a time when the candidate decides that vital matters should be considered."[66] Predictably, nothing came of this proposal. It went against the structural nature of candidate-centered campaigns, Jackson's authoritarian style of decision making and his notion from the outset that the campaign would be a rainbow coalition rather than a black community campaign as envisioned by Walters' committee. Thus, the campaign from its inception through its various stages in 1984 and 1988 was the highly personalized movement of one man.

It is popular among many journalists and intellectuals to criticize Jesse Jackson. And there is much to criticize: his seemingly unrestrained ambition and opportunism, observed from his earliest days in the civil rights movement; his tasteless behavior in the immediate aftermath of Dr. King's murder; his unseemly effort to displace Reverend Abernathy as head of SCLC, and failing that, his less than honest departure from the organization; his lack of bureaucratic competence and his authoritarian leadership style; his mismanagement, if not misappropriation, of Operation PUSH-Excel funds; his tendency toward demagoguery; his failure initially to tell the truth about his "hymie" and "hymietown" remarks; and overall, his tendency to move from issue to issue and place to place without follow through or responsibility. Some or indeed all of these criticisms may be valid,[67] but in terms of their political consequence they are—taken out of context—not particularly relevant. In context, however, they point to the limits of personalized movements in general and Jackson's Rainbow Coalition in particular. Jackson like any person has his strengths and weaknesses and like any political leader he has his admirable and less than admirable qualities. However Jackson's character is weighed, he is with Ronald Reagan arguably the most remarkable political leader of the post–civil rights era and will loom large in the history of the movement's transformation from protest to politics.

After the 1984 campaign Jackson called for the institutionalization of the Rainbow Coalition as a permanent, multiethnic organization devoted to progressive political change that would operate not only as an electoral organization but as a broad-based social movement entity that would include mass demonstrations, rallies, boycotts, and so forth. It was also envisioned that local Rainbows might perhaps run their own candidates (under the Democratic party banner) in local and state elections. In 1986 the Rainbow Coalition was formally incorporated as a national organization with local, congressional district and state affiliates. The revised bylaws require that a state Rainbow have only twenty-five members in a third of a state's congressional districts in order to qualify for a charter. Despite this rather limited membership requirement there has been hardly any local organizational development. Several reasons account for this organizational inertia. First, from the outset there was and there remains a continuing tension between the various "colors" in the Rainbow, especially between white left activists and the neonationalist black activists. Second, although the local and state Rainbows were envisioned as mass membership organizations with a measure of democratic autonomy, in the end Jackson relegated to himself the authority to pick the local leaders, which stunted the development of indigenous leadership.[68] Finally, in predictable Jackson style, he has failed in the interim between campaigns to devote the time and resources to the tedious follow-up work of grassroots organizing. Rather, in typical "Jetstream Jesse" fashion (this termed was coined by Chicago columnist Mike Royko to describe Jackson's peripatetic behavior and his consistent failure to follow through on initiatives he would launch with great fanfare) he has done virtually everything else; from serving as the "Bishop of Black America" preaching funerals and marrying celebrities, hosting two television programs, running and not running for mayor of the District of Columbia and being elected the District's "shadow senator." All of this plus his regular job as the leading black spokesperson on issues ranging from the Persian Gulf war to the appropriate punishment for convicted rapist Mike Tyson. Even for a man with Jackson's abilities and stamina these activities have left little time or resources for organization building. As a result, the National Rainbow Coalition is little more than another paper organization, with one or two functionaries in cities around the country who are willing to assist Jackson as a kind of permanent advance person when he visits.[69] The extensive network of activists and voters mobilized in the campaigns of 1984 and 1988 have been allowed to atrophy, to be activated only if Jackson decides to once again seek the presidency.

This is probably as Jackson wants it, reflecting his personal needs and ambitions. Unlike his mentor Dr. King, Jackson throughout his career has been unwilling to delegate authority. King surrounded himself at SCLC with strong-willed and highly competent leaders, and while remaining clearly in charge was quite willing to delegate authority (Jackson's leadership of Operation Breadbasket is a prime example of this). By contrast, Reynolds describes Jackson's leadership of Operation PUSH in the following way:

> Delegation of authority is another obstacle. Jackson does not transfer his power to anybody beneath him. Everybody responds immediately in a precision like manner to his command, but staff members do not like obeying orders of lesser individuals because

there is little division of authority. All the administrative staff feel they are all on the same level; there is nobody capable of being above them but Jackson.[70]

A similar pattern is apparent in the Rainbow Coalition.[71] Jackson has surrounded himself with a cadre of long-time functionaries rather than independent political leaders and staff, and reserves decisions on critical issues to himself. The Rainbow Coalition as a broadly based, independent progressive political organization has not developed, and given Jackson's leadership, it is not likely to develop. Again, this is as Jackson would have it, preferring a personalized to an institutionalized movement. But, any organization so thoroughly under the control of one person cannot be a viable political entity, one that would provide democratic access to its agenda or strategy.

This may be seen in the role, more precisely the lack of a role, of Jackson in the 1992 Democratic presidential nomination process.[72] Once he reluctantly took himself out of the race, there was sentiment in the organization for Jackson and the Rainbow Coalition to endorse one of the candidates and thus help to shape the outcome of the process in a liberal or progressive direction. Jackson refused himself to endorse a candidate, and refused to allow the organization to do so. The sentiment at the organization's pre-primary national conference (addressed by each of the five major Democratic candidates) was to endorse either Senator Tom Harkin, the only traditional liberal among the five, or former California Governor Jerry Brown, the left insurgent candidate. But Jackson said no, and instead gave his "blessing" to each of the candidates. The result of the 1992 primary process was that Arkansas Governor Bill Clinton—a cofounder of the conservative Democratic Leadership Council and perhaps the least liberal or progressive candidate—won the nomination, in large measure on the basis of overwhelming black support in the Super Tuesday and Illinois, Michigan and New York primaries. Jackson declined to endorse or allow the Rainbow to endorse a candidate for several reasons. First, he wanted to maintain his own *personal* power as the preeminent black broker inside the party establishment and at the convention, unrestrained by the organization. Second, he did not wish to risk his *personal* credibility or that of *his* organization by endorsing Harkins or Brown. Many black elected officials (especially in the south) endorsed Clinton, and it was not clear that if Jackson had endorsed someone else the black vote would have followed his leadership. This would have demonstrated the hollowness of his frequently stated claim that he could deliver "seven million votes" and the weakness of the Rainbow Coalition at the grassroots level. Either would have put at risk his claim of preeminent leadership in the party and nation and his credibility as the principal black broker at the convention and in a subsequent Democratic administration, as well as with the media and the corporate establishment.[73]

Jackson and the Rainbow Coalition had the potential to become a major force for independent, progressive politics in the United States. Jackson, perhaps predictably, blew it. This once again points to the significance of the failure of the National Black Political Convention as an institutional mechanism to discipline the resources of black America and its leaders.

10

Racial Symbolism as "Ideology" in the Post–Civil Rights Era, and a Postscript on the Clinton Administration and the 1994 Election

In 1984 and 1988 the Democratic party's nominees for president were Walter Mondale and Michael Dukakis, persons long identified with its traditional liberal wing. Both lost by large margins. In 1992 the party nominated Bill Clinton, a person identified with its more centrist, southern conservative or moderate wing. Clinton won by a narrow margin in a three-way race. After the 1984 and 1988 elections journalists, politicians and political consultants argued that Mondale and Dukakis lost because they were liberals and because they were too closely identified with "special interest groups," organized labor, feminists, homosexuals but especially blacks. For example, after the 1984 election the Democratic party commissioned several studies to determine why the party lost the presidency. One was conducted by Stanley Greenberg, Clinton's 1992 pollster. It pointed clearly to the party's identification with blacks as the source of its problem. Based on a series of focus group interviews with white "Reagan Democrats" in Macomb County, a Detroit suburb, Greenberg argued that the reason these white middle and working class voters turned against the Democrats was because of their distaste for blacks and because of their association of the party with "them." Greenberg wrote, "These white Democratic defectors express a profound distaste for blacks, a sentiment that pervades almost everything they think about government and politics. . . . Blacks constitute the explanation for their [white defectors] vulnerability and for almost everything that has gone wrong in their lives, not being black is what constitutes being middle class, not living with blacks is what makes a neighborhood a decent place to live. These sentiments have important implications for Democrats, as virtually all progressive symbols have been redefined in racial and pejorative terms."[1] Implicit in Greenberg's report was the notion that if the party was to win the presidency it would have to distance itself—at least symbolically—from blacks and their interests and present itself—again at least symboli- cally—as the party of the white middle class. This notion was made explicit in a report prepared by Milton Kotler and Nelson Rosenbaum for the Democratic National Committee (DNC). In 1985 DNC Chair Paul Kirk paid a private consultant firm more than $250,000 for a study designed to determine why the party lost the presidency in 1984 and what it might do to win in the future. The study, reportedly the largest research project ever undertaken by the party, was based on a series of focus group interviews and a nationwide survey of more than 5,000 voters. Kolter and Rosenbaum concluded that the Democrats needed to "de-market" the party to the social and economic underclass and focus instead on the interests and concerns of the white middle class. Like the Greenberg report, this study concluded that among southern whites and northern urban "ethnic" voters (Irish, Italian and Poles) the party was identified as the "give away party, giving white tax money to blacks and poor people."[2] The study was distributed to a number of party leaders and apparently their reaction to its language and tone was so negative that Kirk refused to release it and reportedly ordered all but a few copies destroyed.[3] While there was a negative reaction to the language of the report, its findings and their strategic implications were not rejected. On the contrary, they resurfaced after the Dukakis defeat in 1988.

Just prior to the 1988 election Harry McPhearson, a former John- son administration functionary, wrote an op-ed essay in the *New York Times* titled "How Race Destroyed the Democrat's Coalition," in which he argued that the party's identification with blacks put it at risk of becoming a permanent minority in presidential elections.[4] The *Times* itself in its post mortem on the 1988 election raised similar concerns in an editorial titled "Does Race Doom the Democrats?"[5] A year after the 1988 election the Democratic Leadership Council (DLC), the organiza- tion of white conservative and centrist Democrats formed after the 1984 election with the avowed purpose of moving the party to the right, published a report similar in substance although not tone to the DNC report Kirk had destroyed in 1985. Called *The Politics of Evasion*, the study published by the DLC's research arm, the Progressive Policy Institute, argued that the party was too liberal, too attentive to "special interests" and had lost touch with the values and interests of middle class voters."[6] The report received widespread attention in the national press and in some ways became a kind of political bible of the party's more conservative elements, finding its way into the rhetoric and pro- posals of Bill Clinton, a DLC founder and its former chairman.

Finally, in 1991 Thomas Edsal, a *Washington Post* reporter, with his wife Mary published an article in the *Atlantic Monthly* simply called "Race," where these arguments about the crippling effects of blacks on the post–civil rights era Democratic Party's presidential coalition were synthesized.[7] Later in a best-selling book, clearly designed to influence the 1992 election, the Edsals once again invoked the spectre of race destroying the Democratic Party. Relying on the Greenberg, Kotler and Rosenbaum, and Karmack and Galston reports, the Edsals argued that the Democratic Party should deemphasize issues of racism, poverty, civil rights and affirmative action and instead focus on the concerns of the middle class in terms of lower taxes, opposition to quotas and a tough approach to welfare and crime. This is almost precisely the script followed by the Clinton strategists. For example, a frequent refrain in Clinton's rhetoric in 1992 was "opportunity plus responsibility," a subtle appeal to the view of many whites that blacks are irresponsible, lazy, preferring to live on welfare than work. This follows the Edsals' notion that "There has been little consistent public emphasis on accompanying responsibilities or on standards of reciprocal obligation. . . . Going further, the Democratic Party failed to understand the *political* need to couple newly granted rights and preferences with a persuasive and visible message of reciprocal obligation" (emphasis by the authors).[8] In his emphasis on "opportunity and responsibility" and in his talk on "ending welfare as we know it," Clinton brought such an emphasis consistently to the 1992 campaign.

The Edsals also argued that Jesse Jackson as the most visible symbol of the party's identification with blacks (a "near-institution" within the party, as they put it) "epitomizes one of the central problems of the Democratic party as it struggle[s] to regain the support of a majority of the electorate in presidential elections."[9] Thus, they suggested that the nominee in 1992 should find a way to distance himself from Jackson, downplay his role at the convention and in the fall campaign while simultaneously not alienating the crucial black vote necessary to win. Clinton—as the analysis below shows—also skillfully followed this part of the Edsals' script. Ironically, then, Jackson, who ran for president to halt the party's drift to the right, became in 1992 a useful symbol to facilitate the nomination and election of a so-called New Democrat, not wedded to traditional party ideology.

Before turning to detailed analysis of the puzzling election of Clinton in 1992, it should be clear that Clinton was not the first Democratic nominee to attempt to distance himself from liberalism, blacks and Jesse Jackson. Although both Mondale and Dukakis clearly came out of the party's liberal wing and tradition, both men in the general election campaigns attempted to present themselves as "pragmatic centrists" rather than as liberals, and attempted to distance themselves from blacks in general and Jackson in particular. Dukakis in particular followed this approach, first by selecting conservative Texas Senator Lloyd Bentsen as his running mate, and second by denying (until the final days of the campaign) that he was a liberal, claiming instead that he was a non-ideological pragmatist interested only in "competence."[10] And in spite of Jackson's considerable success in rallying black voter turnout, Dukakis's campaign reportedly asked Jackson not to campaign or to campaign unobtrusively, in stealth fashion, in several states with large black populations, fearing that his visibility would mobilize more anti-Dukakis white voters than it would black Democrats.[11] Thus, the "dissing," as my children would say, of Jackson, while perhaps done more effectively by Clinton, is nothing new. On the contrary it has been part of the process since Jackson entered presidential politics.

This treatment of Jackson is simply emblematic of what has been described as the new orthodoxy in discussion of race, racism, ideology and partisanship in the post–civil rights era. Namely, that the Democrats embrace of the cause of civil rights and racial justice has resulted in the disaffection of white southerners and the urban white lower-middle class, with the result that it is extraordinarily difficult to forge a majority presidential coalition.

And when Democrats in 1994 lost control of both houses of Congress for the first time in forty years, blacks were once again seen as the culprit, notwithstanding that black turnout was relatively high and overwhelmingly Democratic in a campaign in which white congressional candidates tended to ignore black policy concerns in an effort to appeal to "disgruntled whites" on the racially symbolic issues of crime, welfare and "family values."[12] Yet, shortly after the election, Washington-based columnists Cokie and Steven Roberts wrote an essay with the now familiar, ominous title, "Democrats Must Face Race Issue." The Roberts wrote, "A huge issue that nobody wants to talk about is bedeviling Democrats as they try to absorb the lessons of 1994 and reclaim the center. That issue is race." Noting that given the seniority system blacks in the new Congress will be the ranking member of four committees and the second ranking on two more, they report that party "moderates" urged Richard Gephardt, the Democratic leader, to abandon strict adherence to seniority and select committee leaders on the basis of merit as well as longevity because the presence of so many blacks in leadership positions sends the wrong message to "disgruntled white suburban voters." After reporting that Gephardt rejected the idea because "he's so afraid of the Black Caucus", the Roberts write:

Accordingly, the Democratic leadership in the House will become increasingly weighted toward minorities and thus toward liberal ideas and principles. And to party moderates, this is exactly the wrong direction. They point out that black and Hispanic lawmakers generally represent urban districts dominated by constituents of their own race. As a result, these congressmen seldom meet or talk to the disgruntled white suburban voters who have restored Republicans to power in the House for the first time in forty years.[13]

The Roberts's formulation ignores the fact that whites in congressional leadership positions come from districts dominated by their own race and seldom meet or talk to "disgruntled blacks," suggesting that disgruntled whites should be appeased by the party, but disgruntled blacks should be ignored.

In addition to the pollsters, consultants and pundits who have advanced this thesis, there are sophisticated quantitative and academic studies by political scientists that reach the same conclusions.[14] This line of analysis, only in part correct, has become so widespread that it has been labeled a "new orthodoxy . . . haunting liberal intellectual life, an orthodoxy that waxes nostalgic about the New Deal to blame black (and in some versions, feminist) political demands for the rightward turn in American politics and for the left's collapse."[15] This new orthodoxy is in part correct; however, it is historically misleading, because it assumes that race as a factor in the nation's political life somehow suddenly emerged in the 1960s, when in fact race has been an abiding feature of American politics. At the nadir of Reconstruction, for example, arguments quite similar to the current orthodoxy were being heard.[16] Race was then a problem, divisive and in the minds of the nation's white elites a major impediment to the development of the national economy. The problem was at that time the Republican Party's problem and it eventually resolved it by its abandonment of its black loyalists and ultimately the disenfranchisement of most of the black electorate. This new orthodoxy also assumes that the New Deal coalition was much more working class in its constituent base and policy content than the historical record suggests.[17] Although some important reforms were adopted during the New Deal that served working-class interests, Roosevelt was the reluctant liberal reformer, and much of the legislation adopted during his administrations was severely compromised as a result of the pressures of the party's conservative wing. And from Roosevelt to Kennedy, liberal social and economic reforms were always given priority over the basic civil rights of blacks. Indeed, until the irresistible pressures of the mass protests of the 1960s, liberals ignored blacks with the argument that to pursue civil rights would put in jeopardy working-class programs and policies that would benefit all Americans, black and white. An argument frequently heard today as blacks are urged to eschew race-specific programs in favor of universalist ones that benefit all Americans. Thus, while the 1960s did usher in a new partisan alignment on race that has worked to disadvantage the Democrats in presidential elections, it is only partially correct to assert that this is a new phenomenon, and it is incorrect to imply that prior to the 1960s there was some kind of broad-based class politics that was somehow disrupted by the special pleading of blacks.[18]

The new orthodoxy is correct in its fundamental thesis that in the 1960s there occurred a basic ideological and partisan restructuring of American politics on the basis of race.[19] The critical event was the Kennedy-Johnson administrations' embrace of the civil rights cause. Although the Civil Rights Act of 1964 was adopted with bipartisan support, the Republicans and their nominee in 1964 rejected the legislation, setting in motion a gradual realignment of the parties. The Democratic party became the party of blacks and racial liberalism and the Republican party became the party of racist whites and racial reaction. This process was accelerated in 1968 with the Wallace insurgency and Nixon's southern strategy. By 1972 with the McGovern nomination, the process was complete in the Democratic Party. Blacks had become a core constituency, and the party's embrace of racial liberalism had become near irreversible. The 1980 nomination and election of Ronald Reagan completed the process in the Republican party. Southern whites and a substantial part of the northern working class became core Republican constituent groups and the party's embrace of racial reaction became complete. This much of the new orthodoxy is beyond dispute. It has been exhaustively researched and thoroughly documented in the academic literature. What is in dispute is what is to be made of this outcome; how it and its political consequence is to be interpreted and what the Democrats and blacks should do about it in order to advance their respective interests.

The new orthodoxy focuses on the Democrats and their embrace of racial liberalism rather than the Republicans and their embrace of racial reaction. The Democrats are faulted for their embrace of the cause of racial equality but the Republicans are not held accountable for their embrace of racial reaction. In 1955 Clinton Rossiter, a leading conservative political theorist, wrote that the "problem of the Negro" presented conservatism and Republicans with a choice between expediency—"the cold blooded counting of votes and seats" and principle—"the conscience stricken recognition that the Negro should not have to beg and fight for the ordinary rights of Americans."[20] When confronted with this dilemma the Republicans choose expediency over principle. The party, or more precisely its right wing, which displaced its dominant middle of the road leadership beginning in 1964, choose to count votes and seats rather than follow the dictates of conscience. Yet, except from blacks, one rarely hears criticism of this racist reaction by the Republicans. The Democrats are criticized routinely for becoming the party of blacks but rarely does one hear criticism of the Republicans for becoming the party of whites, not only of whites but racist whites, although this has been its clear strategic objective since Nixon's embrace of the southern strategy in 1968.[21] It is for this reason that this line of thinking with its ominous headlines about "How Race Destroyed the Democratic Party" seems to smack of racism and the familiar blame-the-victim syndrome so familiar in the discourse on race in this country. The headline does not read, as it might, how *racism* destroyed the Democratic Party but how *race* (meaning blacks not whites) did so. This line of reasoning ignores racism and its legacies of poverty, crime and welfare dependency and instead seems to suggest that blacks should have done nothing politically and should do nothing to deal with these racial inequalities because if they do they will run the risk of alienating whites. Which of course may be true. But then, what are blacks to do, remain silent so that a Democrat, *any* Democrat, might be elected president? It is also suggested that blacks should embrace universalist programs rather than race-specific ones. Putting aside for a moment that the problem of racism and its consequences are race specific and therefore may require race-specific programs, in the post–civil rights era the black leadership has, except for the basic civil rights agenda (and its implementation through school busing and affirmative action) pursued essentially a universalist agenda as in its embrace of full employment and national health insurance. The new orthodoxy also mistakes symbolism for substance. While it might *appear* that the Democratic Party has since the 1960s embraced blacks and their agenda, as I show throughout this study this is not the case. On the contrary, the black vote has largely been taken for granted while its principal policy concerns (except in the narrow area of civil rights) in terms of ghetto reconstruction and jobs have been ignored. And at the same time the conditions of the so-called black underclass, neglected for a generation, continue to deteriorate. The new orthodoxy's failure to confront the racism of the Republican Party's strategic calculations and its blindness to the continuing significance of racism and the need for blacks and the society as a whole to confront it forthrightly may itself be a form of subtle racism. As Reed and Bond write, the new orthodoxy "At bottom . . . stems from an inability to perceive black Americans as legitimate, full members of the polity."[22] How else can one explain the fact that when the unemployment rate reaches 8–9 percent among white Americans it leads to immediate calls for emergency, urgent action by the government to deal with the crisis, but when there is a rate twice that among blacks it is ignored by the media and policy elites? And when blacks demand that something be done, their claims are dismissed as special interest pleading.

Nevertheless, this is the situation that blacks confront twenty-five years after the freedom struggle's transition from protest to routine politics. And it is likely to get worse unless there is a radical change in the Democratic Party's strategy or in the way blacks pursue their struggle.

The new orthodoxy, although historically and analytically flawed in several ways, is nevertheless just that, an orthodoxy, widely accepted by the Democratic Party's white establishment. A fundamental assumption of the Democratic Party establishment is that the American people have embraced the anti–social welfare agenda of the right wing.[23] While the Reagan revolution did bring about substantial changes in the context of the debate on the role of government in dealing with the nation's problems (as well as effectively undermining the government's tax base), it is not at all clear that the American people (or even the much smaller American electorate) have embraced a conservative policy agenda. For example, after their analysis of the relevant survey data on the 1980 election, Ferguson and Rogers write, "The conclusion is inescapable. With the exception of the rise of support for military spending, which was itself rapidly reversed, there is little or nothing in public opinion data to support the claim that the American public moved to the right in the years preceding Reagan's 1980 victory."[24] And Wattenberg in *The Rise of Candidate-Centered Politics* demonstrates, I think conclusively, the absence of a conservative policy mandate in the 1980, 1984 and 1988 elections, with large numbers of voters voting for Reagan and Bush although they disagreed with their position on most domestic policy issues.[25] It may be that contrary to the proponents of the new orthodoxy and the DLC the Democrats failed to win recent presidential elections not because they have moved to the left or because they are the captive of blacks or any group of voters. Rather, as Ferguson and Rogers contend, the Democrats may have declined because the party has failed to pursue strategies and policies that would mobilize a progressive mass base. It has failed to do this, they argue, because party elites have "marketed" the party to narrow or special economic interests rather than voters. And these "big investors" in the party are unwilling to permit it to pursue what they call a working class agenda.[26] Ferguson and Rogers's analysis may be correct but it ignores the impact of race and racism historically and in the post–civil rights era in blunting working-class politics in the United States. If a working-class agenda or, more broadly, a national interest agenda is to be effectively pursued, the Democratic Party must not only divest itself of its big investors but must also talk honestly and forthrightly to working-class whites about race and racism and the urgent national need to pursue policies of racial melioration. This is not likely to happen because the party's elites and strategists do not have a program or plan of racial reconciliation that they think can "sale" to the American people. The Democrats and the Republicans, to put it bluntly, are incapable of dealing responsibly with the nation's racial tensions; and since race pervades politics and policy discussion in the post–civil rights era, this means the parties are incapable of dealing with many of the nation's other pressing domestic problems. The 1992 election of Bill Clinton epitomizes this situation.

Paradoxes and Puzzles in the Election of 1992

The post–civil rights era orthodoxy on presidential elections is simply stated by Morris Fiorina: "Absent a truly major recession or costly war, it did not matter who won the Democratic and Republican nominations, a generic Republican would defeat a generic Democrat."[27] So, why did the Democrats win in 1992? Assuming for analytic purposes the accuracy of Fiorina's proposition, three possible explanations (or some combination thereof) may account for Clinton's victory. First, he was not a generic Democrat. Second, Bush was not a generic Republican. Third, there was a major recession in 1992. My purpose here is not to present a full-scale analysis of the 1992 election, but rather, to examine the election in the context of the problem of race, ideology and the post–civil rights era party system.[28] From this perspective Clinton won because, following the script of the new orthodoxy on race, liberalism and partisanship, he was able to effectively "de-market" himself to blacks and poor people while marketing himself to the white middle class as a nongeneric Democrat. In a sense Clinton was the DLC's computer candidate, appealing to the white middle class on the basis of a campaign that symbolically distanced him from blacks while at the same time winning the nomination and the election on the basis of the black vote, demonstrating once again that blacks demand less for their votes—even in terms of mere respect—than any other group.

What is a generic Democrat? What is a generic Republican? A central distinction according to the orthodox analysis is that a generic Democrat is identified with special interest groups: blacks, the poor, homosexuals and feminists; is supportive of civil liberties and consequently is viewed as "soft on crime"; favors less spending on the military and is less willing to use force in international affairs; and tends to favor higher taxes and increased spending on the welfare state. By contrast, a generic Republican is identified by hostility to these so-called special interest groups; favors lower taxes; larger expenditures on the military; fewer social welfare expenditures; a more activist, interventionist foreign policy; adheres to traditional values in terms of family, sexuality and the role of women; and are more concerned about controlling crime than the rights of persons accused of crimes. These distinctions, of course, oversimplify a complex reality but the kernels of truth they embody have since 1972 constituted the raw material for the marketing of partisan campaigns and are code words or shorthand referents used by journalists in their coverage of partisan politics. Underlying all of these issues except military spending and military interventionism is race. That is, it is perceived that issues of crime, law and order, the death penalty, taxes, welfare spending, promiscuous sexuality and the absence of traditional family values are all linked to blacks. The post–civil rights era survey data on white attitudes toward blacks bear out this perception: a majority or near majority of whites tend to agree that blacks are prone to crime and violence, are lazy, prefer welfare to work, are sexually promiscuous and lack family values.[29] Thus, in the post–civil rights era, campaign marketers have learned that they can effectively appeal to antiblack or racist sentiments among whites indirectly through ads that ostensibly focus on crime, welfare or quotas but are really about race and racism. Given this analysis, were Bush and Clinton generic partisans?

Patrick Buchanan and the Republican right wing argue that Bush was not a generic Republican and his deviation from Reagan-era orthodoxy was one of the factors in his defeat. Citing such things as his decision to support a tax increase, his signing of the Civil Rights Act of 1991, his support of the Clean Air Act and Americans with Disabilities Act, right-wing columnists and activists contend that President Bush abandoned Republican orthodoxy and in the process forfeited the domestic issue agenda to the Democrats. In foreign and military affairs the collapse of the Soviet empire removed from the 1992 campaign the issue of competence and leadership in dealing with the Soviet threat. As Mikhail Gorbachev reportedly told President Reagan, "I am going to take your issue away from you," meaning that by ending the cold war the Republican party would lose its capacity to rally its constituents around the threat of the "Russian bear" as Reagan did so effectively in the 1984 campaign.

Although Bush did depart to some extent from hard-core right wing policy preferences on taxes and domestic policy, it was not a sharp or radical departure. Reagan, for example, during his administrations also raised taxes, signed civil rights legislation and in general accommodated, as did Bush, bipartisan congressional majorities in areas of domestic policy where he could not enact a generic Republican program. The differences between Reagan and Bush are therefore more matters of degree, style and personality than substance.

The Clinton case is equally problematic. Clinton's campaign from its emphasis on the problems of the middle class to his selection of a running mate sought to present the candidate as a nongeneric "new Democrat." But the platform adopted in 1992 was decidedly liberal, indeed as liberal as any adopted since 1972. On civil rights, while attacking quotas the platform embraced affirmative action, for the first time embraced full civil rights for homosexuals and adopted the entire feminist agenda in terms of reproductive rights. The platform also endorsed "universal access to quality, affordable health care—not as privilege but as a right"; an expansion of the earned income tax credit for the working poor; an increased and indexed minimum wage; family and medical leave; a "domestic GI bill" enabling *all* Americans to borrow money for college; increased taxes on the wealthy; expansion of Head Start to cover all eligible children; and a reform in welfare that would provide education, job training, health and child care so that all persons on welfare could "go to work within two years in available jobs either in the private sector or in community service to meet unmet needs." Although the platform did not use the term full employment, it did call for a "national public works investment and infrastructure program [that] will provide jobs and strengthen our cities. . . . We will encourage the flow of investment to inner city development and housing through targeted enterprise zones and incentives for private and public pension funds to invest in urban and rural projects."[30] All in all, a quite liberal document that if enacted would have represented the largest expansion of the role of the government in the society and economy and the greatest growth in the welfare state since Lyndon Johnson's Great Society. So the Clinton case, like Bush's, represents something of a paradox: the party platform was generically Democratic but the candidate ran as a nongeneric new Democrat.

The last element of the Fiorina proposition also suggests something of a paradox. The economy in 1991–92 was not in a major recession. Interest rates and inflation were low and unemployment was not high by post-war standards. Yet, throughout the election year, various surveys showed that most Americans thought the economy was in bad shape and getting worse. This pessimism was reinforced by extremely negative coverage by the national press. Finally, although unemployment was, relatively speaking, not high and the economy in 1992 was growing at a modest rate, the impact of joblessness did not follow the traditional pattern of post-war recessions. Not only were blue-collar workers and minorities facing unemployment as is traditionally the case, but also highly educated and affluent white-collar workers were also disproportionately impacted. These newly displaced workers were more likely to take their frustrations out at the ballot box than blue-collar workers and minorities.

The final factor in the economic equation is one that is usually not included in the standard models forecasting elections. The deficit—due in part to the candidacy of Ross Perot—became a major issue in campaign rhetoric and press coverage, serving as a kind of all-purpose symbol of the economy's decline and the government's inability to deal with the nation's problems. Thus, the analysis ends in ambiguity. Bush may have lost because he was not perceived as a generic Republican and/or Clinton was not perceived as a generic Democrat or the economy was perceived to be in major difficulty. But on each of these we are dealing with perceptions as much as reality. In many ways Bush was a generic Republican, Clinton was a generic Democrat and the economy was not in a major recession. Yet Clinton won, suggesting that perhaps any Democrat—even one generic in perceptions as well reality—might have won in the volatile situation of 1992, especially given the Perot factor.[31] But any Democrat did not win, rather, a self proclaimed "New Democrat" centrist and moderate won, which may be interpreted as confirmation of the essential thesis of the DLC orthodoxy. This is because Clinton was successfully marketed to the white middle class as a New Democrat, not beholden or captive to special interests, especially blacks. How Clinton was able to successfully distance himself from blacks while simultaneously winning the election on the basis of the black vote shows the twisted dynamics of race in the post–civil rights era party system.

Symbols, Sister Souljah and Race in the Election of 1992

Bill Clinton could not have been nominated or elected without the overwhelming support of black voters. Yet his campaign was deliberately designed to distance him and the party from blacks. This strategy of "symbolic distance" from blacks was not racist, but it did seek to appeal to underlying antiblack sentiments among the Wallace/Reagan Democrats in the crucial battleground states of the Midwest: Michigan,

Ohio, Illinois and Pennsylvania. The strategy and tactics of the campaign drew on the work of Kotler and Rosenbaum, Karmarck and Galtson, the Edsals and Stanley Greenberg (Greenberg was the campaign's principal pollster and a major strategist). The strategy was a dicey one; to maintain crucial black support in the primaries and the general election while at the same time winning over those white Democratic defectors that Greenberg had written "express a profound distaste for blacks." This "white distaste" for blacks caused these voters to abandon the party because they viewed it as catering to black interests in terms of "welfare handouts," "coddling criminals" and the perceived power of Jesse Jackson in party affairs. In the course of the 1992 campaign, the Clinton strategists found a number of ways to symbolically deal with these white perceptions that effectively allowed the candidate to appear not beholden to blacks and a hard-line New Democrat on issues of welfare, crime and Jesse Jackson.

In 1969 John Mitchell, Nixon's campaign manager and later attorney general, told the civil rights lobby to "watch what we do, not what we say," indicating that the administration for political reasons would give to whites the symbolism of anti–civil rights rhetoric but the substance of policy and programs would go to blacks. In a sense this was the Clinton campaign strategy—substantively a liberal-to-progressive platform but cloaked in the symbolism of a New Democrat, moving away from the party's traditional concern with blacks and the poor toward an emphasis on the middle class. Indeed, I would not be surprised if Clinton did tell his key black supporters among the mayors and members of Congress this essential strategy of the campaign in terms of symbols and substance: In order to win, John [Congressman John Lewis of Georgia], we have to make this symbolic appeal to whites, but watch what we do [for example, read the platform], not what we say.[32]

Clinton pursued this strategy generally by an overarching focus on the middle class with a proposed tax cut and "universalist" non-targeted programs (like health care, expanded college aid, worker retraining programs) rather than programs targeted on the poor and the urban underclass.[33] And although Clinton campaigned in the black community especially during the primaries, in the general election the daily campaign events and the bus trips tended to be scheduled in such a way that the event of the day in terms of the evening news coverage would be in white communities. This strategy led Harlem Congressman Charles Rangel on more than one occasion to compare the campaign's treatment of blacks to how a man treats a concubine or a prostitute. For example, in early October Rangel was quoted as saying, "I don't have any problem when he's talking to black groups. My problem is the campaign and the strategy as it relates to bus trips and speeches given on prime time television where he is addressing crowds other than African Americans. We've got to be courted publicly and we've got to be treated as first class voters and can not be taken for granted." Later Rangel compared the campaign's strategy toward blacks to a man saying to a whore "meet me in the hotel room; I don't want to be seen with you in the lobby."[34]

This strategy was also specifically pursued through three symbolic themes or events during the course of the campaign: the focus on welfare, the execution of Ricky Ray Rector and the Sister Souljah incident.[35] Clinton campaign strategists had assumed that the Republicans would use welfare as the Willie Horton of 1992, with ads linking welfare, race and the Democrats as the Horton ad was used to link crime, race and Dukakis in 1988.[36] In the 1991 Mississippi governor's race Kirk Fordice, the Republican candidate, had used an ad with a black woman holding a baby to link his opponent with support for "welfare giveaways." Knowing the salience of this issue among whites, the Clinton campaign from the outset emphasized "opportunity and responsibility," subtly suggesting that some blacks wanted opportunities but were not responsible. This theme was accompanied by ads that ran in Michigan and Pennsylvania where Clinton pledged to end "welfare as we know it" by limiting eligibility to no more than two years. Clinton's position on welfare is a good example of John Mitchell's maxim of giving symbols to one group and substance to another. Clinton's rhetoric and ads appealed to antiwelfare sentiment among working- and middle-class whites, leaving the impression that there would be a two-year cut off, period. (Senator Daniel Moynihan, the leading congressional authority on welfare, dismissed Clinton's rhetoric on the subject as "boob bait for the bubbas.") However, the substance of his proposal, based on the work of Harvard's David Ellwood (who subsequently became a top official in the Department of Health and Human Services), involved a broad program of expanded social services including health, child care and public sector jobs as a last resort.[37] Such a program, if enacted, would cost more than the current welfare system, at the outset an estimated thirty billion dollars. For this reason alone, it is not likely to have been enacted even by a Democratic Congress, but it is a type of reform that the Congressional Black Caucus has long supported.

The campaign also wished to avoid Dukakis's Willie Horton problem. The Willie Horton ad was used to appeal to attitudes among whites that blacks tend to be criminally inclined and that Democrats tend to be soft on crime. Clinton blunted this possible line of attack first by pledging to put "100,000 new police officers on the street" and second, unlike Dukakis and many liberal Democrats, by supporting the death penalty. And to emphasize his "tough" approach to crime, in the midst of the campaign he canceled appearances in order to return to Arkansas to preside over the execution of Ricky Ray Rector, a retarded black man; so retarded that he apparently was not aware that death was permanent.

All of these symbolic appeals came together in the Sister Souljah incident. As the Edsals pointed out in *Chain Reaction*, Jesse Jackson had come to symbolize what they described as one of the "central problems" of the party as it struggled to recapture the support of white defectors. Thus, they argued that it would be strategically efficacious if the nominee in 1992 could somehow find a way to "stand up" to Jackson without alienating his black constituency. The Sister Souljah affair was orchestrated by Clinton strategists to accomplish this objective. After the Los Angeles riots, Sister Souljah, a little-known rap singer, made remarks that were interpreted as a call for blacks to kill whites. At one of his periodic Rainbow Coalition conferences Jackson invited the rap singer to participate in a workshop. Clinton in a subsequent appearance at the conference seized on this as means to attack Jackson, arguing that in inviting Sister Souljah to his conference Jackson by implication was condoning black violence against whites. In case the press missed the significance of his remarks, Clinton's aides went out of their way to inform reporters that Clinton had shown the courage to stand up to Jackson.[38]

The incident was widely reported in the press (including a *Newsweek* cover story) and apparently had the desired effects. While Jackson and other black leaders grumbled, black support for Clinton remained firm in the polls and apparently his support among whites increased. Clarence Page reports that "Tracking polls show the incident marked the upturn in Clinton's popularity that quickly took him from third place behind Perot to first."[39] Page indicates that the incident came up in focus groups and surveys of suburban and blue-collar "Reagan Democrats," who praised Clinton for standing up to Jackson in addition to his strong stand on welfare and capital punishment.[40]

Ironically, Clinton probably could not have been nominated without Jackson's acquiescence. As Table 10.1 shows, Clinton won 70 percent of the black vote in the twenty-nine primaries conducted during 1992, but only about half of the white and Hispanic vote. If Jackson had run in 1992 it is probable that most of this vote would have gone to him, depriving Clinton of his margin of victory.[41] For example, in the southern Super Tuesday primaries, if Jackson had been in the race Clin-

TABLE 10.1

The Democratic Party Primary Vote in 1992 by Race and Religion

% Total Vote	Race	Clinton	Brown	Tsongas
80%	Whites	47%	23%	25%
14	Blacks	70	15	8
4	Hispanics	51	30	15
	Religion			
50	Protestant	55	14	21
30	Catholic	44	24	24
6	Jewish	45	15	33
	TOTAL	50	21	20

Source: Calculated from exit polls conducted in twenty-nine primary states from February to June, 1992, as reported in *New York Times*, July 12, 1992.

ton may have done only marginally better than Albert Gore in 1988, when Jackson won the deep south states, Dukakis Florida and Texas, and Gore only Tennessee and those states bordering it. The decisive advantage Clinton received in the Super Tuesday primaries provided the momentum that propelled him to victory in the next contests in Illinois and Michigan and in effect the race was over, since the only remaining candidate was Jerry Brown.

Blacks were also an important factor in Clinton's general election victory. Initial exit poll data showed Clinton and Bush getting about the same percentage of the white vote (Clinton 39, Bush 41) but after comparing exit poll results with the actual vote, the Voter Research Project concluded that Bush decisively defeated Clinton among whites, garnering 43 percent to Clinton's 38 percent.[42] Thus, like John Kennedy's election in 1960 and Carter's in 1976, if the election had been held only among whites the Democratic candidate would have lost. And as the data reported in Table 10.2 show, in several states the black share of the total Democratic vote in 1992 exceeded Clinton's margin of victory (Louisiana in 1992 became the first state in history where blacks constituted the majority of a winning presidential candidate's total vote).

But it is not accurate to conclude that "Black Voters Gave Clinton Victory" because as Table 10.3 shows Clinton actually received a smaller proportion of the black vote than Mondale in 1984 (90 percent) and Dukakis in 1988 (85 percent). This again demonstrates that the black vote—as a base rather than a swing vote—is only of marginal consequence in post–civil rights era presidential politics. Although Clinton

TABLE 10.2

The African American Voter Contribution to
Clinton's Margin of Victory in Selected States

	Clinton Margin of Victory	Black Dem. Share of Total Vote	Black Share of Dem. Vote
Georgia	0.6%	17.4%	40%
Louisiana	4.6	23.5	51.5
Maryland	14.2	14.8	29.7
Michigan	7.4	7.7	17.7
New Jersey	2.4	8.4	19.6
Ohio	1.9	8.3	20.7

Source: David Bositis, "African Americans and the Election of 1992" (Washington: Joint Center for Political and Economic Studies, 1993).

TABLE 10.3

Percentage of Black Vote for the
Democratic Nominee for President, 1976–1992

Year	Nominee	% Vote
1976	Carter	88%
1980	Carter	85
1984	Mondale	90
1988	Dukakis	86
1992	Clinton	82

Source: "Portrait of the Electorate," *New York Times*, November 5, 1992.

would not have been elected without the overwhelming support of blacks, Dukakis and Mondale did not win with even higher levels of black support.

What is puzzling about the Clinton election is that he received roughly the same or in some cases even less support among white ethnic and regional groupings than Dukakis. As Table 10.4 shows, only among Jews was there a swing in Clinton's direction as compared to Dukakis (from 64 to 78 percent). Clinton did a little better than Dukakis among southern whites (although he decisively lost his native region vote to Bush) but all in all the white ethnic and regional votes were basically the same as in other post–civil rights era presidential elections. Essentially, then, the election of 1992 was not so much a gain in voter support by Clinton and the Democrats but rather a loss in support

TABLE 10.4

Democratic Percentage of the White Vote in the
Presidential Election by Ethnicity and Region, 1976–1992

	1976	1980	1984	1988	1992
All Whites	47%	36%	35%	40%	39%
Protestants	41	31	27	33	33
White Born-Again Christian	—	33	22	18	15
Catholic	54	42	45	47	44
Jewish	64	45	67	64	78
From the East	49	38	42	45	45
From the Midwest	46	37	35	42	39
From the South	47	35	28	32	34
From the West	44	32	33	41	39

Source: Based on exit polls conducted on election day as reported in "Portrait of the Electorate," *New York Times*, November 5, 1992.

by Bush and the Republicans, a loss not so much to Clinton but to Perot. Like 1980, 1992 was a repudiation of the incumbent rather than a mandate for the challenger.

This suggests that perhaps an openly generic Democrat like New York Governor Mario Cuomo might have won in 1992,[43] contrary to the conventional wisdom that the election of Clinton represents a vindication of the DLC's centrist ideology and the new orthodoxy's strategy of disengagement from blacks and the poor. In a two-party system, at some point in the cycle of elections the "in" party inevitably loses to the "out" party, often without regard to the ideology or policy preferences of its candidate. Reagan won in 1980 in spite of the fact that large numbers of voters supporting him disagreed with his position on many major issues. But since Reagan is a generic Republican and campaigned as one, once in office he could claim a mandate and mobilize public and congressional support for his agenda. By contrast Clinton, who, *if one judges by the platform,* is a generic Democrat, campaigned as if he was not and consequently once in office found it near impossible to mobilize public and congressional support for his agenda.

Conclusion

In his first two years in office, Clinton was barely able to get his economic and deficit reduction program through the Congress (by a single vote in both houses), his modest $11 billion economic stimulus program was killed by senate filibusters, his scaled-down welfare

reform proposal was ignored by the Congress and his ambitious program for national health insurance—the centerpiece of his domestic
reform agenda—was rejected by the Congress. Lacking a mandate from
the campaign, the 1992 platform's broad agenda of liberal reform predictably was rejected or fatally compromised in the interplay of
entrenched Washington interests and the gridlock of congressional politics. And then in an election that surprised academic, professional and
media observers of American politics, the president and his party were
repudiated by the electorate in the 1994 midterm election.

    As a corollary to his proposition that since the 1970s a generic
Republican defeats a generic Democrat unless there is a crisis or scandal
of some sort, Fiorina also proposed (in 1992) that "barring a national
cataclysm the Republicans had no more chance of carrying the House
than the proverbial snowball had surviving the fires of hell."[44] Nothing
cataclysmic occurred in 1994. There was no bloody war, no massive
recession or major scandal. Nor was there a charismatic presidential
candidate whose coattails might have affected the outcome. Thus, why
the enormous advantages of Democratic incumbency collapsed is at
this writing not known; the detailed constituency-level research having
not yet been completed. For purposes of African American politics, the
question is whether the largely race-based conservative Republican
realignment of the vote in presidential elections has now reached down
to the congressional and state levels.

    Since 1970 the question of realignment has been the "external"
question for political scientists and other observers of American politics.[45] The concept of realignment or of a critical election was first
advanced by V. O. Key in his seminal article "A Theory of Critical Elections."[46] Critical or realigning elections, historically associated with high
levels of socioeconomic stress, involve a change in the mass coalitional
bases of the party system, resulting in the emergence of a new majority
party with enduring consequences for public policy. Since the 1970s it
has generally been assumed such a transformation has occurred at the
presidential level involving a shift of blacks to the Democratic coalition and of southern whites and, to a lesser extent, eastern and southern
European ethnic minorities to the Republicans. Accompanying this
transformation in the party coalitions has been a shift of presidential
policy making in a sharp conservative direction. The problem has been
that a similar transformation had not occurred in the other branches of
the federal government and in state politics and policies. By the end of
the Bush administration, the Supreme Court had undergone a conservative realignment and in 1994 both houses of Congress elected conservative Republican majorities, with the Democrats suffering signifi-

cant defeats in all parts of the country except the Northeast.[47] Republicans also won most of the governorships (including all the major states except Florida and six of the traditionally Democratic southern states) and made significant gains in state legislative seats, winning 37 percent in the deep south. Thus, if realignment has not occurred, the outcome of 1994 election points strongly in that direction, although it will probably take a couple of more elections before this eternal question of national politics can be finally answered.[48]

For blacks the 1992 and 1994 elections were emblematic of their irrelevancy in post–civil rights era national politics. In 1992 the party that they have loyally supported for the last twenty-five years decided that it could only recapture the presidency by running a campaign based on a strategy of ignoring them and their policy concerns while pandering to racist and antiblack sentiments among whites. In 1994 the Republican party won majorities in the Congress and among the governors in part by campaigning on the basis of the racially symbolic issues of crime, welfare and the absence of "family values." As the twenty-first century dawns, the status of the race—its society, family, culture and community—are in a state of decline. The strategies employed by post–civil rights era black leadership have not been effective in arresting this situation, let alone reversing it. This suggests a need to rethink strategies both in terms of internal communal action and external political participation. There is nothing, however, not even hints, that suggests that the leaders of black America are willing to do this.

PART V

The most magnificent drama in the last thousand years of human history is the transportation of ten million human beings out of the dark beauty of their mother continent into the new found Eldorado of the West. They descended into hell; and in the third century they arose from the dead, in the finest effort to achieve democracy for the working millions which this world had ever seen. It was a tragedy that beggared the Greek; it was an upheaval of humanity like the Reformation and the French revolution. Yet we are blind and led by the blind. We discern in it no part of our labor movement; no part of our industrial triumph; no part of our religious experience. Before the dumb eyes of ten generations of ten million children, it is made mockery of and spit upon; a degradation of the external mother; a sneer at human effort; with aspiration and art deliberately and elaborately distorted. And why? Because in a day when the human mind aspired to a science of human action, a history and psychology of the mighty effort of the mightiest century we fell under the leadership of those who would compromise with truth in the past in order to make peace in the present and guide policy in the future.

—W.E.B. DuBois (on post-Reconstruction era American leadership)

With the end of the cycle of civil rights advocacy, only one basic option remained for the black leadership. This was internal organization and consolidation of the minority group within a multiracial, multicultural society. This imperative meant that the traditional black civil rights leadership had reached a societal void lacking a road upon which to lead its constituency. The situation called for a new black consensus that was capable of redefining the plausible place of the black minority within the societal complex in which blacks, as a *group*, found themselves by 1980. Such a redefinition of the legitimate place of the black minority within the system had to take into full account the meaning of *plurality*. It meant the systematic reorganization of many areas of black life into first a political bloc, then cultural blocs, and then into whatever internal economic organization are possible within a capitalistic, free market system. In this context an independent black political party becomes the initial step toward a total reorganization of black life over the remainder of the twentieth century. Without such a *total* political, economic, cultural, educational, and institutional reorganization of black life, the American black minority will *not* be able to survive into *whatever* system American society becomes by the year 2000 and after [emphasis in original].

—Harold Cruse (on post–civil rights era black leadership)

11

From Incorporation toward Irrelevance:
The Afro-American Freedom Struggle
in the 21st Century

This book provides dismal, detailed evidence of the irrelevancy of black politics in producing in the last twenty-five years benefits for most blacks, especially the imperative to reconstruct and integrate the ghettos into the mainstream of American society. The problem is multifaceted. First, the political culture and system in the United States is, historically, stubbornly resistant to social change and reform, but especially when such change and reform involves race.[1] Indeed, without a systemic crisis of some sort the American political system has *never* responded to citizen demands for fundamental change in its class or racial hierarchies.[2] Second, American political institutions in the last twenty-five years have become increasingly weak and fragmented, as a consequence of the decline in the party system and the presidency, the ever-increasing influence of ever narrower, special interest groups and the growth in power of political pollsters, consultants and assorted hucksters, and of a trivia and sensation seeking media. It is very difficult therefore for the government to produce coherent public policies in the public interest, and the public, knowing this, does not trust it to do so. Third, the white establishment or power elite in the last twenty-five years has essentially rejected the idea that the federal government has a role to play in dealing with the problems of the ghetto poor, arguing that blacks are to blame for their own conditions. Finally, the leadership of black America instead of pursuing the leadership, organization and mobilization of its core community has instead pursued integration into systemic institutions and processes in the classic top-down hierarchical tradition of middle-class liberal reformers.

In this chapter I summarize the results of this study in terms of these four facets of the problem and note what I take to be the implications for the future of Afro-American society, and racial politics and democracy in the United States.

In the post–civil rights era virtually all of the talent and resources of the leadership of black America has been devoted to integration or incorporation into the institutions of the American society and polity. Meanwhile the core community that they would purport to lead has become increasingly segregated and isolated, and its society, economy, culture and institutions of internal uplift and governance have decayed. There is a systemic or structural logic to these processes, one that was probably inevitable and is perhaps irreversible.

The logic of the civil rights movement was systemic integration. Thus, as opportunities for entry and advancement in the institutions of the larger society became available, those blacks with the talent, resources or luck necessary to take advantage of them did so. This process, without a comprehensive plan of ghetto reconstruction along the lines proposed by the Urban League in its domestic Marshall Plan, would necessarily leave substantial numbers of persons behind, even if racism as an active force in American society disappeared. That is, the historical consequences of racism, even in an open society, would mean that a substantial number of blacks for a substantial period of time would lack the skills and resources necessary to effectively integrate into the system. If racism lingered, as it almost surely would, then the situation would be exacerbated.[3] This is essentially what has occurred in the last twenty-five years; all in some senses predictable and predicted.

This predictable bifurcation of black leadership and community has been made worse by ongoing changes in the economy and culture of the larger society that matured at roughly the same time as the civil rights revolution. The economic changes involved, first, a decline in the nation's manufacturing base, resulting in a loss of low-skilled, well-paid employment. Related to this was a fairly systematic and ongoing relocation of employment opportunities beyond the core black community. The cultural changes, communicated and shaped by an increasingly pervasive mass media, involved a loosening of traditional or communal constraints—with respect to family, sex, children, education, violence and drugs—that in the past tended to hold together communities in the face of adversity.[4] The result is a crisis in the black community and leadership of unprecedented magnitude.

At a lecture at Prairie View A & M University in 1989, in response to a question asking him to evaluate black leaders, Harold Cruse responded, "What leaders? We have no leaders." The puzzled student questioner responded by listing the familiar names of the heads of the civil rights organizations, members of Congress and big city mayors. Cruse, responding with evident irritation, said that those persons were not leaders because they had no plan, no program of action and no organization to mobilize or lead blacks in a direction that would deal with their communal problems. This book documents the acuity of Cruse's observation.[5] The civil rights organizations are moribund and largely irrelevant, operating more as relics of the past than instruments for action in the present or future. The black mayors, congresspersons, cabinet officers and the rest are unable to deliver on promises and programs to meliorate conditions in the communities, and increasingly even consider themselves leaders of American institutions who just happen to be black.[6] Even Jesse Jackson, the preeminent "black leader" of the post–civil rights era, subordinated his campaigns for president to the needs of the Democratic Party and the Washington establishment rather than those of blacks. Compared to the experience of other ethnic groups in the United States this situation is near unprecedented. The integration or incorporation of Irish, Jewish, Polish and Italian American leaders into the institutions of the society and polity roughly paralleled the integration of their communities as a whole. In contrast, black leaders are integrated but their core community is segregated, impoverished and increasingly in the post–civil rights era marginalized, denigrated and criminalized.

Again, this situation was a logical outcome of the civil rights movement's integrationist impulse and the system's cooptative response to social movement pressures. As Cruse argues, the only possibility of dealing with this logic was for post–civil rights era black leadership to confront what he calls the "plural" nature of blacks in American society and develop a consensus program for the internal organization and consolidation of blacks as a separate and distinct group in the United States.[7] At the outset of the post–civil rights era most leaders of black America recognized this imperative and throughout the 1970s attempted to act on it. They failed; and since the 1980s blacks have fell under an institutionalized leadership that seems incapable of dealing honestly and realistically with the situation of its constituency internally or in its relationship to the larger society. Rather, as in the post-Reconstruction era it appears that once again "we are blind and led by the blind," with a leadership more interested in the trappings and symbols of power than in internal communal development and mobilization.

There is also a logic and predictability to the failure of internal black leadership organization and mobilization in the post–civil rights era. Twice before, such efforts to build and sustain what the Reverend Lewis Woodson in 1830 called a "national institution . . . that would unite and harmonize the distant and discordant parts of our population" were attempted, and twice before they failed. The previous attempts and the 1970 effort failed for essentially the same reason: the discordant parts of the black community probably cannot be brought together in a single national institution because the discordances—institutional and ideological—are unbridgeable. First, because the middle class leadership establishment is wedded ideologically, institutionally and economically to white structures of power and is therefore adverse to independent or radical thought and action, having as one of its foremost concerns quiescence in the black community and stability in American society. The material conditions in the black community, however, necessarily give rise to radical and nationalistic thought and action, which in turn makes race group solidarity and action all but impossible. This is especially so since the traditions of radicalism and nationalism in black America tend often toward the apocalyptic and the utopian. This historical dilemma in black political life is exacerbated today, since unlike in the 1830s and 1930s, black leaders have responsibilities for managing the institutions of American society as well as looking out for the interests of black people as a whole.

Three consequences flow from the post–civil rights era leadership's inability to act. First, in spite of—indeed in a sense because of—a bewildering variety of organized groups, old and new, the black community today remains largely unorganized. Second, blacks remain dependent on a decaying party (and party system) that attempts to maintain itself in power by ignoring black policy interests and symbolically distancing itself from black people altogether, although blacks provide the party a fifth of its national vote. Third, as a result in part of a lack of effective organization and dependency on the Democratic Party, blacks have been unable to develop the requisite pressures to get the system to respond to its most pressing post–civil rights era demand: the need for employment in the context of some kind of overall program of internal ghetto reconstruction and development. The result is a core black community, euphemistically referred to as the inner city, that is increasingly poor, dispossessed and alienated.[8] Meanwhile the leaders of white America respond with neglect, contemptuously suggesting that unless there is a change in the "values" of African Americans, nothing can be done about the deterioration of their communities.

The civil rights revolution generated a sense of optimism about the prospects for equality, integration and acceptance in American society. Twenty-five years later, blacks now increasingly experience a sense of alarm, a turning back of the clock, a renewed sense of apartness, of being outsiders in a hostile world. Alexis de Tocqueville, that most acute observer of American democracy, did not believe that blacks and whites would ever live together in America on the basis of equality. Instead, he saw inequality and violent conflict between the races as more or less inevitable. Tocqueville saw this problem as inherent in American democracy. He wrote:

> I do not imagine that the white and black races will ever live in any country upon an equal footing. But I believe the difficulty to be still greater in the United States than elsewhere. . . . A despot who should subject the Americans and their former slaves to the same yoke, might perhaps succeed in commingling the races; but as long as the American democracy remains at the head of affairs, no one will undertake so difficult a task; and it may be foreseen that the freer the white population of the United States becomes, the more isolated will it remain.[9]

Twenty-five years after the great civil rights revolution and as American democracy approaches its third century, it is still not possible to conclude that Tocqueville got it wrong.

Appendix

A Comparison of Democratic Party Platform Language on Full Employment, 1944–1992

1944
To speed victory, establish and maintain peace, guarantee full employment and provide prosperity—this is our platform.

1948
To serve the interests of all and not the few . . . to achieve security, full production and full employment—this is our platform.

1952
The Democratic administration prudently passed the Employment Act of 1946 declaring it to be national policy never again to permit large-scale unemployment to stalk the land. We will assure the transition from defense production to peace-time production without the ravages of unemployment. We pledge ourselves at all times to the maintenance of maximum production and purchasing power in the American economy.

1954
We repudiate the Republican stunting of economic growth, and we reassert the principles of the Full Employment Act.

1960
The Democratic party reaffirms its support of full employment as a permanent objective of national policy. For nearly thirty months the rate of unemployment has been between 5 and 7.5 percent of the labor force. A pool of three to four million citizens, able and willing to work but unable to find jobs, has been written off by the Republican administration as a "normal" readjustment of the economic system. The policies of a Democratic administration to restore economic growth will reduce current unemployment to a minimum. Thereafter, if recessionary trends appear, we will act promptly with countermeasures such as public works or temporary tax cuts. We will not stand idly by and permit recessions to run their course as the Republican administration has done.

1964

Full employment is an end in itself and must be insisted upon as a priority objective. It is the national purpose, and our commitment that every man or woman who is willing and able to work is entitled to a job and to a fair wage for doing it.

1968

Every American in need of work should have opportunity not only for meaningful employment, but also for the education, training, counseling and other services that enable him to take advantage of available jobs. *To the maximum possible extent, our national goal of full employment should be realized through creation of jobs in the private economy,* where six of every seven Americans now work. We will continue the Job Opportunities in the Business Sector (JOBS) program, which for the first time has mobilized the energies of business and industry on a nationwide scale to provide training and employment to the hardcore unemployed. We will develop whatever additional incentives may be necessary to maximize the opportunities in the private sector for hardcore unemployed. We will continue also to finance the operation by local communities of a wide range of training programs for youth and retraining for older workers whose skills have become obsolete, coupled with related services necessary to enable people to undertake training and accept jobs—including improved recruitment and placement services, day-care centers, and transportation between work and home. *For those who can work but cannot find jobs, we pledge to expand public job and job training programs, including the Neighborhood Youth Corps,* to provide meaningful employment by state and local government and nonprofit institutions. *For those who cannot obtain other employment, the federal government will be the employer of last resort, either through federal assistance to state and local projects or through federally sponsored projects.*

1972

Full employment—a guaranteed job for all—is the primary objective of the Democratic Party. The Democratic Party is committed to a job for every American who seeks work. Only through full employment can we reduce the burden on working people. We are determined to make economic security a matter of right. This means a job with decent pay and good working conditions for everyone willing and able to work and an adequate income for those unable to work. It means abolition of the present welfare system. To assure jobs and economic security for all the next Democratic administration should support: A full employment economy, making full use of fiscal and monetary policy. Tax reform directed toward equitable distribution of income and wealth and fair sharing of the cost of government. Full enforcement of all equal employment opportunity laws, including federal contract compliance and federally regulated industries and giving the Equal Employment Opportunity Commission adequate staff and resources and power to issue cease and desist orders promptly. Vastly increased efforts to open education at all levels and in all fields to minorities, women and other under-represented groups.

1976
We have met the goals of full employment with stable prices in the past and can do it again. The Democratic Party is committed to the right of all adult Americans willing, able and seeking work to have opportunities for useful jobs at living wages. To make that commitment meaningful, we pledge ourselves to the support of legislation that will make every responsible effort to reduce adult unemployment to 3 per cent within 4 years.

1980
We specifically reaffirm our commitment to achieve all the goals of the Humphrey-Hawkins Full Employment Act within the currently prescribed dates in the Act, especially those relating to a joint reduction in unemployment and inflation. Full employment is important to the achievement of a rising standard of living, to the pursuit of social justice, and to the strength and vitality of America.

1984
For the 1980s, the Democratic Party will emphasize two fundamental economic goals. We will restore rising living standards in our country. And we will offer every American the opportunity for secure and productive employment. Our program will be bold and comprehensive. It will ask restraint and cooperation from all sectors of the economy. It will rely heavily on the private sector as the prime source of expanding employment.

1988
We believe that we can rebuild America, creating jobs at good wages through a national reinvestment strategy to construct new housing, repair our sewers, rebuild our roads and replace our bridges. We believe that we must pursue needed investment through innovative partnerships and creative financing mechanisms such as a voluntary

program to invest private pension funds as a steady source of investment capital by guaranteeing security and a fair rate of return and
assuring sound project management.

1992
We will [emphasize] a national public works investment and infrastructure program [that] will provide jobs and strengthen our cities. . . .
We will encourage the flow of investment to inner city development
and housing through targeted enterprise zones and incentives for private and public pension funds to invest in urban and rural projects.

Emphasis in original of the texts.

SOURCE: Kirk Porter and Donald Johnson (eds.), *National Party Platforms* (Urbana: University of Illinois Press, 1976) supplements.

Notes

Preface

1. Gunnar Myrdal, *Objectivity in Social Research* (New York: Pantheon Books, 1969): 4–5.

2. Matthew Holden, Jr. *The Politics of the Black "Nation"* (New York: Chandler, 1973): 137.

3. The related work is *Racism in the Post Civil Rights Era: Now You See It, Now You Don't* (Albany: SUNY Press, 1995).

Chapter 1

1. Social movements are often identified with extra-systemic political methods such as mass demonstrations, strikes, boycotts and riots; however, these are not defining attributes, rather as Tilly writes a social movement is correctly understood as any "organized, sustained self-conscious challenge to existing authorities," whatever the political methods or tactics employed. See Charles Tilly, "Social Movements and National Politics," in C. Bright and S. Harding (eds.) *State Making and Social Movements: Essays in History and Theory* (Ann Arbor: University of Michigan Press, 1984): 304.

2. Sidney Tarrow, "Aiming at a Moving Target: Social Science and the Recent Rebellions in Eastern Europe," *PS* 24(1991): 12. This short essay is a fine review of the literature on social movements since the 1960s.

3. Douglas McAdams, *Political Process and the Development of Black Insurgency, 1930–1970* (Chicago: University of Chicago Press, 1982): 1, 3.

4. This generally negative view of social movements was substantially corrected by scholarship on the 1960s movements where it was found that movement participants were in general not alienated or fanatical but rather tended to share the characteristics of established interest groups and in the case of the civil rights movement were well integrated into the structure of the black community. See Aldon Morris, *The Origins of the Civil Rights Movement* (New York: Free Press, 1984). See also James Max Fendrich, *Ideal Citizens: The Legacy of the Civil Rights Movement* (Albany: SUNY Press, 1993).

5. McAdams, *Political Process and the Development of Black Insurgency*, p. 3. This point is also made by Robert Salisbury in "Political Movements in Ameri-

can Politics: An Essay on Concept and Analysis," *National Political Science Review* 1(1989): 15–30.

6. The bare bones of this framework and its preliminary application appeared originally as Chapter 6 in R. Gomes and L. Williams, *From Exclusion to Inclusion: The Long Struggle for African American Political Power* (Westport, CT: Greenwood Press, 1992): 97–126.

7. The origins and evolution of the civil rights movement is one of the most thoroughly researched and documented occurrences in the twentieth-century history of the United States. For a concise overview of this vast literature see Stephen Lawson, "Freedom Then, Freedom Now: The Historiography of the Civil Rights Movement," *The American Historical Review* 96(1991): 456–71.

8. David Easton, *A Framework for Political Analysis* (Englewood Cliffs, NJ: Prentice Hall, 1965): X. The other two volumes in the tetralogy are *The Political System* (New York: Knopf, 1953) and *A Systems Analysis of Political Life* (New York: John Wiley & Sons, 1969). The basic outlines of the central concepts of the framework are in "An Approach to the Analysis of Political Systems," *World Politics* 9(1957): 383–400.

9. Harry Scoble, "A Process Model to Study Political Repression" (manuscript, Department of Political Science, UCLA, 1971).

10. Easton, *A Framework for Political Analysis*, p. 78.

11. Ibid., p. 81.

12. As this is first written in late 1992, Somalia is a case where the political system has completely collapsed in that there is no effective government; no means to make and enforce binding decisions for the society. By the time this is published it is almost certain that some new political system or government will have emerged.

13. Even Mikhail Gorbachev in the Soviet Union did not seek the complete transformation of the system but rather its restructuring so as to make it more viable. Unfortunately for him and the Soviet system, the reforms once underway got out of hand and the system was transformed from authoritarian communism to incipient democratic capitalism.

14. Easton, *A Framework for Political Analysis*, p. 90–91.

15. Ibid., p. 92. Gabriel Almond notes that four types of problems are likely to cause stress on systems: state building, nation building, demands for increased participation and demands for the redistribution of resources. See Roger Scott, "System Analysis Without Tears: Easton and Almond," *Politics* 7(1972): 79. The major demands of African Americans have dealt with increased participation and to some extent resource redistribution.

16. Ibid.

17. Whether peaceful protests—marches, strikes, boycotts and civil disobedience—are systemic or nonsystemic methods not only varies by political system but also by historical circumstances. For example, the civil rights demonstrations of the 1960s were viewed by many as nonsystemic but today may be considered systemic. That is, protest since the 1960s may have become institutionalized. But even today a peaceful Tinimen Square-type demonstration on the Washington Mall after some time would be considered nonsystemic.

18. Easton, *A Framework for Political Analysis*, p. 100. Some of Scoble's outputs are also implicit in the work of other scholars. See for examples Frances Fox Piven and Richard Cloward, *Poor Peoples Movements: Why They Succeed, Why They Fail* (New York: Vintage Books, 1977): 27–32 and William Gamson, *The Strategy of Protest* (Homewood, IL: Dorsey Press, 1975) Chaps. 3, 6.

19. Ibid., p. 127. The best work on the use and manipulation of symbols in politics is still Murray Edelman, *The Symbolic Uses of Politics* (Chicago: University of Illinois Press, 1964).

20. Phillip Selznick, *TVA and the Grassroots* (Berkeley: University of California Press, 1949): 13.

21. In the United States it is powerful economic interest groups that typically are informally coopted. The classic study is Grant McConnell, *Private Power and American Democracy* (New York: Vintage Books, 1966).

22. Alan Wolfe, *The Seamy Side of Democracy: Repression in the United States* (New York: David McKay, 1973): 6, and Robert Goldstein, *Political Repression in Modern America* (Cambridge: Schenkman, 1978): Xvi.

23. Scoble, "A Process Model . . . ," p. 3.

24. Gunnar Myrdal, *An American Dilemma: The Negro Problem and Modern Democracy* (New York: Harper & Row, 1944): lXXi. In an empirical test of the Myrdal thesis Frank Westie found that most Americans recognized the dilemma and were prepared to accord blacks equality rather than abandon the principles of democracy and equality. See "An American Dilemma: An Empirical Test," *American Sociological Review* 30(1965): 524–38.

25. Charles Silberman, *Crisis in Black and White* (New York: Vintage Books, 1964): 10.

26. Cited in Leronne Bennett, *Confrontation Black and White* (Baltimore: Penguin, 1965): 103.

27. Ibid.

28. See Louis Harlan's *Booker T. Washington: The Making of A Black Leader, 1865–1910* (New York: Oxford University Press, 1972), and his *Booker T. Washington: The Wizard of Tuskegee* (New York: Oxford University Press, 1983). See also August Meier, *Negro Thought in America: 1880–1915* (Ann Arbor: University

of Michigan Press, 1963), and David Levering Lewis, *W.E.B. DuBois: Biography of a Race, 1868–1919* (New York: Henry Holt & Co., 1993): Chaps. 14 and 15.

29. The March on Washington project organized in 1941 is an example of the overlap between stages in the movement. Organized by A. Phillip Randolph, this effort demonstrated that blacks could be organized on a national basis for mass action. This project was in a sense the forerunner of the 1960s protest phase, influencing the work of CORE, a principal 1960s protest organization, and providing early socialization in protest planning to persons such as Bayard Rustin and James Farmer. On the March see Herbert Garfinkle, *When Negroes March: The March on Washington Movement and the Organizational Politics for FEPC* (New York: Atheneum, 1969).

30. Rayford Logan, *The Betrayal of the Negro* (New York: Collier Books, 1963).

31. See Lewis, *W.E.B. DuBois*, chaps. 15, 17. See also Daniel Walden (ed.), *W.E.B. DuBois: The Crisis Writings* (Greenwich, CT: Fawcett Books, 1972).

32. See Robert Zangrando, *The NAACP Crusade Against Lynching, 1909–1950* (Philadelphia: Temple University Press, 1980).

33. Ira Katznelson, *Black Men, White Cities* (New York: Oxford University Press, 1973): 108.

34. On Roosevelt's role see Zangrando, *The NAACP Crusade Against Lynching* and Nancy Weiss, *Farewell to the Party of Lincoln: Black Politics in the Age of FDR* (Princeton: Princeton University Press, 1983).

35. The NAACP's lobbying strategy during this period was not completely fruitless. In 1917 it organized a successful lobbying campaign against the passage of an amendment to an immigration bill that would have barred the entry of persons of African descent and in the 1930s the Association in coalition with organized labor played an important role in the defeat of John Parker's nomination to the Supreme Court. Parker was accused of racist and anti-labor sentiments. On the immigration bill see Cruse, *Plural But Equal: Blacks and Minorities in America's Plural Society* (New York: William Morrow, 1987): 83 and on the Parker case see Gilbert Ware, "Lobbying As a Means of Protest: The NAACP As An Agent of Equality," *Journal of Negro Education* 33(1964): 103–07.

36. Denton Watson, *Lion in the Lobby: Clarence Mitchell and the Black Struggle for Freedom* (New York: William Morrow, 1990).

37. See Genna MacNeil, *Groundwork: Charles Hamilton Houston and the Struggle for Civil Rights* (College Park, MD: University of Maryland Press, 1983) and MacNeil's "Justiciable Cause: Howard University Law School and the Struggle for Civil Rights," *Howard Law Journal* 22(1979): 108–32.

38. For a discussion of the NAACP's early use of litigation see William B. Hixson, "Moorfeild Storey and the Struggle for Equality," *Journal of American*

History 55(1968): 77–102. The hesitanc, of the Association to embrace litigation is understandable given the role of the Supreme Court in gutting the civil war amendments and the Reconstruction era civil rights laws. See J. Morgan Kouser, *Dead End: The Development of Nineteenth Century Litigation on Racial Discrimination in Schools* (New York: Oxford University Press, 1986).

39. The most comprehensive accounts of the litigation phase are Mark Tushnet, *The NAACP's Legal Strategy Against Segregated Education, 1925–50* (Chapel Hill: University of North Carol `:.`, 1987), and Richard Kluger, *Simple Justice: History of Brown vs Board of Education and Black America's Struggle for Racial Equality* (New York: Vintage Books, 1975).

40. On the absence of any substantive changes in school segregation as a result of *Brown* and its progeny see Gerald Ronsenberg, *The Hollow Hope: Can the Courts Bring About Social Change?* (Chicago: University of Chicago, 1991), and on the inconsequential results of the *Smith* case on black voting see Stephen Lawson, *Black Ballots: Voting Rights in the South, 1944–1969* (New York: Columbia University Press, 1976).

41. In the south any political action by blacks—assembly, organization, litigation, voting—was viewed as system challenging and frequently repressed. In a another sense then blacks in the south employed extra systemic methods because systemic methods were seldom available.

42. See Michael Lipsky, "Protest As a Political Resource," *American Political Science Review* 62(1968): 1144–58 and David Garrow, *Protest at Selma* (New Haven: Yale University Press, 1978), especially chap. 7. The allies activated to bring pressure on national authorities included not only domestic groups (business, labor, church groups) but also leaders of the emerging nations of Asia and Africa. Since the United States saw itself involved in a struggle with the Soviet Union for what was euphemistically called the "hearts and minds" of the largely colored third world this in effec. became an important movement resource. See Mary Dudziak, "Desegregation As A Cold War Imperative," *Standford Law Review* 41(1988): 1147–75.

43. According to a remarkable piece of investigative journalism by the *Memphis Commercial Appeal* the US Army began spying, infiltration and harassment of the civil rights movement as early as 1917. Dr. King, for example, was targeted by Army intelligence as early as 1947, seven years before he emerged as a movement leader at age twenty three in Montgomery. See Stephen Tompkins, "Army Feared King, Secretly Watched Him, Spying on Blacks Started 75 Years Ago," *Memphis Commercial Appeal*, March 21, 1993. See also Kenneth O'Reilly, *Racial Matters: The FBI's Secret File on Black America, 1960–72* (New York: Carroll & Graf, 1994).

44. Tarrow, "Aiming At A Moving Target," p. 15. See also Tarrow's *Democracy and Disorders: Protest and Politics in Italy, 1965–75* (New York: Oxford University Press, 1989): Chap. 12.

45. The Meredith March was initially organized by James Meredith, the first known African American to be graduated from the University of Mississippi, as a "march against fear" designed to demonstrate to blacks in his native state that they need not fear to exercise their newly gained civil rights. On the second day of the march Meredith was shot and wounded. The civil rights leadership then decided to continue the march in Meredith's honor and as means to demonstrate to Mississippi blacks and the nation the continuing climate of fear and violence in the state.

46. Julian Bond was denied his seat in the Georgia Legislature because of his support of a SNCC statement opposing the war in Vietnam.

47. The most thorough account of the origins of black power is in Claybourne Carson *In Struggle: SNCC and the Black Awakening of the 1960s* (Cambridge: Harvard University Press, 1981): chaps. 13–15.

48. Joel Aberbach and Jack Walker, "The Meaning of Black Power: A Comparison of Black and White Interpretations of A Political Slogan," *American Political Science Review* 64(1970): 370 and Carson, *In Struggle*, 215–28.

49. On this interpretation of black power's meaning see Paul Peterson, "Organizational Imperatives and Ideological Change: The Case of Black Power," *Urban affairs Quarterly* 14(1979): 465–84, Donald McCormack, "Stokely Carmichael and Pan Africanism: Back to Black Power," *Journal of Politics* 35(1973): 386–409 and Robert C. Smith, "Black Power and the Transformation From Protest to Politics," *Political Science Quarterly* 96(1981): 431–44.

50. On the Black Panthers see Reginald Major, *A Panther is a Black Cat: A Study in Depth of the Black Panther Party—Its Origins, Its Goals, Its struggle for Survival* (New York: William Morrow, 1970), Gene Marine, *The Black Panthers* (New York: New American Library, 1969) and Chris Booker, *The Rise and Fall of the Black Panther Party*, unpublished manuscript, 1987.

51. Quoted in John Gerassi, "Havana: A New International is Born" in I. Horowitz, Josue de Castro and Gerassi (eds.) *Latin American Radicalism: A Documentary Report on Left and Nationalist Movements* (New York: Vintage Books, 1969): 532. Later in the year Carmichael toured Third World socialist and communist countries (including North Vietnam) where he made similar declarations. Upon his return he wrote an article in which he argued that black power had moved beyond the politics of interest group pluralism in the United States to the revolutionary ideology of Pan Africanism. See "Pan Africanism: Land and Power," *Black Scholar* 1(1969): 36–54. The following year H. Rap Brown, Carmichael's successor as SNCC Chair, called on blacks to arm themselves for the coming revolution. Army intelligence was informed by Mexican authorities that Cuba and China had funneled money through OLAS to Carmichael and other "militant" blacks to wage guerilla war in the United States. The Mexican report said "American Negroes were sighted with automatic weapons training

at an urban guerilla camp near Chiapas in southern Mexico. See Tompkins "Army Feared King, Secretly Watched Him."

52. See U.S. Senate, *Final Report of the Select Committee to Study Government Operations With Respect to Intelligence Operations*, Washington S.R. #94–755, 94th Congress, 2nd session, 1976, Kenneth O'Reilly, *Racial Matters: The FBI's Secret File On Black America, 1960–72*, David Garrow, *The FBI and Martin Luther King, Jr.* (New York: Penguin Books, 1981), Ward Churchill and Jim Wall, *The FBI's Secret War Against the Black Panther Party and the American Indian Movement* (Boston: South End Press, 1988), and Tompkins, "Army Feared King, Secretly Watched Him."

53. See *Final Report of the Select Committee to Study Government Operations*, p. 179. In Hoover's analysis King, after the death of Malcolm X, was seen as the one figure able to bring together the various factions of the movement in such a radical direction. Writing of King the Hoover memorandum said he could "be a very real threat should he abandon his supposed 'obedience' to white liberal doctrines (nonviolence) and embrace black nationalism. . . . The man has the necessary charisma to be a real threat in this way." Hoover's musings were also shared by the Army which feared there were not enough troops in the country to suppress the riots, let alone the armed revolt many officers expected. At one point some analysts reportedly even considered withdrawing troops from Viet Nam and Europe to react to the anticipated violence. See Tompkins "Army Feared King, Secretly Watched Him."

54. Evidence of this process of formal cooptation may be seen in terms of an ongoing series of "first Negro who" appointments in the Johnson administration of black cabinet officers, judges and other high-level officials. Especially important in this regard was the highly visible role the Congressional Black Caucus began to play in national politics in the early 1970s (with highly flattering cover stories in *Newsweek*, *Ebony* and *Jet*) and the election of a string of big city mayors, again widely celebrated in the black and white media. *Time* for example captioned its cover story on the election of Cleveland Mayor Carl Stokes as "The Real Black Power."

55. Selznick, *TVA and the Grassroots*, p. 112.

56. Robert Tucker uses the notion of institutionalization to explain how a society responds to large and powerful revolutionary or radical movements. See his "The Deradicalization of Marxist Movements," *American Political Science Review* 61(1967): 346–48. Shefter uses the term "extrusion" to describe the process whereby ideologically radical or unacceptable contenders for the leadership of previously excluded groups are purged as those groups become incorporated into the political system. See Martin Shefter, "Political Incorporation and the Extrusion of the Left: Party Politics and Social Forces in New York City," *Studies in American Political Development*, 1(1988):86.

57. To some extent the concept institutionalization is viewed in the same way. That is, when a radical or system challenging movement is institutional-

ized its leadership tends to come to accept the values of the system. As Arthur Stinchcombe puts it the system's values and practices rather than those of the movement come "to exert a continuous force in [their] favor ...so that the more powerful a man is the more likely he is to hold the value." See *Constructing Social Theories* (New York: Harcourt, Brace & World, 1968): 153.

58. Bayard Rustin, "From Protest to Politics: The Future of the Civil Rights Movement," in *Down The Line: The Collected Writings of Bayard Rustin* (Chicago: Quadrangle Books, 1971): 118.

59. Ibid., p. 119.

60. Stinchcombe, *Constructing Social Theories*, p. 176–77.

61. Ibid.

62. Rufus Browning, Dale Marshall and David Tabb, *Protest is Not Enough: The Struggle of Blacks and Hispanics in Urban Politics* (Berkeley: University of California Press, 1984): 242–43.

63. For example, several of the major demonstrations in the post–civil rights era have been commemorative celebrations rather than protests, such as the March on Washington in 1988 to celebrate the twenty-fifth anniversary of the 1963 March or the several marches on or, more precisely, rallies in Washington led by Stevie Wonder, the entertainer, to press for passage of the Martin Luther King holiday bill. Even the demonstrations in the late 1980s at the South African Embassy designed to press for United States sanctions were largely ceremonial, celebrity, media-driven events rather than authentic protests. Indeed, one literally had to make an appointment in order to get arrested at the Embassy. Only celebrities or well-known political leaders could get an appointment to go—briefly—to jail.

64. Black leaders ritualistically condemn outbreaks of mass violence in the ghettos, as in the case of the Miami revolt in 1980 and the Los Angeles uprising in 1992. Their refrain is always that the causes of the violence are understandable but it is "unjustifiable." With respect to violence, then, black leaders seek to have it both ways. On the one hand they condemn it but on the other hand they seek to use violence or the threat of it as a means to leverage or pressure the system.

65. Rustin, "From Protest to Politics," p. 117.

66. Ibid., p. 118.

67. "Seven Point Mandate," *Focus*, 14(1976): 8.

68. On the homogeneous, near-monolithic liberal ideological policy preferences of African Americans on economic and social welfare issues see Norman Nie, Sydney Verba and John Petrocik, *The Changing American Voter* (Cambridge: Harvard University Press, 1976): 254–56, and Robert C. Smith and

Richard Seltzer *Race, Class and Culture: A Study in Afro-American Mass Opinion* (Albany: SUNY Press, 1992): 64–81.

69. Charles Hamilton, "Full Employment as a Viable Issue" in *When The Marching Stopped: An Analysis of Black Issues in the 1970s* (New York: National Urban League, 1971): 90–91.

Chapter 2

1. Twice before—in the 1830s and 1930s—black Americans attempted to develop and sustain all inclusive race congresses or conventions. In both periods they failed for essentially the same reasons that the effort in the 1970s failed: ideological factionalism and institutional conflicts. On the National Negro Convention of 1830s see Howard Bell's "A Survey of the Negro Convention Movement, 1830–1861," doctoral dissertation, Northwestern University, 1953. See also Bell's "National Negro Conventions of the Middle 1840s: Moral Suasion vs. Political Action," *Journal of Negro History* 22(1957): 247–60; Bella Gross, "The First National Negro Convention," *Journal of Negro History* 31(1966): 435–43; William and Jane Pease, "The Negro Convention Movement" in N. Huggins, M. Kilson and D. Fox (eds.) *Key Issues in the Afro-American Experience*, vol. 1(New York: Harcourt, Brace & Jovanovich, 1971): 191–205, and their "Black Power: The Debate in 1840," *Phylon* 29(1969): 19–26. On the 1930s convention see John B. Streeter, "The National Negro Congress: 1936–47," doctoral dissertation, University of Cincinnati, 1980; C. Alvin Hughes, "The National Negro Congress Movement," doctoral dissertation, The Ohio State University, 1982 and Lawrence Wittner, "The National Negro Congress: A Reassessment" *American Quarterly* 22(1968): 883–901. And on the centrality of ideology and ideological conflict between nationalists, integrationists and radicals in Afro-American politics see Robert C. Smith, "Ideology as the Enduring Dilemma of Black Politics," in G. Persons (ed.) *Dilemmas of Black Politics: Issues of Leadership and Strategy* (New York: Harper/Collins, 1993): 211–24.

2. On this interpretation of black power see the articles cited in Chapter 1, n. 50. See also Charles Hamilton's "Afterword, 1992" in the twenty-fifth anniversary edition of *Black Power* (New York: Vintage Books, 1992).

3. Claybourne Carson, *In Struggle: SNCC and the Black Awakening of the 1960s* (Cambridge: Harvard University Press, 1981): 215.

4. See Stokely Carmichael, "What We Want," *New York Review of Books,* September 22, 1966, and his "Toward Black Liberation," *Massachusetts Review* 7(1966): 639–51, and Carmichael and Hamilton, *Black Power* (New York: Vintage Books, 1967).

5. Stokely Carmichael, "Pan Africanism: Land and Power," *Black Scholar* 1(1969): 7–15. This article was seminal in the growing influence of the Pan

African variety of nationalism in the early 1970s, which resulted in much ideological confusion throughout the period.

6. Charles Hamilton, "An Advocate of Black Power Defines It," *New York Times Magazine*, April 14, 1968, p. 8.

7. Smith, "Black Power and the Transformation from Protest to Politics," pp. 438–40, and more generally Robert Allen, *Black Awakening in Capitalist America* (New York: Anchor Books, 1969).

8. Powell in a sense saw himself as the originator of the concept, since he had used the phrase as early as 1963. In a speech to the graduating class at Howard in May 1966, a week before Carmichael used black power on the Meredith March, Powell told the students to seek "black power . . . an audacious black power . . . the power to build black institutions of splendid achievement." See Chuck Stone, "The National Conference on Black Power," in Floyd Barbour (ed.), *The Black Power Revolt* (Boston: Extending Horizon Books, 1968): 189. For Powell's essentially reformist view of black power see his statement inserted in the *Congressional Record* as reprinted in Barbour's collection of essays (pp. 257–60). Barbour's volume is a useful documentary of early black power thinking, with contributions from the full variety of black power activists including radicals, nationalists and establishment figures. Reading it is a good precursor to the debates five years later at Gary.

9. Carson, *In Struggle*, pp. 223–24.

10. Powell, by now excluded from Congress, was scheduled to give the Conference's major address but he declined to attend for fear of arrest—on an outstanding civil warrant—if he entered New York City's airports.

11. Stone, "The National Black Power Conference," p. 191.

12. Ibid.

13. Ibid., pp. 195–96.

14. Ibid.

15. On the Chicago new politics conference, see the coverage in the *New York Times*, September 1–4, 1967, James Ridgeway, "Freak-Out in Chicago," *New Republic*, September 16, 1967, pp. 9–12, and the account in Irwin Unger, *The Movement: A History of the American New Left*, (New York: Dodd & Mead, 1974): 137–38.

16. See Imamu Amiri Baraka, "A Black Value System," *Black Scholar* 1(1969): 54–60.

17. At the 1967 National Black Power Conference held in Newark, a "spirit of the conference" resolution was adopted calling for the establishment of a "task force to assist in the Newark recall election of Mayor Hugh

Addonizio." Baraka also gained national attention as a result of his long, bitter struggle with Tony Imperiale, a leader of Newark's Italian-American community, over the location of a black housing and cultural complex within a predominantly Italian-American neighborhood.

18. Amiri Baraka (ed.), *African Congress: A Documentary of the First Modern Pan-African Congress* (New York: William Morrow, 1972): VIII.

19. See Carmichael, "Pan Africanism: Land and Power."

20. Charles Hamilton, "Pan Africanism and the Black Struggle in the U.S." *Black Scholar* 2(1971): 10–15.

21. For example, see Ronald Walters, "In World Relations: The Future of Pan Africanism," *Black World* 24(1974): 4–18.

22. Baraka, *African Congress*, p. 25.

23. Ibid., p. 64.

24. Ibid., p. IX. Baraka elaborated this notion of a world African party in his "The African Party and the Black Struggle," *Black Scholar* 2(1971): 24–33. In his speech Mayor Kenneth Gibson also proposed a black political party "on the basis of nationalism" and as an institutional manifestation of "a new black politics." After invoking the slogan "Nation time," he said "we need a black political organization along the lines of the one-party African states. We need an organization which will be a need (sic) for us to do as Malcolm said—'Get in the closet and settle our differences.'"

25. Ibid., p. 42.

26. Ibid., p. 171.

27. Imari Obadele, President of the Republic of New Africa is a man of principle who has put his liberty and life on the line in pursuit of his goal of a separate black nation, socialist in character, to be carved out of several states in the deep south. Indeed, within a year of the Atlanta meeting, Obadele and several of his followers were victims of a predawn raid by FBI and state police at the group's Jackson, Mississippi headquarters. During the raid, which involved use of an armored car and tear gas, a state police officer was killed. As a result, Obadele and several of his colleagues spent several years in state prison. Obadele, now on the faculty of Prairie View A & M University, outlines the philosophical and legal basis for his proposed plebiscite and discusses the strategy of organization and propaganda leading ultimately to a "peoples war" that would force the government to conduct the plebiscite and abide by its results in his "The Struggle is for Land," *Black Scholar* 3(1972): 54–60. Whatever one thinks of Obadele's ideology (and it is clearly utopian), it deserves to be taken seriously, debated and rejected, and not patronizingly adopted as a resolution in ritualistic obedience to some notion of "unity without uniformity" which implies

that any and all ideas advanced by blacks as a program for liberation are equally valid. Obadele provides an account of the Republic of New Africa's history through the 1980s in *Free the Land* (Washington: Songhay Press, 1984).

28. The Jewish Kahillah eventually collapsed after a decade or so for many of the same reasons as did the black congresses or conventions—ideology (socialism), nationalism (zionism) and nationality (East Europeans v. Germans) as well as the usual conflicts of organization and personality. On the Kahillah see Arthur Goren, *New York Jews and the Quest for Community* (New York: Columbia University Press, 1970).

29. Holden, *The Politics of the Black "Nation"*, (New York:Chandler, 1973): 172. To continue the analogy with Jewish Americans, in New York Jews have been able to develop and sustain reasonably well-developed mechanisms of collective or communal discussion and action to deal with their internal problems and differences and engage in communal philanthropic work. And Jewish political leaders also created and sustained a reasonably successful "Jewish" political party in New York, although it of course was not called the Jewish party but rather the Liberal party, open to all but with Jews as its core, dominating constituency.

30. U.S. Congress, House, Representative Diggs, "Congressional Black Caucus Recommendations to President Nixon," 92nd Congress, 1st session, March 30, 1971, *Congressional Record*, vol. 117.

31. In developing its agenda for presentation to President Nixon the Caucus conducted a wide-ranging series of hearings and conferences in an effort to solicit information and recommendations from a broad range of interests and individuals, except nationalists. Specifically, the Caucus attempted to exclude nationalist testimony and proposals on black education which rejected school busing in favor of community control. Only after protests by CORE's Roy Innis did the Caucus permit this view to be included in the record of its education hearings, and in its recommendations to the President the CORE position was flatly rejected. On the conflict between the Caucus and CORE on school busing see Robert C. Smith, "Black Elites and Black Groups in the Federal Policy Process: A Study in Interest Articulation," doctoral dissertation, Howard University, 1976: chap. 6, and *Proceedings of the National Policy Conference on Education For Blacks* (Washington: Congressional Black Caucus, 1972): 131.

32. Several participants in the meetings (led by Congressman Hawkins) argued against any black strategy, agenda or candidate because they would only antagonize the party nominee and other groups in the Democratic coalition whose support blacks would later need to defeat Nixon.

33. Amiri Baraka, "Toward the Creation of Political Institutions for All African Peoples," *Black World* 21(1972): 60. Earlier Baraka's CAP had called for a series of regional black conventions to name candidates and develop strategies

and agendas, which would culminate in a national meeting to develop a plan to influence the 1972 election.

34. Shirley Chisholm, *The Good Fight* (New York: Harper & Row, 1973): 25.

35. Chisholm describes the origins of her candidacy as follows: "Running for president was not my idea originally. It was a number of college students who started me thinking about it, against what I first thought was my better judgment. . . . A young man at a southern college asked why didn't I run. . . . I said I am black, I am a Woman. . . . He said, "Don't worry, we will be voting soon and we will support you. . . . The germ of the decision began here." *The Good Fight*, pp. 13, 15–16.

36. See for example Baraka, "Toward the Creation of Political Institutions," p. 58; Chisholm, *The Good Fight*, p. 28 and Marable, "Black Nationalism in the 1970s: Through the Prism of Race and Class," *Socialist Review* 10(1980): 105.

37. Baraka, "Toward the Creation of Political Institutions," p. 62.

38. Ibid, pp. 62–63.

39. Ibid., p. 63.

40. *New York Times*, November 21, 1971. The press release also said the convention would be "open to all black people regardless of party affiliation or ideology, to reflect the full diversity of interest of 25 million blacks."

41. Bryant Rollins, "The Importance of Gary," *Amsterdam News*, March 3–11, 1972.

42. James Stephens, "The State Delegations," *Jet*, March 30, 1972.

43. Three thousand five hundred delegates were formally certified by the Credentials Committee (initially a $25 registration fee was required for delegate certification but after much criticism this rule was dropped) representing the District of Columbia and all except six states with small black populations— Alaska, Montana, West Virginia, Wyoming and South and North Dakota. The largest delegations were New York (339), Michigan (254) and California (212). In addition to the delegates another 5500 persons attended as observers.

44. The most detailed account in the press of the opening session is Simeon Booker, "Black Political Convention is Successful Despite Splits and Tactical Differences," *Jet*, March 30, 1972.

45. On the importance and significance of Baraka's leadership role see the article by Booker above, Thomas Johnson, "Black Assembly Voted at Parley," *New York Times*, March 13, 1972, *Newsweek's* "Emergence of A New Leader," March 27, 1972, Edwin Jaffe, "Coming Together at Gary," *Nation*, April 3, 1972, and Ronald Walters, "The New Black Political Culture," *Black World* 21(1972): 4–17. Walters, the Howard University political scientist and active

staff person at the convention, was rhapsodic in his praise of Baraka, writing, "Baraka is not only a man, he is himself a movement with an effective organization. . . . The man himself was poetry in motion, he was a master politician wielding the gavel of power on the podium. . . . It was his skill and respect among the masses which moved the business of the convention along in a way which others could not. . . . The Black nation owes a great deal to the philosophy of Imamu Baraka." Pp. 8, 16.

46. On the grumbling at the time by delegates and others about the poor planning and resulting confusion, see Virginia Thrower, "Observers Criticize Planning," *The Gary Post-Tribune*, March 3, 1972, and Tom Knightly, "Confusion Normal, Diggs," *The Gary Post-Tribune*, March 12, 1972.

47. The draft preamble was prepared by the staff of Atlanta's Institute of the Black World.

48. See Roy Wilkins, "Minorities Are the Losers When They Play Ethnic Politics," *Sacramento Bee*, February 12, 1972.

49. See Gary Slaughter, "NAACP Blasts Preamble," *Gary Post-Tribune*, March 11, 1972 and Thomas Johnson, "Blacks at Parley Divided on Basic Role in Politics," *New York Times*, March 12, 1972.

50. The full text of the preamble is in "Call To The Convention," *Amsterdam News*, March 3–11, 1972. In order that the reader might appreciate the full flavor of the convention processes, dialogue and debate, I shall quote liberally from the relevant proceedings and documents.

51. Slaughter, "NAACP Blasts Preamble." See also Barbara Reynolds, "Dems Target At Black Parley," *Chicago Today*, March 12, 1972. The memorandum in revised form was reprinted as "The NAACP and the Black Political Convention," *The Crisis* 79(1972): 229–30.

52. The NAACP did send its fifteen allotted delegates to the convention but with specific instructions "not to commit the NAACP to any position, nor any endorsement of any kind." However, neither Wilkins nor any of his principal assistants attended. Urban League Director Vernon Jordan, attended the convention briefly in what he called "an unofficial capacity" but the organization declined to send official delegates, claiming its tax exempt status prohibited involvement in political activities, while SCLC—the other major civil rights organization—sent an official delegation, but Ralph Abernathy its President did not attend. On the participation of the major civil rights organizations see Faith Christmas, "Questions Rights Group's Role at Gary Meeting," *Chicago Defender*, March 11–17, 1972.

53. Slaughter, "Blacks at Parley Divided on Basic Role in Politics."

54. The original plan had been for the committee to receive platform planks from the state delegations prior to the convention and then a small

working group of staff was to pull together a draft platform. Again, time did not permit this; however, a Howard University working group under the direction of Carl Holman of the National Urban Coalition did prepare a series of proposals that constituted a working draft.

55. Mickey Thrower, "Rep. Chisholm, Busing Hot Issues at Convention," *Gary Post-Tribune*, March 10, 1972. The possible male chauvinist character of this decision was blunted when the two most prominent women at the convention—Coretta King and Dorothy Height, President of the National Council of Negro Women—opposed the Chisholm endorsement, arguing that the convention should deal with issues not candidates and that endorsements would be divisive. See Geraldine Fields and Virginia Thrower, "Women Agree: No Endorsements," *The Gary Post-Tribune*, March 13, 1972. Interestingly, in its waning moments with only a few hundred delegates present the convention adopted a resolution to support Chisholm. This is further evidence of confusion in the convention proceedings. On the last-minute Chisholm endorsement see Mickey Thrower, "60 To Continue Parley's Work," *Gary Post-Tribune*, March 13, 1972.

56. The text of the Hatcher address is in the *Chicago Defender*, March 18, 1972 and the *Black Scholar* 4(1972): 17–22.

57. Jackson is quoted in Grayson Mitchell and David Robinson, "Blacks Give Ultimatums and Edge to New Party," *Chicago Sun Times*, March 12, 1972.

58. On the Jackson-Hatcher speeches and subsequent convention comments see Gary Slaughter, "Black 3rd Party—Now? Wait?" *Gary Post-Tribune*, March 12, 1972.

59. Jackson, for example, in a post-convention interview indicated the continuing mechanism created by the convention—the National Black Political Assembly—might become "the cradle of a third party, in fact if not name." See Thrower, "60 To Continue Parley's Work."

60. The most detailed press account of the agenda's content was in the *Gary Post-Tribune*. See Gary Slaughter, "Blacks Ask Radical Changes in System," March 13, 1972. The national press tended to downplay these radical proposals, focusing instead on the school busing and Middle East resolutions. See for examples Thomas Johnson, "Black Assembly Voted At Parley," *New York Times*, March 13, 1972 and *Newsweek*, "Black Politics: The Gary Convention," March 27, 1972.

61. *The Gary Post-Tribune*, "Anti-busing Resolution OKd," March 13, 1972.

62. It was also one factor that prompted the Congressional Black Caucus several weeks after the convention to issue its own alternative to the convention agenda, which predictably unreservedly endorsed busing as a tool to desegregate the schools.

63. Quoted from Ronald Walters, *Black Presidential Politics in America: A Strategic Approach* (Albany: SUNY Press, 1988): 89.

64. Quoted in *Chicago Defender*, "Gary Convention Failed to Live Up To Its Roseate Promise," March 18–24, 1972. Black columnist Ethel Payne questioned the motives of Innis in proposing the resolution, asking "who is bankrolling the anti-busing campaign of CORE? . . . Why is Innis so friendly with certain well known segregationists, including some U.S. Senators?" See "The Moment of Truth at Gary and Beyond," *Chicago Defender*, March 18–24, 1972. Earlier in the month George Wallace had won the Florida Democratic primary on a largely anti-busing platform.

65. *The National Black Political Agenda*, p. 13.

66. DuBois's uncompromising support of Israel is representative of establishment black opinion at that time. On his views and how they developed see Horne, *Black and Red: W. E. B. DuBois and the Afro-American Response to the Cold War* (Albany: SUNY Press, 1986).

67. As with opposition to the Vietnam War SNCC was the first major black leadership group to articulate this pro-Palestine position. See Carson, *In Struggle*, pp. 267–69.

68. For the text of the original resolution adopted by the convention and its revision by the Steering Committee, see Walters, *Black Presidential Politics*, pp. 90–91.

69. An interesting footnote here on the convention's handling of controversial issues, Yvonne Day, Chair of Gary's Committee on the Status of Women sought to have the convention go on record in favor of legalization of abortion. It never came to vote as it was roundly condemned by the male leadership (including Jesse Jackson) as "genocide." See Thrower, "Rep. Chisholm, Busing are Hot Issues."

70. See Nadine Brown, "Diggs Peacemaker in Gary Walkout Hassle," *Michigan Chronicle*, March 25, 1972.

71. Ibid.

72. Ibid. Speaking for the minority faction in the delegation Sherry Shuttles charged that Young had refused to let non-UAW blacks speak during the convention and that Young's majority faction was "highly organized and politically sophisticated, but largely reflects the so-called 'friends' of the Negro, groups like the UAW and the Democratic party. Therefore, they have not dealt with the very fundamentals of this Gary experience. They are still trying to limit the struggle of Black folks to the confines others created."

73. John Dean, "Black Political Assembly: Birth of a New Force?" *Focus* 2(November 1973): 4.

74. *New York Times*, March 12, 1972. For views similar to Johnson's see the *Amsterdam News* editorial "The Experiment in Gary," March 18, 1972; Carlos Russell, "A Journey We Must Make," *Amsterdam News*, March 18, 1972; Simeon Booker, "Black Convention is Successful Despite Splits and Differences;" "If We Failed" editorial in *Michigan Chronicle*, March 25, 1972; and Austin Scott, "Impact of Black Parley Assessed by AP Newsman," *Gary Post-Tribune*, March 14, 1972.

75. "Gary Convention Failed to Live Up to its Roseate Promise."

76. "The Black Declaration of Independence and Bill of Rights," Washington, Congressional Black Caucus, 1972.

77. Fauntroy controlled the fifteen-person District of Columbia delegation as a favorite son candidate. He had persuaded Chisholm not to enter the District's primary so that he might have a cohesive bloc of delegates to bargain with at the Democratic convention. Chisholm claims he pledged to release the delegates to her on the second ballot. See *The Good Fight*, pp. 49–50.

78. If the busing and Middle East resolutions were the only items in the Gary agenda that McGovern objected to it indicates that either he and his staff had not read it or did not take its more radical planks seriously. It is more likely the former, since busing and the Middle East items were given widespread attention in the national press and in all likelihood this is all McGovern and his staff knew or cared about the document. McGovern does not discuss the Gary convention or issues related to it in his campaign memoir. See *Grassroots* (New York: Random House, 1977).

79. Fauntroy could not live up to his part of the bargain, since within days of its announcement many of the unpledged delegates Fauntroy had offered to McGovern indicated to the press that Fauntroy could not speak for them and in many instances had not even been contacted by him prior to his announcement.

80. Quoted in Walters, *Black Presidential Politics*, p.92.

81. Among the blacks in the administration who were delegates at Gary were White House aide Robert Browne, HEW Assistant Secretary Edward Sylvester (who chaired its Rules Committee), Arthur Fletcher and John Wilks of the Labor Department and HUD Assistant Secretary Samuel Jackson.

82. Baraka, "Toward the Creation of Political Institutions," p. 73.

83. Ibid., p. 72.

84. Ibid., p. 73–74. On the issue of unity with establishment black leaders Baraka wrote, "There is an essential difference, one day it will be a deadly difference, between black people who view political movement as one means of attaining black power and these colored folks who are 'in politics' only for their

personal gains, or the white boys! This difference must be brought into easily defined relief. We are for black unity, umaja. But at some point we probably must consider what is to be done about those Negroes whose values are so destroyed that they are adamantly, almost militantly, opposed to working for black peoples interests." P. 61.

85. Walters in his contribution to this *Black World* special on the convention also chided black elected officials for their behavior but in language more restrained than Baraka's. Writing that black elected officials were unduly influenced if not controlled by whites because many may be "dependent upon votes and money much of which is white and a large percentage of which is Jewish." While "others may not be directly controlled by whites but feel they are, in a similar sense constrained by the internalized behavior of white acculturation and by the need to be 'realistic,'" see "The New Black Political Culture," p. 14. Congressman Clay, one of the Caucus members least supportive of the convening of the convention at Gary, nevertheless used his contribution to warn the Democratic party that unless it shared power with blacks and stopped taking the black vote for granted, the Gary convention provided the vehicle to serve as an alternative to continued black support. See "Emerging New Black Politics," p. 37. Clay's allusion to a black political party was an explicit focus of William Strickland's essay, "The Gary Convention," although his conception of a party that would, for example, include elements of the Viet Cong and the Tupamaros (a Latin American urban guerilla organization) is hardly one that Congressman Clay would have found acceptable.

86. Dean, "Black Political Assembly."

87. Ronald Walter, "African-American Nationalism," *Black World* 22(1973): 9.

88. Ibid.

89. Ibid.

90. Ibid., p. 21.

91. Malcolm X delivered the "Ballot of the Bullet" speech initially in a debate with Louis Lomax held in Cleveland on April 3, 1964. See George Brietman (ed.) *Malcolm X Speaks* (New York: Grove Press, 1965): 23–44. I am quoting from a subsequent version of the speech from the album *Ballots or Bullets*, First Amendment Records, Distributed Jamie/Guyden Distributing Corp.

92. See Austin Scott, "Black Convention: Defining Differences," *Washington Post*, March 23, 1974, Gregory Sims, "Political Convention Ends As It Begins, Amidst Controversy," *Jet*, March 30, 1974, and Harold Cruse, "The Little Rock National Black Political Convention, Part 2," *Black World* 24(1974): 4–23.

93. Cited in Harold Cruse, "Black Politics Series: The Methodology of Pan Africanism," *Black World* 24(1975): 19.

94. William Greider, "Deep Differences Cripple Black Unity," *Washington Post*, March 18, 1974. Wilkins claimed that he was not invited but in a formal statement released later the group said "The absence from Little Rock of the NAACP and thousands who attended the first meeting at Gary, Indiana was not due to a lack of a desire for unity in facing racial problems but was and is due to the separatist and nationalist ideology set forth by the dominant factions at Gary." See *The Crisis* 81(1974): 3.

95. See the *Washington Afro-American*, "Some of the Radicalism Went Out of National Black Convention," March 26–30, 1974.

96. Greider, "Deep Differences Cripple Black Unity."

97. Paul Delaney, "Black Political Group Facing Problems of Unity and Leaders," *New York Times*, March 15, 1974 and Scott, "Black Convention: Defining Differences."

98. Sims, "Political Convention Ends As It Begins."

99. The only substantive resolution of significance considered at the convention again dealt with Middle East policy. The resolution did not reaffirm the position adopted at Gary; rather, it indicated support for Arabs in the conflict and condemned black congressmen for voting for military aid to Israel. See Austin Scott, "Two Resolutions Held Threat to Unity of Black Convention," *Washington Post*, March 17, 1974, and Paul Delaney, "Hatcher Criticizes Blacks Absent from Convention," *New York Times*, March 18, 1974.

100. Reflecting to some extent Baraka's evolving Marxist-Leninist ideological stance, there was, unlike at Gary, a significant Marxist faction at Little Rock which only further complicated the efforts at unity within the various nationalist sects and between them and the establishment forces. See Cruse, "Methodology and Pan Africanism," p. 7.

101. Robert Allen, *Black Awakening in Capitalist America*, p. 273.

102. *Washington Afro-American*, "Some of the Radicalism went out of the National Black Convention."

103. Greider, "Deep Differences Cripple Black Unity."

104. Cruse, "The Methodology of Pan Africanism," pp. 14–18.

105. Baraka's view of such a party had in all likelihood become even more radical given his disappointment with the Gibson mayoral administration in Newark and his evolving Marxist-Leninist ideology. For example, at Little Rock he argued that blacks must "develop a revolutionary ideology, that is socialist and anti-capitalist. . . . Either you will help destroy America or you will be destroyed with it. You don't have any choice." See Scott, "Black Convention Defining Differences."

106. Strickland, "The Gary Convention," pp. 25–26.

107. This view of the party was elaborated early on by Chuck Stone, "Black Politics: Third Force, Third Party or Third Class Influence?" *Black Scholar* 1(December, 1969): 11–17.

108. Cruse, "Methodology and Pan Africanism," p. 15.

109. Greider, "Deep Differences Divide Convention," p. 109.

110. Ibid. Clay's observation was dramatically demonstrated the year before in the Newark mayoral election. Baraka, a veteran of the campaign that initially elected Gibson, could be safely ignored by the mayor in his reelection campaign because he was confident that Baraka and his organization could not deliver sufficient votes to affect the outcome of the election. This is all the more telling since Baraka at the time had probably the best local organization of any nationalist leader.

111. Quoted in Cruse, "Methodology and Pan Africanism," p. 17. But Cruse notes elsewhere in this article that Conyer's opinion may also have been informed by Conyer's pessimistic judgment that "at this point there is no elected [black] Democratic leader in the nation who can run off the Democratic ticket and win," presumably himself included.

112. Amiri Baraka, "Toward Ideological Clarity," *Black World* 24(1974): 89, 95.

113. Ibid., p. 86. By calling for a simultaneous struggle against racism and capitalism Baraka in this paper, for the time being, sidestepped the ideological debate about which should be given causal primacy in explaining black oppression and therefore guiding the struggle. This omission caused as much consternation among his sectarian nationalist colleagues as did his adoption of communism amongst the black establishment.

114. Within a month of Baraka's announcement of his new ideology, Oklahoma State Representative Hanna Atkins, one of the handful of elected officials still active in the assembly, resigned her post as treasurer (although not her assembly membership) saying "I cannot remain in a leadership position in an organization with an avowed scientific socialist," adding that Baraka was seeking to philosophically dominate or destroy the organization. Baraka issued a statement regretting Atkins' resignation, saying the assembly should be a broad-based body comprising all different philosophies, adding, "I ask why Hanna Atkins can be in the Democratic Party with [Alabama] Governor Wallace and she can't be here with me." See "State Rep. Atkins Quits Black Assembly Post," *Jet*, February 25, 1975.

115. Amiri Baraka, "Why I Changed My Ideology: Black Nationalism and Socialist Revolution," *Black World* 24(1975): 30.

116. Ibid., pp. 32–33.

117. Ibid., pp. 36–37.

118. Ibid., p. 33. Baraka does not address here how a revolutionary communist organization of blacks will deal with the traditional Marxist notion of a multiethnic working class solidarity, admitting no place for whites in his organization and rejecting association with the CPUSA and such black communists as, for example, Angela Davis.

119. "Ron Daniels Interview—The National Black Political Assembly: Its Position and Future," *Black World* 24(1975): 30.

120. This race-class debate is largely academic, with little consequence then or now for the realities of the struggle. And as an issue in academic discourse it is probably unresolvable historically, theoretically or empirically by the methods of science. Thus, whether one attaches primacy to race or class in explanation of the subordinate status of Africans is a matter of ideological tastes rather than objective historical or theoretically informed empiricism.

121. "Daniels Interview," p. 30.

122. Ibid., pp. 34–35. The statement of principles was essentially a modified version of the preamble adopted at the Gary convention, which linked black oppression to the "twin foundations of white racism and white capitalism" and the "mobilization of the broadest possible spectrum of philosophies and constituencies in support of the struggle to destroy racism and capitalism." See "New Politics for Black People: A Statement of Principles, Goals, Guidelines and Direction for the National Black Political Assembly," *Black World* 24(1975): 61–65.

123. "Daniels Interview," p. 35.

124. Hanna Atkins, "Why I Resigned From the NBPA," *Black World* 24(1975): 45–46.

125. Ibid., p. 45.

126. Amiri Baraka, "Statement on the National Black Assembly," *Black World* 24(1975): 43.

127. Ibid.

128. Gary Mayor Hatcher, the Assembly's other principal leader, declined to respond to questions posed by *Black World*, indicating as Daniels put it that he was preparing to take a less active, leadership role in the assembly.

129. "Daniels Interview," p. 33. As possible candidates he mentioned Julian Bond, Dick Gregory and Congressman Ronald Dellums. Daniels argued that with such a prominent candidate the campaign might attract as many as ten

million votes. But even without a prominent candidate Daniels said the party would nominate someone in order to "educate the masses."

130. Marable, "Black Nationalism in the 1970s," p. 88.

131. The utopian mind set—guided by wishful representation and a will so strong to transform society that it ignores reality—is not unknown among all strata of activist-intellectuals but the tendency is especially pronounced among those from oppressed groups. And it is probably exaggerated among literary or creative intellectuals such as a Baraka. Thus, it is probably wise that creative intellectuals—as most usually do—avoid overt leadership roles in political movements because as in Baraka's case both their creative output and the movement are likely to suffer.

132. The assembly briefly formed a working group to try to develop the basis of a coalition with progressive white activists so that a multiethnic progressive "peoples" campaign rather than a strictly black effort might be undertaken. However, nothing came of this effort. See Walters, *Black Presidential Politics*, p. 147.

133. "Daniels Interview," p. 33.

134. Austin Scott, "Dellums Declines," *Washington Post*, March 22, 1976.

135. "Blacks to Form Political Party," *New Orleans Times-Picayune*, August 24, 1980, and Roger Wilkins, "Blacks Look Outside Two Parties in Search of Influence," *Washington Star*, October 24, 1980.

136. The Chavis resolution stipulated that the assembly should continue to exist with state and local chapters having the option to affiliate with the party. See "Motion Calling for An Independent National Black Political Party," N.D.

137. Ibid. See also Press Statement of National Black Political Assembly, September 4, 1980.

138. Mack Jones, "A National Black Independent Political Party: Preliminary Questions" (discussion paper prepared for the Annual Olive-Harvey Afro-American Studies Conference, Chicago, April 9–11, 1981), p. 1.

139. Walters, *Black Presidential Politics*, p. 149.

140. See Ronald Walters, "Black Presidential Politics: Bargaining or Begging," *Black Scholar* 11(1980): 22–31 and more generally *Black Presidential Politics*.

141. Manning Marable, "Anatomy of Black Politics," *Review of Black Political Economy* 8(1978): 381. Professor Marable, now Director of Columbia University's Institute for African American Studies, has apparently changed his views on these matters, if one is to judge by his recent lectures and columns.

142. "Proposed Statement of Principles and Charter for a National Black Independent Political Party" (prepared for presentation to Delegates of the Founding Convention, November 21–23, 1980, Philadelphia).

143. Walters, *Black Presidential Politics*, p. 150.

144. On SWP's view of its role in the NBIPP see Nan Bailey, Malik Miah and Mac Warren, *The National Black Independent Party* (New York: Pathfinder Press, 1981). I should like to thank Kwame Somburu for information and extended discussion of the role of the SWP in the NBIPP. Somburu (then Paul Boutelle) was the SWP's 1968 vice presidential candidate.

145. Paulette Pierce, "The Roots of the Rainbow Coalition," *Black Scholar* 19(1988): 2–17.

146. Amiri Baraka, "Black Power 20 Years Later," *New York Newsday*, August 17, 1986 cited in Ibid.

147. Of utopian thinking Karl Mannheim writes that "certain oppressed groups are intellectually so strongly interested in the destruction and transformation of a given condition of society that they unwillingly see only those elements in the situation which tend to negate it. Their thinking is incapable of correctly diagnosing an existing condition of society. They are not at all concerned with what really exists, rather in their thinking they already seek to change the situation that exists. Their thought is never a diagnosis of the situation; it can only be used as a direction for action," see *Ideology and Utopia* (New York: Harcourt Brace, 1936): 40.

148. This definition is from Milton Morris, *The Politics of Black America* (New York: Harper & Row, 1975): 92.

149. Walters, *Black Presidential Politics*, p. 156.

150. See *An Insight Into the Black Community* (Chicago: Johnson Publications, 1972):12–13; Gary Marx, *Protest and Prejudice* (New York: Harper & Row, 1967): 28–29; William Brink and Louis Harris, *The Negro Revolution*, (New York: Simon & Shuster, 1963): 119–20; and Angus Campbell and Howard Schuman, *Racial Attitudes in Fifteen American Cities* (Ann Arbor: University of Michigan, Institute for Social Research, 1971):15–17.

151. See the harshly critical editorial of the Black Caucus's efforts to develop ties with Farrakhan and the Nation of Islam, "The Black Caucus Gets Mugged," in the *New York Times*, September 25, 1993.

152. Campbell and Schuman, *Racial Attitudes in Fifteen American Cities*, p. 18. *Ebony's* 1972 survey found 6 percent support for a separate black nation. See *An Insight into the Black Community*, p. 13.

153. Apart from social class—the least educated and affluent—the only other demographic variables associated with support for black nationalism are

age and region, with younger and rural southern blacks much more supportive. See Richard Allen, Michael Dawson and Ronald Brown, "A Schema Based Approach to Modeling an African American Belief System," *American Political Science Review* 83(1989): 421–41, and Patricia Gurin, Shirley Hatchett and James Jackson, *Hope and Independence: Black Response to Electoral and Party Politics* (New York: Russell Sage, 1991): 183.

154. See Michael Dawson, "Structure and Ideology: The Shaping of Black Public Opinion." Paper prepared for presentation at the 1995 Annual Meeting of the Midwest Political Science Association, Chicago, p. 29.

155. Holden, *The Politics of the Black "Nation"*, p. 172.

156. See Bell, "A Survey of the Negro Convention Movement," p. 39.

157. In 1983 the Leadership Roundtable under the direction of Congressman Fauntroy developed a fairly detailed plan for the internal reorganization of black America, including a development bank and a political action network involving the entire range of religious, civic, civil rights, fraternal and political organizations. See *The Black Leadership Family Plan for the Unity, Survival and Progress of Black People* (Washington: Congressional Black Caucus, 1983). The plan was never implemented, in part because the Roundtable itself never became a functioning organization.

158. "African-American Summit '89," *Unity*, February 16, 1989.

159. Press statement, "The African-American Summit," N.D.

160. There were also rumblings of discontent among some that the summit was a thinly disguised process to advance Jesse Jackson's political ambitions, which led others to stay away. But the critical reason that attendance was sparse is probably that few people saw any meaningful reason to convene.

161. Quoted in Ronald Smothers, "Blacks Discussing Routes to Power," *New York Times*, April 24, 1989. Ronald Brown, newly installed as the first black chair of the Democratic National Committee, reportedly was chagrined by his participation in the meeting. Ronald Kutner reports, "Last April, the Chairman found himself attending a poorly staffed 'Black Summit' in New Orleans where, after having been assured that no black radicals were involved, he was appalled to find Louis Farrakhan on the program. He gave his speech, and got out of town before Farrakhan arrived." See "Ron Brown's Party Line," *New York Times Magazine*, December 3, 1989, p. 129.

162. Sometimes it seems that the principal activity of post–civil rights era black leadership has been developing the "black agenda." Since the late 1960s a bewildering series of conventions, meetings, leadership summits, congresses, institutes, etc., have replaced rallies, marches, demonstrations and lawsuits as a principal routine activity yielding an equally bewildering set of documents variously described as the "black agenda." In a systematic canvas of such

national agenda-building meetings and manifestos I counted sixteen since 1967, all more or less equivalent. And I probably missed a couple.

163. These structural barriers include the winner-take-all provision of the electoral college, the single-member district system of electing members of the House, the maze of fifty separate state ballot access laws and the presidential campaign finance laws.

164. Gurin, Hatchett and Jackson, *Hope and Deliverance*.

Chapter 3

1. Charles Hamilton, "The Patron-Recipient Relationship and Minority Politics in New York City," *Political Science Quarterly* 94(1979): 211–28.

2. Carmichael and Hamilton, *Black Power*, p. 39.

3. One might argue that Jesse Jackson's departure from SCLC was an important factor in that organization's decline, since in leaving he took with him the resources of Operation Breadbasket, the organization's most effective northern organizational base.

4. On the decline of SNCC and CORE see respectively Clayborne Carson, *In Struggle: SNCC and the Black Awakening of the 1960s* and August Meier and E. Rudwick, *CORE: A Study in the Civil Rights Movement, 1942–68* (New York: Oxford University Press, 1973); and also James Q. Wilson, *Political Organizations* (New York: Basic Books, 1973): chap. 9.

5. Kenneth Clark, "The Civil Rights Movement: Momentum and Organization," in T. Parsons and K. Clark (eds.) *The Negro American* (Boston: Beacon Press, 1966): 623. On this point more specifically see H. H. Haines, "Black Radicalization and the Funding of Civil Rights Organizations," *Social Problems* 37(October 1984):31–43.

6. CORE is dead but its ghost remains in parts of the country under the autocratic and quixotic leadership of Roy Innis, who has functioned as executive director since Lyndon Johnson was president.

7. Clark, "The Civil Rights Movement," p. 612.

8. See "A Troubled Operation PUSH Struggles to Focus Mission," *New York Times*, April 1, 1991.

9. Gunnar Myrdal, *An American Dilemma*, p. 819.

10. Clark, "The Civil Rights Movement," p. 619–20.

11. Clark shares this assessment of the increasing irrelevance of the civil rights organizations in the post–civil rights era, at least the NAACP. If any-

thing, he is more negative in his assessment than I am in this analysis. See his "The NAACP: Verging on Irrelevance," *New York Times*, July 14, 1985.

12. Clark, "The Civil Rights Movement," p. 605.

13. The increasingly active role of the board chairman in the day-to-day operations of the association and as a visible spokesperson is one of the important changes in the organization since the 1960s. The ascendancy of the role of the former board chairman, William Gibson, resulted in internal in-fighting and, some argue, undermined the effectiveness of the national staff.

14. See Tuseda Griggs, "Group Seeking Younger Members," *West County Times*, April 6, 1992.

15. NAACP, *Annual Report*, 1987, p. 18.

16. These tensions and conflicts within the Leadership Conference and the civil rights lobby generally are revealed quite sharply in the campaign to defeat Supreme Court nominee Robert Bork and in the 1982 renewal of the Voting Rights Act. On the Bork nomination see Michael Pertschok and Wendy Schaelzel, *The People Rising: The Campaign Against the Bork Nomination* (New York: Thunder Mouth's Press, 1989) and on the Voting Rights Act see Dianne Pinderhughes, "Black Interest Groups and the 1982 Voting Rights Act," unpublished manuscript, Urbana, University of Illinois, 1991.

17. Denton Watson, *Lion in the Lobby: Clarence Mitchell's Struggle to Pass Civil Rights Laws* (New York: William Morrow, 1990).

18. Clark, "The Civil Rights Movement," p. 621.

19. See Haines, "Black Radicalization and the Funding of Civil Rights Organizations," and Charles Henry, "Big Philanthropy and the Funding of Black Organizations," *Review of Black Political Economy* 9(1979): 174–90.

20. NAACP, *Annual Report*, 1987.

21. On NAACP funding sources from 1968 to 1977 see Henry, "Big Philanthropy and the Funding of Black Organizations." The association's annual dues are extremely modest, ten dollars for basic membership (the local branches keep four dollars and six are forwarded to the national office) and fifteen dollars for a membership that includes a subscription to *The Crisis*.

22. NAACP, *Annual Report*, 1992, pp. 111, 131,. The NAACP Special Contribution Fund is a separate "publicly supported" trust established in 1964 to support the association's activities. Figures from the association's annual reports should be accepted with caution. In the wake of the controversy surrounding the firing of Benjamin Chavis, the American Institute of Philanthropy, which rates the financial management of nonprofit organizations, reported that the NAACP's accounting procedures were so confused that the budget could not be understood. See Peter Kilborn "Financial Problems Hinder the Work of the

NAACP," *New York Times*, November 4, 1994. In 1994, facing a reported $3.5 million deficit, the association placed its entire national staff on a three-month unpaid furlough. See Steven Holmes, "NAACP Plans to Rehire Most of Its Staff in Early '95," *New York Times*, December 31, 1994.

23. On the confusion surrounding the selection process see Clarence Lusane, *African Americans at the Crossroads* (Boston: South End Press, 1994): 27–29. A sure indicator of this confusion is that the selection committee and the board apparently seriously considered Jesse Jackson—a man without administrative skill or interest and who has never subjected himself to organizational discipline and is probably incapable of doing so—for the position.

24. Quoted in Steven Holmes, "NAACP Chief's Meeting Upsets Board" *New York Times*, April 10, 1994.

25. Ibid. The *New York Times*, the principal organ of the liberal establishment, also, rather arrogantly, criticized Chavis for his embrace of Farrakhan and other nationalist leaders. See the editorial "The NAACP's Mistake," March 7, 1994.

26. This was initially written prior to Chavis's dismissal in August of 1994. I had expected Chavis to be removed for ideological and political reasons and although such factors may have played a role, the proximate cause of his removal was the disclosure that he had agreed without the knowledge of the association's board to pay $332,000 in NAACP funds to settle a sexual discrimination suit brought by a former female employee. In the wake of the controversy surrounding the firing of Chavis there were charges and countercharges of widespread corruption, personal favoritism, excessive salaries and extravagant perks. Critics also charged poor management and administration at the national office; that the sixty-four-member board was too large; is selected in an undemocratic manner and is too acquiescence to its chairman. See Clarence Lusane and James Steele, "A Fatal Attraction: The Firing of Ben Chavis by the NAACP," *Black Political Agenda* 2(1994):1, 10–13.

27. Clark, "The Civil Rights Movement," p. 607. Clark goes on to write, "The ghettos of northern cities and the forces which perpetuate such ghettos are clearly beyond the scope of an agency such as the Urban League or any private agency."

28. See Nancy Weiss, *The National Urban League, 1910–1940* (New York: Oxford University Press, 1974), and her *Whitney M. Young and the Struggle for Civil Rights* (Princeton: Princeton University Press, 1989).

29. On the largely stillborn efforts of blacks in the 1960s and 1970s to create a black equivalent of the United Jewish Appeal, see the series of articles in the special issue of the *Black Scholar*, "Black Fund Raising," 8(1976), and King Davis, "Funding the Black Agenda in the 1980s" (paper prepared for the 1981 Annual Congressional Black Caucus Legislative Weekend), September, Washington, D.C.

30. National Urban League, *Report to the Delegate Assembly*, 1992, p. 12.

31. Affiliate dues accounted for 5 percent of the league's 1994 budget. Affiliates are separately incorporated and dues to the National office are based on 4.5 percent of their local United Way allocations, up to a maximum of $50,000.

32. National Urban League, *Annual Report*, 1985. I should note that in 1980 Alpha Phi Alpha, the fraternal group, pledged to raise and give one million dollars to the Urban League, the NAACP and the United Negro College Fund. A year later it made its first installment of $165,000 to each group.

33. Clark, "The Civil Rights Movement," p. 622.

34. By contrast the NAACP has very little research or independent analytic capacity and even its journal, *The Crisis* (which it claims has a circulation of 346,000, making it the fourth largest black circulation magazine), continues to publish but is a far cry from its glory days under DuBois's editorship when it was a forum for what DuBois called "hammering at the truth," presenting some of the best work on the problems of the race and racism. One reason for its decline is that its editor was, until his retirement, Benjamin Hooks rather than an individual who knew what he was doing with respect to publication of a good journal of opinion and analysis. It was DuBois's independent, critical editing of *The Crisis* that in part resulted in his dismissal from the NAACP in the 1930s, a lesson subsequent leaders of the association may have learned all too well.

35. National Urban League, *Annual Report*, 1985, p. 8.

36. Ibid. pp. 5–6.

37. The institutional consequence of Dr. King's effect on the traditional black clergy and church was the formation of the Progressive Baptist Convention. This organization broke away from the traditionalist National Baptist Convention in part because it was dissatisfied with its conservative, anticivil rights stance.

38. The most comprehensive history of the NBC is in C. Eric Lincoln and Lawrence Mamiya, *The Black Church in America* (Durham: Duke University Press, 1990).

39. Taylor Branch, "Of Kings and Dynasties: How Black Baptists Healed Themselves," *Washington Weekly*, September 24, 1984, p. 11.

40. While the black "church" (the church is of course not a monolith) has become more politically active and socially conscious, it still has not become a force at the national level in terms of lobbying and voter mobilization as has, for example, the white evangelical Christian church. Contrary to the arguments of some, religiosity in the post–civil rights era black community is not an apolitical, otherworldly force, rather the more religiously inclined blacks are the more

active in the organizational life of the community and are more likely to register and vote. For data and analysis on the role of religiosity in the post–civil rights era black community see Robert C. Smith and Richard Seltzer, *Race, Class and Culture*, pp. 125–32, Michael C. Dawson, Ronald Brown and Richard Allen, "Racial Belief Systems, Religious Guidance and African American Political Participation," *National Political Science Review* 2(1992): 22–44 and Ronald Brown and Monica L. Wolford, "Religious Resources and African American Participation," *National Political Science Review* 4(1994):30–48. However, the role of the black church in politics should not be exaggerated. The National Black Election Survey conducted in 1984 found that only 22 percent of blacks said they attended a meeting at their church in support of a candidate; only 10 percent said they did work for a candidate through their church and only 19 percent said their church took up a collection for a candidate during the election year. See Katherine Tate et al., *The 1984 National Black Election Study Sourcebook*, (Ann Arbor, University of Michigan, Institute of Social Research, 1988): tables 19.1–19.3. Lincoln and Mamiya found in a 1983 survey of more than 1800 black clergymen that only about half supported use of the church to achieve political and social change. These politically active clergy tend to be well educated and their congregations tend to be middle and upper class rather than working and poor. See *The Black Church in America*, p. 198.

41. Like the NAACP, the National Baptist Convention faces serious financial and administrative problems. In 1994 Rev. Henry Lyons of St. Petersburg, Florida defeated Jemison in an acrimonious race for convention president. Upon assuming office, Lyons reported that the organization faced a deficit of $765,000 and was unable to pay its bills. He also indicated that the group did not have a written budget nor a full-time executive director to manage its day-to-day affairs. Lyons also reported that in the past the convention had grossly exaggerated its membership, indicating that it was constituted by 33,000 affiliate churches and 8.2 million members. In fact, Lyons said the group probably includes no more than 3,000 churches and 700,000 members. See "New National Baptist Leaders Face Big Money Problems," and "National Baptist President Tells Group's Money Status," *Richmond Free Press*, January 12–14, February 16–18, 1995.

42. A serious biography of Mr. Muhammad is sorely needed, because as C. Eric Lincoln points out, he was one of the most remarkable men of the twentieth century. Largely unlettered, he made an enormous contribution to the dignity and self-esteem of blacks in the United States, in addition to making Islam a respectable force in the black community. See Lincoln's "The American Muslim Mission in Context." Paper presented at the Conference on Islam in North America, University of Alberta, Edmonton, Canada (1980), p. 21, and his seminal study *The Black Muslims in America* (Boston: Beacon Press, 1961). See also Louis Wright's interesting discussion of the philosophical groundings of Mr. Muhammad's thought "Elijah Muhammad's Political Thought on God and Authority," *21 Century Afro Review* 1(1994): 63–102.

43. Ibid., p. 23.

44. In its unrelenting condemnation of whites, white supremacy and racism and in its call for racial separatism, the Nation may be viewed as a radical organization, however, its doctrines have always included many elements that may be considered conservative in the context of American politics. Its emphasis on economic nationalism in terms of small-scale entrepreneurship, its focus on moral reform and traditional values with respect to family life, sex, alcohol and drug use as well as its condemnation of welfare dependency are all quite compatible with the right wing's approach to race in the United States.

45. Lincoln, "The American Muslim Mission in Context," p. 20.

46. Ibid. An indicator of Warith Muhuammad's acceptability and respectability in American society is that in 1992 he was invited to give the opening prayer in the U.S. Senate and was later guest at a reception in his honor hosted by Senators Paul Simon of Illinois and Orin Hatch of Utah. See Don Terry, "Black Muslims Enter Islamic Mainstream, *New York Times*, May 3, 1993.

47. Lawrence Mamiya, "From Black Muslim to Bialian: The Evolution of a Movement," *Journal for the Scientific Study of Religion* 21(1982): 141.

48. Ibid. In 1985 Warith Muhammad disbanded the American Muslim Mission and urged his followers to avoid any separatist movement or organization and instead associate themselves with the established Muslim Mosques in their local communities. In a simultaneous telephone hookup he told his followers "If you follow my advice, you would put down the term 'American Muslim Mission': you would put it down and never pick up any term that lumps you all together in one community. You would be members of a Muslim community that's international." See M. Hyer, "Black Muslim Leader Disbands Separatists," *Washington Post*, April 10, 1985.

49. Perry Lang, "Farrakhan is Seeking Larger Political Base," *San Francisco Chronicle*, May 28, 1990, and George Curry, "Farrakhan: An Interview," *Emerge*, August 1990, pp. 30–37.

50. Farrakhan's doctrinal shifts, however, have been tentative and ambivalent in part because he might fear a counter schism within the Nation itself or a loss of part of his following to some of the more doctrinally pure sects that claim adherence to the philosophy of Mr. Muhammad.

51. Louis Farrakhan, "The Final Call." Personal notes from a speech delivered at Howard University, December, 1984. On his endorsement of Harold Washington, Farrakhan claimed that he discovered in "careful study" of Mr. Muhammad's teachings that he had said "If a politician arose among us who was fearless, who would stand up and plead our cause and would not sell us out, that kind of politician deserves and should get the full backing and support of our entire people." See E. R. Shipp, "Candidacy of Jackson Highlights Split Among Black Muslims," *New York Times*, February 27, 1984.

52. William Henry, III, "Pride and Prejudice," *Time*, February 28, 1994, p.26.

53. Because of its unfamiliarity with the nationalist tradition and perhaps also because of a bit of overt ill will, the establishment press is incapable of reporting accurately on this aspect of black politics. Thus, its reporting always tends to be alarmist, taking literally and seriously the rhetoric of Minister Farrakhan (as for example his so-called death threat against a *Washington Post* reporter during the 1984 campaign). Farrakhan, who views himself as a prophet in the Old Testament tradition, uses apocalyptic language of righteous indignation and religious metaphor, demanding justice and damnation in the name of God. Such rhetoric is not taken literally and does not alarm those familiar with the nationalist tradition or the tradition of the religious jeremiad in Afro American culture (see David Howard-Pitney, *The Afro-American Jeremiad: Appeals for Justice in America*, Philadelphia, Temple University Press, 1990). Malcolm X was similarly portrayed during his career, especially for his use of the rhetoric of the white devil and his repeated use of animal imagery (dog, wolf, fox, etc.) to refer to whites in their relationship to blacks. On Malcolm's use of these rhetorical devices see Hank Flick and Larry Powell, "Animal Imagery in the Rhetoric of Malcolm X," *Journal of Black Studies* 18(1988): 435–51.

54. A 1994 poll by *Time* found that 73 percent of blacks were familiar with Farrakhan, making him along with Jesse Jackson the best-known black leader of the post–civil rights era. Most blacks familiar with Farrakhan viewed him favorably, with 65 percent saying he was an effective leader, 63 percent that he speaks the truth and 62 percent that he was good for the black community. By contrast only 34 percent viewed him as a bigot or racist. See Henry, "Pride and Prejudice," p. 22.

55. Mamiya, "From Black Muslim to Bialian," p. 144. The nationally distributed newspaper, *The Final Call*, also serves as a recruiting device. Prior to the mid-1980s Farrakhan did not grant interviews to the white press; however, since then he has regularly granted such interviews and appears from time to time on television news and talk shows. He also has a weekly radio and cable television program broadcast in most large cities.

56. This line of criticism is pursued by Adolph Reed in his "False Prophet II: All for One, None for All," *Nation*, January 28, 1991.

57. Of all the national black organizations including the church, the Nation is the only one that has an effective presence on the street corners of black America and on the campuses of the nation's colleges and universities.

58. James D. Barber, *The Presidential Character: Predicting Performance in the White House* (Englewood Cliffs, N.J.: Prentice & Hall, 1985): 7. See also Jeffrey Tillis, *The Rhetorical Presidency* (Princeton: Princeton University Press, 1967).

59. On the role of oratorical competence and a leadership of defiance in Afro-American political culture, see Holden, *The Politics of the Black "Nation"*, pp. 16–24.

60. Bruce Perry, *Malcolm: The Life of A Man Who Changed Black America* (Barrytown, N.Y.: Station Hill, 1991): 380.

61. Myrdal, *An American Dilemma*, p. 749.

62. Clark, "The Civil Rights Movement," p. 598.

63. The twelve were Clark, Richard Hatcher, Percy Sutton, California legislators William Greene and Mervyn Dymally, Clarence Townes of the Republican National Committee, Louis Martin of the Democratic National Committee, Vernon Jordan then of the Voter Education Project, Alderwoman Louise Reynolds of Louisville, Alderman Q.V. Williamson of Atlanta and Frank Reeves of the Howard law faculty.

64. Joint Center for Political Studies, *Newsletter* 1(1970):2.

65. Similar caucuses of black elected officials have been formed at the state and local levels, especially at the state legislative level.

66. Holden, *The Politics of the Black "Nation"*, pp. 70–71.

67. *Shaw et al. v. Reno et al.*, 92-357, 1993 (slip opinion).

68. In *Miller v. Johnson*, 94-631, 1995 (slip opinion) the Supreme Court continued its attack on the drawing of majority black legislative districts pursuant to the Voting Rights Act by holding that not only irregularly shaped districts but that use of race itself as the "predominant" factor in redistricting was presumptively unconstitutional. This 5-4 decision invalidated Georgia's 11th congressional district and by implication suggested that at least half the majority black congressional districts, north and south, might be subject to challenge. At a minimum, the decision invites further litigation and suggests to state legislatures that in future redistricting they might—without violating the Voting Rights Act—refrain from creating majority black districts. Like much of its recent civil rights jurisprudence (see Chapter 6), the Court in this case, while not explicitly abandoning the basic precedent or doctrine established in *United Jewish Organizations*, renders a judgment that nevertheless undermines its practical application. In *United Jewish Organizations v. Carey*, 430, U.S. 144(1977), Justice White, writing for a 7-2 majority, said ". . . a reapportionment plan cannot violate the Fourteenth or Fifteenth Amendments merely because a state uses specific numerical quotas in a certain number of majority black districts."

69. See Robert C. Smith, "Financing Black Politics: A Study of Congressional Elections," *Review of Black Political Economy* 17(1988): 5–30.

70. This is in part because their challengers usually do not raise sufficient funds to mount competitive races. See Ibid., pp. 15, 27–28.

71. Holden, *The Politics of the Black "Nation,"* p. 202.

72. Personal Interview.

73. See "President to See Hill Black Caucus," *Washington Star*, February 14, 1971.

74. NBC News, "Meet The Press," May 23, 1971.

75. Congressional Black Caucus, Press Release, June 19, 1975. See also "Congress' Black Caucus Rejects White Member," *Washington Star*, June 19, 1975. In 1988 at the urging of Missouri's Congressman Wheat, the Caucus created an associate member category for whites. As associates, whites may not vote or attend closed meetings and dues were one rather than four thousand dollars a year. As of 1990 forty whites had become associate members. See Carol Swain, *Black Faces, Black Interests: The Representation of African American Interests in Congress*, (Cambridge: Harvard University Press, 1991): 37.

76. On Franks, see Georgia Persons, "The Election of Gary Franks and the Ascendancy of the New Black Conservatives," in Persons (ed.) *Dilemmas of Black Politics* (New York: Harper/Collins, 1993): 194–208.

77. Frequently, the Caucus will dissolve itself into the "Democratic Black Caucus" as a means to exclude Franks. This happened so frequently in the first year of the Clinton Administration that Franks briefly threatened to resign in protest. Unlike Franks, Oklahoma Congressman J. C. Watts, elected in 1994, declined to join the group.

78. See *In Opposition to Clarence Thomas: Where We Must Stand and Why* (Washington: Congressional Black Caucus Foundation, 1991), and Ronald Walters, "Thomas Estranged from His Blackness," *Washington Post*, July 16, 1991.

79. In a rather ironic twist on this, in a hearing before his subcommittee on health, Stark denounced Health Secretary Louis Sullivan, who is black, as an Uncle Tom and a disgrace to his race because of Sullivan's failure to support national health insurance. See Chapter 5.

80. On the changing role orientations of the Caucus see Charles Jones, "An Overview of the Congressional Black Caucus, 1970–85," in F. Jones et al., *Readings in American Political Issues*, (Dubuque, Iowa: Kendal/Hunt, 1987):219–40. In general, the Caucus is quite cohesive in its voting behavior, constituting the core of the Democratic party's liberal bloc in the House. This may change to some extent with the influx of the new group of rural, southern congressman, who might be expected to take a more conservative position on social and moral issues, school prayer, gun control and crime.

81. In 1982 the House adopted a rule prohibiting informal House groups from accepting outside funds. As a result, the Caucus had to divide itself into two organizations: the Congressional Black Caucus (supported by member con-

tributions) and the Congressional Black Caucus Foundation (supported by tax-deductible contributions and the annual fund raising dinner). When the Republicans took control of the House after the 1994 elections they adopted rules prohibiting House caucuses (although not the caucus foundations) from receiving member contributions, using House office space, staff or equipment. In addition, substantial contributions from outside sources were also prohibited. This change in rules will inhibit, to some extent, the Caucus's internal and external communication networks and impede its capacity as a group to develop independent legislative analysis or alternative legislative programs such as its annual budgets.

Interestingly, in a move that anticipated the decision of the House Republican majority, in 1985 the Democratic National Committee (DNC) also withdrew official recognition from its minority group caucuses, preventing them from using party money or staff to support their operation. DNC Chair Paul Kirk said the decision was necessary because the party was too closely identified with "special interests," but Texas Congressman Mickey Leland described it as an "abomination" because "The caucuses have been a means for blacks and Hispanics to participate and generate interest in the Party and this is going to stifle them." See James Dickinson, "DNC Withdraws Recognition of 7 Caucuses" *Washington Post*, May 18, 1985.

82. Charles Jones, "Testing a Legislative Strategy: Congressional Black Caucus Action Alert Communication Network," *Legislative Studies Quarterly* 12(1989): 532.

83. Quoted from Darlene Clark Hines, "A History of the Joint Center: 1970–1990," in *Annual Report*, 1989 (Washington: Joint Center for Political and Economic Studies, 1989): 6. Professor Hines's short essay in the Center's 1989 Annual Report is excerpted from an authorized history of the Center. Although Professor Hines, a distinguished historian, completed the study, the Center elected not to publish it, in part because it disagreed with aspects of her interpretation of the Center's history and role in post–civil rights era black politics (Personal Interview with Professor Hines).

84. See Lewis, *W.E.B. DuBois*, chaps. 8–9.

85. *Jet*, "Farmer to Set Up First Think Tank for Blacks," June 21, 1973. Nothing came of Farmer's efforts.

86. Holden, *The Politics of the Black "Nation"*, p. 180.

87. Henry, "Big Philanthropy and Black Civil Rights Organizations," p. 187.

88. R. Kent Weaver, "The Changing Role of Think Tanks," *PS* 22(1989): 570. For an analysis of the increasingly important role of think tanks in the modern era see James Smith, *The Idea Brokers: Think Tanks and the Rise of the New Policy Elite* (New York: The Free Press, 1991).

89. The Joint Center's ideological focus on the conventional liberal-con-servative cleavage in mainstream American politics is a distortion of the rich ideological diversity of mainstream black politics. This focus misleads the press and public, which depend on the Center for the "black perspective" on politics and public policy. For example, the available survey data indicate that Minister Farrakhan and black nationalism has far more support in black America than do black Republicans or conservatism, but one would hardly know this from the Center's conferences and publications.

90. See his inspirational history: Vincent Harding, *There Is a River: The Black Struggle for Freedom in America* (New York: Harcourt, Brace & Jovanovich, 1981).

91. Vincent Harding, personal interview with author.

92. Henry, "Big Philanthropy and Civil Rights Organizations," p. 183.

93. Metropolitan Applied Research Center, *First Annual Report*, 1967, quoted in Ibid., p. 183.

94. In 1975 Clark left MARC and was succeeded as director by Charles Hamilton. Ford eventually dropped its support and MARC shortly thereafter closed.

95. Weaver, "The Changing Role of Think Tanks," p. 370.

96. Joint Center for Political Studies, *Annual Report*, 1991, p.3.

97. Data on the Center's budget from its 1991 annual report and the fig-ures on the budgets of the other Washington based think tanks are from Weaver, "The Changing Role of Think Tanks," p. 573.

98. Probably the best work the Center has done is its series of studies on the Voting Rights Act. These include technical monographs such as Barbara Phillips, *How to use Section 5 of the Voting Rights Act*, and more academic studies such as Chandler Davidson's edited volume *Minority Vote Dilution* (Washing-ton: Howard University Press, 1984) and Frank Parker's *Black Votes Count* (Chapel Hill: University of North Carolina Press, 1990).

99. This quip is quoted from Weaver, "The Changing Role of Think Tanks," who is citing from Peter Kelly, "Think Tanks Fall Between Pure Research and Lobbying," *Houston Chronicle*, March 9, 1988.

100. Thomas Dye, *Who is Running America?* (Englewood Cliffs, NJ: Pren-tice Hall, 1990): chap. 9. Most Washington think tanks encourage their staff to move in and out of government in a revolving door process. Thus far this prac-tice has not characterized the behavior of the Center's staff, although given its liberal bent this may be because in its twenty-year history there has been only one Democratic administration. The Center does, however, frequently engage policy makers from the executive branch in its proceedings and has often had in residence U.S. Ambassadors and military officers. And in the Clinton adminis-tration Edwin Dorn, a former deputy director of research at the Center and its

specialist on race and the armed services, was appointed Assistant Secretary for Personnel Management at the Defense Department. At the time of his appointment Dorn had left the Center to join the staff at Brookings.

101. In its research, publications and commentaries on black politics the Center, like the mainstream black media (*Ebony, Essence, Black Enterprises*), tends to take a celebratory, noncritical stance toward black political leaders and organizations, avoiding critical discussion and analyses about black politics and leadership, or the U.S. political economy and culture.

102. At the local level there are hundreds of grassroots, community-based self-help or development organizations supported by private and foundation funds. The effect they have on dealing with the internal problems of the community or organizing it is not known. Similarly, in many cities there are a number of small nationalist and radical groups but they tend to be narrowly sectarian and to work in isolation from each other.

103. *New York Times*, "Groups Join to Aid Blacks," August 20, 1990. A year earlier James Cheek, the former Howard University President, announced the formation of yet another organization—the National Organization of African Americans—as a new "voice on the national scene advocating a new agenda and different direction for African Americans." On this new organization see Cheek's press statement in *Directions*, (October 1992), the group's inaugural newsletter.

104. During consideration of the Humphrey-Hawkins Act, a series of slick Madison Avenue ads, televised nationally, dramatizing the unemployment problem in black America and discussing jobs as an alternative to welfare and crime *may* have helped to generate public pressure on the Congress and the president to enact more responsible legislation.

105. One explanation may be the relatively higher level of suspiciousness and lack of trust—interpersonally and socially—that exists in the Afro-American community, which would lead to both elite and mass unwillingness to sustain such an effort because of suspiciousness of the motives of those who would run it. On this lack of trust historically see R. Jones, "The Myth of Afro-American Communalism: Elements of a Black Political Psychology" (unpublished manuscript, Brown University, 1990); on its manifestation in contemporary Afro-American culture see Robert C. Smith and Richard Seltzer, *Race, Class and Culture: A Study in Afro-American Mass Opinion*, pp. 31–32, and on its consequences politically see Holden, *The Politics of the Black "Nation"*, pp. 23–24.

Chapter 4

1. C. Wright Mills, *The Power Elite* (New York: Oxford University Press, 1956).

2. Ibid., p. 9.

3. Thomas Dye, *Who's Running America: The Bush Years* (Englewood Cliffs, NJ: Prentice Hall, 1990): 10. Dye and his colleagues since 1976 have published six editions of this study covering administrations from Nixon to Clinton.

4. Dye, *Who's Running America?*, p. 12. Inevitably there are methodological problems in trying to identify systematically those persons who constitute a group as elusive as a national power elite (not the least being that many powerful do not wish to be identified). But Dye's method is at least systematic and probably offers as close an approximation of this elusive reality as is possible.

5. Mills, *The Power Elite*, p. 256.

6. Ibid.

7. Paul Peterson, *City Limits* (Chicago: University of Chicago Press, 1981).

8. Of the many studies of post–civil rights era Atlanta see Mack Jones, "Black Political Empowerment in Atlanta: Myth and Reality," *The Annals* 439(1978): 90–117; Floyd Hunter, *Community Power Succession: Atlanta's Policy Makers Revisited* (Chapel Hill: University of North Carolina Press, 1980); Adolph Reed, "The Black Urban Regime: Structural Origins and Constraints," in Michael Smith (ed.), *Power, Community and the City: Comparative Urban Community Research* (New Brunswick: Transaction, 1988); and Clarence Stone, *Regime Politics* (Lawrence, Kansas: University of Kansas Press, 1989).

9. For more detailed analysis of the growth and development of black elected officials since the 1960s see Linda Williams, "Black Political Progress in the 1970s: The Electoral Arena," in M. Preston, L. Henderson and P. Puryear (eds.), *The New Black Politics* (New York: Longman, 1982):97–135, and Theresa Chambliss, "The Growth and Significance of African American Elected Officials," in R. Gomes and L. Williams (eds.), *From Exclusion to Inclusion* (Westport, CT: Greenwood Press, 1992):53–70.

10. These figures are from the Joint Center's annual *Roster of Black Elected Officials*.

11. See for example Chambliss, "The Growth and Significance of African American Elected Officials."

12. Descriptive or statistical representation in government is symbolically important in a democratic polity, especially for a previously excluded group, even if such representation has little impact on substantive policy outcomes. It is also a measure, albeit a crude one, of a group's power. As G. William Domhoff puts it, "If a group or class is highly overrepresented or underrepresented in relation to its proportion of the population, it can be inferred that the group is relatively powerful or powerless. . . . Similarly, when it is determined that a minority group has only a small percentage of its members in leadership positions, even though it comprises 10 to 20 percent of the

population, then the basic processes of power inclusion or exclusion are inferred to be at work." See *Who Rules America?* (Englewood Cliffs, NJ: Prentice Hall, 1967):12.

13. See James Mock, "The Black Political Executive and Black Interests, 1961–80," Doctoral dissertation, University of Tennessee, 1981, and his "The Black Vote Output: Black Political Executives, 1961–80," Paper prepared for presentation at the Annual Meeting of the Midwest Political Science Association, Milwaukee, 1982. See also Robert C. Smith, "Black Appointed Officials: A Neglected Category of Political Participation Research," *Journal of Black Studies* 14(1984): 369–88.

14. Estimates of the percentage of black appointees in the Johnson, Nixon and Carter administrations are from Smith, "Black Appointed Officials." Estimates of the Reagan and Bush percentages are from the Associated Press. See Tim Bovee, "Most Early Appointees White, Mid-age Males," *West County Times,* March 8, 1993.

15. In the first years of his administration President Clinton appointed blacks to about one third of the cabinet posts and to about 13 percent of his overall appointments. At a comparable point in the Carter administration blacks constituted less than 5 percent of his appointees. This suggests that by its end the Clinton administration may meet or exceed the 20 percent patronage threshold.

16. Since 1972 black delegate representation has averaged about 3 percent at the Republican Conventions and blacks have constituted less than 5 percent of the Republican vote in national elections. See Pearl Robinson, "Whither the Future of Blacks in the Republican Party," *Political Science Quarterly* 97(1982): 207–32.

17. See Byron Shafer, *Quiet Revolution: The Struggle for the Democratic Party and the Shaping of Reform* (New York: Russell Sage, 1983).

18. On the negotiations leading up to the adoption of the Charter language on affirmative action see Ronald Walters, *Black Presidential Politics*, pp. 53–64.

19. Ibid, p. 67.

20. The *Ebony* list is not based on scientific criteria of identification and selection and therefore it is only a crude, suggestive indicator of changes in leadership composition.

21. The *Ebony* lists from 1963 to 1980 are analyzed in detail in Robert C. Smith, "Leadership in Negro and Black: Retrospect and Prospect," *Urban League Review* 9(1985): 8–19, and Robert C. Smith, *Black Leadership: A Survey of Theory and Research* (Washington: Howard University, Institute for Urban Affairs, 1983): chap. 3. See also Charles Henry, "Ebony's Elite: America's Most Influential

Blacks," *Phylon* 42(1981): 120–32, and Clarence Lusanne, *African American Leadership At the Crossroads* (Boston: South End Press, 1994): 23–25.

22. Nathan Huggins, "Afro-Americans," in J. Higham (ed.), *Ethnic Leadership in America* (Baltimore: John Hopkins, 1978): 92. The other major change in the *Ebony* list during this near-thirty-year period is the dramatic increase in the leadership of fraternal groups, from 1 percent in 1963 to 20 percent in 1990. Since these organizations existed in the earlier period it is difficult to explain the increase in their influence as judged by *Ebony's* editors. It might be because these organizations have become larger and more socially active or it might represent some bias in the selection process.

23. The disaffection of young inner-city blacks from traditional black leadership including Jesse Jackson, black mayors and celebrity "leaders" such as Magic Johnson and Bill Cosby has been documented in a couple of studies. See Carl Taylor, *Dangerous Society* (East Lansing: Michigan State University Press, 1990), and Kathy Cohen and Michael Dawson, "Neighborhood Poverty and African American Politics," *American Political Science Review* 87(1993): 298–99.

24. John Saloma describes the network of conservative individuals and institutions and the strategies they employed to create and nurture this new conservative black intelligentsia. See his *Ominous Politics: The New Conservative Labyrinth* (New York: Hill & Wang, 1984): 130–37.

25. Quoted in Fred Barnes, "Invent A Negro Inc.," *New Republic*, April 15, 1985, p. 9.

26. Ibid.

27. In 1981 Woodson founded an organization called the National Center for Neighborhood Enterprise, which is described as a nonprofit, nonpartisan, research and demonstration organization devoted to the empowerment of low income Americans through the philosophy of self-help and market-oriented approaches. More than 90 percent of its budget of more than two million dollars is derived from foundation and corporation donations. See *Programs and Activities: The National Center for Neighborhood Enterprise* (Washington: National Center for Neighborhood Enterprise, 1993). See also Woodson's "Leading From Our Strengths," *Urban League Review* 9(1985): 46–54. Reportedly, Woodson's organization was asked to organize a task force to advise House Speaker Newt Gingrich on welfare reform and other poverty related issues. See Serge Kovaleski, "Some Gingrich Statements are Full of 'Misinformation,'" *West County Times*, March 2, 1995.

28. Thomas' marriage to a white woman although rarely discussed in the public press was frequently mentioned by blacks, especially women, as a further basis to oppose his confirmation. My 95 year old mother for example supported Thomas throughout but her support begin to waver when she discovered at the swearing-in that his wife was white.

29. A. Parsons, "Thomas Nomination Divides the Black Community," *West County Times,* July 28, 1991.

30. A. Clymer, "Most Americans Undecided on Court Nomination, Poll Finds," *New York Times,* September 10, 1991.

31. It is legitimate to raise questions about Thomas' integrity in this regard, since, as someone quipped during the hearings, Thomas "may have taken the right turn to the top when he saw the left lane was crowded." That is, Thomas may have reasoned that given the relatively smaller number of black conservatives compared to the larger number of liberal blacks he could more likely rapidly advance his career by becoming a conservative Republican, ideological principles notwithstanding. This point about Thomas' evolution from moderate to radical right wing ideologue is traced in Timothy Phelps and Helen Winternitz, *Capitol Games:Clarence Thomas, Anita Hill and the Story of a Supreme Court Nomination,* (New York: Hyperion, 1992): 94–124.

32. Thomas is not alone in playing this double game of using and not using race. For example, when Bush nominated William Lucas, a marginally qualified individual, to be the assistant attorney general in charge of civil rights, Senator Dennis DeConcini explained his support for Lucas, notwithstanding his minimal qualifications and hostility to the traditional civil rights agenda, by saying, "He is a product of what the civil rights movement is all about, a black individual who has literally come from the kind of background that none of us [the all-white Senate Judiciary Committee] can ever appreciate. I find it really sad to see this man picked apart by those who have fought so hard to see that people like Bill Lucas have a fair chance to prove themselves and continue to advance." DeConcini's view nicely illustrates the dilemma, as in his view any black, qualifications and philosophy aside, who has overcome racism and poverty merits appointment. This literally means almost any black professional since all have had to overcome one or both of these barriers. DeConcini is quoted in "Six Members of Senate Panel Explain Their Vote on Lucas," *New York Times,* August 2, 1989. The Judiciary Committee on a tie vote rejected Lucas' nomination.

Chapter 5

1. The analysis in this chapter is based on several sources. First, during 1973–74 I conducted personal interviews with twenty of the approximately thirty or so black appointees of the Nixon-Ford administrations. During the Carter administration I administered a mail questionnaire during the summer of 1978 to all black appointees in the administration. Of thirty-two such persons, twenty (63 percent) responded. In addition, I rely on press reports and, for the Carter and Reagan administrations, a systematic analysis of more than one hundred books written by journalists, academics and former officials in the

administrations. These volumes were reviewed and cross-checked with each other and other sources for information on decision making on race-related issues and the roles of black appointees. These sources are not definitive and in no way substitute for needed research by historians in the presidential and agency and departmental archives. Nevertheless, taken as a whole they do provide the first empirical data on the role of blacks in executive branch decision making during the last twenty-five years.

2. On the Taft black cabinet see Louis Harlan, *Booker T. Washington: The Wizard of Tuskegee* (New York: Oxford University Press, 1982): 351–54, and on the Roosevelt group see Nancy Weiss, *Farewell to the Party of Lincoln: Black Politics in the Age of FDR* (Princeton: Princeton University Press, 1982): chap. 7.

3. Hobart Taylor, a staff assistant to Vice President Johnson while he chaired President Kennedy's Committee on Equal Employment Opportunity and Clifford Alexander, a staff assistant to Johnson in the White House and Samuel Jackson, a Johnson appointee to the EEOC played roles in the shaping of early government policy on affirmative action. Taylor in fact claims credit for inserting the phrase affirmative action in President Kennedy's 1961 Executive Order 10925, which required nondiscrimination and affirmative action in employment by government contractors. Jackson was instrumental at the EEOC in the late 1960s in the Commission's decision to start collecting statistics on employment by race and its adoption of an effects test to determine employment discrimination, a test that went beyond the narrow strictures of Title VII of the 1964 Civil Rights Act. On the roles played by Taylor, Alexander, and Jackson see Hugh Davis Graham, *The Civil Rights Era: Origins and Development of National Policy* (New York: Oxford University Press, 1990): 33, 238, 249. The roles of these low-level staff aides to the president in influencing administration decision making on this seminal post–civil rights policy stands in sharp contrast to the inconsequential, near invisible role of E. Fredric Murrow, Eisenhower's lone White House aide. See Murrow's memoirs, *Black Man in the White House* (New York: Coward-McCann, 1963), Charles Hamilton, *Adam Clayton Powell: The Political Biography of an American Dilemma* (New York: Atheneum, 1991): 261–63, 286, and Milton Katz, "E. Fredric Murrow and Civil Rights in the Eisenhower Administration," *Phylon* 62(1980): 133–44.

4. Although he conspicuously did not appoint a black to his cabinet, in the nationally televised presentation of his cabinet Nixon, consistent with his style, conspicuously trotted out Walter Washington, announcing his reappointment as District of Columbia Mayor, alongside his cabinet. Thus, the nation was not left with the symbolism of an all-white government.

5. On the origins and organizational properties of the Council of Black Appointees see Robert C. Smith, "The Political Behavior of Black Presidential Appointees: 1960–80," *Western Journal of Black Studies* 8(1984): 139–47.

6. Unless otherwise noted all direct quotes are from personal interviews or the mail questionnaires.

7. Paul Delaney, "Nixon Seeking to Placate Black Aides Ready to Quit," *New York Times*, January 4, 1971.

8. The origins and development of the Philadelphia Plan are detailed in Graham, *The Civil Rights Era*, and in J. Larry Hood, "The Nixon Administration and the Revised Philadelphia Plan: A Study in Expanding Presidential Power and Divided Government," *Presidential Studies Quarterly* 23(1993): 145–67.

9. Executive Order 11246 was issued by President Johnson as part of his implementation of the Civil Rights Act of 1964. Under the order as a prerequisite for the award of a government contract, recipients were required to take "affirmative action" to assure nondiscrimination in employment.

10. Graham, *The Civil Rights Era*, p. 285.

11. George Meany, the President of the AFL-CIO, described the Nixon administration's revived Philadelphia Plan as a "concoction and contrivance of some bureaucrat's imagination to offset criticism of the administration's civil rights record." Although his biographer Denton Watson reports that Clarence Mitchell "remained neutral" during the battle over the plan but after its adoption became one of its strongest supporters, he was quoted during the debate as calling the plan a "calculated attempt coming right from the President's desk to break up the coalition between Negroes and labor unions. Most of the progress in this country has come from this alliance." Meany and Mitchell are quoted in *Civil Rights Progress Report* (Washington, Congressional Quarterly Press, 1971): 57–58, and see Watson's *Lion in the Lobby* (New York: William Morrow, 1991): 730. On Mitchell's initial skeptical attitude toward affirmative action see also Hood, "The Nixon Administration and the Revised Philadelphia Plan," p.148 and Graham, *The Civil Rights Era*, p. 199.

12. Graham, *The Civil Rights Era*, p. 326.

13. Ibid., pp. 326–27.

14. The comptroller general also ruled that the president lacked the authority to promulgate any plan that employed race as a criteria in employment decisions.

15. Arguably this vote on the Philadelphia Plan was one of the most important of the post–civil rights era because it put the Congress on record as to its view of the validity of affirmative action under the 1964 Civil Rights Act. This was critical in providing guidance to the courts in their interpretation not only of the Philadelphia Plan but also subsequent affirmative action programs in education and employment in both the private and public sectors.

16. Ibid., p. 343.

17. Gaddis Smith, *Morality, Reason and Power*, (New York: Hill & Wang, 1986): 134. Betty Glad in *Jimmy Carter: In Search of the Great White House* (New

York: W. W. Norton, 1980): 449, writes that Young could have been a more effective force in influencing African and South African policies if he had not been so controversial.

18. In their memoirs neither Cyrus Vance or Zbigniew Brzezinski attribute a major policy role on African policy making to Young. See Cyrus Vance, *Hard Choices: Critical Years in American Foreign Policy* (New York: Simon & Shuster, 1983), and Zbigniew K. Brzezinski, *Power and Principle: Memoirs of the National Security Advisor, 1977–81* (New York: Farrar, Straus & Giroux, 1982).

19. Glen Abernathy et al., *The Carter Years*, (London: Frances Printers, 1980): 60–61.

20. Ibid.

21. Clark Mollenhoff, *The President Who Failed: Carter Out of Control* (New York: MacMillan, 1980): 226.

22. Smith, *Morality, Reason and Power*, p. 135.

23. The several available biographical studies of Young are largely descriptive; however, they also document his strong advocacy on African issues, especially southern Africa, but shed no light on his effectiveness in shaping administration policy. See Lee Clement, *Andrew Young at the United Nations* (Salisbury, NC.: Documentary Publications, 1978), Carl Gardner, *Andrew Young: A Biography* (New York: Drake, 1978) and H.E. Newsum and O. Abegrunin, *United States Foreign Policy Towards Southern Africa: Andrew Young and Beyond* (New York: St. Martin's Press, 1987). Young's own memoir *A Way Out of No Way: The Spiritual Memoir of Andrew Young* (Nashville, Tn.: T. Nelson, 1994) is completely useless in this regard, since he does not discuss his role in Carter administration decision making.

24. Stephen Shull, *The President and Civil Rights Policy*, (Westport, CT: Greenwood Press, 1989): 124.

25. See Shull, *The President and Civil Rights Policy*, Lawrence Lynn, *The President as Policy Maker: Jimmy Carter and Welfare Reform* (Philadelphia: Temple University Press, 1981); Abernathy, *The Carter Years*; Joseph Califano, *Governing America* (New York: Simon & Shuster, 1981); and Harold Wolman and Astrid A.E. Merget, "The President and Policy Formulation: President Carter and Urban Policy," *Presidential Studies Quarterly* 10(1980): 402–15.

26. See Wolman and Merget, "The Presidency and Policy Formulation: President Carter and Urban Policy," p. 404.

27. See Ernest Holsendolph, "Jordan urges Carter to Visit Looted Areas," and "President Rejects Jordan's Criticism," *New York Times*, July 26, 1977.

28. Wolman and Merget, "The Presidency and Policy Formulation: President Carter and Urban Policy," pp. 408–10.

29. Ibid., p. 404.

30. Lynn, *The President as Policy Maker*, p. 197. See also Califano, *Governing America*, p. 331.

31. Califano, *Governing America*, p. 331.

32. There is evidence that Title VII housing discrimination complaints were processed more effectively by HUD under Harris' leadership than under the tenure of her predecessors in the Nixon and Ford administrations and her successor in the Reagan administration. See Charles Lamb, "Fair Housing Implementation: From Nixon to Reagan." Paper presented at the 1991 meeting of the American Political Science Association, San Francisco, p. 12, and Hanes Walton, Jr., *When the Marching Stopped* (Albany: SUNY Press, 1988), chap. 4.

33. My account of the case is drawn from press accounts and Alan Sindler, *Bakke, Defunis and Minority Admissions: The Quest for Equal Opportunity* (New York: Longman, 1978); Joel Dreyfuss and Charles Lawrence, *The Bakke Case: The Politics of Inequality* (New York: Longman, 1979); Bernard Schwarz, *Behind Bakke: Affirmative Action and the Supreme Court* (New York: New York University Press, 1988); and Califano, *Governing America*, pp. 236–41.

34. Eleanor Holmes Norton, "The Role of Black Appointees," *Urban League Review* 9(1985): 109.

35. On the initial and revised briefs see John Osborne, "Carter's Brief," *New Republic*, October 15, 1977, pp. 6–9, and James Signer, "A Brief in Detail," *National Journal*, October 1, 1977.

36. Matthew Holden, an official in the administration, writes, "There was a variety of meetings, some by black government executives, to discuss the implications of the decision, and to urge the White House to take a vigorous posture in defense of *Bakke* principles, and to make clear that there would be no backing off the affirmative action course. People wanted the president personally to take such a position and wanted Ambassador Young to go to the President to urge such a course. Young refused. 'The president appointed you' he said to the assembled group, 'that's your department.'" See his "The President, Congress and Race Relations," Ernest Patterson Lecture, University of Colorado, Boulder, October 11, 1984, p. 39.

37. Sources differ as to how the final draft was prepared. Sindler, Dreyfuss and Lawrence suggest it was personally rewritten by McCree while Schwarz argues it was actually rewritten in the White House.

38. *New York Times*, February 17, 1977.

39. Dreyfuss and Lawrence, *The Bakke Case*, p. 190.

40. Sindler, *Bakke, Defunis and Minority Admissions*, p. 171. Sindler suggests that McCree's concerns about affirmative action reflected less the per-

ceived institutional constraints of his role but more the fears among some blacks that affirmative action would cheapen the achievements of minorities such as himself. Califano suggests that McCree might have been unduly influenced by two young white holdover aides from the Nixon administration. At a meeting with McCree to urge that he rewrite the brief, Califano writes that McCree's young aides "did not disguise their distaste for affirmative action" and that McCree "seemed to acquiesce in the argument of his aides. My God, I thought, he's bending over backward. I remembered what Lyndon Johnson said when he put the first black, Andrew Brimmer—who like McCree, was Harvard-educated—on the Federal Reserve Board: 'I want to be Goddamn sure he hasn't forgotten what it's like to be black.' . . . I was afraid that McCree was carrying so much personal freight on this issue that he could not decide objectively." See *Governing America*, p. 237.

41. In his exhaustive study of Paul Volcker's tenure as Federal Reserve Board Chair, William Greider makes reference to Carter administration appointee Emmett Rice's support of Volcker's high interest rate policy in order to lower inflation by generating a massive recession. This policy, which resulted in 1981–83 in the worst recession since the depression, was consistently supported by Rice although blacks were predictably among its principal victims. In board deliberations only Nancy Teeters—its only female member—consistently opposed Volcker's policies as too harsh, and she was accused by her colleagues of being too soft, of bringing a "feminist perspective" to the decision making process. Rice did not bring a similar "black perspective" to the process. (It is worth noting here that Federal Reserve Board governors do not serve at the president's pleasure but rather have fourteen-year fixed terms). See Greider, *Secrets of the Temple: How the Federal Reserve Runs the Country* (New York: Simon & Shuster, 1987): 406.

42. Robert Thompson, "The Commission on Civil Rights," in T. Yarbourgh (ed.), *The Reagan Years* (New York: Praeger, 1985): 188. Pendelton consistently argued that affirmative action programs that required "goals and timetables" could not be distinguished from quotas and that such programs should be abolished because they operated to discriminate against white men.

43. Ibid.

44. Ibid.

45. Ronnie Dugger, *On Reagan: The Man and His Presidency* (New York: McGraw-Hill, 1983): 217–18.

46. See Edwin Meese, "A New Beginning," in *The Fairmount Papers: Black Alternatives Conference* (San Francisco: Institute for Contemporary Studies, 1981): 159.

47. See Herbert Denton, "White House Names Black Aides in Move to Improve Ties," *Washington Post*, April 20, 1982, and Lawrence Barrett, *Gam-*

bling With History: Ronald Reagan in the White House, (New York: Doubleday, 1983): 428.

48. Rowland Evans and Robert Novak, *The Reagan Revolution* (New York: E.P. Dutton, 1981): 134.

49. Samuel Pierce, "The Republican Alternative," in J. Elliot (ed.), *Black Voices in American Politics* (New York: Harcourt Brace Jovanovich, 1986): 120.

50. Evans and Novak, *The Reagan Revolution*, p. 134. David Stockman in his memoirs makes a similar observation about Pierce's defense of HUD programs. See *The Triumph of Politics* (New York: Harper & Row, 1986): 142.

51. Dugger, *On Reagan*, p. 127.

52. Ronald Brownstein, *Reagan's Ruling Class* (New York: Pantheon, 1983): 120..

53. Stockman, *The Triumph of Politics*, p. 142. Pierce discusses his conflicts with Stockman and the president over the HUD budget in "The Republican Alternative," pp. 126–27.

54. See Bill McAllister, "HUD's Stealth Secretary," *Washington Post*, January 24, 1987, Joseph McCormick, "In Search of Low Income Housing," *Urban League Review* 8(1984): 44–56, and Charles Moore and Patricia Hoban-Moore, "Some Lessons from Reagan's HUD: Housing Policy and Public Service," *PS* 23(1990): 13–18.

55. Irvin Mololsky, "Reagan's Housing Chief Says Never Mind to Critics," *New York Times*, January 20, 1989.

56. Pierce, "The Republican Alternative."

57. Ibid., pp. 126–27.

58. Lamb, "Fair Housing Implementation," p. 6.

59. See James Kushner, "The Fair Housing Act of 1988: The Second Generation of Fair Housing," *Vanderbilt Law Review* 42(1989): 1049–1120.

60. Lamb, "Fair Housing Implementation," p. 5. Lamb notes that while the enforcement provisions of the fair housing law were strengthened by the Reagan administration, the implementation record at HUD under Pierce's tenure was the least effective of any administration since 1968 (see p. 12).

61. Pierce, "The Republican Alternative," p. 123.

62. When information was leaked that the administration was considering repealing all forms of gender or race preferences within its discretion, seventy senators and 240 representatives began drafting legislation that would have codified the provisions of the executive order.

63. Howard Kurz, "Affirmative Action Policy Gains a Reprieve," *Washington Post*, October 25, 1985.

64. Barrett, *Gambling With History*, p. 418.

65. Ibid., p. 419. On the Bob Jones controversy and decision-making process see also Lou Cannon, *President Reagan: The Role of a Lifetime* (New York: G. P. Putnam, 1982): 520–25.

66. Ibid., p. 415. Both Cannon and Barrett agree that Reagan made the decision on the basis of a memo from then Mississippi Congressman Trent Lott, which said, "regarding pending cases concerning the tax exempt status of church schools . . . Supreme Court has now agreed to review the case of 'Bob Jones v. United States.' I urge you to intervene. . . ." Reagan is said to have scribbled on the margins "I think we should" (Ibid., p. 149).

67. Ibid., p. 416.

68. *Bob Jones University v. United States*, 103 Sup.Ct. 2017 (1983).

69. The one exception to this is Bob Woodward's *The Commanders* (New York: Simon & Shuster, 1992), an account of the administration's decision to go to war in the Persian Gulf. This war, opposed by the Congressional Black Caucus and a majority of the black population, according to Woodward's account was also opposed in internal deliberations by General Powell, the Chairman of the Joint Chiefs. Woodward claims that Powell argued for the use of sanctions rather than force to secure Iraqi withdrawal from Kuwait, the alternative preferred by the Democratic Party majority. Powell is also said to have urged a quick end to the war in order to avoid the needless slaughter of Iraqi soldiers.

70. The Fiesta Bowl was prompted to create the minority scholarship program in King's honor in response to widespread protests by blacks and others to holding the game in Arizona because of that state's refusal to legislate a state holiday on King's birthday.

71. M. Dowd, "Cavazos Leaves Education Department Under Pressure," *New York Times*, December 13, 1991.

72. M. Dowd, "President Orders Aides to Review New Minority Scholarship Policy," *New York Times*, December 15, 1990.

73. Ibid.

74. *Hearings*, Committee on Government Operations, Subcommittee on Human Resources and Intergovernmental Relations, House, March 19–20, 1991. Cited in *Focus* 19(1991).

75. Anthony DePalma, "A Two Sided Ruling on Scholarships," *New York Times*, December 7, 1991. This is entirely consistent with Williams's original formulation, as in his letter to the Fiesta Bowl he indicated, "You may wish to

consider changing the Martin Luther King, Jr. fund from a race exclusive program to a program in which race is considered a positive factor among similarly qualified individuals. . . ." See Michael Williams letter to John Booker, Executive Director, Fiesta Bowl, December 4, 1990, p. 2.

76. Four years later the Supreme Court, without comment, let stand a decision by the Fourth Circuit Court of Appeals that a University of Maryland program which set aside scholarship money exclusively for about thirty black students a year violated the equal protection clause of the Fourteenth Amendment. See Steven Holmes "Minority Scholarship Loans Are Dealt Setback by Court," *New York Times*, May 23, 1995.

77. "Stark Calls Sullivan Disgrace to His Race," *West County Times*, August 3, 1990.

78. Twenty percent of blacks are uninsured compared to 12 percent of whites. Dr. George Lundberg, editor of the *Journal of the American Medical Association*, suggests that lack of national health insurance in the United States may itself be an indicator of racism, writing that it was "no coincidence that the United States and South Africa were the only developed countries that lack a national health policy insuring access to basic care to all." Overall, Lundberg concludes that the racial disparity in health between blacks and whites is in large part a product of inequality in access to health care. See his "National Health Care Reform," *Journal of the American Medical Association* 265(1991):2566.

79. "Stark Calls Sullivan Disgrace to His Race." Stark also said Sullivan had reversed his position on abortion at the urging of Bush administration officials before taking his cabinet post.

80. Ibid.

81. Press accounts of administration decision making on national health care policy suggest that Sullivan did not play a major role in the development of the policy he articulated. Rather, the policy was largely made by Richard Darman, the Director of the Office of Management and Budget. See Robert Pear, "Health Issues At Fore, Not Secretary," *New York Times*, October 25, 1991.

82. "Lawmaker Says His Racial Insult of Health Secretary Was Mistake," *New York Times*, October 25, 1991. While Sullivan refused to challenge Darman's dominance in the formation of national health policy, reportedly he did in budget decisions challenge Darman's proposals for huge cuts in medicaid and other programs for the disabled and the poor. See the report on a detailed memorandum he sent to Darman forcefully rejecting his proposed cuts as a threat to health services for the disadvantaged in Robert Pear, "Health Secretary Rejects Demands on Spending Cuts," *New York Times*, December 12, 1990.

83. Robert Pear, "Administration Rejects Proposals for New Anti-Poverty Programs," *New York Times*, July 6, 1990.

84. Ibid.

85. Once again, a definitive assessment of the role of black appointees in executive branch decision making in the last twenty-five years requires detailed inquiry into the archives of the various presidents and the relevant departments and agencies, as well as biographies and memoirs by the major appointees themselves (Robert Weaver, Patricia Harris, Andrew Young, William Coleman, Donald McHenry, Samuel Pierce, etc.). Thus far only Carl Rowan who served in the Johnson administration has written his memoirs and Alex Poinsett is at work on a biography of Louis Martin who held high-level positions in the Johnson and Carter administrations. Rowan's memoir is *Breaking Barriers* (New York: Harper Perennial, 1991).

86. Holden, *The Politics of the Black "Nation"*, p. 206.

Chapter 6

1. See Hanes Walton, Jr., *When the Marching Stopped: The Politics of Civil Rights Regulatory Agencies* (Albany: SUNY Press, 1988), especially chap. 1, "The Institutionalization of the Civil Rights Revolution," and Hugh Davis Graham, *The Civil Rights Era: Origins and Development of National Policy* (New York: Oxford University Press, 1990), especially the concluding chapter. This point is also made from a somewhat different perspective by Robert Detlefsen, *Civil Rights Under Reagan* (San Francisco: Institute for Contemporary Studies, 1991).

2. Graham, *The Civil Rights Era*, pp. 468–70.

3. Charles V. and Dana L. Hamilton, "The Dual Agenda: Social Policies of Civil Rights Organizations, New Deal to the Present," (paper prepared for delivery at the 1991 annual meeting of the American Political Science Association, Washington, D.C.). See also Michael Brown, *Divergent Fates: Race and Class in the Making of the American Welfare State, 1935–85* (forthcoming) and Dana Hamilton, "The National Urban League During the Depression, 1930–39" (Ph.D diss., Columbia University, 1982).

4. Matthew Holden, Jr., "The President, Congress and Race Relations" (Ernest Patterson Memorial Lecture, University of Colorado, Boulder, 1986), p. 69.

5. Ibid., p. 10. This "significant position of blacks in the legislative process" was lost as a result of the 1994 election of Republican congressional majorities, placing in jeopardy the twenty-five year civil rights consensus analyzed in this chapter.

6. In *Grove City College v. Bell*, 465 U.S. 55 (1984) the Supreme Court interpreted Title IX of the 1972 Education Amendments to mean that it prevented discrimination in a particular program or activity at a university receiv-

ing federal grants, requiring cutting off funds to that particular program but not the institution as a whole. In 1988 the Civil Rights Restoration Act reversed this decision of the Court declaring that discrimination in one program or activity required a cutting off of funds to the institution as a whole.

7. For a good collection of papers that provide a summary and overview of the legal and political issues and the research on the effects of school desegregation on the educational attainments of black and white kids see Nicholas Mills (ed.), *The Great School Bus Controversy* (New York: Teachers College Press, 1973).

8. Spencer Rich, "House Acts Against Busing," *Washington Post*, June 28, 1974.

9. Spencer Rich, "Bus Ban Defeated 47 to 46," *Washington Post*, May 16, 1974.

10. Denton Watson, *Lion in the Lobby: Clarence Mitchell and the Struggle for Civil Rights* (New York: William Morrow, 1991).

11. In *Miliken v. Bradley* 418 U.S. 717 (1974) the Court strictly speaking only prohibited cross-district busing as had been ordered by the lower federal courts in the Detroit area and even there left open the possibility of the constitutionality of such cross districting schemes, given a showing of cross district violations. However, the decision was widely and correctly read at that time to mean as the *Washington Post* said editorially that "neither the constitution nor the federal courts are going to be able to compel solutions to problems of racial isolation in our urban school systems." See "The Detroit Ruling," *Washington Post*, July 29, 1974.

12. See Rowland Evans and Robert Novak, "The Busing Compromise that Failed," *Washington Post*, September 24, 1973. Evans and Novak, opponents of busing, may not be the most reliable of sources. However, the essential facts of their account was confirmed at the time in personal interviews with NAACP lobbyists and black members of Congress and staff. Also the National office of the NAACP suspended the president of its Atlanta Chapter for accepting a similar busing compromise in the Atlanta school district. See R. Drummond Ayres, "Atlanta Strikes an Integration Bargain," *New York Times*, April 25, 1973.

13. J. Francis Polhaus, NAACP Washington Bureau, interview.

14. William Raspberry, "Integration: A White Option," *Washington Post*, July 26, 1974.

15. Harold Cruse argues that northern white liberals and black leaders made a similar error in the post Reconstruction era when they opposed the Blair Education bill (which would have spent large federal sums on public education) because it would have provided federal support for segregated schools in the south. See *Plural but Equal* (New York: William Morrow, 1987): 9–24.

16. See David Armor, "The Evidence on Busing," and Thomas Pettigrew et al., "Busing: A Review of the Evidence" in Mills (ed.), *The Great School Bus Controversy.* These articles provide a thorough reading of the research on the effects of school desegregation on the educational performance of black and white children.

17. For a succinct analysis of the history of the Supreme Court and its decisions on race see Eugene Walton, "Will the Supreme Court Revert to Racism?" *Black World* 21 (1972): 46–48.

18. See the discussion of these cases later in this chapter in terms of their reversal by the Civil Rights Act of 1991.

19. While the battle for the Court was eventually lost, it was not an easy or quick victory for the right. Rather, it took more than twenty years, four presidents and thirteen nominees before conservatives could claim a narrow working majority. President Nixon was able to place only one strong ideological conservative -Rehnquist—on the Court, in part because of the opposition of the civil rights liberal-labor coalition. The rejection of Judges Haynsworth and Carswell in the Nixon administration led Nixon and Ford to choose more moderate nominees—Blackmun, Powell and Stevens—who could more easily win confirmation. Reagan came to office with a more determined ideological agenda than Nixon and Ford and was more successful in appointing conservatives— O'Connor, Scalia and Kennedy—and Bush's nomination of Clarence Thomas reinforced this conservative tendency. But as a consequence of the Bork battle, Reagan and Bush were able to do this only by selecting "stealth" candidates; nominees without any clear record on the major legal and constitutional conflicts of the time, especially civil rights. This was because the defeat of Judge Bork made it clear that a nominee with a clear record of opposition to civil rights, broadly construed, or to affirmative action specifically could not win approval of the Senate. On the significance of the Bork nomination see Ethan Bronner, *Battle for Justice: How the Bork Nomination Shook America* (New York: W.W. Norton, 1983), Patrick McGuigan and David Weyrich, *Ninth Justice: The Fight for Bork* (Lanham, MD.: University Press of America, 1990), and Bork's *The Tempting of America: The Seduction of American Law* (New York: New York University Press, 1989).

20. This point about the limited ability of the courts in fostering social change or liberal reform is made persuasively by Gerald Ronsenberg in *The Hollow Hope: Can Courts Bring About Social Change?* (Chicago: University of Chicago Press, 1991). See especially his detailed analysis of the limited role the courts played in school desegregation. See also Girardeau A. Spann, *Race Against the Court: The Supreme Court and Minorities in Contemporary America* (New York: New York University Press, 1993).

21. Justice Marshall made these remarks in his annual address to First Circuit Appeals Court Judges. See Linda Greenhouse, "Marshall Says Court's

Rulings Imperil Rights," *New York Times*, September 9, 1989. This point is also made by Spann in *Race Against the Court* where he writes, "Racial minorities have now accumulated sufficient power to participate meaningfully in the political process, and historically, minority interests have fared better before the representative branches of the government than before the Supreme Court" (p. 3). Spann, perhaps, overstates the degree of minority influence in the political process but in any event he notes that the "inevitability of Supreme Court review" renders even meaningful gains in ordinary politics vulnerable.

22. In its previous term the Court had significantly narrowed affirmative action in the area of minority contract set asides. See *City of Richmond v. J.A. Carson* 488 U.S. 469 (1989).

23. Data on the Reagan and Bush approval ratings are from Gallup surveys reported in *The Ladd Report*, (New York: W.W. Norton, 1991): 13.

24. Steven Holmes, "Lawmakers Seek a Rights Compromise," *New York Times*, May 18, 1990.

25. See Edward Carmines and James Stimson, *Issue Evolution: Race and the Transformation of American Politics* (Princeton: Princeton University Press, 1989), chap. 3.

26. Ibid., p. 72.

27. The Leadership Conference on Civil Rights rates members of Congress on support for civil rights, with 100 indicating complete support. In 1989 the Conference scored northern Democrats at 90, southern Democrats at 73, northern Republicans at 43 and southern Republicans at 13. See "A Civil Rights Record for the 100th Congress" (Washington, 1989). See also Cheryl Miller and Hanes Walton, Jr., "Congressional Support of Civil Rights Policy: From Bipartisan to Partisan Convergence," *Congress & Presidency* 21(1974): 11–27.

28. Although only eleven Republicans voted to override Bush's veto, perhaps at least a half dozen or more supported the bill but voted to sustain the veto in loyalty to the president. Thus, the number of Republican racial liberals may be in the range of 17 to 20.

29. Adam Clymer, "Public Left Out in Rights Bill Debate," *New York Times*, May 29, 1991.

30. See *The Ladd Report* (p. 13) for Gallup poll data for late 1990 through July 1991.

31. See Joan Biskupic, "New Struggle Over Civil Rights Brings Shift in Strategy," *Congressional Quarterly Weekly Report*, February 9, 1991, p. 368. See also on this point Judy Mann, "Women as Beneficiaries," *Washington Post*, May 22, 1991.

The *New York Times* poll indicated that the public in general did not think additional laws to protect against job discrimination were needed for either blacks or women. But more said that women needed additional protection than said blacks, 41 percent and 36 percent respectively. see Clymer, "Public Left Out of Rights Debate."

32. Steven Holmes, "Affirmative Action Plans Are Now Part of the Normal Corporate Way of Life," *New York Times*, November 22, 1991.

33. Steven Holmes, "Talks on Rights Split Business," *New York Times*, April 19, 1991.

34. See "Major Differences on Civil Rights" for a line by line comparison of the major provisions of the three bills in the *New York Times*, June 5, 1991.

35. The definition of quota in the bill was adapted from Justice O'Connor's opinion in *Sheet Metal Workers International Association et al. v. EEOC, City of New York and New York Department of Human Services*, 478 U.S. 421 (1986). She defined it as a "fixed number or percentage of persons of a particular race, color, religion, sex or national origin which must be attained, or which can not be exceeded, regardless of whether such persons meet the necessary qualifications to perform the job."

36. This one-vote margin was nearly missed as Congressman Craig Washington, a black Democrat from Texas, who had supported the Caucus bill, initially voted no on the Democratic bill to protest its limits on damages for women. The women members of Congress prevailed on him to change his vote so as to provide the one-vote margin over 1990. See Gwen Ifill, "Goal Eludes Democrats As 9 in GOP Switch," *New York Times*, June 6, 1991.

37. Ibid.

38. The administration bill was defeated 266 to 162 and the Caucus bill by a margin of 277 to 152. See the *Congressional Record, House*, June 4–5, 1991.

39. These included districts in Mississippi, Louisiana and Georgia.

40. Hispanic Congresswoman Ros Lehtinen of Florida, a Republican, voted for the bill. Her district in Miami is majority Hispanic.

41. Adam Clymer, "President Rejects Senate Agreement on Rights Measure," *New York Times*, August 2, 1991.

42. Ibid.

43. Adam Clymer, "Dole, Bush's Point Man in the Senate, is Considering Life Behind the Lines," *New York Times*, December 12, 1991.

44. See the *New York Times*, "The Compromise on Civil Rights," December 12, 1991 for comparison of the major provisions of the compromise agreement with the original Danforth position on the key issues in disagreement, which shows that on all of them the president basically accepted the position of the

senator. See also Charles Dale, *The Civil Rights Act of 1991: A Legal Analysis of Various Proposals to Reform the Federal Equal Employment Opportunity Laws* (Washington: Congressional Research Service, 1991).

45. *New York Times*, "The Compromise On Civil Rights.

46. Ibid.

47. Ibid.

48. Ibid.

49. David Lauter, "White House Would Kill Anti Bias Rules," *West County Times*, November 21, 1991.

50. Adam Clymer, "Reaffirming Commitment, Bush Signs Civil Rights Bill," *New York Times*, November 22, 1991.

51. See the *Congressional Record, Senate* November 22, 23, 1991, and "Thumbing Nose at Congress: Mr. Bush Signs—and Undermines—the Rights Bill," *New York Times*, November 22, 1991.

52. In the 1992–93 term the Court's five-person majority continued to undermine long-established civil rights principles and precedents. In Chapter 6 I discussed *Shaw v. Reno*, a case which Justice White said in his dissent the majority "choose not to overrule, but rather to sidestep" its 1977 precedent in *United Jewish Organizations of Williamsburg v. Carey*. Similarly in a Title VII case the Court, in a ruling much like the *Wards Cove* case of 1989, repudiated a twenty-year precedent. In *St. Mary's Honor et al. v. Hicks*, 92–602 (1983 slip opinion). Justice Souter in dissent wrote "I cannot join the majority in turning our back on these earlier decisions. 'Considerations of stare decisis have special force in the area of statutory interpretation, for here unlike in the context of constitutional interpretation, the legislative power is implicated, and Congress remains free to alter what we have done.' It is not as though Congress is unaware of our decisions concerning Title VII and recent experience [referring to the Civil Rights Act of 1991] indicates that Congress is ready to act if we adopt interpretations of this statutory scheme it finds to be mistaken."

53. Again, the election in 1994 of Republican majorities in both Houses of Congress, but especially the House of Representatives threatens to substantially diminish this twenty-five-year consensus and coalition. This is especially the case in the House because a substantial number of the Republicans elected in 1994 are from the south, and southern Republicans have been least supportive of civil rights during the last twenty-five years (see note 32 in this chapter).

54. See Thomas Sowell, *Civil Rights: Rhetoric and Reality* (New York: William Morrow, 1984) for a cogent statement of this view.

55. See Frank Parker, *Black Votes Count* (Chapel Hill: University of North Carolina Press, 1990), Robert C. Smith, "Liberal Jurisprudence and the Quest for

Racial Representation," *Southern University Law Review* 15(1988): 1–51, and Bernard Grofman, "Identifying and Remedying Racial Gerrymandering," *The Journal of Law & Politics* 8(1992): 345–404.

56. Steven Holmes, "Lawyers Expect Ambiguities in New Rights Laws to Bring Years of Lawsuits," *New York Times*, December 12, 1991.

57. Steven Holmes, "States May No Longer Raise Minority Scores on Job Tests," *New York Times*, December 14, 1991.

58. Recent studies show that employment discrimination is still widespread. See M. Turner, M. Fix and R. Struyk, *Opportunities Denied, Opportunities Diminished: Discrimination in Hiring* (Washington: Urban Institute, 1991), J. Kirsherman and K. Neckerman, "We'd Love to Hire Them But . . . : The Meaning of Race for Employers," in C. Jencks (ed.), *The Urban Underclass* (Washington: Brookings Institution, 1992), and more generally Robert C. Smith, *Racism in the Post–civil Rights Era: Now You See It, Now You Don't* (Albany: SUNY Press, 1995): chap. 4.

59. A study by the *New York Times* of black employment in the construction trades in Philadelphia twenty-five years after the adoption of the Philadelphia Plan found very little long-term progress in the employment of blacks. The *Times'* study in fact described affirmative action in the City's construction industry as "something of a hollow victory." See Louis Uchitelle, "Union Goals of Equality Fail," *New York Times*, July 9, 1995.

60. Paul Burstein, *Discrimination, Jobs and Politics* (Chicago: University of Chicago Press, 1985): chap. 6, and Jonathan Leonard, "Employment and Occupational Advance Under Affirmative Action," *Review of Economic and Statistics* 66(1984): 377–85.

61. The extensive econometrics literature on affirmative actions clearly show that its effects on the employment and earnings of blacks has been modest, frequently so modest as to be barely measurable. For a recent review see L. Badgett and H. Hartmann, "The Effectiveness of Equal Employment Opportunity Policies" in M. Sims (ed.), *Economic Perspectives On Affirmative Action* (Lanham, M.D: University Press of America, 1995).

62. On the use of quotas as a means to accomplish affirmative action objectives see *Sheetmetal Workers et al. v. E.E.O.C. . . .* and *United States v. Paradise*, 480 U.S. 92(1987).

63. This approach toward affirmative action would have to be used with caution, however, since as Justice Brennan wrote in the *Bakke* case "with respect to any factor (such as poverty or family educational background) that may be used as a substitute for race or as an indicator of past discrimination, whites outnumber racial minorities simply because whites make up a far larger percentage of the total population and therefore outnumber minorities in absolute terms at every socioeconomic level." For example, while about a third of the black pop-

ulation is poor compared to less than 10 percent of whites there are more than twice as many poor whites as poor blacks—twenty-two million compared to about nine million. See U.S. Bureau of the Census, *Current Population Reports, Money, Income and Poverty Status of Families and Persons in the United States,* Series P-60 #57(1987): 5–6.

64. My experience serving as a reviewer for the National Science Foundation's Minority Doctoral Fellowship Program suggests to me that minority students selected under this program should have been competitive in the NSF's general doctoral fellowship program, which is open to all students without regard to race or ethnicity. Assuming, that is, that the general program is equitably administered. I should note that in the Minority Doctoral Program, once a qualified pool of applicants is selected an effort is made to achieve a gender, regional and ethnic balance in the choice of persons who will receive awards. Similar considerations of course could be used in the general program.

65. As with busing, I had anticipated that the Supreme Court would eventually terminate affirmative action on constitutional grounds. While in *Adarand Constructors v. Pena* 93-1841 (1995, slip opinion) the Court did substantially narrow the range and scope of federal affirmative action programs, as a result of the 1994 election it now appears more likely that the Congress will seek to enact a stature banning affirmative action, at least in several of its forms.

Chapter 7

1. Ralph Bunche, "The Programs of Organizations Devoted to the Improvement of the Negro," *Journal of Negro Education* 8(1939): 542–43. Bunche developed this point more extensively in his "Critique of New Deal Planning As It Affects the Negro," *Journal of Negro Education* 5(1936): 59–65. On the role of race and class in the making of New Deal social welfare policies see Michael Brown, *Divergent Fates: Race and Class in the Making of the American Welfare State, 1935–85.*

2. Hugh Davis Graham, *The Civil Rights Era: Origins and Development of National Policy, 1960–72* (New York: Oxford University Press, 1990): 101.

3. Ibid.

4. See Whitney Young's *To be Equal* (New York: McGraw-Hill, 1964) for an outline of the League's five billion dollar, multi-year ten point "Marshall Plan."

5. David Garrow, *Bearing the Cross,* (New York: William Morrow, 1986).

6. Ibid. King's clearest statement of the democratic socialist implication of his evolving stance is in his last SCLC presidential address, "Where Do We

Go From Here?" in James Washington (ed.), *A Testament of Hope: The Essential Writings of Martin Luther King, Jr.* (San Francisco: Harper San Francisco, 1986): 256.

7. As of now there is not available a full-scale study of the poor peoples campaign.

8. There was some discussion in the last year of the Johnson administration about fundamental reform in the welfare system, including some kind of guaranteed income. See Daniel Moynihan, *The Politics of A Guaranteed Income* (New York: Vintage Books, 1973): 580.

9. Lyndon Johnson had lost his consensus and capacity to govern as a result of the Vietnam War and the black rebellion in the cities and had withdrawn from the presidential race, and the Congress was increasingly hostile to black demands and was more interested in passing federal antiriot legislation. For example, the Fair Housing Act was stalled in Congress with little prospect for passage. Indeed, it was in part the guilt generated by King's murder that resulted in final passage of the bill as a kind of memorial to him.

10. Bayard Rustin, "From Protest to Politics: The Future of the Civil Rights Movement," *Commentary* 39(1965): 28–29.

11. History repeats itself. This familiar observation might be used to charcterize the full employment legislative process of the 1970s, since in many ways the process of the 1970s closely parallels what happened in 1946 when the first full employment bill was enacted. On the 1946 Act see Stephen Bailey's classic study, *Congress Makes the Law: The Story Behind the Employment Act of 1946* (New York: Vintage Books, 1950). See also G. William Domhoff, *The Power Elite and the State: How Policy is Made in America*, (Hawthorne, New York: Aldine de Gruyter, 1990): chap. 7.

12. See C. Hunter-Gault, "Black Leaders Agree Full Employment is Overriding Issue of the 1970s," *New York Times*, August 31, 1977. Even black nationalists and radical leaders supported the idea of full employment. Their view, however, was that full employment was not possible in a capitalist, racist economy; a view they shared with a broad spectrum of white liberal and conservative economists.

13. In addition to my own interviews and reading of the record I rely on Essie Seck's dissertation, "Political Decision Making on Full Employment Policy: Implications for Social Work Intervention," University of Southern California, 1981. Although situated in the social work literature, this massive, thoroughly researched study includes material on the mobilization processes and legislative struggle.

14. The proceedings of the UCLA conference were edited by Paul Bullock in *A Full Employment Policy for America* (Los Angeles: University of California, Institute of Industrial Relations, 1973).

15. See the *Congressional Record, House,* June 6, 1974 for a summary and explanation of the original bill. In August of 1974 Senator Humphrey introduced the bill in the Senate. It is not clear when Humphrey became involved with the legislation or whether he participated in writing the initial bill. He did, however, testify at the first series of hearings held by Hawkins on the bill where he described it as a "job guarantee bill" and talked of a job as a basic or fundamental right. See *Hearings HR 15476,* Subcommittee on Employment Opportunities, Committee on Education and Labor, 93rd Congress, 2nd session, October 8, 1974, p. 24.

16. Bailey, *Congress Makes A Law,* p.47.

17. The "lib-lab" lobby organized itself formally as the Continuation Group and engaged in traditional lobbying activities including letters and visits to members of Congress, public education campaigns (publications and newsletters), testimony before congressional committees and negotiations on the various revisions of the bill. There was also an effort to stimulate local activity in support of the bill. Among the groups included in the coalition were the AFL, the CIO, church, religious and civil rights groups and the National Farmers Union, which authored the original proposal and was one of the few organizations that actively worked for a bill from the outset. The black community was represented in the Coalition by the NAACP. William Haste representing the Association said "The Negro has the most to lose if the objectives [of the bill] are not achieved. The fact must be brought home to minority groups that they will never be able to make progress unless there are adequate jobs for the people." Quoted in Bailey, *Congress Makes A Law,* p. 87. The NAACP considered asking that a nondiscrimination in hiring provision be included in the bill but elected not to pursue the matter because white liberals in the coalition argued this would endanger the entire bill. See Charles and Dana Hamilton, "The Dual Agenda: Social Policies of Civil Rights Organizations, New Deal to the Present," (paper presented at the 1991 Annual Meeting of the American Political Science Association, Washington), p. 10.

18. Seck, "Political Decision Making on Full Employment," p. 400.

19. After the right to sue was eliminated the AFL-CIO announced the bill was its number one legislative priority. See its statement of March 12, 1976 cited in Ibid., p. 440.

20. See Augustus Hawkins, "Planning for Personal Choice: The Equal Opportunity and Full Employment Act" and Hubert Humphrey, "Guaranteed Jobs for Human Rights", *The Annals of the American Academy of Political and Social Science* 418(1975): 13–16, 17–25.

21. M. Hyer, "Jesse Jackson Sees Protests for Jobs, Housing," *Washington Post,* January 7, 1975, and M. O'Neil, "600 Ministers Back March to D.C. Over Jobless Rate," *Washington Afro-American,* December 10, 1974. See also "A Leadership Role for Black Ministers," *Ebony,* April 1975, pp. 66–70.

22. Seck, Political Decision Making on Full Employment," p. 445–46.

23. See the *Hearings*, Subcommittee on Employment Opportunities, Committee on Education & Labor, House, January 18–19, 1978, and *Hearings*, Committee on Banking, Housing and Urban Affairs, May 8–10, 1978 for a good representation of business attitudes toward the revised bill. I should note that leading black business organizations—the National Association of Black Manufacturers and the National Association of Minority Contractors testified in support of the bill. See the *Hearings*, Equal Opportunities Subcommittee, Committee on Education and Labor, House, June 22, 1978.

24. Ralph Miliband, *The State in Capitalist Society* (New York: Basic Books, 1969): 147, 50.

25. See *Congressional Record House*, March 8–16, 1978, pp. 6122.

26. Seck, "Political Decision Making on Full Employment," p. 390. Seck writes that the bill "was all the rage in Washington and appeared ready to waltz through the Democratic controlled Congress to force a politically embarrassing veto by President Ford. Then the respected Shultz attacked the bill." On this point about Shultz's role see the remarks by Senator Eagleton during the Senate debate. See the *Congressional Record, Senate*, October 13, 1978, p. 36786.

27. Committee On Labor and Public Welfare, Subcommittee on Employment, Poverty and Migratory Labor, Senate, *Hearings on S.50 and S.472* May 14, 17, 18, 19, 1976, p. 141.

28. Charles McCamey, "The 1976 Primaries: The Black Vote," *Focus*, 4(1976): 4.

29. For a discussion of the origins and outcome of the "ethnic purity" flap see Jules Witcover, *Marathon: The Pursuit of the Presidency, 1972–76* (New York: Viking Press, 1977): 302–08.

30. Ibid.

31. Seck, "Political Decision Making on Full Employment," p. 356.

32. See *The Platform of Democratic Party*, 1972.

33. Seck, "Political Decision Making on Full Employment, p. 357.

34. See Chapter 5.

35. Allen Ehrenhardt, "Black Caucus: Wary Carter Ally," *Congressional Quarterly Weekly Report*, March 7, 1977.

36. "Carter Puts Priority on Full Employment," *New York Times*, September 8, 1977.

37. Marshall, the distinguished labor economist, was a student of the problem of race and discrimination in the labor market and was therefore thor-

oughly familiar with the problem of black joblessness and the imperative of some kind of government remedy. Interestingly, an article of his own on the problem was published during the congressional debate. See "The Economics of Racial Discrimination: A Survey," *Journal of Economic Literature* (1978): 849–71.

38. Seck, "Political Decision Making on Full Employment," p. 392.

39. Paul Houston, "Black Congressmen, Carter Clash Over Employment Bill," *Los Angeles Times*, September 27, 1977.

40. "Background on the White House Coverup on the Humphrey-Hawkins Full Employment Bill," (press release, office of Congressman John Conyers, October 3, 1978). See also Houston, "Black Congressmen, Carter Clash Over Employment Bill."

41. Transcript of address cited in Seck, "Political Decision Making on Full Employment," p. 377.

42. *Congressional Record, Senate*, 95th Congress, 2nd session, October 13, 1978, p. 36741.

43. Quoted from Seck, "Political Decision Making on Full Employment," p. 458. On support in general for the compromise by the Black Caucus and others see "Backers Defend Revised Humphrey-Hawkins Bill," *Congressional Quarterly Weekly Report*, November 26, 1977, pp. 2475–76.

44. The National Association of Black Social Workers, for example, in a statement said, "It is quite clear that the revised version fails to address many of the important problems dealt with in the original. . . . Most importantly the guarantee of the original bill that enough jobs will be developed in the public sector to reach designated full employment levels." See Seck, "Political Decision Making on Full Employment," p. 130.

45. "The Cruel Hoax of Humphrey-Hawkins," *New York Times*, February 21, 1978.

46. Technically the bill was an amendment to Section 2 of the Employment Act of 1946.

47. *Congressional Record, House*, March 8–16, 1978, p. 6102.

48. Ibid., p. 6094.

49. Ibid., p. 6091.

50. Ibid.

51. Ibid., p. 7041.

52. Ibid., p. 6107. Many observers indeed agree that passage of the bill, especially in the Senate, was in large measure a tribute to Senator Humphrey

and to his wife Muriel who succeeded him in the Senate and worked for its passage in negotiations with the administration and Senate colleagues.

53. Ibid., p. 7331.

54. *Congressional Record, Senate*, October 10, 1978.

55. They were removed in the final House-Senate conference on the bill, replaced by general language requiring the president to pursue with equal emphasis full employment as well as other goals.

56. *Congressional Record, Senate*, October 13, 1978, p. 36746.

57. See the remarks of Senator Jake Garn of Utah in Ibid., p. 36806.

58. Ibid., p. 36808.

59. *Administration of Jimmy Carter, Public Papers of the President*, "Full Employment and Comprehensive Training Bill," Remarks on Signing on HR50 and S2570, p. 1872.

60. Ibid.

61. Congressman Conyers makes this argument in "Humphrey-Hawkins: A Framework for Full Employment?" *In These Times*, November, 1978, pp. 8–16.

62. Augustus Hawkins, "Whatever Happened to Full Employment?" *Urban League Review* 10(1986): 11.

63. F. Thayer, "A Bipartisan Fear of Full Employment," *New York Times*, October 12, 1988.

64. Post-war Gallup polls have shown over the years variable support for the abstract idea that the government should see to it that every person who wants to work should be able to find a job but how this translates into support for specific legislation, especially a bill that would mandate government spending to create jobs in the public sector is ambiguous.

65. The distinction between an electoral coalition and a governing coalition is useful here. Blacks were an essential component of the coalition that Carter and the Democrats needed to get elected but not to govern, while business was an insignificant part of Carter's electoral coalition (in terms of votes, but not money) but an indispensable part of the coalition needed to govern. Only if blacks had made it difficult for the administration to govern—through mass pressure or disorders—might this strategic calculus been altered in the Humphrey-Hawkins legislative struggle.

66. Four percent of course is not full employment in the sense of more job vacancies than applicants. Four or any percent unemployment is arbitrary, which is why in both the 1946 Act and the 1978 legislation the drafters initially resisted the notion of any quantitative definition or indicator of full employ-

ment. In *Full Employment in a Free Society*, (London: G. Allen Unwin, 1944), Sir William Beveridge defined full employment as meaning "always more vacant jobs than unemployed men . . . the jobs at fair wages of such a kind, and so located that the unemployed men can be reasonably expected to take them." Cited in Kemp, *Congress Makes a Law*, p. 49.

67. See *Congressional Record, Senate*, October 13, 1978, p. 36787.

68. On this point see Richard Gill, *Economics and the Public Interest*, (Pacific Palisades, CA: Goodyear, 1968): 186–88.

69. See, for example, Phillip Harvey, *Securing the Right to Employment: Social Welfare Policy and the Unemployed in the United States* (Princeton: Princeton University Press, 1989).

70. See R. Hershey, "U.S. Unemployment Rate Drops to 4.9%, Lowest Mark Since 1973," *New York Times*, April 8, 1989, and K. Noble, "America is Fully Employed, But Some Still Need Jobs," *New York Times*, December 11, 1988.

Chapter 8

1. Parts of this chapter originally appeared in my "'Politics' Is Not Enough: On the Institutionalization of the Afro-American Freedom Movement," in R. Gomes and L. Williams (eds.), *From Exclusion to Inclusion: The Long Struggle for African American Political Power* (New York: Greenwood Press, 1992): 97–126.

2. Murray Edelman, *The Symbolic Uses of Politics* (Urbana: University of Illinois Press, 1964):5.

3. For a descriptive overview of these budgets see Sula Richardson, "An Overview of the Congressional Black Caucus' Constructive Alternative Budget Proposals, FY 1982–FY 1986" (Washington: Congressional Research Service, typescript, 1985), and for a more sophisticated analysis in the context of the congressional budget process see Alvin Thornton, "Alternative Budgets of the Congressional Black Caucus: Participation of an Ideological Minority in the Budgetary Process" (paper presented at the 1983 Annual Meeting of the National Conference of Black Political Scientists, Houston, TX).

4. Thomas Edsal, "Liberals Out of Balance in New House Equation," *Washington Post*, May 22, 1985.

5. Thornton, "Alternative Budgets of the Congressional Black Caucus."

6. On the Reagan contextual revolution in politics and policy see Robert C. Smith and Hanes Walton, Jr., "U-Turn: Martin Kilson and Black Conser-

vatism," *Transition* 62(1994): 209–16, and more generally Walton's *African American Power and Politics: The Political Context Variable* (forthcoming).

7. Thornton, "Alternative Budgets of the Congressional Black Caucus", p. 27.

8. *Congressional Record, House*, May 24, 1982, pp. 11511–38.

9. Congressman Ronald Dellums as the only black member of the Armed Services Committee was responsible for developing and presenting in floor debate the Caucus's defense alternative. When the Armed Services Committee refused to hold hearings on the Caucus proposals, the Caucus raised its own funds in order to sponsor a six-day series of hearings on the domestic and national security implications of the Reagan defense program. For Dellums' views on the budget implications of military spending in the context of a full employment economy see his "Welfare State vs. Warfare State: The Legislative Struggle for Full Employment," *Urban League Review* 10(1986): 49–60.

10. The debates and roll call votes on these budgets are reported in the *Congressional Record, House* on the following dates: May 6, 1981, May 24, 1982, April 5, 1984 May 22, 1985 and April 9, 1987. The Caucus's budget in 1986 was referred to the Budget Committee but there was no floor debate or vote.

11. On the pattern of congressional support in the post–civil rights era for black policy concerns see Michael Combs, John Hibbings and Susan Welch, "Black Constituents and Congressional Roll Call Votes," *Western Political Quarterly* 40(1985): 424–34, and Kenny Whitby, "Measuring Congressional Responsiveness to the Policy Interests of Black Constituents," *Social Science Quarterly* 68(1987): 367–77. During the 1984 debate, Congressman Major Owens challenged his white southern Democratic colleagues on this issue, arguing:

> It should be noted that there are more than fifty white members of the Congress who represent a substantial black population. Among these are four districts in Alabama, three districts in Florida, five districts in Georgia, six districts in Louisiana, five districts in South Carolina, four districts in Mississippi, three districts in Texas and five districts in Virginia. Special note must be given to the fact that the sponsor of the conservative budget, the gentleman from the fourth district in Louisiana represents a district which has a 31 percent black population. . . . If the congressmen in this House would begin to truly represent their constituencies there would be enough votes to pass the CBC budget.

See the *Congressional Record, House*, April 5, 1984, p. 2379. As a result of the 1990 reapportionment process, many of the districts referred to by Owens are now represented by blacks.

12. See the comments along these lines by then Majority Leader Wright and Representatives Obey, Hoyer, Ottinger and Scheur among others during the 1982 debate. And similar comments are to be found in floor discussion of

each of the budgets. For example, in 1987 then Majority Leader Thomas Foley voted for the CBC budget, although he was opposed to its fundamental priorities and intended in the end to support the proposals of the Democratic majority on the Budget Committee. Nevertheless in faint praise he said:

> I cannot say that I agree with every aspect of the Congressional Black Caucus budget. I strongly support the Committee's budget and I intend to vote for it even if this amendment should pass. But I will vote for this budget at this time because I believe that this sincere effort by the Congressional Black Caucus to address the budget deficit is worthy of commendation.

See the *Congressional Record, House,* April 9, 1987, p. 1981.

13. *Congressional Record, House,* April 5, 1984, p. 2377.

14. Before he retired from the House, Congressman Parren Mitchell remarked "I don't want to use the word 'isolated' to describe how I feel. The 'new' liberals [like] Leon Panetta and Richard Gephardt consult with me regularly, but I just don't feel anywhere near as comfortable with the ideological direction the party is taking nowadays." Mitchell estimated that when he came to the House in 1970 there were about 180 liberals but in 1985, he said, there were little more than 100. See Edsal "Liberals out of Balance in New House Equation.

15. *Congressional Record, House,* May 24, 1982, p. 11524.

16. Ibid, 11530–31.

17. Ibid., p. 11533.

18. *Congressional Record, House,* May 22, 1985, p. 13090.

19. David Broder, "Invisible Budget," *Washington Post,* May 30, 1982.

20. On the key role played by the Caucus in the Gramm-Rudman exemptions see Edward Walsh, "Democrats Get Taste of Unity," *Washington Post,* November 6, 1985. Hawkins is quoted on the welfare reform bill in Martin Tolchin, "Congress Leaders and White House Agree on Welfare," *New York Times,* September 27, 1988, and the black college act's passage is analyzed in William Blakey, "A Legislative Victory" *New Directions* 14(1987): 1–19.

21. *Congressional Record, House,* April 9, 1987, p. 1974.

22. The quote is from an article by Gray in an Urban League symposium on black leadership edited by Ronald Walters and Robert C. Smith. See "Leadership in the Legislative Process," *Urban League Review* 9(1985): 105. In his last year as Budget Chair, liberals on the committee refused to sign a Gray-negotiated conference report unless its priorities were reordered to lower defense

outlays and modestly increase social welfare spending. see Tom Kenworthy, "House Liberals Balk At Budget Compromise," *Washington Post*, June 5, 1987.

23. This practice was also followed by former Caucus member Michael Epsy in his term on the Budget Committee.

24. Eric Pianin, "Black Caucus Members Face Dilemma of Hill Loyalties," *Washington Post*, September 23, 1987. On Gray's early tenure as Budget Chair see Pamela Fessler, "New House Budget Chief Gray Weighs Local, National Claims," *Congressional Quarterly Weekly Report*, February 2, 1985, and more generally on Caucus institutional versus race or constituency loyalities see D. D. Fears, "A Time of Testing for Black Caucus As Its members Rise to Power in House," *National Journal*, April 27, 1985.

25. On Gray's initial appointment as Budget Chair, Conyers indicated that he understood Gray could not support the Caucus's alternative budgets because "Gray has an establishment position that will preclude him from advancing the Black Caucus's views. He is faced with serious controversy on the committee. We can't expect him to push the alternative." See Nadine Cohodas, "Black House Members Striving for Influence," *Congressional Quarterly Weekly Report*, April 13, 1985.

26. Arthur Stinchcombe, *Constructing Social Theories* (New York: Harcourt, Brace & World, 1968): 153.

27. This may also be seen in the career of Congressman Ronald Dellums as he rose in seniority on the Armed Services Committee. Dellums, a democratic socialist and a product of the radical left culture of the San Francisco Bay area, made his reputation in the House as an outspoken, uncompromising critic of what he frequently called the "bloated, irrational, insane" defense budget. But as a subcommittee chair he would routinely report and vigorously defend in floor debates bills that he would subsequently vote against. And once he became chair of the full committee in 1993 he for the first time in his more than twenty years in the House voted for a defense authorization bill, which at $263 billion was almost as much as the military spending of all other nations combined. I profile Dellums in an essay in David DeLeon (ed.), *Leaders From the 1960s Generation: A Biographical Sourcebook* (Westport, CT: Greenwood Press, 1994): 504–08. On Dellums' longstanding view of the military budget see his *Defense Sense: The Search for A Rational Military Policy* (Cambridge: Ballinger, 1983). On his appointment as chair of the Armed Services Committee see Graham Browning, "Dellums Turn," *National Journal*, May 22, 1993, and "Dove to Head Armed Services Committee, Despite Opposition to Arms Buildup Rep. Dellums viewed as 'Pragmatic,'" *Washington Post*, December 23, 1992.

28. On press commentary of this sort see Jeffrey Katz, "Growing Black Caucus May Have New Voice," *Congressional Quarterly Weekly Report*, January 2, 1993, and Kenneth Cooper, "For Enlarged Congressional Black Caucus, A New Kind Of Impact," *Washington Post*, September 19, 1993.

29. These quotes are from Douglas Harris, "On Symbolic and Material Caucus Power: The Congressional Black Caucus, 92nd–103rd Congress", (p. 5). Paper prepared for presentation at the 1994 Annual Meeting of the American Political Science Association, New York. Professor Harris's paper also pursues this line of analysis, suggesting the Caucus was an increasingly powerful force in House decision making.

30. The Caucus's alternative budget and the debate on it are in the *Congressional Record, House*, March 17–18, 1993, pp. 1370–1484.

31. The remarks of Mfume and Washington are from my notes of C-Span's broadcast of the hearings on January 13, 1994.

32. See "Caucus Members Help Win Battle for New Crime Bill," *Jet*, September 19, 1994. Mfume said he was persuaded to support final passage on the basis of a promise by the president that he would issue an executive order calling for racial fairness in application of the death penalty in federal cases.

33. As the ranking or senior Democratic member of these committees and subcommittees, blacks will continue to exercise some leverage in committee decision making since they will direct the minority party staff and play a role in shaping committee hearings and floor debate.

34. Lani Guinier, "The Triumph of Tokenism: The Voting Rights Act and the Theory of Black Electoral Success," p. 10. I am quoting here from a 1990 typescript of this paper, which was subsequently published in the *Michigan Law Review* 89 (1991). Professor Guinier follows the same line of reasoning in her "No Two Seats: The Elusive Quest for Political Equality," *Virginia Law Review* 77(1991): 1413–1495. See also her *The Tyranny of the Majority*, (New York: Free Press, 1994).

35.Guinier, "The Triumph of Tokenism," p. 9.

36. Ibid., p. 114.

37. Ibid., p. 140.

38. Ibid., p. 155.

39. Former Iowa Congressman H. R. Gross built his career by delaying and disruptive tactics designed to slow down the work of the House. A fiscal conservative, Gross argued that the best way to stop government spending was to slow House proceedings. Thus, he employed every parliamentary rule—quorum calls, points of order, points of personal privilege and repeated requests for roll call rather than voice votes—in an ongoing one-man filibuster.

40. *The Langston Hughes Reader*, (New York: George Braziller, 1958): 191.

Chapter 9

1. Actually, before Jackson there had been six black candidates for president in the nation's history, all save Shirley Chisholm running as third-party candidates. For a list of the candidates and the number of votes they received see Hanes Walton, Jr., and Ronald Clark, "Black Presidential Candidates Past and Present," *New South*, Spring 1972, p. 21.

2. See "A Black for President Among Jesse's Goals," *Chicago Sun Times*, March 28, 1971. A *Jet* magazine survey in the summer of 1971 found that 98 percent of its readers thought that a black should run for president in 1972, with 93 percent favoring Julian Bond's candidacy. See Ronald Kisney "Blacks Pick Man They Prefer as Candidate for U.S. President," *Jet*, August 26, 1971, pp. 13–14.

3. The idea of running for president was urged on Dr. King as early as 1968 as part of an independent peace challenge to President Johnson.

4. Hamilton Jordan, "Can the Whole Be More Than the Sum of Its Parts: Mondale's Choice," *New Republic*, June 6, 1983, pp. 15–19.

5. Ronald Walters, "A Black Presidential Strategy for the 1984 Election" (unpublished manuscript, Howard University, 1983, p. 10).

6. "Interview: Jesse Jackson," *Playboy*, July 1984, p. 74.

7. Ibid.

8. "Outlook for A Black Presidential Candidacy: A Background Paper" prepared by the Joint Center for Political Studies, March 10, 1983, pp. 12–13. The Center estimated that at best a black candidate would win no more than 200 delegates and James Lengle, a Georgetown University Political Scientist, who prepared a separate estimate for the Joint Center of a black candidate's possible delegate strength estimated it at 226–325 delegates (Jackson in 1984 won 384 delegates). See Lengle, "To Run or Not to Run: Estimates of a Black Contenders Delegate strength at the 1984 Convention," Joint Center for Political Studies, ND, p. 5.

9. Ibid., pp. 13–14. Atlanta Mayor Andrew Young forcefully endorsed this notion that a black candidacy might make the nominee appear the captive of blacks, telling the *Atlanta Journal* (May 29, 1983), "If you make the Democratic candidate mortgage himself to the special interests of a black constituency . . . it almost makes him unelectable."

10. See Milton Coleman, "Black '84 Candidacy Called A 'Hoax' by NAACP Leadership," *Washington Post*, July 14, 1983.

11. John Jacobs, "Against a Black candidacy," *New York Times*, May 10, 1983; Ronald Walters, "Black Candidacy in 1984 is No Joke," *Los Angeles Times*,

June 12, 1983; John Conyers, "Transforming Politics With a Coalition of the Rejected," *Washington Post*, July 21, 1983; and Jesse Jackson, "Hey You Democrats: We'll all Benefit If A Black Runs for President," *Washington Post*, April 10, 1983.

12. Adolph Reed, *The Jesse Jackson Phenomenon* (New Haven: Yale University Press, 1986): 8.

13. Neither the National Black Leadership Roundtable or the smaller Black Leadership Forum were convened to discuss and decide the issue. This in spite of the fact that these two organizations were specifically set up as mechanisms to deliberate and decide such issues for the national black community. Yet, both were ignored although many of the persons in the ad hoc group were instrumental in the formation of both groups.

14. Howell Raines, "Group of Black Leaders Support Idea of Bid by Black for President," *New York Times*, June 21, 1983. The group also approved the draft of the "Peoples Platform" which was described as the black agenda upon which all presidential candidates were to be evaluated.

15. Joseph Lowry of the SCLC, the spokesman for the group, reported that of the twenty persons at the meeting two-thirds had voted in favor of the idea.

16. Compared to 1984, the 1988 campaign was more professionally organized and included less militant, more establishment type blacks such as Ronald Brown and Eleanor Holmes Norton and many more whites (including Democratic party establishment figures such as Bert Lance and Ann Lewis) in important staff and advisory positions. The campaign in 1988, unlike in 1984, was also adequately financed, with sufficient funds to support a paid staff and to run a sophisticated media campaign. Finally, the 1988 campaign was supported by virtually the entire black leadership establishment in contrast to 1984 when leading blacks in Congress, big city mayors and the heads of the major civil rights organizations opposed Jackson's candidacy. Overall, the 1984 campaign had more elements of a movement-style insurgency, while the campaign in 1988 was a more routine, traditional presidential campaign. See Robert C. Smith, "From Insurgency Toward Inclusion: The Jackson Campaigns of 1984 and 1988," in L. Morris (ed.), *The Social and Political Implications of the 1984 Jesse Jackson Campaign*, (New York: Praeger, 1990): 215–30.

17. See Anthony Broh's comprehensive study of press coverage of the 1984 campaign where these points are made, *A Horse of A Different Color* (Washington: Joint Center for Political Studies, 1985).

18. Reed, *The Jesse Jackson Phenomenon*, p. 115.

19. See Elliot Skinner, "The Jesse Jackson Campaign and Foreign Policy," and David Coolidge, "The Rev. Jesse Jackson and the Palestinian Question," in Morris (ed.), *The Social and Political Implications . . .*, pp. 169–78, 157–68.

20. Rodney Green and Finley Campbell, "The Jesse Jackson Economic Platform: A Critique and Alternative," in Ibid., pp. 99–124.

21. See *"Playboy* Interview", p. 132.

22. Robert Browne, "The Economic Policy of the Jackson Candidacy," in Morris (ed.), *The Social and Political Implications . . .* , p. 92.

23. Christopher Edley, "Jesse Jackson vs. the Rules," *Washington Post,* December 28, 1984.

24. The second primary, widely used in the south, requires a runoff in case no candidate receives a majority of the vote. Jackson argued this procedure resulted in the defeat of black candidates who otherwise might win their party's nomination.

25. See Joseph McCormick, "Anatomy of a Tactical Miscalculation: Jackson's 1984 Attack on the Runoff Primary System," in Morris (ed.), *The Social and Political Implications. . . .*

26. See Ronald Walters, "The Issue Politics of the Jesse Jackson Campaign for President" in Ibid., pp. 37–40.

27. See, for example, his proposed use of worker pension funds to finance various infrastructure job creation programs. Gwen Ifill, "Jackson Details Pension Loan Plan," *Washington Post,* March 18, 1988.

28. On the definition and role of valence issues in voter choice see Donald Stokes, "Spatial Models of Party Competition," in Angus Campbell et al. (eds.), *Elections and the Political Order* (New York: John Wiley & Sons, 1966): 170–71.

29. Teenage pregnancy and the use of illegal drugs are clearly valence issues. Survey data show there is near universal opposition to both, with no statistically significant partisan, class, gender, regional or racial differences.

30. For example, Benjamin Ginsberg examined party platforms, U.S. statutes and aggregate voting statistics and found a relationship between platforms, voter choices and public policy. See "Elections and Public Policy," *American Political Science Review* 70(1976): 41–49. And Ian Budge and Richard Hofferbert also found a linkage between post-war (1948–85) platforms and government outputs. See "Mandates and Policy Outputs: US Party Platforms and Federal Expenditure," *American Political Science Review* 84(1990): 111–13.

31. See Warren Weaver, "Democratic Panel Nears Completion of Fall Platform," *New York Times,* June 24, 1984. And David Broder, "Parties Resharpen Decades-Old Ideological Clash," *Washington Post,* August 18, 1984.

32. Gallup Poll data just prior to the opening of the 1980 primaries showed Carter's job approval rating among blacks at 30 percent compared with 29 percent among whites. See *The Ladd Report,* p. 13.

33. Walters, *Black Presidential Politics in America*, especially chaps. 1, 6.

34. The first use of the rainbow motif was by the Detroit area White Panthers—a white 1960s student group sympathetic to the Black Panthers. In 1971 they changed their name to "Rainbow Peoples Party." See Kathleen Rout, *Eldridge Cleaver* (Boston: Twayne Publishers, 1991): 151. Gary Mayor Richard Hatcher employed the rainbow motif in his keynote address at the 1972 Black Political Convention where he said "And when, if they leave us no choice—and if we form a third political movement, we shall take with us Chicanos, Puerto Ricans, Indians and Oriental, a wonderful kaleidoscope of colors." The text of Hatcher's address is in *The Black Scholar* 4(1972): 17–22.

35. Thomas Cavanagh and Lorn Foster, *Jesse Jackson's Campaign: The Primaries and Caucuses* (Washington: Joint Center for Political Studies, 1984):17.

36. Estimates of the black vote in the 1984 and 1988 primaries are based on the *New York Times* exit polls.

37. James Q. Wilson, "The Negro in Politics," in T. Parsons and K. Clark (eds.), *The Negro American* (Boston: Beacon Press, 1966): 427. This point is also made by Walter Dean Burnham in "Party Systems and the Political Process," in Burnham and William Chambers (eds.), *The American Party System* (New York: Oxford University Press, 1975): 17–22.

38. Carmichael and Hamilton, *Black Power*, p. 82.

39. Linda Williams, "White/Black Perceptions of the Electability of Black Political Candidates," *National Political Science Review* 2(1990): 53.

40. Ibid.

41. Thomas Schelling, *Micromotives and Macrobehavior*, as cited in Robert Huckfeldt and Carol Kohfeld, *Race and the Decline of Class in American Politics*, (Urbana: University of Illinois Press, 1989): 16.

42. Robert Bostch, *We Shall Not Overcome* (Chapel Hill: University of North Carolina, 1981): 196.

43. See Frances Fox Piven and Richard Cloward, *Poor Peoples Movement: Why They Succeed, Why They Fail*, (New York: Vintage Books, 1977): chap. 3, and Michael Goldfield, *The Decline of Organized Labor in the United States* (Chicago: University of Chicago Press, 1987). In the last twenty-five years blacks have been more effective in pursuing their narrow race-specific, civil rights agenda than labor has been in pursuit of its trade union specific agenda, i.e., an indexed minimum wage, common situs picketing, plant closing notification, striker replacement legislation or repeal of section 14B of the Taft-Hartley Act. The courts and the labor-management regulatory agencies during this period have also ruled more adversely on labor issues than they have on race issues.

44. On Jackson's campaign appeals to the white working class see T. R. Reid, "Jackson's Ode to the Working Poor," *Washington Post*, April 18, 1988,

and Haynes Johnson and Gwen Ifill, "Jackson Stirs White Underdogs," *Washington Post*, April 2, 1988.

45. See Percy Cohen, *Jewish Radicals and Radical Jews* (London: Academic Press, 1980), Arthur Liebman, *Jews and the Left* (New York: John Wiley & Son, 1979), and W. D. Rubenstein, *The Left, the Right and Jews* (New York: Universe Books, 1982). See also David Lewis, "Parallels and Divergences: Assimilationist Strategies of Afro-American and Jewish Elites from 1910 to the Early 1930s," *Journal of American History* 71(1984): 543–64.

46. It is estimated that more than half of the funds to support Democratic candidates for federal office comes from Jews. See Stephen Issacs, *Jews and American Politics* (Garden City, NJ: Doubleday, 1974): 121, and Earl Raab and Seymour Martin Lipset, *The Political Future of American Jews* (New York: American Jewish Committee, N.D.): 4.

47. Raab and Lipset, *The Future of American Jews*, p. 7.

48. Ibid., p. 12. See also Lipset's "Jews are Still Liberal and Proud of It," *Washington Post*, December 20, 1984.

49. The general pattern of white support for big city mayoral candidates is among Jews and upper income, well-educated persons. This is the same for Jackson in 1988 except for Jews.

50. Raab and Lipset, *The Future of American Jews*, p. 15. For a detailed analysis of Jackson's approach to foreign policy see Karin Stanford, *Beyond the Boundaries: Reverend Jesse Jackson in International Relations* (Albany: SUNY Press, forthcoming).

51. See Coolidge, "The Reverend Jesse Jackson and the Palestinian Question." See also Stanford, *Beyond the Boundaries*.

52. Progressive Jewish politics is distorted by Zionism, an issue irrelevant to the internal dynamics of American politics. This was a great fear of anti-zionist Jews in this century; that if the state was established it would inevitably tend to turn Jewish ideology away from its progressive inclinations toward whatever parties, policies or groups necessary to preserve the state. Zionism then always has the potential to align Jews with otherwise inhospitable forces who control or influence the United States government.

53. Gerald Boyd, "Jackson Assesses Low White Vote," *New York Times*, March 22, 1984.

54. See Coleman McCarthy, "Jackson's Reversal on Abortion," *Washington Post*, May 21, 1988, and Nat Hentoff, "Dred Scott, Abortion and Jesse Jackson," *Village Voice*, February 24, 1989.

55. Jackson also fully embraced the agenda of gays and lesbians. On this as well as the abortion issue he was going against mainstream black opinion,

which tends to be more conservative or traditional on these issues. See Smith and Seltzer, *Race, Class and Culture*, pp. 36–42.

56. Armando Gutierrez, "The Jackson Campaign in the Hispanic Community," in Lucius Barker and Ronald Walters, *Jesse Jackson's 1984 Presidential Campaign* (Urbana: University of Illinois Press): 108–25.

57. National Conference of Christians and Jews, *Taking America's Pulse: The Full Report of the National Conference Survey on Inter-Group Relations* (New York: National Conference of Christians and Jews, 1994): 7.

58. Ibid.

59. Rodolfo O. de la Garza, et al., *Latino Voices: Mexican, Puerto Rican and Cuban Perspectives in American Politics* (Boulder: Westview Press, 1992).

60. Lorenzo Morris and Linda Williams, "The Coalition at the End of the Rainbow," in *Ibid.*, pp. 229–36.

61. Arthur Schlesinger, *The Cycles of History*, (Boston: Houghton Mifflin, 1986):273.

62. Walter Dean Burnham, *Critical Elections and the Mainsprings of American Democracy* (New York: W.W. Norton, 1970): 113.

63. See Leon Epstein, "The Scholarly Commitment to Parties," in A. Finifter, *The State of the Discipline* (Washington: American Political Science Association, 1983): 127–54.

64. Martin Wattenberg, *The Rise of Candidate-Centered Politics: Presidential Elections n the 1980s* (Cambridge: Harvard University Press, 1989).

65. Ronald Walters, "A National Campaign Committee for the Black Presidential Bid," unpublished memorandum, N.D.

66. Ibid.

67. Most of these allegations or criticisms of Jackson are convincingly documented in Barbara Reynolds, *Jesse Jackson: The Man, The Movement and the Myth*, (Chicago: Nelson-Hall, 1975), republished in 1985 as *Jesse Jackson: America's David*. Although the text of both versions of the book are the same, in *America's David* Reynolds added a new introduction that paints Jackson in a much more sympathetic light. A more sympathetic portrayal of Jackson's career is also presented in Marshall Frady's "Profiles," which also cover his presidential campaigns. See *The New Yorker*, February 3, 10 and 17, 1992.

68. One can sympathize with the concern of Jackson and his staff to exercise some hierarchical control on local chapters or affiliates in terms of organization and leadership to prevent them, as one Jackson aide put it, from being taken over by "the crazies." To some extent both the National Negro Congress

of the 1930s and the National Black Political Convention of 1970s were sub-verted by well-organized but fringe black nationalist and white left factions.

69. This contrast, for example, with the Christian Coalition created by former presidential candidate the Reverend Pat Robertson. Robertson's orga-nization has developed into an influential grassroots movement at state, local and congressional district levels and increasingly is playing an important—in some places decisive—role in the nomination and election of Republican can-didates.

70. Reynolds, *Jesse Jackson, The Man, The Movement and the Myth*, p. 121.

71. On this theme of authoritarianism in Jackson's conduct of his presi-dential campaign see Elizabeth Colton (Jackson's 1988 press secretary), *The Jesse Jackson Phenomenon: The Man, The Power, The Message* (New York: Doubleday, 1989).

72. It was also strikingly demonstrated in 1993 when Jackson mounted an unseemly campaign to succeed Benjamin Hooks as head of the NAACP, willing apparently to simply abandon the Rainbow Coalition as cavalierly as he aban-doned SCLC and Operation PUSH.

73. Although Jackson has frequently challenged the prerogatives of cor-porate America in his rhetoric and some issue stances, the Rainbow Coalition receives support of various sorts from major corporations. For example, its 1991 convention was underwritten in part by a number of major corporations, just as was the meeting that year of the more conservative DLC. Unfortunately, the Rainbow Coalition does not make available an annual report or other docu-ments that would permit analysis of the sources of receipts or the nature of expenditures.

Chapter 10

1. Stanley Greenberg, *Report On Democratic Defection*, (Washington, D.C., 1985): 13, 18, as quoted in Thomas Edsal and Mary Edsal, *Chain Reaction: The Impact of Race, Rights and Taxes On American Politics* (New York: W.W. Norton, 1992): 182.

2. Milton Kotler and Nelson Rosenbaum, "Strengthening the Demo-cratic Party through Strategic Marketing: Voters and Donors," a confidential report for the Democratic National Committee by the CRG Research Institute, Washington, D.C. 1985. I am grateful to Professor Hanes Walton, Jr. for sharing excerpts from this report with me. See also Peter Brown, "85 Dem. Report Urges "De-Marketing of Party," *Houston Chronicle*, April 17, 1989.

3. Brown, "85 Dem Report Urges De-Marketing of Party."

4. Harry McPhearson, "How Race Destroyed the Democrat's Coalition," *New York Times*, October 28, 1988.

5. "Does Race Doom the Democrats?" *New York Times*, November 20, 1988.

6. See Elaine Kamarck and William Galston, *The Politics of Evasion* (Washington: Progressive Policy Institute, 1989).

7. Thomas Edsal and Mary Edsal, "Race," *The Atlantic Monthly*, May, 1991, pp. 53–86.

8. Edsal and Edsal, *Chain Reaction*, pp. 278, 282.

9. Ibid., pp. 291–92.

10. In the last weekend of the campaign Dukakis, sensing the election was lost, embraced liberalism and began to campaign more actively in the black community. Interestingly, when he used the word liberal to describe himself he defined it in his own terms, declaring "I'm a liberal in the tradition of Franklin Roosevelt, Harry Truman and John Kennedy." This formulation of course left out Lyndon Johnson, the quintessential liberal of the post-war era, closely identified with the cause of civil rights and government programs to deal with poverty and racial injustice. See Robin Toner, "Dukakis Asserts He is a Liberal, Invoking 3 Venerated Presidents," *New York Times*, October 31, 1988.

11. Michael Oreskes, "Jackson Aides Say Dukakis Wants to Limit Campaign," *New York Times*, September 1, 1988.

12. The data are ambiguous on black turnout in the 1994 election. *The Wall Street Journal* calculates on the basis of exit polls that black turnout increased by 20 percent over the 1990 midterm elections and that the black share of the total vote doubled to 10 percent. See Michael Frisby, "Blacks are Searching for New Ways to Make Voting Strength Count," February 6, 1995. However, the Census Bureau's survey found that black turnout was slightly down in 1994, 37 percent compared to 39.2 percent in 1990. See Randolph Schmid, "Low Income Voters Skipped Election That Swept in GOP," *West County Times*, June 9, 1995. A further source of ambiguity here is that black respondents are more likely than whites to report having voted when they did not. See Paul Abramson and William Claggett, "Race Related Differences in Self Reported and Validated Turnout in 1986," *Journal of Politics* 5(1989): 397–407. On black attitudes toward the 1994 campaign see Isabel Wilkerson, "Many Blacks See Betrayal in This Year's Campaign," *New York Times*, November 10, 1994.

13. Cokie and Steven Roberts, "Democrats Must Face Race Issue," *West County Times*, December 16, 1994.

14. The best of the academic studies are Edward Carmines and James Stimson, *Issue Evolution: Race and the Transformation of American Politics* (Prince-

ton: Princeton University Press, 1989), Robert Huckfeldt and Carol Kohlfeld, *Race and the Decline of Class in American Politics* (Urbana: University of Illinois Press, 1989), and Earl Black and Merle Black, *Politics and Society in the South* (Cambridge: Harvard University Press, 1989).

15. Adolph Reed, "Race and the Disruption of the New Deal Coalition," *Urban affairs Quarterly* 27(1991): 336. This essay is a review of the major academic studies of this problem. Reed (with Julian Bond) also reviews the Edsals' book and other popular studies in "Equality: Why We Can't Wait," *Nation*, December 9, 1991.

16. See Forrest Wood, *Black Scare: The Racist Response to Emancipation and Reconstruction* (Berkeley: University of California Press, 1968).

17. The level of class voting during the New Deal was modest, reaching its peak in President Truman's 1948 campaign and then declining thereafter. See Paul Abramson, John Aldrich and David Rohde, *Change and Continuity in the 1988 Elections*, (Washington: Congressional Quarterly Press, 1991): 139–41.

18. It should also be noted that in the post–World War II period there has been a substantial decline in class voting in all western democracies. See Mark Franklin, et al., *Electoral Change: Responses to Evolving Social and Attitudinal Structures in Western Countries* (New York: Cambridge University Press, 1992).

19. Other issues that emerged at the same time as the civil rights revolution—the Vietnam War, abortion and issues of sexual morality and lifestyles— also played a part in the partisan transformation of the last twenty-five years. But race was the catalytic factor.

20. Clinton Rossiter, *Conservatism in America* (New York: Vintage Books, 1955): 247.

21. According to Nixon aide John Ehrlichman, Charles Colson in a 1972 memo to Nixon on strategy wrote "The key voter blocs to go after are Catholics, organized labor and the racists." and Ehrlichman notes "That the subliminal appeal to the anti-black voter was always in Nixon's statements and speeches on schools and housing. . . ." See *Witness to Power* (New York: Auburn House, 1982): 222–23. See also Kevin Phillips, *The Emerging Republican Majority* (New York: Doubleday, 1970).

22. Reed and Bond, "Equality: Why We Can't Wait," p. 736.

23. This is the basic thesis of Kamarck and Galston, *The Politics of Evasion*.

24. Thomas Ferguson and Joel Rogers, *Right Turn: The Decline of the Democrats and the Future of American Politics* (New York: Hill & Wang, 1986): 28. Ferguson and Rogers analyze the data from a left liberal perspective but even neoconservative social scientists frequently reach the same judgment. For

example, in analysis of a broad range of polls and surveys early in the first Reagan administration Lipset concluded that most Americans remain opposed to most reductions in most social programs and committed to the basic assumptions of the welfare state. See Seymour M. Lipset "Poll After Poll After Poll After Poll Warns President Reagan on Program," *New York Times*, January 13, 1982. Indeed, it is probably the case—the data are not clear—that if the words welfare or welfare state were not associated with blacks and laden with white supremacist stereotypes, then, support for the welfare state among whites would be as high as it is in the European social democracies. On this point see Don Muir, "The Liberal Progressive Agenda and the Rebirth of the Democratic Party" (Masters Thesis, San Francisco State University, 1990) and Michael Brown, "Welfare State and Democracy in America: Reflections on Race and Social Policy, 1935–94" (paper prepared for presentation at the 1994 Annual Meeting of the American Political Science Association, New York).

25. Martin Wattenberg, *The Rise of Candidate-Centered Politics: Presidential Elections in the 1980s* (Cambridge: Harvard University Press, 1991).

26. Ferguson and Rogers, *Right Turn*, p. 43. In addition to the dominance of the Democratic party by powerful economic interests (not a new phenomenon), in the post–civil rights era American elections have come to be dominated also by pollsters, media consultants and other hucksters who, lacking political principles, will do anything to win, selling the presidency like toothpaste.

27. Morris Fiorina, *Divided Government* (New York: MacMillan, 1992): 2.

28. Robert Loevy, *The Flawed Path to the Presidency 1992* (Albany: SUNY Press, 1995) is a useful early analysis of the 1992 campaign.

29. See National Conference of Christians and Jews, *Taking America's Pulse: The Full Report of the National Conference Survey on Inter-Group Relations* (New York: National Conference of Christians and Jews, 1994): chap. 2 and Robert C. Smith, *Racism in the Post–Civil Rights Era: Now You See It, Now You Don't* (Albany: SUNY Press, 1995): chap. 3.

30. *A New Covenant*, Democratic Party Platform, 1992. The language on the use of private pension funds as a source of investment capital for public projects was advanced by Jackson in his 1988 campaign.

31. Perot's voters came disproportionately from demographic and attitudinal groups that traditionally support Republican candidates. Although in the exit poll 38 percent of Perot voters said absent Perot they would have voted for Clinton and 37 percent for Bush, the critical data bearing on Perot's impact is that 56 percent of his voters said they voted for Bush in 1988 and only 17 percent for Dukakis.

32. A cooperative press was necessary in the success of this strategy. The national news media for a variety of reasons (including ideological and gener-

ational compatibility with Clinton and the wish to have a new story line after twelve years of Republican president versus Democratic Congress stories) gave Clinton quite favorably coverage compared to Bush, including highly negative reporting on the economy, less than thorough inquiry into the Jennifer Flowers allegations regarding Clinton's sexual indiscretion and presentation of Clinton as a new, centrist Democrat in spite of the liberal platform adopted at the New York convention.

33. Frances Cline, "Campaign is a 'Fraud' to Urban Underclass," *New York Times*, October 3, 1993.

34. See for the first quote Sam Roberts, "When Race is an Issue in Politics," *New York Times*, October 12, 1992, and for the second Clarence Page, "Clinton's Debt to Sister Souljah," *West County Times*, October 30, 1992.

35. Clinton also sought to inoculate himself from a Jesse Helms-like attack on him as a "quota" candidate (In his 1990 Senate campaign Helms ran an ad attacking racial quotas by showing white hands crumbling a rejection letter while the announcer said the man had lost his job to a black although he was better qualified). Clinton early on denounced quotas while supporting affirmative action and diversity but to some extent the Bush campaign could not raise this issue since Bush signed the Civil Rights Act of 1991, which Patrick Buchanan and congressional conservatives called a quota bill. Thus, the Bush campaign could not use the issue in the clear-cut fashion of Helms.

36. On the use and effectiveness of the Willie Horton ad during the 1988 campaign see Martin Schram, "The Making of Willie Horton," *The New Republic*, May 28, 1990 and Kathleen Hall Jamieson, *Dirty Politics: Deception, Distraction and Democracy* (New York: Oxford University Press, 1992): 131–35.

37. David Ellwood outlines his reform proposals in *Poor Support* (New York: Basic Books, 1988).

38. See the brief account of the incident in Bob Woodward's *The Agenda* (New York: Simon & Shuster, 1995): 29–33. Woodward reports that "After the speech Jackson tried to hand Clinton a long memo outlining the strengths he would bring to the Democratic ticket should Clinton choose him as his vice presidential running mate. Clinton declined. "I'm not going to put you through what Fritz Mondale or Mike Dukakis did"(p.33). Clinton was referring to Mondale and Dukakis telling Jackson that he was on their lists of possible running mates when in fact they had no intention of choosing him.

39. Page, "Clinton's Debt to Sister Souljah."

40. Ibid.

41. Even a Jackson endorsement of one of the more liberal candidates— Harkins or Brown—might have negatively affected Clinton's support among blacks. That Clinton was acutely aware of the possible impact of a Jackson

endorsement was revealed when he was mistakenly told on the eve of Super Tuesday that Jackson had endorsed Harkins. Unaware that he was being filmed, Clinton became visibly disturbed and angry, accusing Jackson of betrayal.

42. Clarence Page, "Black Voters Gave Clinton Victory," *West County Times*, November 20, 1992.

43. No post–civil rights era national white political leader spoke more honestly, eloquently and passionately about racism, its legacy and the imperative of racial reform than Governor Cuomo. In 1990 for example, speaking informally to working- and middle-class whites in Queens, Cuomo said:

> We are cognizant of the fact that for a long period of time we deprived them not just of their civil rights, we deprived them of their human rights. And so in a kind of weak attempt to in some way compensate for that we constructed special programs called affirmative action. I don't understand people who resent it. Because they [blacks] are different. Because the Italian Americans were not locked in chains and dragged from Naples and then tied to machines and made to haul them like beasts of burden. It's a different experience and you have to recognize that.

See Sam Howe Verhovek, "Cuomo, Strolling Discusses Slavery," *New York Times*, June 2, 1990. Cuomo's remarks are all the more remarkable when compared with Clinton's strategic pandering to whites in 1992 when it came to issues of race and racism.

44. Fiorina, *Divided Government*, p. 1.

45. William Schneider, "Realignment: The Eternal Question," *PS* 15(1982): 449–57. See also Evertt Carl Ladd, "Like Waiting for Godot: The Uselessness of Realignment for Understanding Change in Contemporary American Politics," *Polity* 25(1990): 511–25.

46. V.O. Key, "A Theory of Critical Elections," *Journal of Politics* 17(1955):3–18. Walter Dean Burnham presents a historical analysis of the phenomenon in his *Critical Elections and the Mainsprings of American Politics*, (New York: W.W. Norton, 1970).

47. The Democrats lost fifty-five House seats, six in the northeast, fifteen in the midwest, seventeen in the west and seventeen in the south and border states. The southern congressional delegation after 1994 for the first time ever has a Republican majority, sixty-four Republicans, sixty-one Democrats (including the twelve blacks representing majority black districts).

48. Historically, critical elections produce enduring partisan and policy majorities (historians generally agree that there have been only five critical elections in the country's history, those of 1800, 1828, 1860, 1896 and 1932). Thus, the question is whether the Republican majorities will endure. The guess here is no, and that instead we are likely to see shifting partisan majorities in national

elections and periodic third-party or independent presidential campaigns. This is ultimately because neither of the two major parties have a coherent set of programs to deal with the electorate's concerns about crime, welfare and the education of its children; but especially policies and programs to deal with the problem of the ongoing decline in living standards precipitated by the restructuring of the American labor market in the context of a global economy.

Chapter 11

1. The political culture is resistant to change because of the absence of a tradition of cross-ethnic working class solidarity and organization; racism and the ideology of white supremacy; an individualistic, antistatist, commercial ethos; and the tendency among the people toward apathy and ignorance regarding politics. The political system is resistant to change because of federalism, the separation of powers, the separate and staggered terms of the executive and the Congress, the antimajoritarian character of the Senate in terms of its constituency and its rules and procedures, and the "winner take all" provision in the allocation of House seats and electoral college votes.

2. Reflecting on these systemic and cultural obstacles to change as well as the "privileged position of business" in shaping government decisions, an eminent student of American democracy concludes "it may be true that our best, yet dismal, hope for structural change is through a transitory catastrophe." See Charles Lindbloom, "Comment On Manley," *American Political Science Review* 77(1983): 368–83. Implicit in Lindbloom's notion is that a crisis or system catastrophe will result in structural changes that are progressive in character, as has been the case historically in the United States. However, theoretically at least, such a crisis might result in regressive social policies and political repression.

3. On the persistence of racism and white supremacist attitudes in the last twenty-five years see Robert C. Smith, *Racism in the Post Civil Rights Era: Now You See It, Now You Don't* (Albany: SUNY Press, 1995). See also Joe Feagin, "A Slavery Unwilling to Die," *Journal of Black Studies* 18(1988): 415–69 and Feagin and Hernan Vera, *White Racism: The Basics* (New York: Routledge, 1995).

4. The economic changes in general and with respect to the black community in terms of their consequences have been thoroughly researched and are by now well known. The cultural changes in general or with respect to blacks in particular are less thoroughly researched or understood. The best treatment, in my view, of the general problem of cultural changes in the 1960s and their consequences is Christopher Lasch, *The Culture of Narcissism: American Life in An Age of Diminishing Expectations* (New York: W.W. Norton, 1978) and his *Haven in a Heartless World: The Family Besieged* (New York: Basic Books, 1973). There is no good book-length treatment of the race-specific component or consequences of these broader cultural changes.

5. Harold Cruse, "New Black Leadership Required," *New Politics* 2(1990): 39–49. See also Mack Jones, "The Increasing Irrelevancy of Black Leadership"

(paper prepared for presentation at the 1981 Annual Meeting of the National Conference of Black Political Scientists, Baltimore).

6. See Huey Perry (ed.), "A Minisymposium Exploring the Meaning and Implications of Deracialization in African American Politics," *Urban Affairs Quarterly* 27(1991): 198–226 and Perry (ed.), "Black Electoral Success in 1989," *PS* 23(1990): 141–60. See also Georgia Persons (ed.), *Dilemmas of Black Politics: Issues of Leadership and Strategy* (New York: Harper/Collins, 1993).

7. Harold Cruse, *Plural But Equal: Blacks and Minorities in America's Plural Society* (New York: William Morrow, 1987). Cruse did not systematically develop the idea of black plurality but compared to the other ethnic racial minorities (Latinos and Asian Americans) the African American community is much more of a plural or distinct society. Politically, it is much more ideologically distinct; socially its members face far higher levels of discrimination in housing, employment and education than other ethnic racial minorities; and African Americans tend to be more conscious of their separate and subordinate status than the various Latino and Asian American minority communities. The concept of a plural society was first advanced by M. G. Smith in his *The Plural Society of British West Indies* (Berkeley: University of California Press, 1965). See also Ira Katznelson, "Comparative Studies of Race and Ethnicity: Plural Analysis and Beyond," *Comparative Politics* 1 (1972): 135–54. Although she does not use the concept or idea of black plurality (preferring instead the legal term "insular group") it is central to the line of analysis pursued by Lani Guinier in her law review articles. Finally, see the recent paper by David Sears, Jack Citrin and Colettee Van Laar, "Black Exceptionalism in Multicultural Society" (presented at the 1995 Annual Meeting of the American Political Science Association, Chicago).

8. Poor blacks are not only alienated from mainstream American politics and leaders but also increasingly from black establishment leadership and politics. While generally supportive of the liberal policy initiatives of the black establishment, poor blacks are also more nationalist in outlook, disengaged from traditional black organizations and in general feel that no leaders or organizations represent their interests or concerns in national politics. These generalizations are documented quite effectively in a fine case study of Detroit's inner city black community. See Cathy Cohen and Michael Dawson, "Neighborhood Poverty and African American Politics," *American Political Science Review* 87(1993): 298–99.

9. Alexis de Tocqueville, *Democracy in America* (Garden City, N.J.: Doubleday, 1848; 1969): 356. The extraordinarily high incidence of violent crime committed by blacks; and the society's increasingly violent, almost it seems near militaristic response to it, while less dramatic than open rebellions like the 1992 Los Angeles riots are probably the best indicator of the violent polarization of the races, although most of these acts of violence are intraracial. The ill advised war on drugs, which in effect and implementation, has become a war on poor blacks, only exacerbates the overall violence associated with the war on crime.

Index

Printed in the United States
66750LVS00003B/25-33

9 780791 431368